Gender Relations in Early India

Gender Relations in Early India

Vinita Chandra

RAWAT PUBLICATIONS
Jaipur • New Delhi • Bangalore • Hyderabad • Guwahati

ISBN 81-316-0379-2

Published by
Prem Rawat for **Rawat Publications**
Satyam Apts, Sector 3, Jawahar Nagar, Jaipur 302 004 (India)
Phone: 0141 265 1748/7006 Fax: 0141 265 1748
E-mail: info@rawatbooks.com
Website: www.rawatbooks.com

New Delhi Office
4858/24, Ansari Road, Daryaganj, New Delhi 110 002
Phone: 011 2326 3290

Also at Bangalore, Hyderabad and Guwahati

Typeset by Rawat Computers, Jaipur
Printed at Chaman Enterprises, New Delhi

To my Mumma
for her courage, warmth, perseverance and precision

To my Husband
for being a truly 'gender-sensitive' husband,
also for his determination, purposefulness, equanimity,
and child-like simplicity and joyousness

Contents

Acknowledgements **ix**

Abbreviations **xi**

1 Introduction **1**

- Meaning of *Dharma* 9
- Sources of *Dharma* 10
- Origin and Evolution of the *Dharmaśāstras* 10
- *Dharmaśāstras: Number and Dates* 13
- The Socio-political and Economic Life 19
- Religion 30
- Social Conditions 32

2 Gender Dynamics within the Household **40**

- The Ideology of the *Gṛha* in the *Dharmaśāstras* 42
- Birth 44
- Marriage 46
- Forms of Marriage 54
- Choice Regarding the Decision to Get Married 65
- Dowry 67
- Bride Price 68
- Remarriage 70
- Death 72
- Upbringing of Children 72
- Conjugal Relations 75
- Duties of the Husband/Householder 82
- Polygamy 92
- Menstrual Taboos 94
- Women as the Daughter-in-Law 99

- Motherhood 99
- Other Women as Relatives 101
- Exclusion from the Household 102
- Adultery vs *Varṇa* Identity 104
- Adultery and Gender Identity 106
- Rape 114
- Husband's Death: Widowhood, *Niyoga* and *Sati* 115
- Desertion 123
- Opting-out of the Household 124

3 Property and Legal Rights 151

- Rights 151
- Ownership and Property in Ancient India 152
- Concept of Law in Ancient India 154
- Property Rights 154
- Inheritance and Partition of Immovable Property 155
- Women's Right to Movable Property: *Strīdhana* (Women's Property) 159
- Succession to *Strīdhana* 167
- Women's Dominion over *Strīdhana* 171
- Legal Rights 174

4 The Ideal and the Reality 186

- Women in the Epics 187
- Characters in the *Vālmīki Rāmāyaṇa* 190
- Characters in the *Mahābhārata* 209
- Women in the *Śangam* Society 233
- Women in the Epigraphic Records 243
- Deviations from the Norm of Ideal Wifehood 244
- Deviation from the Norm Regarding the Name of Women 247
- Deviations from the Norms Regarding Exogamy 248
- Deviations from the Norm: Use of Metronymics 250
- Deviation from the Prohibition upon Performance of Religious Penances, or Sacrifices by Women 251
- Within the Sphere of Influence: The Cases of Identity Construction in Accordance with the Norms 252

5 Conclusion 278

Bibliography **319**

Index **328**

Acknowledgements

The completion of this research work has been the result of the aspirations, efforts and blessings of many people. I have an intense gratitude towards my supervisor Dr R.K. Pant for affectionate and patient guidance.

I would also like to thank the Indian Council for Historical Research, New Delhi for providing me with the Junior Research Fellowship, which facilitated my work.

I am also immensely thankful to Dr Sati Chatterji (Jadavpur University) and Prof. Sadanand More (University of Pune) for their encouraging comments on the work.

It would have been impossible for me to complete my research if not for the constant motivation of my husband, Dr Abhishek Chandra. His companionship has been the great blessing I have received in life.

No words to thank Mumma. She has been my strength and my hope. She has taught me to walk through the darkest, and remain a warrior of light.

Nana and Papa have kept on inspiring me towards a mightier purpose of worldly existence even after having physically left the world.

The concern of Nanaji and Naniji for the completion of this work has been overwhelming. Without their blessings, this would not have been possible.

I am immensely thankful to Mama (my mother-in-law), Prof. Chandrakala Padia, for encouraging me all through the research. The insightful discussions on the subject held very frequently between us; and her scholarly presence have significantly contributed to the completion of this work.

I have no words to express my gratitude to Ms Prabha Ginodia, Ms Manju Pandey, Shri P.K. Vijai, Shri B.K. Chaturvedi and my brother Ankur, who have all kept on encouraging and supporting me.

Prof. Sunil Ray, Institute of Development Studies, Jaipur has been a constant source of encouragement, motivation and guidance. His constant encouragement to write something original instead of 'reproducing knowledge', has been inspiring me all through this work.

I am also thankful towards the library staffs of the Central Library, University of Rajasthan, BHU and JNU; as well as all the other libraries which I consulted. I am also immensely thankful to Ms Priti Singh, Mr Alok Kumar Singh, Ms Archana, Dr Manisha Shukla and Rajeshji for helping me in a number of ways.

If anybody had to pay a cost for the completion of my work, he is my little son Parth, who had to stay away from me for around three months. For his sweet little understanding of the fact that 'Mama has to study', I am beholden. Parth has been a blessing for my life and my work.

My acknowledgement would remain incomplete if I do not thank Dr Kumkum Roy and Dr Uma Chakravarti for their invaluable writings in the field. I have been reading them with constant admiration and rare differences.

I am also thankful to Mr Pranit Rawat of Rawat Publications for the efficient and speedy publication of the work.

Vinita Chandra

Abbreviations

A.Br.	:	*Aitareya Brāhmaṇa*
Angiras	:	*Angiras Samhitā*
Āpas.Dh.S.	:	*Āpastamba Dharmasūtra*
A.S.W.I.	:	Archaeological Survey of Western India.
Atri	:	*Atri Samhitā*
Baudh.Dh.S.	:	*Baudhāyana Dharmasūtra*
B.O.R.I.	:	*Bhandarkar Oriental Research Institute*
Bṛ.Up.	:	*Bṛhadāraṇyaka Upaniṣad*
Bṛhas	:	*Bṛhaspati Smṛti*
Ch.Up.	:	*Chhāndogya Upaniṣad*
Dakśa	:	*Dakśa Samhitā*
E.I.	:	*Epigraphia Indica*
Gautama	:	*Gautama Samhitā*
Hārita	:	*Hārīta Dharmasūtra*
H.I.S.W.K.	:	*The History and Inscriptions of the Sātavāhanas and Western Kshatrapas*
Kātyāyana	:	*Kātyāyana Smṛti*
Likhita	:	*Likhita Samhitā*
Manu	:	*Manusmṛti*
Mbh	:	*Mahābhārata*
Nārada	:	*Nārada Smṛti*
Pārāśara	:	*Pārāśara Smṛti*
ṚV	:	*Ṛgveda*
S.I.	:	*Select Inscriptions Bearing on Indian History and Civilization*
Samvarta	:	*Samvarta Samhitā*
Śankha	:	*Śankha Samhitā*

Śātātapa	:	*Śātātapa Samhitā*
S.B.E.	:	*Sacred Books of the East*
T.S.	:	*Taittirīya Samhitā*
Uśanā	:	*Uśanā Samhitā*
Vasiṣṭha	:	*Vasiṣṭha Dharmaśāstra*
Viṣṇu	:	*Viṣṇu Smṛti*
Vyāsa	:	*Vyāsa Samhitā*
Yama	:	*Yama Samhitā*
Yāj	:	*Yājñavalkya Smṛti*

1

Introduction

History has been a 'history by males' as well as of males. For until not very remote times, history was merely a record of battles and wars, with males as the principle or the only protagonists. All the activities which received historical attention were principally male achievements. Gerda Lerner observes, "As long as historians considered as significant activities mainly the control, exercise and transmission of political and military power, women, who were outside the power structure… were of necessity ignored. At best their contribution to power was peripheral and could be easily passed over as [only an indirect] 'influence'."[1] A woman received attention by the historians only when she displayed some of the characteristics, which are perceived as and believed to be 'intrinsically male'. Also, the principal authors of history have been males. This came as natural to a male dominated society. According to social anthropologist Edwin Ardener, the dominant modes of expression in any society have been generated by the dominant structure.[2] Only the dominant mode is 'heard'. Any subdominant group, either learns to express its views 'in-terms' of the dominant mode – thus women turn into what Veena Das[3] calls 'female patriarchs', i.e., women speaking on behalf of men,[4] or remain inarticulate, i.e., 'muted'.[5]

Even when history tried to widen its scope by inclusion of other aspects of human life as well as histories of people whose lives had dimensions other than the aforementioned, it could not effectively include the facts and analyses related to the lives of women. For example, though the rise of social history during the 1960's acted as a curtain-raiser from the experiences of the powerless and the inarticulate, it could not function in the same manner as far as women's marginalization in history was concerned. Disappointingly, the work of social historians took cognizance only of the experiences of powerless men and completely overlooked the experiences of women in similar plight. Thus, while 'class' emerged as a category of historical analysis, 'gender' remained invisible to the eyes of even the socialist and labour historians. Such was also the case with Marxist history. The most illustrious of Marxists historians remained oblivious of women as a part of the exploited lot, while coining the term 'social class' with specific connotations. For Karl Marx, the only stratification which exists in a capitalist society is on two levels, i.e., the bourgeoisie who own and control the means of production; and the proletariat who own nothing but their own labour which they, so to say, sell to the bourgeoisie. However, both these terms are defined in the terms of male sex only and women lack any mention or specification. What is more, even 'family history' is deeply fraught with patriarchal biases and assumptions. Though questions relating to the work done by women are dealt with, it is done with a patriarchal mindset. Unmarried and widowed women are almost excluded from the family history, as if they did not exist. Such neglect is starkly visible in monograph studies like those done by Philip Greven where family history is confined to a study of father-son relationship and the property matters affecting them. The equally important father-daughter and mother child relationships are provided no space in them.[6]

One of the reasons is that women have more than often been conditioned to remain silent and passive, assuming stereotypical roles within the 'private' sphere of life, which remained changeless over time, and therefore irrelevant to the "intellectually interesting questions of historical change".[7] The tasks of child bearing and rearing, and housekeeping, besides others that women might have performed from time to time during different periods of history, were considered to be of little importance at best and hence remained absent from the pages of history. The long-standing dichotomies; as against mere distinctions; of nature and culture, work and family, public and private have unjustifiably, if incidentally, worked as an unholy alliance in just opposing woman to man, ousting her from participation in many important areas of human activity, and so violating the very concept of historiography.[8] Needless to say that any history, written with an inherent androcentric bias, is bound to be incomplete and biased in its representation of the totality of human life and existence.

Thus, in order to render women's voices audible, several layers of accumulated dust have to be removed. The past few decades have, however, seen many scholars making significant efforts to bring women's voices into the mainstream history. The result has been the coining of a new term "Women's History", which may seem to allude to a history of the women alone. However, the term has wider connotations. It stands for a history where women are not relegated to the silence of the background; rather their existence as authors of and actors in history is recognized. What is aimed at is not an utter exclusion of references to men, but a reinterpretation of historical events with a realization that women have had a vital and not peripheral role in the making of history. This line of change in thought has provided room for deeper reflections upon the history of mankind, and fresh interpretations based on a 're-looking' at the events and stages with respect to the contributions women might have made to their shaping up, as well as their impact upon the lives of women. Women's history tends to focus on both, how women have shaped history, i.e., the role they might have played in processes of historical change and how processes of historical change might haves shaped women's lives over the ages. This requires a relentless reworking over facts available and analyses already made, and the present work is a humble attempt in the same direction.

Though the aforesaid discussion holds true for history of women through out the world, our focus is primarily on the history of women in India. The Indian situation represents an example of the relative visibility of women in historical writing particularly with regard to 'ancient' India wherein historians created a certain space for women in the reconstruction of the past[9] Women in ancient India as a subject of research caught the attention of scholars since the 19th century. Both Indian and Western scholars studied the position of women in ancient India, though with different perspectives. The works of pre-independence authors include those of Indra[10], Bader[11], Horner[12], Upadhyaya[13], Altekar[14] and Meyer[15]. While varied aspects were taken up by these authors for study, those by the Western scholars have been criticized by Chakravarti and Roy for lacking analytical rigour; having an unquestioning dependence on textual sources, which were the compositions of males schooled in patriarchal ideology and hence suffered from an inherent andro-centric bias which significantly influenced the conclusions that were drawn; and exhibiting a tendency to romanticize the early Indian situation.[16] At times, one also comes across certain racist and sexist assumptions implicit in the writing of these texts. However, in spite of such drawbacks, they have been significant so far as they provided an impetus for the study of women in early India and the wealth of details they incorporated. Coming to the works by the Indian authors, it may be noted, first, that these works were a response to the then existing social conditions where the "search for origins and for an ideal situation was both a means of instilling national pride, as well as a reflection of it"[17]. The preoccupation of these works with questions such as sati, female infanticide, child marriage, widow remarriage and enforced widowhood, and an attempt to find answers for them in the ancient sources, with the underlying assumption that the older the source, the greater its authenticity; has to be seen in the backdrop of the social reform movements of the 19th century. Altekar was the most influential of authors of this category, who provided a *paradigm* for several other authors on the historiography of women in India for years to come. Later, Chakravarti has made a forceful plea to move *beyond the Altekarian Paradigm* in one of her thought provoking papers.[18] A number of shortcomings and inherent bias of the paradigm that Altekar presented have been rightly pointed out. Criticisms apart, however, even the works belonging to this category have to be acknowledged to have set the study of women in history into motion and for providing several details.

Among the works of post-independence authors are J.B. Chaudhuri[19], R.M. Das[20], M.Talim[21], Moti Chandra[22], P. Mukherji[23], S. Gulati[24], Jayal[25] and others. These works were, in turn, not free from prejudices and "the influence of nationalist historians manifested itself at a number of levels in these works"[26]. The unity in underlying assumptions and concerns of most post-independence scholarship is reflected in the continued reliance on virtually fixed patterns of explanation.[27] There were only a few scholars like Jayal[28] and Mukherji[29] who show glimpses of attempts to move away from hitherto used sources and methods, for example, recognition of the need to interpret data in terms of a sociological or anthropological approach.

As recognized by Chakravarti and Roy, "It will thus be evident that despite a certain tacit recognition of the inadequacies of some of the earlier studies, no radical breakthrough is discernible in post-independence works which concern themselves exclusively with women in early India. This seems to be remarkable in view of the fact that socio-economic history in general, of which women's history should have ideally formed an integral and crucial part, has made considerable progress in the past few decades, and one would have expected these developments to be reflected in the studies on women. If this has not followed, however, the reasons need to be explored".[30] Subsequently they have pointed towards the almost absolute absence of women as a category of analysis in the writings of such pioneers as Kosambi, Thapar and R.S. Sharma and a few significant contributions in the form of papers such as the one by Jaiswal[31]. However, the lacunae pointed towards by Chakravarti and Roy have been considerably sought to be filled in by their own writings in the last decades of the 20th century to the present times, besides many others who have been more analytical in their approach and have tried to study the social structures, and taken recourse to sources other than the textual only, for example, using the anthropological and archaeological evidences. Other than Chakravarti and Roy, the list of such scholars includes Sukumari Bhattacharji, Suvira Jaiswal, Mandakranata Bose, Shalini Shah, Kirit K. Shah and others. Chakravarti and Roy, in their numerous writings, have presented a meticulous examination of concepts and structures, put to question existing explanations and analyses, pointed towards fallacies, and also have tried to open new vistas in research in Women's history by pointing towards the areas which deserve to be looked into. Mandakranta Bose's well known volume[32] includes thought provoking papers on issues dealing with lives of women in the different periods of Indian history. Shalni Shah, in her work[33], has studied gender relations in *Mahābhārata* in the light of anthropological findings, thus adopting a newer approach. She has also dealt with several issues related with women in *Mahābhārata* and women in ancient Indian society in general. Kirit K. Shah's work[34] is unique in that he has used the epigraphic evidences to find out deviations from the norms set by the lawgivers, thus making an attempt to bring the 'silent voices' of women to the fore, and trying to uncover reality. Few of the historians have explicitly dealt with prostitution in ancient India. These include the work of Sinha and Basu[35], which gives a detailed description of the practice of and attitude towards prostitution in ancient India.

Not many scholars have delved into the issue of property rights of women in ancient India. However, there are some significant studies. Again, however, most of these works have been written from a legal point of view, and lack the analytical insight of a historian, resulting into a more factual rendering rather than the analysis of property rights. The first authoritative work on Hindu law was H.T. Colebrook's *A Digest of Hindu Law on Contracts and Succession* with a commentary by Jagannath Tarkapanchanan.[36] Along with other aspects of Hindu law, this work contains sections on *strīdhana*. In the 19th century, among the major publications of legal treatises dealing with *strīdhana*, mention may be made of Thomas Strange's *Hindu Law*.[37] However, the most authoritative work dealing with this aspect of Hindu law was Sir Gooroo Das Bannerjee's *Hindu Law of Marriage and Strīdhana*, which subsequently underwent numerous editions.[38]

The 20th and 21st centuries saw a remarkable rise in the publication of legal literature, most of which dealt with the question of *strīdhana* at length. Among such publications, mention may be made of the works of K.P. Jayaswal,[39] N.C. Sengupta,[40] L. Sternbach,[41] B.S. Narang,[42] Justice M. Rama Jois,[43] Werner F. Menski[44] etc. However, admittedly most of the works listed above discuss the concept of *strīdhana* from purely a legal perspective and suffer from a lack of analysis from the historical and sociological perspectives. P.V. Kane's work[45] is one of those few works wherein a historical perspective has been adopted to discuss the topic of *strīdhana*. Among the papers written on the economic or property rights of women in ancient India are Sukumari Bhattacharji's *Economic Rights of Ancient Indian Women*[46] and N.N. Bhattacharyya's *Proprietary Rights of Women in Ancient India*[47].

It is evident that in the last few years, women's history in early India has no more remained a neglected area. It has been drawing the attention of more and more number of scholars. Though the spirit of innovation and analysis has penetrated into the study of women in early India, this is not to deny the fact that there is still a long terrain that has remained unexplored. There is specially a need for further studies which make comparative estimate of the picture that emerges out of the prescriptive texts and the one that emerges out of a study of non-conventional sources like the anthropological and archaeological sources. The present research is a humble attempt in that direction. A closer study of the *dharmaśāstras* is taken up to find out the prescribed position of women in the period under study, which would subsequently be compared with the picture that emerges out of a study of other textual and epigraphic sources. The dichotomy between prescription and practice is necessary to be sought out in order to unearth the reality regarding the position of women in the then society.

When it comes to a study of women's history in the context of ancient Indian society, one comes across several contradictions and ambiguities. This was the time when the society gradually established itself as patriarchal, controlling every aspect of women's existence. The *dharmaśāstras*, which were the treatises on law, tried to lay down the bases of women's status, roles, rights and duties. Considered to be the foundational documents of the Hindu way of life, that codified both social relations and personal belief as religious imperatives, they are believed to have exerted deep impact on women's lives and conduct through history. It is believed that their teachings have not entirely lost their force to this day. They are thus, some of the most useful sources for understanding women's lives in India. The present research, therefore, seeks to study women in the *dharmaśāstras*. Among the works on *dharmaśāstras*, the earliest and the most detailed are the volumes authored by P.V. Kane.[48] Among these, volume IV focuses specifically on rules laid down for women in the *dharmaśāstras*. There have been a few other works which have taken up the study of women in the *dharmaśāstra* texts. These include the works by Shakuntala Rao Shastri,[49] R.M. Das,[50] Manjushree[51] etc. However, as already discussed, the works of Chakravarti and Roy have far surpassed the others as far as the depth of analysis is concerned. However, while most of the works have focused on the textual sources, a few have relied on the epigraphic sources only. A comparative study of both the sources is an enterprise yet waiting to be undertaken comprehensively. The present research is a humble attempt in this direction.

At the very outset, it has to be borne in mind that these were the writings of men schooled and indoctrinated in patriarchal ideology. Again, one finds that what is being prescribed by these texts is not in consonance with reality. Several deviations from the norms set in these texts can be found on studying the other textual and epigraphic sources. Also, change can be marked out in the attitude of different *dharmaśāstrakāras*. Not only this, contradictory statements can be found within a single text. The present research will enquire into the attitude of *dharmaśāstrakāras* towards women, changes in it and relating both of these to the changing socio-religio-economic frame of reference, thus making a modest attempt to find the factors accounting for such an attitude. Underlying this is the supposition that the attitude towards women in these texts might have been a response to or reflection of the then existing conditions in the socio-religio-economic context.

To sum up, the objectives of the present study are:

- To undertake an intensive and exhaustive study of the select *dharmaśāstra* texts, and find out all that is said about women in them, as also finding out points of contradictions within a text, and changes in different texts.
- To undertake a study of other textual sources as well as some epigraphic sources, and find out the scenario regarding the position of women.
- Comparison between the prescription (based on *dharmaśāstras)*, and practice (based on other texts and epigraphic sources), finding out the degrees of consistency and inconsistency, marking out deviations from the norms; thus finally unearthing the reality shrouded in myth regarding the actual position of women in the then society.
- Making an attempt to relate the line of thinking of the authors of these texts with the then existing socio-political and economic conditions.
- To find out if the *dharmaśāstras* were really the foundational documents of Hindu view of life, as is believed, or whether if they had only a limited sphere of influence.

The study has been divided into five chapters. The present (first) chapter briefly discusses the need for studying women's history, provides a preliminary survey of studies taken up on related topics, thereby justifying the relevance of the subject of the present study and delineating the objectives with which the study is undertaken. A general introduction to the concept of *dharma* and the *dharmaśāstras* as well as the dates of these texts are also discussed. Dates of the texts are discussed very briefly, along with providing a background of the social, political, economic and religious conditions of the period. The second chapter discusses whether the *dharmaśāstras* had a bearing on the lives of women. An effort has been made to go into details and provide an unbiased analysis. The third chapter discusses the property and legal rights given to the women by the authors of the *dharmaśāstras*. The fourth chapter gives space to a study of women in the epics, *Śangam* society, and the epigraphic records, thereby making an effort to compare and contrast the picture with the one that emerges out of a study of the *dharmaśāstras*, thus estimating the actual position of women and gender relations in the then society. The last chapter discusses the inferences drawn out of the study and delves into some theoretical issues related to the lives of women.

Meaning of *Dharma*

In order to understand the nature and objective of the *dharmaśāstras*, to understand the meaning of *dharma* is imperative. However, the actual meaning of *dharma* has kept changing during the ancient times of Indian history. The word has been used in several widely different senses. In its most general sense, it is derived from the root *dhṛ*, which means, to uphold, to support, to sustain or to nourish.[52] Thus, '*dharma* is what is firm and durable, what sustains and maintains, what hinders fainting and falling'.[53] The word appears to be used in the same sense in a few of the passages of the ancient-most documents of Vedic language.[54] In most of the other cases, the word *dharma* carries the meaning 'religious ordinances or rites'[55]. In some other passages, the contextual meaning of the word appears to be, 'fixed principles or rules of conduct'[56]. In the *Aitareya Brāhmaṇa*, the word *dharma* seems to have been used in an abstract sense, viz,. 'the whole body of religious duties'[57]. In the *Bṛhadāraṇyaka Upaniṣad*, *Dharma* and *Satya* (truth) are treated as equivalent.[58] According to a passage in the *Chhāndogya Upaniṣad*, 'There are three branches of *dharma*, one is (constituted by) sacrifice, study and charity (i.e., the stage of householder), the second is (constituted by) austerities (i.e., the stage of being a hermit), the third is the *brahmacārī* dwelling in the house of his teacher and making himself stay with the family of his teacher till the last; all these attain to the worlds of meritorious men; one who abides firmly in *brahman* attains immortality'.[59] As the word *brahmacārī* itself occurs in this passage, it is clearly indicated that here *dharma* stands for the peculiar duties of the *āśramas*. The foregoing points make it clear that the meaning of the word *dharma* passed through several transitions. However, ultimately its most prominent significance came to be 'the privileges, duties and obligations of a man, his standard of conduct as a member of the *Āryan* community, as a member of one of the castes, as a person in a particular stage of life.'[60] It is in this sense that the word is employed in the *dharmaśāstra* literature.[61] According to the *Manusmṛti*, the sages requested Manu to impart instruction in the *dharmas* of all the *varṇas*.[62] It is employed in the same sense in the *Yājñavalkya Smṛti*.[63] Medhātithī commenting on Manu says that the expounders of *smṛti* dilate upon *dharma* as five-fold, viz., *varṇadharma, āśrama-dharma, varṇāśramadharma, naimittikadharma* (such as *prāyascitta*) and *guṇadharma* (the duty of the crowned king, whether *kśatriya* or not, to protect).[64] It may be noted that the *Mitākśarā* on Yājñavalkya (I.1) after mentioning the five-fold *dharmas* and illustrating them, adds a sixth category, viz., '*Sādhāraṇa-dharma*', meaning duties common to all men (including even *cāṇḍālas*) such as *ahimsā*.[65]

Sources of *Dharma*

The *Gautama Dharmasūtra* says, "the *Veda* is the source of *dharma* and the tradition and practice of those that know it (the *Veda*)".[66] So Āpastamba says, "the authority (for the *dharma*) is the consensus of those that know *dharma* and the *Vedas*".[67] Same is the view expressed in *Vasiṣṭha Dharmasūtra*.[68] The *dharmasūtras* in general enumerate three sources of *dharma*: the *Veda*, tradition and 'good custom'. The *Manusmṛti* lays down five different sources of *dharma*, "the whole Veda is (the foremost) source of *dharma*, and (next) the tradition and practice of those that know it; and further usages of virtuous men and self-satisfaction".[69] Yājñavalkya declares the sources in a similar strain- "The *Veda*, traditional lore, the usages of good men, what is agreeable to one's self and desire born of due deliberation – this is traditionally recognized as the source of *dharma*".[70] Thus, the codes of Manu and Yājñavalkya add one more as the source of *dharma*, i.e., inner contentment. The commentators on Manu add the hypothesis that where one has a choice between two ways of acting, conscience will show which is to be preferred.

Origin and Evolution of the *Dharmaśāstras*

Though the *Vedas* are counted as the foremost among the sources of *dharma*, they do not profess to be formal treatises on *dharma*; they only contain disconnected statements on the various aspects of *dharma*. Lingat writes, "Strictly speaking, the *Vedas* do not even include a single positive precept which could be used directly as a rule of conduct. One can find there only references to usage which falls within the scope of *dharma*."[71] The *Vedas* are considered as *śruti,* i.e., revelation, while the *smṛti,* i.e., tradition is the second important source of *dharma*. *Smṛti* comprises of the six *Vedāngas,* the epics and the *Purāṇas*. Rules of *dharma* are contained in all these works. However, those whose special object is to expound them belong to the class of the *Vedāngas*. The *Vedāngas* are considered as the auxiliary sciences required for the interpretation of the *Veda*s. They are sub-divided into six kinds of treatises bearing (1) on phonetics and more especially on the euphonic rules peculiar to the *Vedas*; (2) on meters; (3) on linguistic analysis and grammar; (4) on astronomy, especially for the Vedic calendar which fixes days propitious for sacrifices; (5) on the explanation of the difficult terms of the *Veda* i.e., etymology; and lastly (6) on the rituals to observe in the sacrifices i.e., *kalpa*.

All of the aforementioned works are written in the form of *sūtra*, i.e., in the form of aphorisms or highly condensed and abstract sentences.[72] Among these, the *kalpa-sūtras* are in turn divided into three categories of work – the *śrauta-sūtras*, which deal with the great sacrifices; *gṛhya-sūtras*, which deal with domestic cults and the *dharmasūtras,* which specifically deal with the duties and the privileges which are attached to the status of membership in the *Āryan* community. Among these, the *śrauta-sūtras* elaborate upon the rituals of the sacrifices which belong directly to the *śruti* or great sacrifices, while the *gṛhya-sūtras* are concerned with domestic rites which those scriptures mention only incidentally. Thus even the *gṛhya-sūtras* consist of rituals essentially. They touch upon topics which fall under the category of *dharma* only incidentally.

However, it seems that in the post-Vedic era, a need must have arisen for the composition of manuals devoted exclusively to the topics related to *dharma*. In the post-Vedic era, there was an affirmation of the supremacy of the *brāhmaṇas*.[73] They were to play the role of preceptors, and they had to compose manuals in which the teachings which they wished to inculcate in their pupils were condensed, in the form of formulae. Apart from this, appeals must have been commonly made to the *brāhmaṇas* to arbitrate between parties to a dispute or to give advice as to which rule should be followed in the case of a particular difficulty.[74] At the royal courts also, the *brāhmaṇas* had to play the role of confessor or councillor, or of judge. These must have been the reasons which would have prompted the development of a literature which was specifically devoted to *dharma:* these are the *dharmasūtras*.[75] Thus, each school has, in addition to its *samhitā* and its *brāhmaṇas,* its threefold series (at least in theory) of the *kalpa-sūtra*: *śraūta, gṛhya,* and *dharma.* According to Winternitz too, "The oldest manuals on *dharma*, the *dharmasūtras*, originated in the closest association with the literature of rituals (*Vedānga-kalpa*)."[76] Kane also writes, "It seems that originally many, though not all, of the *dharmasūtras* formed part of the *kalpasūtras* and were studied in distinct *sūtracaraṇas*."[77] Thus, originally it seems that most of the *dharmasūtras* were attached to a particular Vedic school. But of all those which have come down to us, 'it is only in the case of the Āpastamba, Hiraṇyakeśī and Baudhāyana *sūtracaraṇas* that we have a complete *kalpa* tradition with its three components of *Śrauta, Gṛhya and Dharmasūtras*.[78] The *dharma-sūtras* bear a close relation to the *gṛhya-sūtras* in all respects. The connection is not only linguistic but also as regards the subject matter.[79] Kane also says that the *Dharmasūtras* were closely connected with the *gṛhya-sūtras* in subjects and topics.[80] Like the *gṛhya-sūtras,* the *dharma-sūtras* contain rules about the *saṁskāras*, including marriage; on the *āśramas,* including the duties of the *brahmacārī*, and the householder; on funeral oblations, etc. But they seldom describe the rituals of domestic life; they touch upon it only in passing. They intend above all to propound the rules to govern men's conduct. This lead to the appearance of precepts of a juridical character which can be found in the *dharmasūtras*. At a later stage, it seems, *dharma* was subjected to a specialized study. It was at this time that *dharma* began to be studied in special schools no longer attached to any one *caraṇa,* to any particular Vedic school.[81]

A science of *dharma* grew up, in which the rule of conduct was taught more systematically than in the *dharmasūtras*.[82] The new treatises were called *dharmaśāstras*. It is generally agreed that these great treatises on *dharma*, followed, historically speaking, immediately after the latter.[83] However, as Kane has mentioned, there are certain points that distinguish the *dharmasūtras* from the *dharmaśāstras*[84]*:* (a) Many *dharmasūtras* are either parts of the *Kalpa* belonging to each *sūtracaraṇa* or are intimately connected with the *gṛhyasūtras*; (b) The *dharmasūtras* sometimes betray some partiality in their Vedic quotations for the text of the Veda to which they belong or in the *caraṇas* of which they are studied; (c) The authors of the (older) *dharmasūtras* do not claim to be inspired seers or superhuman beings, while the *Smṛtis* such as those of Manu and Yājñavalkya are ascribed to gods like Brahma; (d) The *dharmasūtras* are in prose or mixed prose and verse, the *Smṛtis* are in verse only; (e) The language of the *dharmasūtras* is generally more archaic than that of other *Smṛtis*; (f) The *dharmasūtras* do not proceed upon any orderly arrangement of topics, while the *Smṛtis* arrange their contents and treat of the subjects under three principal heads, viz., *ācāra, vyavahāra* and *prāyaścitta*; (g) Most of the *dharmasūtras* are older than the *Smṛtis*.

Dharmaśāstras: Number and Dates

The number of *dharmaśāstras* is many, starting from the *dharmasūtras*, which were composed in the period around 6th or 7th century BC; down to the composition of digests and commentaries which continued to be written until after the 18th century AD. Kane estimates the number of these works known to writers of the Middle Ages at about a hundred. Some survive only in the form of abridgements, and the majority is known to us only from quotations which the authors of commentaries and digests preserve for us. However, other scholars have excluded the *dharmasūtras* as well as the digests and commentaries from the category of *dharmaśāstras* and included only the *Smṛtis* in it. For the purpose of our study, we have taken into account a few major *dharmasūtras* in it, besides some major and minor *smṛti* works.

Gautama Dharmasūtra

In all probabilities the oldest of all the *dharmasūtras*, that have come down to us, is that of *Gautama*, or of the *Gautama* school, the *Gautamīya Dharmaśāstra*. It is difficult to say whether it was composed by a single author or it arose in the Vedic school going by the name of Gautama. The text which has come down to us is unattached. However, it may be believed to have earlier formed part of the *kalpa-sūtra* of one of the Vedic schools, which were founded by the members of the ancient *brāhmaṇa* family known by the name Gautama.[85] All these schools were attached to the *Sāma Veda*. It seems to belong to the *Rāṇāyanīya* school of the *Sāma Veda*.[86]

The *Gautama Dharmasūtra* cites the authority of none other but Manu who might have been someone other than the author of *Manusmṛti*. However, he often alludes to the opinions professed by various *ācāryas* (teachers), which implies that there were others who had taught *dharma* before him. This proves that Gautama's *dharmasūtra* must not have been the first treatise on *dharma*. Also the language in which the text is written is less archaic and more conformable to the grammatical rules of Panini than the *dharmasūtras* of Āpastamba and Baudhāyana. The earliest work to refer to Gautama as a writer on *dharma* is the *Baudhāyana Dharmasūtra*.[87] The age of the latter ranges between 500–200 BC.[88] If the above Gautama be identical with ours, and if Baudhāyana was the borrower, then Gautama may be taken to have flourished earlier than the above date. Kane places this text between 600 and 400 BC.[89]

The Dharmasūtra of Vasiṣṭha

Vasiṣṭha is the name of one of the most famous *Ṛṣis* of the *Ṛgveda*. Regarding the authorship and origin, Keith comments, "The ancient tradition mentions as the author of this work one ṛsi Vasiṣṭha, to whom a large number of hymns of Book VII of the *Ṛgveda* are too attributed. This position is in accord with the well-established tradition, already known to Kumārila, according to which the *Vasiṣṭha Dharmasūtra* originally belonged to a school of the *Ṛgveda* and later became authoritative for all the *brāhmaṇas*.[90] In any case the relationship between this work and a school of the *Ṛgveda* is established beyond doubt. Several of Vasiṣṭha's opinions are archaic and in many respects differ from those of ancient authors like Gautama and Baudhāyana. Kane places it between 300 and 100 BC.[91] Keith agrees with Kane.[92]

Viṣṇu Smṛti

This work is known by various names including *Viṣṇu Smṛti*, *Viṣṇu Sūtra* and *Vaiṣṇava dharmaśāstra*. It is unique in the sense that while the other *dharmasūtras* represent themselves as human products, this work is attributed to the god Viṣṇu. He addresses them to the goddess Earth when, under the *avatāra* in the form the Boar, he raises the Earth above the waters. Thus there is no clue regarding its real authors. Further, the work is far more extensive than the old *dharmasūtras*. The work, as it has reached us, seems to be of a fairly recent redaction and on the basis of several internal evidences, Kane has placed this edition about 400 to 600 AD, while placing the original one about 300 BC to 100 AD.[93]

However, some of the portions seem to refer to its composition in a much older period. Bühler, followed by Jolly, suggested that there are traces of a much older *dharmasūtra* which has been retouched at some recent period by a member of a Vaisnavite sect. They concluded that the *Viṣṇu Smṛti* was, in its original form, the *dharmasūtra* of the *kaṭha* school of the Black *Yajurveda*[94] and that it is actually much more ancient than Āpastamba, even earlier than the fourth or fifth century BC.[95] P.V. Kane also points out that there is a close relationship of the work with the *Kaṭhaka* school of the *Yajurveda*.[96]

Yājñavalkya mentions *Viṣṇu* among the writers on *Dharmaśāstra*.[97] It is not certain whether or not this *Viṣṇu* was identical with the author of *Viṣṇu Smṛti* or it is a reference to an older writer.

Manusmṛti

The *Manusmṛti* is considered to be the most authoritative work among the *dharmaśāstras*. In the traditional list of writers on *dharma*, contained in the *Yājñavalkya Smṛti*[98], Manu is mentioned first of all. Much more celebrated than any other *smṛti* in India, the popularity of *Manusmṛti* spread far beyond the confines of India. It has enjoyed a similar prestige in Champa, Cambodia and Indonesia.

Manusmṛti ascribes to itself a mythical origin. Verses fourth to fifty-ninth in the first chapter are put in the mouth of Manu, while verse sixty-one onwards, Bhṛgu is the speaker. The code or the institutes of the sacred law are said to have been taught by the Brahmā to Manu, who in turn taught them to Marīci and other sages.[99] The question of the origin of *Manusmṛti* has evoked widespread interest among the scholars. A group of scholars believed that the metrical *Manusmṛti* did not begin all of a sudden and at a given date, rather the germs of the text lay in the older *sūtras*. Max Müller was one of the chief proponents of this hypothesis.[100] This hypothesis gained currency among many scholars including Hopkins,[101] Bühler,[102] and Jolly.[103] However, this earlier attempt did not prove successful and, it evoked many questions. The recovery of the manuals of the so-called *Mānava* school, contradicted the hypothesis rather than confirming it, as the doctrines of the *Mānavagṛhyasūtra* differed from those of the *Mānavadharmaśāstra* in a significant way.

It is also argued by many that the original work underwent a considerable number of additions, alterations and revisions before it reached the present form. In the *Manusmṛti*, as it has come down to us, Manu says, he taught the institutes taught to him by Brahmā to Marīci and other sages[104], which in a previous verse[105] were told to have numbered ten including Atri, Angirās, Pulastya, Pulaha, Kratu, Prācetas, Vasiṣṭha, Bhṛgu, and Nārada, besides Marīci. Also, this text is a narration by Bhṛgu after the sixtieth verse. As Lingat writes, "So, the *Manusmṛti* ought to be attributed not to Manu, but to Bhṛgu, or at least ought to be considered to be the Bhṛgu (i.e., Bhārgava) recension of the *Mānavadharmaśāstra*".[106] Further, Lingat makes a reference to the citations taken by the medieval digests from a "*Bṛhan*-Manu" (Great Manu) and a "*Vṛddha* Manu" (Old Manu), and suggests that these were later amplified versions of the text. He finally expresses the opinion that the version of Bhṛgu seems to be the earliest.[107] While the statements made by Lingat seem to hold some ground, nothing could be said conclusively about it.

Further, the mythological references to Manu are confusing. The question of the historical identity of Manu, or the Manus, needs to be ascertained before it can be satisfactorily resolved. Parnasabari Bhattacharyya has tried to make an analysis of the historical references to Manu in the ancient Indian texts.[108] Here, she has referred to the *Taittirīya Samhitā* and the *Tāṇḍyāmahābrāhmaṇa* where it is said that whatever Manu said is medicine. Besides others, mention has been made of the many passages in the *Mahābhārata* which refer to various Manus in connection with legal and moral questions. The *Arthaśāstra* also refers to Manu and the *Mānava* school a number of times. Also, many statements are common to both the *Arthaśāstra* and *Manusmṛti*. Whether the author of *Arthaśāstra* derived these from *Manusmṛti* or both the texts derived them from some anterior common source is doubtful. Bhattacharyya has further referred to stray references to Manu in the Buddhist and Jaina literature, as well as in a number of epigraphic records. From all the references she has made, the historicity of Manu is fairly established; however, some questions await their satisfactory solutions. Whether Manu was an individual propagator of law, or were there a number of Manus starting from a Manu of hoary antiquity, or if Manu represented a school of thought which had its origins in the Vedic past; are few to mention.

However, regarding the date of the extant *Manusmṛti*, there are sufficient grounds to believe that the text succeeded the *dharmasūtras* and preceded the other *dharmaśāstras*. So there is a general consensus among the historians that *Manusmṛti* is older than the other *dharmaśāstras*. Kane assigns the extant *Manusmṛti* to a period between the second century BC and second centûry AD.[109]

Manusmṛti has been commented upon by more number of scholars than any other *smṛti* text. Among the commentators, Medhātithī (c. 825–800 AD) is the oldest, and Kulluka (before 1300 AD) is the most popular. Their commentaries are called *Bhāṣya* and *Mānvārthamuktāvalī* respectively. The other commentators are Govindarāja, Nārāyaṇa, Rāghavānanda, Nandana and Rāmacandra. Asahāya also seems to have written a commentary. The *Vivādaratnākara* quotes a commentary on Manu by Udayākara.

Yājñavalkya Smṛti

Yājñavalkya too is a mythical personage and figures amongst the most illustrious sages of the Vedic age. However, it is difficult to establish a definite relationship between the Vedic sage and the author of *Yājñavalkya Smṛti*. On the basis of some internal evidence suggesting some connections with the White *Yajurveda*, Jolly proposed that the *smṛti* arose from a *dharmasūtra* belonging to a school attached to that *Veda*.[110] Again, he suggests that connections also exist between the *Yājñavalkya Smṛti* and the *gṛhyasūtra* of the *Mānava* school which itself belongs to the Black *Yajurveda*.[111] However, all that that can be conceded according to Kane, is that the author of the *smṛti* must have been a student of the White *Yajurveda*, and that no conclusions may be drawn that there was a *dharmasūtra* of the White *Yajurveda*, on which the *Yājñavalkya Smṛti* was based.[112]

Whoever might be the author of the *Smṛti*, it occupies a very important position among the *dharmaśāstras*. This is attested to by the numerous commentaries written upon it. The intrinsic qualities of the work make it worthy of such an appreciation. It is certainly the best composed of all the *Smṛtis* which have come down to us. The three subjects of *ācāra*, *vyavahāra* and *prāyascitta* have received a very systematic treatment in this work. The portion on *vyavahāra* (secular law) is the most famous. The section on *dāyabhāga* (inheritance and succession), included in *vyavahāra*, has given rise to two schools of law, viz., *Mitākśarā* governing the whole of India excepting Bengal (i.e., the region included in the present-day West Bengal and Bangladesh), and *dāyabhāga* prevailing in Bengal. The *Yājñavalkya Smṛti* is in general very close to Manu, but it occasionally evidences a remarkable independence.

The evident progress in the style and form of writing of the work leaves little room for doubting the hypothesis that its composition must be later than that of the code of Manu. Yet debate rages on the question of the date of its composition. Jayaswal puts *Yājñavalkya Smṛti* between 150 AD and 200 AD.[113] Kane placed the composition of the work between the first century BC and the third century AD.[114]

Of the many commentaries on the *Yājñavalkya Smṛti*, those of Viśvarūpa (c. 800–25 AD), Vijñṛneśvara (c. 1070–1100 AD.), Aparārka or Aparāditya (first half of the 12th century) and Śūlapāṇi (sometime between 11th and 15th centuries) are famous.

Nārada Smṛti

There are two versions of the *smṛti* attributed to Nārada, a smaller and a larger one.[115] The short version was translated into English by Jolly in

1876. The longer version, which is believed to represent the original work, was published by Jolly in 1885, but since the manuscript ended with verse 22 of section V, the text had to be completed with the aid of the short version. Further, Jolly added under the title of appendix (*pariśiṣtam*) a chapter on theft taken from an old Nepalese manuscript. Later, Jolly published a new translation in 1889 in which he added more than a hundred other verses which are attributed to Nārada by commentators or authors of digests and were not a part of the text which he edited earlier.

It shall be noticed that the *Nārada Smṛti* follows the *Manusmṛti* to a considerable extent in the nomenclature and arrangement of the eighteen titles.[116] However, on certain vital matters, Nārada differs from Manu. A comparison of the contents of these two *Smṛtis* fully confirms that Manu was the senior in age. Nārada's treatment is more analytical than Manu's. It is an important work on *vyavahāra*. Jolly suggested that the *Smṛti* can hardly belong to a period earlier than the fifth or sixth century AD at the very latest.[117] Kane suggested the date of its composition to be between 100 and 300 AD.[118]

Bṛhaspati Smṛti

Bṛhaspati is the name of one of the deities in the *Ṛgveda*. The *dharmaśāstra* bearing his name seems to have enjoyed a considerable authority amongst the commentators.

Bṛhaspati follows the *Manusmṛti* very closely and considers it as the highest authority. He refers to and quotes it often, and many times he seems to be merely a commentator on Manu, explaining and developing his precepts. Though at times, he deviates from the decisions recommended by Manu, especially in the context of his favourable treatment of the rights of women in their father's or husband's property.

Bṛhaspati is undoubtedly later than Manu. According to Jolly, the earlier date of the composition of this *Smṛti* must be the first century AD.[119] Kane places him after Manu and Yājñavalkya, and assigns the date 200 AD to 400 AD to the *Smṛti*.[120]

Pārāśara Smṛti

Pārāśara is also one of the Vedic sages, being the author of several Vedic hymns and known in mythology as the father of the celebrated author of *Mahābhārata*, Ṛṣi Vyāsa. The extant *smṛti* is written in twelve chapters comprising 592 verses. It deals only with *ācāra* and *prāyascitta*.

Pārāśara is mentioned by Yājñavalkya among the ancient writers on *dharma*.[121] But, the extant *Pārāśara Smṛti* mentions Yājñavalkya in the first chapter.[122] It is doubtful if we possess the ancient *smṛti* of Pārāśara.[123] So, it is later than the *Yājñavalkya Smṛti*. It may be that the older work of Pārāśara was recast at a later date. According to Kane, the age of this work is between 100 and 500 AD.[124]

Kātyāyana Smṛti

Kātyāyana is frequently cited by both ancient and modern commentators. Some evidences suggest that Kātyāyana might have authored a more extensive work, which has not been retrieved yet. Kātyāyana is also named in the *Yājñavalkya Smṛti* amongst the sages who had codified *dharma*.[125] According to Kane, the author took Nārada and Bṛhaspati as his models in the order and treatment of the subjects to be dealt with on *vyavahāra*.[126] Frequent references to the opinion of Bhṛgu are found in the text, which may be taken to refer to Manu. However, the rules which he attributes to Bhṛgu can not always to be traced in the *Manusmṛti*. This has strengthened the argument for the theory of successive recensions of Manu. Kātyāyana deals in considerable detail with the personal property of women (*strīdhana*). In fact, he is the first *smṛti* author to have dealt with this issue in detail. Kane places this text sometime between 400 and 600 AD.[127]

The Socio-political and Economic Life

The period under review is characterized by a fluid situation in the political arena with numerous hordes of foreigners coming, and settling as a part of the ruling aristocracy; and as traders due to the brisk economic activity. This gave rise to a social scene where processes of transition and reconciliation started along with attempts to maintain the status quo by some of the dominant sections of the society. Religion had its own significant role to play. A study of the political, economic, social and religious conditions of the time is imperative before the discussion is taken further.

The Political Scene

Political scene in the Mauryan period was characterized by centralized monarchy. However, events in the post-Mauryan period became diffuse. During this period, with the disintegration of large kingdoms, a number of small kingdoms and tribal republics rose. Even though this period was marked by the absence of a large empire like that of the Mauryas, the centuries that followed the Mauryan rule were historically important and witnessed significant developments.

The Śungas established the rule of their dynasty, usurping the throne from the last Maurya ruler, who was assassinated by Puśyamitra Śunga sometime around 185 BC. They are usually regarded as *brāhmaṇas* belonging to the Bhāradwṛja clan, and are said to have been the revivalists of Vedic Brāhmanism. This period also witnessed the growing importance of the Bhagwatism. The Śungas remained occupied with wars, and finally, the last king was killed by his minister Vasudeva in 73 BC, who subsequently founded the Kāṇva dynasty. The Kāṇva kings reigned uneventfully for a period of about forty-five years, after which, they were overthrown by the Ṛndhras. However, the Ṛndhra conquest of Magadha does not seem to have resulted in a permanent occupation, and petty kings ruled the region after their withdrawal.

Tribal polities also reappeared in Punjab, Haryana and Rajasthan during this period. The Arjunāyanas, Kuniṇḍas, Auḍambaras, Trigartas, Ṛgastyas, Śibis and Yaudheyas are known from their coins which were issued in the period between the 2nd century BC and AD. Some of them later migrated to adjoining areas. Many of these clans claimed a *kśatriya* status. Some of the chiefs took titles suited to kings; however, their coins were minted in the name of the *gaṇa* or the *janapada*, indicating them to be more of republican polities.

Another powerful kingdom that rose out of the ruins of Magadha was Kalinga under Khāravela, who was a powerful monarch and a devout Jaina. According to R.C. Majumdar, his conquering expeditions indicate a state of political chaos and confusion such as would have naturally followed the downfall of the Magadha Empire.[128] After his fall, the history of Kalinga becomes obscure.

In the Deccan, the Sātavāhanas appeared as successors of the Mauryas in the first century BC and ruled for more than four centuries. They were sometimes called the Ṛndhras or the Ṛndhrabhṛtyas, leading to a doubt of their having a low origin. According to Romila Thapar, the rise of Sātavāhanas follows the pattern of transition from chiefdom to kingdom, with the newly established kings performing Vedic sacrifices as an act of legitimization.[129] The kings of this dynasty did not assume any lofty titles, rather were content with the simple title of *rājan*. This was in tandem with their administrative system, where power was distributed throughout the hierarchy of officials. The first king who gained wide recognition was Śātakarṇī, who ruled around 50 BC, known for his policy of military expansion. He claimed to have destroyed the *khatiyas* (*kśatriyas*). The Sātavāhana power faced a blow due to the invasions of western Kśatrapas for a brief period of twelve years, however, they rose to glorious heights during the reign of Gautamiputra Śātakarṇī. It is said that he uprooted the Śakas, destroyed the pride of the *kśatriyas*, stopped the inter-mingling of the four *varṇas*, and furthered the interests of the twice-born. It is interesting to note that some Sātavāhana rulers use metronymics. The period of the Sātavāhanas recorded significant growth in trade and maritime activity, along with art and architecture. However, the third century saw the gradual weakening of the Sātavāhana power, as local governors began to claim independent status. After their fall a number of kingdoms came into being. In the north-western Deccan the Abhiras came into prominence; in Maharashtra and Kuntala, the Chutus and after them the Kadambas became powerful. The Ikśvākus established themselves in Ṛndhradeśa; in the south-eastern part of the former Sātavāhana empire the Pallavas founded an independent dynasty and expanded into a great power by the middle of the sixth century. The Vākāṭakas became powerful in the region of Vidarbha (Berar).

In the South, the period was marked with frequent conflicts between the Ceras, Colas and Pāṇḍyas. Accordingly, poems were composed on the themes of war and love by the Sangam poets. In the farther south, this was a period of transition from the chiefdoms to the kingdoms, with the formation of the states.

The north-west was affected by the happenings in central Asia. The north-western provinces of the Magadha Empire were wrested by Demetrius, the Bactrian king, about the beginning of the second century BC. Thus, he established Indo-Greek power in India. They made forays into the Ganges heartland. Pātañjali's *Mahābhāṣya* refers to Yavana raids in the western Ganga plain and Rajasthan. The most widely known Indo-Greek ruler was Menander, whose fame is immortalized by the Buddhist text, *Milindapañho*. He ruled in the period from c. 150 to 135 BC and patronized Buddhism. He stabilized the Greek power, besides extending its frontiers in India. The Indo-Greek rule in the Punjab and adjoining territories lasted for over a century and a half. These rulers adopted the provincial organization of the Hellenistic kings – the Greek *satrapies* with their *strategoi* and *medriarchs*. Trade between India and the west increased considerably as a result of the Greek conquest. The Indo-Greek rule exerted considerable influence in other areas too like art and architecture.

The Greeks were not the only foreigners to have entered and influenced India in this period. The Pārthians, Śakas and Kuśāṇas were the other people who entered India by turns. An independent national kingdom was established in Parthia about the middle of the third century BC. In the middle of the second century BC, Parthian king Mithradates-I had carried arms till the *Sindhu*. Towards the close of the first century AD, Parthian chiefs were involved in a struggle for power in the lower Sindh. Some Parthian kings also ruled in the Peshawar valley.

The Śaka power was established by king Maues or Maga in Gandhāra in c. 80 BC. Three important Śaka principalities can be traced in India. Two of them were in northern India, with Mathurā and Takshaśilā as the capitals respectively. The third comprised Malwa and Kathiawar peninsula in Western India. The previous two are known as northern Kśatraps, while the latter are known as the Western Kśatraps. The western Kśatraps ruled for nearly three centuries. The rulers called themselves *Satraps*. The Kuṣāṇas, the last of the foreign invaders, belonged to a nomadic Turkish tribe, Yueh-Chih. By the beginning of the first century BC, they gave up their nomadic habits and divided themselves into five groups or principalities. Nearly a century after this division, Kujula Kadphises I, the king of one of the principalities, attacked and subjugated the other four principalities. This lead to the establishment of a large empire in India. The greatest Kuṣāṇa king was Kaniṣka who ruled in the first century AD. He was a patron of Buddhism. Four kings of this dynasty ruled for a period of about one hundred years. However, the overthrow of the Kuṣāṇa empire did not mean an end of the Kusāṇa power in India. The later Kuṣāṇas ruled in Kabul and a part of the Punjab valley for a long time. They were ousted by another branch of the same clan, known as the Kidāra Kuṣāṇas.

To sum up, the political history of India from the first century BC to the third century AD presents a confusing picture of advancing waves of contending tribes, kings, and invaders. Most of the kingdoms in the post-Maurya period were small, except for the Śaka-Kuṣāṇas in the north and the north-west, and the Sātavāhanas in the Deccan, who ruled over large areas. They did not exercise rigid centralized control over their territories like the Mauryas. The Kuṣāṇas entered into a feudatory relationship with a number of small kings. They also seem to have practised a hereditary dual rule; in some cases a father and his son ruled at one and the same time. The Sātavāhanas had several vassals such as the Maharaṭhīs and the Ikśvākus who founded independent kingdoms on the ruins of the domains of their overlords. The centrifugal forces of the post-Maurya period were sought to be counterbalanced by the association of divine elements with the ruler.

With the eclipse of the Kuṣāṇas in the north India and of the Sātavāhanas in the Deccan in the third century, there prevailed a period of political disintegration, which paved the way for the emergence of several minor powers and new ruling families. It was in this period that the Guptas laid the foundation of an empire. The first two Guptas, Śrigupta and Ghaṭotkaca, were rulers of no consequence. The first ruler who deserves mention is Chandragupta I, whose accession to the throne in about AD 319–320 can be considered to be the real beginning of the Gupta era. He sought to gain in prestige by diplomatically entering into marriage alliance with a Licchhavi princess. His rule remained confined to Magadha and part of eastern Uttar Pradesh. He was succeeded by his son Samudragupta. The states overpowered by Samudragupta make a fairly long list and covered a large part of the subcontinent. But it is generally believed that Samudragupta exercised direct administrative control only over northern India. The kings of the Deccan and the south merely paid him homage; the Śakas in western India seem to have remained unconquered. The empire of Samudragupta was further extended and consolidated by Chandragupta II, who ruled from AD 375 to 415. Chandragupta II's campaign against the Śakas resulted in their final defeat and the annexation of western India to the Gupta empire. Kumāragupta and then Skandagupta succeeded him. Skandagupta faced the Hūṇa threat and fought them bravely but the situation became complicated owing to several domestic problems. However, he appears to have won the battle. But his death in about 467 AD was followed by a succession of several kings who could not keep the empire intact. A major blow to Gupta power came towards the end of the fifth century, when the Hūṇas entered north India in hordes.

The dissolution of the Gupta empire coincides with the establishment of the Hūṇa kingdom in north India as far as Eran in Madhya Pradesh. The disintegration of Gupta power cannot be fully explained by the Hūṇa invasion. Perhaps it was the inevitable result of the manner in which the empire was organized. In contrast to the Mauryas, the Guptas do not seem to have possessed a large professional army. Neither did they possess an elaborate and organized bureaucracy.

The Economic Scene

Though the political scene seems to present a situation of chaos in the post-Mauryan period, the period is marked with brisk economic activity and a fabulous expansion in trade and industry. As Romila Thapar writes, the dynasties of this period had a relatively quick turnover, yet beneath these changes the most stable factor was trade.[130] However, a decline in the long distance trade and concomitant ruralization of arts and crafts ensued from the Gupta period onwards.

Agrarian Structure and Agriculture

During the Mauryan period, there were state farms being worked by slaves and hired labourers under the supervision of the superintendent of agriculture. However, in the post-Mauryan period, individual possession of the farms seems to have been promoted. *Milindapañho* refers to the individual who clears the forest and takes other steps to make the land fit for cultivation; and by virtue of doing these things, becomes the owner of the land.[131] Echo of this is also found in the *Manusmṛti* where it is said that the sages declare a field belongs to one who cleared away the timber.[132] Thus theoretically the investment of physical labour in a piece of unclaimed property was supposed to confer on the individual the title to that property.[133] Perhaps a need was felt to encourage cultivation of untilled lands. This is further supported by a verse in *Manusmṛti*, which states that the acceptance of an untilled field by the *brāhmana* is less blameable than a tilled field.[134] Though land was possessed by individual farmers, the idea of state ownership was not altogether absent. Textual and epigraphic references corroborate the idea that the state effectively exercised the rights of ownership over land. The practice of making religious land grants by the rulers had come into vogue, perhaps to make lands arable. On their part the Sātavāhanas started the practice of donating land with fiscal and administrative immunities to *brāhmaṇas* and Buddhist monks. This gradually weakened their central authority. The gifted villages tended to become semi-independent administrative pockets, which loosened royal control over the countryside. In the Sātavāhana kingdom, even the individuals are recorded to have made such grants to the Buddhist monks. The Sātavāhanas did not posses the vast bureaucracy of the Mauryas. They could not, therefore regulate various economic activities, as the Mauryas had done. The clearing of forests and the founding of new settlements under the aegis of the state was not possible, and agricultural expansion depended on individual effort. A contemporary Buddhist work refers to individual farmers in large numbers working hard and engaged in cultivation.

However, no references to the purchase or sale of land for secular purposes are found. This seems to have limited the scope of individual ownership. Though no epigraphic references are found indicating the grant of land to administrative officers, some verses in *Manusmṛti* provide for the assignment of land to revenue officials in charge of one, ten, twenty, a hundred or a thousand villages.[135] Perhaps the state enforced laws in the post-Maurya period to protect agriculture. *Manusmṛti* lays down the punishment of mutilation for selling false seed corn, taking up seed already sown and for destroying boundary marks; and enjoins punishment for theft of agricultural implements.[136]

As mentioned earlier, an increase in the practice of granting land and villages to priests and temples, which had begun in the Sātavāhana period and which gained in strength during the rule of the Vākāṭakas, caused a decentralization of administrative authority. The Guptas have very few such grants to their credit. The transfer of magisterial and police powers together with fiscal rights to the donees not only weakened the royal authority but also led to the oppression of peasants and inhabitants of the gifted villages. Thus, the land grants led to the growth of feudal society. That the peasants were attached to their land even when it was given away is indicated by several inscriptions belonging to that period. This led to the emergence of serfdom. As a matter of fact, the recipients of the donations enjoyed the right of subinfeudation which eroded the rights of the peasantry. The donated land could be assigned to tenants on certain terms. This implied the donees' right to evict tenants from their land. The practice of subinfeudation, therefore, reduced permanent tenants to the position of tenants-at-will.[137]

From the Gupta period onwards, the imposition of forced labour (*viṣṭi*) and several new levies and taxes further undermined the position of peasants. The practice of making land grants thus gave rise to feudal agrarian relations and forms of exploitation which generated social tension of which we have considerable evidence in later times. But at the same time it led to agrarian expansion in the peripheral and backward areas where donations of land were often made and where *brāhmaṇa* beneficiaries carried their advanced agricultural knowledge. The extension of agriculture helped the process of the formation of new states by providing a stable agrarian base from the late Gupta period, when trade ceased to pay a major role in socio-political transformation.[138]

Industrial Arts and Crafts

The period between the second century BC and AD witnessed remarkable growth in arts and crafts. It seems that the state exercised almost no control over them. A steep rise in commercial activity and the consequent growth of money economy also facilitated the proliferation of arts and crafts, which led to greater specialization than ever before and consequently to the achievement of greater technical skill in certain spheres of production. So many artisans as mentioned in the texts belonging to this period were never to be found in the earlier Buddhist texts or even the *Arthaśāstra.* The *Dīgha Nikāya* mentions nearly two dozen trades, but the *Mahāvastu* gives a list of thirty-six kinds of workers living in the town of Rājagṛha. The *Milindapañho* enumerates as many as seventy-five occupations. The period is also marked with the growth and specialization of crafts. Mining and metallurgy, textile, silk weaving, pearl-fishing and gem-cutting, and several other industries grew during this period. The inscriptions belonging to the period, mention the weavers, goldsmiths, dyers, workers in ivory and metal, jewellers, sculptors, fishermen, smiths, perfumers (*gandhika)* etc., who figure as donors of caves, pillars, tablets, cisterns etc. to the Buddhist monks. It seems that the artisans were prosperous citizens.

However, a decline in the long distance trade seems to have set in from the Gupta period onwards. With this, the linkages between coastal towns and their hinterland became weak. This in turn resulted in the fall of commodity production. The movement of artisans and traders from one part of the country to the other became redundant. Thus rendered constrained, the artisans remained confined to villages and in course of time, they were also transferred to the donees like the peasants. Consequent upon this, the arts and crafts were ruralized.

Trade and Commerce

The most striking development of the period following the decline of Mauryan empire from the economic point of view was the thriving trade between India and the Western world. The Mauryas, who are said to have greatly improved internal communications, had provided the initial basis for the growth of trade. There was an extraordinary growth of both inland and external trade. Thus there was also a corresponding increase of imports and exports, opening up of new markets, elaboration of urban settlements and consequent improvement in the level of prosperity. Also characteristic of this period was the opening up of the remote parts of the country and the discovery of new channels of communication. It seems that trade was conducted in the luxury items more than the essential goods. This also marks the prosperity of the people in those times. From an economic point of view, the most important development of the period was the thriving trade between India and the Roman empire. India enjoyed a favourable balance of trade in the transactions with the Romans, as is evidenced by the complaint of Pliny that bullion was flowing out of the Roman Empire into India. This is also evidenced by the numerous hoards of gold coins discovered in the southern India. In the textual sources, several ports have been mentioned indicating a thriving maritime trade. External trade was carried on not only with Rome, but also with Egypt, South-east Asia and China. It has been pointed out that while the north India was engaged in 'transit trade', the south was dominated by 'territorial trade'.

However, as mentioned earlier, a decline in the long distance trade seems to have set in from the Gupta period onwards. Though this had little impact on the internal economy of the country, it gradually led to the ruralization of arts and crafts and decay of many towns in the third and fourth centuries. The query regarding the relative paucity of metal money from the Gupta period onwards also finds an answer in the decline of trade.

Organization of Industry and Trade: The Śreṇī

The increase in trade in the post-Mauryan period demanded efficient organization of production and distribution. Production and exchange were facilitated through the institution of *śreṇī.* It is in this period that we get the earliest epigraphic evidence of the existence of guilds of artisans. The artisans were organized under their headman, the *jyeṣṭha*, who perhaps enjoyed the favour of the king. Literary evidences also indicate a significant growth in the number of guilds in this period. The important ones were the guilds of potters, metal-workers, weavers, goldsmiths, bead and glass makers, ivory workers and carpenters. The *śreṇī* fixed rules of work, as well as the quality of finished product and its prices. Banking and financing functions were also associated with the guild. They received deposits on regular interests and also lent money. Also, it seems that the occupations were hereditary. There are references in the *Jātakas* to industries being localized at particular towns and villages. Besides this, the guilds had rules for their respective classes. There were judges and the disputes related to the members of a guild were settled by them. The court monitored the behaviour of the members of the guild and ensured the customary usage of the guild, the *śreṇī-dharma.* Thus the guilds had judicial functions too. That the guild also intervened in the personal matters of the members is clear from the regulation that, in order to join the Buddhist order as a nun, a married woman had to seek the permission of the guild.

The goods produced by the artisans, individually or through the guilds, were purchased by the merchants, the *vaṇij.* The transportation of merchandise to long distances was facilitated through the *sārthavāha*, the caravan leader, with a number of caravans travelling together for protection from the brigands. The *Jātakas* also refer to the *sārthavāhā*, the (caravan leader), whose directions were obeyed by the caravans along the trade routes. Organizations associated with these assisting in the commercial activities, but less powerful than the guilds, were the *puga, goṣṭhi* and the *nigama*; the corporations, committees and locations where exchanges were conducted. The towns of Taxilā, Kauśāmbi and Bhaṭṭiprolu are associated with the *nigamas.* Excavations have brought to light a number of seals with the emblems of the guilds and corporations. In several cities they seem to have issued coins, which was ordinarily done by sovereign powers.

Urbanization

Due to unprecedented growth of trade and commerce in the period following the decline of Mauryas, urbanism reached a high point during the first centuries of the Christian era. Many towns emerged as centres of crafts and commerce and became hubs of economic activity. Most of them took the form of special local markets for the sale of particular products, due to localization of industry as a result of the formation of guilds and occupational castes. The urban culture brought with it better living conditions for the people. The excavations of many urban centres of the period provide evidences to prove that there was a rise in the standard of living of the people. Several new trade routes were formed both for internal and external trade.

However, the slump in trade and the general decline in commodity production consequent upon the ruralization of arts and crafts led to the decay of many towns in the third and fourth centuries. In north India many urban settlements of the Kuṣāṇa period like Kauśāmbi, Hastināpur, Ahichchhatra, and Taxilā show signs of decay. This is also true of most of the Sātavāhana urban centres, like Kaundinyapura, Paiṭhan, and Nāsik (Maharashtra), Amarāvati and Dharnikoṭā (Andhra Pradesh), Vadgaon-Madhavpur, Brahmagiri and Chandravalli (Karnataka). In the far south Arikameḍu was the most important town which ceased to be economically active after the third century. In the heartland of the Gupta empire the evidence of urban decay can be seen at many places. Admittedly urban centres did not disappear altogether in the Gupta period, and prosperous town dwellers living in comfort and ease were not entirely absent.

Growth of Money Economy

Connected with the phenomenon of growth of trade was the growth of a money economy in the early centuries before and after the Christian era. This period is characterized by the extensive use of coins. It has been suggested that since India had not known the use of silver and gold currency, the imported coins could only have been used as bullion. But some silver coins ascribable to the Sātavāhanas have been found, and epigraphic evidence suggests the use of the silver *paṇa.* It seems that the Roman coins were not only valued for their intrinsic value, but were also circulated in the transactions. In the north-west, the Indo-Greek rulers issued a few gold coins but the Kuṣāṇas issued them in large numbers. For day to day transactions, however, lead and copper coins were used. Kuṣāṇas issued a large number of copper coins. The Sātavāhanas issued coins of lead or potin. This suggests that money economy had become prevalent in the Deccan and coastal areas. Coinage also allowed the possibility of forward speculation in goods and capital.[139] With the expansion of commercial activity, weights and measures also became detailed and complex. Trade and coinage were inextricably linked with the process of urbanization. Again, there is a relative paucity of metal money from Gupta period onwards. This can be explained on the basis of a slump in trade and commercial activity. Though the Guptas issued the largest number of gold coins in ancient India, these could be used only in heavy economic transactions. They could have hardly flowed into day-to-day retailing.

Religion

The religious history of India is probably the most vital factor determining the trends of history itself, particularly in the ancient period.[140] This seems true at least to the extent that religion played an important role in shaping people's lives in ancient India, and hence, also the course of history. During the period under study, there were significant developments in the field of religion. One of the main aspects of the religious history of this period is the emergence of neo-Brahmanism more or less in the form in which we know it in later periods or even now. Neo-Brahmanism emerged as a conglomeration of beliefs, opinions, usages, religious creeds and observances derived from the manifold sources, heretic or popular, Vedic or non-Vedic, native or foreign, Aryan or non-Aryan, orthodox or heterodox. It seems to have been an attempt at synthesis, the process stretched over a long period, though it assumed a tangible shape in the epic literature.

The most important principle that operated to bring these Brahmanical sects about is *bhakti*, primarily the loving adoration of some persons by others, but secondarily the deep affection and mystic devotion for some personal deity who is the principal object of worship to his devotees (*bhaktas)*.[141] The principal sects that emerged were *Vaiṣṇavism* and *Śaivism.* The doctrine of *bhakti*, enunciated first in the *Gītā* and a vital force in *Vaiṣṇavism* and *Śaivism* became socially more relevant from the Gupta period onwards. It preached that one could obtain final liberation only through devotion to and faith in God, and not just by performing sacrifices. God was attainable to all through *bhakti.*

One of the earliest religious schools centred upon a personal God who seems to have been originally a human hero was that of the *Bhāgavatas* or the *Pañcarātras.* It was this school which came to be designated later as the *Vaiṣṇava* and became one of the foremost Brahmanical creeds of India. According to the epic and purānic traditions, the *Bhāgavatas* worshipped Vāsudeva Kṛṣṇa, the Sātvata or Vṛṣṇi chief and some of his relations. The historicity of Vāsudeva Kṛṣṇa is doubted by historians, who have variously tried to identify him. Several supernatural myths were associated with him in due course of time.

Śaivism, associated with the worship of Śiva, or Rūdra Śiva, was the other cult that developed in this period. However, it seems to have found origins long before. Rūdra was the Vedic god with dual nature being a terrible and at the same time a benign deity. He was identified with the pre-Vedic divinity who came to be known chiefly as Śiva to the later Vedic and subsequent ages. The worship of some such god, described as the prototype of Śiva-Paśupati, seems to have been prevalent even among the Indus valley people. Perhaps it is from the amalgamation of this god of the Indus valley and the allied god-concepts of pre-Vedic, Vedic and post-Vedic ages, that the *Śaiva* cult gradually emerged.

The messianic aspect of *Vaiṣṇavism* and to a lesser extent *Śaivism*, also became socially more meaningful in the context of the emerging feudal social structure of the time. It consisted in the theory of incarnation, first mentioned in the Gītā and developed under the influence of the Buddhist doctrine of the *Bodhisattvas*.[142] According to this theory, *Viṣṇu* is said to have appeared in each of the incarnations as a saviour, and at the end of the Kali age would appear to uproot the *mlecchhas* and restore *dharma*. Thus, the theory of incarnations (*avatāravāda*) fostered a hopeful belief in the coming of a redeemer who would deliver his devotees from the miseries of the world. This vision must have appealed particularly to the lower social orders. The doctrine was also adopted by *Śaivism*, though Śiva continued to be worshipped chiefly in the form of a *linga* (phallus).[143]

The three other well known sects during this period were the *Śākta*, *Saura* and *Gāṇapatya.* They centred respectively on the worship of Śakti (the female principle, conveniently called Durgā or Pārvatī), Sūrya (the sun god) and Gaṇapati. Female divinities, were mostly of tribal origin. They began to attain positions of importance in the Gupta period. Though the worship of Mother goddesses was not earlier unknown, it was now that they came to be clearly associated with important Brahmanical gods. Śrī or Śrī-Lakśmī, the goddess of wealth and plenty, became popular among the *vaiśyas* and the *śūdras*, and was recognized as the wife of Viṣṇu, and Pārvati became the spouse of Śiva. The assimilation of female deities into the Brahmanical pantheon led to the growth of the Śakti cult which preached that the male could be activated only through union with a female. The phenomenon owed much to the interaction between Brahmanical and tribal ideas, facilitated by the ever increasing number of brahmana settlements in the backward areas; it later became the central feature of the Tantric religion.[144] The other group of devotees in ancient India were the worshippers of the war god Subrahmanya or Kārttikeya. But they were not included in the orthodox list of the five sects.

During this period, Jainism prospered in different centres. This period was marked by many important developments. The schisms in Jainism occurred in this period. Some date around AD 80 may be taken to mark the definitive rupture between the Śvetāmbaras and Digambaras.[145] The two developed into rival sects, and the unity of the sect was forever lost. During this period also the canons of the Jain sacred literature was fixed. However, it was not as yet perhaps written. This was done at a Council held in AD 453 at Valabhi. Several other important Jaina works were composed in this duration. Jainism expanded beyond Bihar, the land of its birth, and spread to the rest of India including the far south. Jainism did receive patronage from some rulers, but largely supported by the merchant community. In some respects, this period witnessed the greatest activity of the church and marked the heyday of the faith. Jainism largely remained conservative but by the Gupta period seems to have developed icons.

The rapid extension of Buddhism after the time of Aśoka to various parts of India resulted in the rise of approximately eighteen Buddhist sects. These sects arose on account of geographical conditions rather than doctrinal differences except in certain cases. With the spread of Buddhism, communities were founded in various parts of the country and as there was no coordinating organization, many of them developed their own traditions respecting the ancient teachings. The differences between many of them were so small that a number of them died out or merged in a short time with others. It was in this period that Buddhism was adopted by the Greeks in the north, from whom Buddhism received widespread royal patronage. Both Buddhism and Jainism developed into influential philosophical systems during this period. During the Gupta period, the Mahāyāna sect, through its emphasis on *bhakti* and images and its enlarged pantheon which included male and female deities, came closer to the Brahmanical religion. With the decline of trade, however, much of the support that Buddhism had received earlier from the mercantile class ceased in the subsequent period and its establishments became increasingly dependent on the grants of land and villages in course of time.

Social Conditions

The changes in the political and economic scene influenced the social scenario of the period in a significant way. It was both, political chaos and flourishing trade, that brought the foreigners in India. The influx of large hordes of people form western and central Asia contributed towards a new and alien population. Those who came were initially alien in custom and belief, but the mutations that occurred among them and in the host societies expanded their cultural experience.[146] Also, thriving economic activity gave rise to the prosperous classes of artisans and merchants. Again, in the post-Mauryan period, artisans and craftsmen were generally drawn from the *śūdras*, who gained in wealth and status on account of the progress of crafts and commerce. However, since most of the artisans were confined to urban centres like Taxilā and Mathurā in the north and coastal towns and their hinterlands in the Deccan and the south, it is difficult to postulate any major change in the living conditions of the *śūdras*. They generally had to face discrimination, which must have given rise to discontent in them leading to tension in the society. Several early Purāṇic passages of the late third and early fourth century indicate that the society was passing through a phase of crisis known as the Kaliyuga when the institutions of family, private property, and the *varṇa* system were under attack.[147] The situation must have got further complicated with the influx of numerous hordes of foreigners. Such situations might have posed a threat to the existing social order. This is corroborated by the gloomy prophecies made in the Brahmanical literature of the period.[148] It would have been difficult to find a place for the new emerging classes in the extant social structure. *Varṇāśrama* system formed the core of Indian society earlier. Though the *varṇas* were never marked with tight compartmentalization, and it was perhaps this which gave way to further adjustments. An attempt to come to terms with the new elements within the social structure can be found in the acceptance of the foreign rulers as "degenerate *kśatriyas*". No doubt that the foreigners too had a significant role to play in this as they too made attempts at assimilation into the new society. They adopted conciliatory propaganda measures to smoothen the hostility of the indigenous society.[149] Another such attempt at reconciliation is found in the theory of "*varṇasaṁkara*" (mixed castes) which were said to have originated out of the *anuloma* and *pratiloma* marriages. This category was perhaps formed to include those of the lowest *varṇa*, who had gained economic opulence due to a spurt in the economic activity and would have tried to improve their caste status by associating with the newcomers. The social structure was undergoing changes in the Gupta period. Pronounced *varṇa* distinctions in various spheres of life can be noticed in the contemporary writings.

Religion played no less a role in determining the direction of the social responses. The prosperous community of the merchants patronized Buddhism and Jainism. There are references to donations being made by the guilds to the monks in the literature of the time. Also, many of the foreign ruling dynasties patronized Buddhism and Jainism. Buddhism in particular, reflected more flexible attitudes towards the social stratification. A sharpening of stratification at the theoretical level observed in the texts like *Manusmṛti* may have been a response to such flexibility. Theoretically, the *varṇas* were precisely and clearly defined, but this seems to have been far from the social reality. The urban population seems to have been very fluid and this might have been the reason for which the urban life seems to be downplayed in the *dharmaśāstras.* The attempt made by the lower in the social rung to exploit the demands of urban life to improve their social status, coupled with the influx of foreigners, might have generated fear psychosis in the Brahmanical class. This explains the continuous reiteration in the *Manusmṛti* of the inherent superiority of the *brāhmaṇas* as compared to the other classes. To provide authority to what is said in the text, a divine origin was ascribed to it.

An analysis of the social conditions of the time presents a picture where the influx of foreigners and a spurt in economic activity, coupled with developments in religion, set a process of transition in the society. The pressure of the circumstances threatened the disintegration of the existent social order. Attempts at reconciliation led to an increase in the social mobility. However, a closer analysis reveals that the threads of the initial social fabric were loosened and the social reality was far removed from the normative models set by the Brahmanical texts.

Notes

1. Lerner, Gerda, *Teaching Women's History*, American Historical Association, Washington, 1981, p. 6.
2. Ardener, Shirley (ed.), *Perceiving Women,* Dent Publishers, London, 1975, pp. 21–23.
3. Chanana, Karuna (ed.), *Socialization, Education and Women,* Orient Longman, New Delhi, 1988, p. 200.

4. Umā-Maheśvara *Saṁvāda* in the *Anuśāsana Parvan* is an example of this. Umā lectures on *strīdharma* which is men's view of what women ought to be, when she is asked by Śiva to do so.
5. Shah, Shalini, *The Making of Womanhood: Gender Relations in the Mahābhārata,* Manohar, New Delhi, 1995, p. 3.
6. Philip. J. Greven, Jr., *Four Generations: Population, Land and Family in Colonial Andover*, Ithaca, Massachusetts, 1970.
7. Carroll, Berenice (ed.), *Liberating Women's History: Theoretical and Critical Essays*, University of Illinois Press, Urbana, 1976, p. xi.
8. Bock, Gisela, "Challenging Dichotomies" in Karen Offen, et al. (ed.), *Writing Women's History: International Perspective*, Macmillan, London, 1991.
9. Chakravarti, Uma and Roy, Kumkum, "In Search of Our Past: A Review of the Limitations and Possibilities of the Historiography of Women in Early India" in *Economic and Political Weekly*, Vol. 23, No. 18, April 30, 1988, pp. WS–2 to WS–10.
10. Indra, *The Status of Women in Ancient India,* The Minerva Book Shop, Lahore, 1940.
11. Bader, Clarisse, *Women in Ancient India: Moral and Literary Studies,* Chowkhamba Sanskrit Series Office, Varanasi, 2nd ed., 1964.
12. Horner, I.B., *Women Under Primitive Buddhism: Laywomen and Almswomen,* G. Routledge & Sons Ltd., London, 1930.
13. Upadhyaya, B.S., *Women in Rigveda,* 3rd revised ed., S. Chand & Co., New Delhi, 1974.
14. Altekar, A.S., *The Position of Women in the Hindu Civilization,* 2nd ed., 5th reprint, Motilal Banarsidass, Delhi, 1987.
15. Meyer, J.J., *Sexual Life in Ancient India,* Motilal Banarsidass, Delhi, 1971.
16. Chakravarti, Uma and Roy, Kumkum, op. cit., pp. WS–2 to WS–4.
17. Ibid., p. WS–3.
18. Chakravarti, Uma, "Beyond the Altekarian Paradigm: Towards a New Understanding of Gender Relations in Early India", in Roy, Kumkum (ed.), *Women in Early Indian Societies*, Manohar, New Delhi, 1997.
19. Chaudhuri, J.B., *The Position of Women in the Vedic Ritual*, The Author, Calcutta, 1956.
20. Das, R.M., *Women in Manu and His Seven Commentators,* Kanchana Publications, Bodh Gaya, 1962.
21. Talim, M., *Women in Early Buddhism,* University of Bombay, Bombay, 1972.
22. Moti Chandra, *The World of Courtesans,* Vikas, New Delhi, 1973.
23. Mukherji, P., *Hindu Women,* Orient Longman, New Delhi, 1978.
24. Gulati, S., *Women and Society,* Chanakya Publications, Delhi, 1985.
25. Jayal, Shakambari, *The Status of Women in the Epics*, Motilal Banarsidass, Delhi, 1966.

26. Chakravarti, Uma and Roy, Kumkum, op. cit., p. WS–5.
27. Ibid, p. WS–5.
28. Jayal, Shakambari, op. cit.
29. Mukherji, P., op. cit.
30. Ibid, WS–6.
31. Jaiswal, Suvira, "Women in Early India: Problems and Perspectives", in *Proceedings of Indian History Congress*, Vol. 42, Magadh University, Bodhgaya, 1981, pp. 54–60.
32. Bose, Mandakranta, *Faces of the feminine in Ancient, Medieval, and Modern India*, Oxford University Press, New Delhi, 2000.
33. Shah, Shalini, *The Making of Womanhood: Gender Relations in the Mahābhārata*, Manohar, New Delhi, 1995.
34. Shah, Kirit K., *The Problem of Identity: Women in Early Indian Inscriptions*, OUP, New Delhi, 2001.
35. Sinha, S.N. and Basu, N. K., *Women in Ancient India: Vedic to Vatsyayana*, Khama Publishers, Delhi, 2002.
36. Colebrook, H.T., *A Digest of Hindu Law on Contracts and Successions*, Vols. I-IV, Calcutta, 1797–98.
37. Strange, Thomas A. L., *Hindu Law*, Parbury, Allen, London, 1830.
38. Banerjee, Gooroo Das, *Hindu Law of Marriage and Strīdhana*, firstly in 1878, reprint, Mittal Publications, Delhi, 1984.
39. Jayaswal, K.P., *Manu and Yājñavalkya: A Comparison and a Contrast: A Treatise on the basic Hindu Law*, Butterworth (India), Calcutta, 1930.
40. Sengupta, N.C., *Evolution of Ancient Indian Law*, Eastern Law House Ltd., Calcutta, 1953.
41. Sternbach, L., *Juridical Studies in Ancient Indian Law*, Vols. I & II, Motilal Banarsidass, Delhi, 1965–67.
42. Narang, B.S., *Concept of Strīdhana in Ancient India*, Parimal Publications, Delhi, 1990.
43. Jois, M. Rama, *Ancient India Law: Eternal Values in Manusmriti*, Universal Law Publishing Company, Delhi, 2002.
44. Menski, W.F., *Hindu Law*; *Beyond Tradition and Modernity*, OUP, New Delhi, 2003.
45. Kane, P.V., *History of Dharmaśāstra (Ancient and Medieval Religious and Civil Law in India)*, 5 Vols., B.O.R.I., Poona, 1930–1946.
46. Bhattacharji, Sukumari, "Economic Rights of Ancient Indian Women", in *Economic and Political Weekly*, Vol. 26, No. 9–10, March 2–8, 1991, pp. 507–512.
47. Bhattacharyya, N.N., "Proprietary Rights of Women in Ancient India", in Roy, Kumkum (ed.), *Women in Early Indian Societies*, Manohar, New Delhi, 1999.
48. Kane, P.V., op. cit.
49. Shastri, Shakuntala Rao, *Women in the Sacred Law*, Bhartiya Vidya Bhawan, Bombay, 1953.

50. Das, R.M., *Women in Manu and His Seven Commentators*, Kanchana Publications, Bodh Gaya, 1962.
51. Manjushree, *Position of Women in the "Yājñavalkyasmṛti"*, Prachi Publishers, New Delhi, 1990.
52. Kane, P.V., *History of Dharmaśāstra (Ancient and Medieval Religious and Civil Law in India)*, Vol. I, Part I, 2nd ed.., B.O.R.I., Poona, 1968, p. 1.
53. Lingat, Robert, *The Classical Law of India,* Thomson Press (India) Ltd., New Delhi, 1973, p. 3.
54. *ṚV*.I.187.1, X.92.2.
55. *ṚV*.I.22.18, V.26.6, VIII.43.24, IX.64.1.
56. *ṚV*.IV.53.3, V.63.7, VI.70.1, VII.89.5.
57. *A.Br*.VIII.13.
58. *Bṛ.Up*.I.14.14.
59. *Ch.Up*.2.23.
60. Kane, P.V., op. cit., p. 3.
61. Ibid., p. 4.
62. *Manu*.I.2.
63. *Yāj*.I.1.1.
64. Kane, P.V., op. cit., p. 4.
65. Ibid.
66. *Gautama*.I.1–2.
67. *Āpas.Dh.S*.I.1.1.2.
68. *Vasiṣṭha.I.4–6.*
69. *Manu* II.6.
70. *Yāj*.I.1.7.
71. Lingat, Robert, op. cit., p. 8.
72. Ibid., p. 10.
73. Ibid., p. 12.
74. Ibid.
75. Ibid.
76. Winternitz, Maurice, *History of Sanskrit Literature*, translated by Subhadra Jha, Motilal Banarsidass, Delhi, 1998, pp. 575–576.
77. Kane, P.V., op. cit., p. 19.
78. Ibid., p. 20.
79. Lingat, Robert, op. cit., p. 18.
80. Kane, P.V., op. cit., p. 20.
81. Lingat, Robert, op. cit., p. 12.
82. Ibid.
83. Ibid., p. 73.
84. Kane, P.V., op. cit., p. 21.
85. Lingat, Robert, op. cit., p. 19.
86. Keith, A.B., *A History of Sanskrit Literature*, OUP, London, 1953, p. 437.

87. *Baudh.Dh.S.*I.2.7, II.4.17.
88. Kane, P.V., op. cit., p. 30.
89. Ibid., p. 36.
90. Keith, A.B., op. cit., pp. 578–579.
91. Kane, P.V., op. cit., p. 59.
92. Keith, A.B., op. cit., p. 579.
93. Kane, P.V., op. cit., p. 125.
94. *The Institutes of Vishnu, S.B.E.* Vol. VII, ed. by F. Max Müller, translated by Julius Jolly, reprinted, Motilal Banarsidass, Delhi, 1965, p. xii.
95. Ibid., p. xvi.
96. Kane, P.V., op. cit., p. 124.
97. *Yāj.*I.1.4.
98. *Yāj.*I.1.4–5.
99. *Manu.* I.58.
100. Max Müller, *History of Ancient Sanskrit Literature*, Williams and Norgate, London, 1859.
101. Hopkins, E.W., *The Ordinances of Manu*, Trübner & Co., London, 1884.
102. Bühler, G., *The Laws of Manu, translated, With Extracts from Seven Commentaries*, Clarendon Press, Oxford, 1886.
103. Jolly, Julius, *Recht und Sitte*, translated by Batakrishna Ghosh, Bharatiya Publishing House, Varanasi, 1975.
104. *Manu.*I.58.
105. *Manu.*I.35.
106. Lingat, Robert, op. cit., p 91.
107. Ibid., p. 92.
108. Bhattacharyya, Parnasabari, *Conceptualizations in the Manusmṛti*, Manohar, New Delhi, 1996, pp. 65–92.
109. Kane, P.V., op. cit., p. 344.
110. Cited in Kane, P.V., op. cit., p. 441.
111. Ibid.
112. Kane, P.V., op. cit., p. 441.
113. Jayaswal, *Manu and Yājñavalkya: A Comparison and a Contrast: A Treatise on the basic Hindu Law*, Butterworth (India), Calcutta, p. 61.
114. Kane, P.V., op. cit., p. 443.
115. Ibid., p. 467.
116. Ibid., p. 468.
117. *The Minor Law Books, S.B.E.*, Vol. XXXIII, Part I, ed. By F. Max Müller, translated by Julius Jolly, reprinted, Motilal Banarsidass, Delhi, 1965, p. xviii.
118. Kane, P.V., op. cit., p. 477.
119. *The Minor Law Books, S.B.E.*, Vol. XXXIII, Part I, ed. By F. Max Müller, translated by Julius Jolly, reprinted, Motilal Banarsidass, Delhi, 1965, p. 275.
120. Kane, P.V., op. cit., p. 488.

121. *Yāj*.I.4.
122. *Pārāśara*.I.8.
123. Kane, P.V., op. cit., p. 460.
124. Ibid., p 464.
125. *Yāj*.I.1.4.
126. Kane, P.V., op. cit., p. 496.
127. Ibid., p. 502.
128. Majumdar, R.C., *Ancient India*, Motilal Banarsidass, Delhi, 1952, p. 132.
129. Thapar, Romila, *Early India*, Penguin, New Delhi, 2002, p. 226.
130. Ibid., p. 245.
131. *Milindapañho, being dialogues between King Milinda and the Buddhist sage Nagasena: the Pali Text*, ed. by V. Trenckner, The Royal Asiatic Society, London, 1928, p. 219.
132. *Manu*.IX.44.
133. Sharma, R.S. (ed.), *Perspectives in Social and Economic History of Early India*, Munshiram Manoharlal, Delhi, 1983, p. 137.
134. *Manu*.X.114.
135. *Manu*.VII.115–120.
136. *Manu*.IX.291, 293.
137. Jha, D.N., *Early India: A Concise History*, Manohar, New Delhi, 2004, p. 163.
138. Ibid., pp. 163–165.
139. Thapar, Romila, op. cit., p. 252.
140. Banerjee, P., *Early Indian Religions*, Vikas, New Delhi, 1973, p. v.
141. Sastri, K.A. Nilakanta, *A Comprehensive History of India*, Vol. Two, 2nd reprint, People's Publishing House, New Delhi, 1987, p. 379.
142. Jha, D.N., op. cit., p. 169.
143. Ibid., p. 170.
144. Ibid.
145. Sastri, K.A. Nilakanta, op. cit., p. 357.
146. Sastri, K.A. Nilakanta, op. cit., p. 223.
147. Jha, D.N., op. cit., p. 137.
148. The *Gārgī Samhitā* states that at the end of the *Kali* age people of all four castes will observe a similar moral code and wear similar clothes (*GS, Yuga Purāṇa,* 100–101). The *Viṣṇu Purāna* goes further to say that in the *Kali* age people of all castes would become like *Śūdras* (*Viṣṇu Purāna*, VI. 1,53). The *Mahābhārata* also echoes similar sentiments (*Mbh, Āranyaka P.*, 188.29).
149. Thapliyal, Uma Prasad, *Foreign Elements in Indian Society: 2nd century BC to 7th century AD*, Munshiram Manoharlal, New Delhi, 1979, pp. 129–130.

2

Gender Dynamics within the Household

Family has been the basic social unit since ages. When and how family came into existence is a topic of separate research. However, a brief discussion and understanding of the origins of family is called for in order to understand gender relations within the household dynamics.

It is not that only humans are social beings. Even the animals are found to live in some kinds of communities or better said, groups. For any single being, human or otherwise; the challenges posed by nature are harsh to bear. This necessitates the existence of some kind of organization within the living beings. Human life, in its initial phases, was nothing but collective hunting, gathering and living. There might have been a gradual extension of community life, as also the rise of a unit called family. The domestic or family ideology presents another explanation for the rise of family. According to it, family is the only viable option to organize reproduction and production, and to pass down the bloodline the control of property to successive generations.[1] However, as Chakravarti has observed, "This aspect of the ideology does not present a major obstruction in studying the family; however, what is an impediment is the very core of the domestic ideology which has constructed the family as *a non-conflict zone* (emphasis added), a realm of affect where members are linked to each other through mutual duties and obligations. Further, according to the ideology, while some members of the family may wield authority, it is nevertheless outside the realm of power. Most importantly, what is actually paternalistic dominance[2] within the family with members having unequal access to material assets and the right to make decisions is recast as a consensual arrangement amongst its members. *What is systematically obscured and not recognized in the ideological construction of the family is that power is a factor of relationships within the family just as it is in other institutions in civil society, and that there are competing interests in reality* (emphasis added)".[3] It is in this light that gender relations within the family at a particular point of time and changes in it with the passage of time has to be studied. This chapter proposes to study gender relations which the *dharmaśāstrakāras* sought to accord to the women within the ambit of domestic life and family.

It is of interest that the structure of family kept on changing with time. The matriarchal family in the initial phases gradually gave way to a patriarchal organization with the change in economic activity. Though originated as a consequence of the challenges nature posed, the interactions of individuals within the family further gave rise to other challenges. The nature of the challenges these interactions posed did not threaten its survival immediately. Family has been intended to grow as a protective umbrella for individuals not only for physical protection and development, but also to provide a platform for their mental, emotional and spiritual development. The fact that these objectives the family has achieved, even though partially, cannot be outright rejected. However, the other side of the truth is that family also has been a battleground of the interests of individuals members of the family; the continuous struggle between those who are powerful and the others who are powerless. Just as any other social unit, family also carried within it the seeds of exploitation. Just like the contrary cannot be rejected, this fact also can not be denied completely that family has been as much a locus of conflict and exploitation. With the establishment of patriarchy; characterized by male dominance, or more specifically, dominance of the male head of the family; the relations between the two sexes became skewed, leading to the general subjugation of women. Relations between the sexes are thus, not natural attributes, but 'social constructs', and with the institutionalization of patriarchy, construction of gender as a means of differentiation, or better said, discrimination; became the order too; the feminine being subordinated to the masculine. The male dominance expressed, among other things, unequal social relations. Actually it is not possible to pinpoint the time of this new patriarchal set-up for it was not an 'event' but a process developing at different pace and at different times. What is important is to delineate the historical processes by which patriarchy became established and institutionalized. Also, what are the modes of the expression of male dominance? And finally, how and to what extent does it affect a woman's life? Womanhood, in patriarchy, is an ascribed status, defined by certain norms which are indispensable for the continuance and furtherance of patriarchy. The family organization being patriarchal, there is a definite and very significant correlation between womanhood and family life. A close understanding of this is critical for understanding of women's position in such a society. The study of gender relations within the family is thus, inalienable from the understanding of women within the society.

With the growth of economic activity, household emerged as a crucial unit of production, distribution and consumption, as also reproduction, within which individuals were 'differentially socialized'[4]. Though not synonymous, the definitions of family and household have been closely related and even overlapping. The family being the social unit, household formed the economic unit of the society. At times, the family could easily slide into the household as far as the identification of the members is concerned. Also, an understanding of the economics within the family is crucial to the understanding of women's position within the family and household and as such, within the society by and large. The present chapter will, have the, focus on studying the position of women within the family and the household, as prescribed by the normative literature.

The Ideology of the *Gṛha* in the *Dharmaśāstras*

During the period of the composition of the *dharmaśāstras*, and may be even before that, the importance of household assumed enormous proportions, as is evident from the overwhelming importance that was assigned to the order or stage of the householder as compared to the other three orders of life (*āśramas*). The *gṛha* i.e., the household; controlled by the patriarch, the *gṛhapati;* is recognized as the central institution in the *dharmasūtras* as well as the *dharmaśāstras*. In fact, the *gṛhastha* was viewed as providing support and sustenance to the rest of the three orders of life. Manu has upheld the importance of the order of the householder over the rest of the three orders. He says, as all living creatures subsist by receiving support from air, similarly the members of all the orders subsist by receiving support in the form of gifts of sacred knowledge and food from the householder. Hence, the order of the householder is the most sacred of all.[5] He further ascribes the origin of other three orders to the order of the householder,[6] and says that just as all rivers, both great and small, find a resting-place in the ocean, even so men of all orders find protection from householders.[7] Other *dharmaśāstrakāras* also repeated such statements.[8]

In line with the overarching importance being given to *gṛha* in the prescriptive literature, there are certain functions ascribed to the *gṛha* as an institution, the due performance of which is deemed necessary to the sustenance of the social organization envisaged by the authors of such texts. These include providing shelter to the other three orders by giving alms, propitiation of the gods and ancestors, extending hospitality to the *atithi* and providing succour and shelter to the weak and dependent. Both production and distribution were carried out by the householder only. This becomes clear from the injunction of Vyāsa which enjoins upon the householder to 'acquire that which has not been already acquired, and having obtained it, distribute it as soon as possible'.[9] The role women were expected to play in the performance of these functions determined the gender relations within and outside the household.

Quite in consonance with the importance ascribed to the *gṛha,* the points of entry to and exit from the household were attributed a high degree of significance. Accordingly, norms regarding participation in rituals marked to symbolize their significance are elaborated. In all the rituals, the principle performer remained the householder, thus distinguishing him from other members of the household and according to him a position, superior to all the rest. Again, not only the performance, but participation was to be guided by norms.

It becomes important to study this dimension with reference to gender. It is also important to study the position and bargaining power of women at various points of entry to the household, as well as the specificities of the roles and functions of women, while she remains a part of the household. The connections of the household with the extra-domestic world and the role, if any, played by women assume significance in this regard, besides other issues that will subsequently come up. No less important is to study the chances of exclusion from the household, if any, for example, in the case of adultery. Widowhood and desertion by the husband will also be studied in this context. A study of women within the sphere of the household will remain incomplete without a study of women who attempted to opt out of the household. This included those who abandoned their husband or took recourse to a heretical life.

Entry to and Exit from the Household

Birth

Birth was a significant occasion in that it marks as the point of entry to the household.[10] We can learn a lot about the status of a female child from the manner in which her birth is received in the society. In fact, there was a marked difference in the way birth of a girl child and a male child was taken by the prescribers of the code of social conduct. Sacred rites as that of *pumsavana* were prescribed solely with the aim of securing the birth of a son. All the prayers of this rite are transparently aimed at preventing the birth of daughters, so that only a son be born. The sacred rites to be performed upon the birth of a girl child were to be performed without the recitation of mantras.[11] For them, only the marriage ceremony had to be performed with mantras.[12] This is important in the light of the fact that no initiation, the ceremony which bestowed upon an individual the status of a *dvija* (twice-born), was prescribed for women, and marriage alone was considered to be their initiation.[13] This marks a mere tacit acceptance of the daughter as the part of the father's family. A ritual status was conferred upon her only with the assumption of the role of the wife.

Thus defined, the membership of the daughter within the household would have been at best partial.[14] However, this is not to say that the birth of a girl child was looked down upon completely. Manu considers one's daughter as the highest object of tenderness.[15] However, again, there is little doubt in the acceptance of the fact that the birth of a son was favoured. The eagerness to beget a male child becomes evident from the prescription of days when the husband should approach the wife so as to obtain a son. Manu lays down rules giving details of days when the husband should approach the wife and when he should not with reference to her monthly courses.[16] In the following two verses, an attempt has been made to explain the birth of a daughter or a son. Yājñavalkya says that women have sixteen nights during the menstruation cycle and one should enjoy coition with them on even nights. A person observing this rule is considered a *brahmacārī*.[17] He should, however, abandon the first four nights and days like *Amāvasyā*, *Purṇimā*, *Aṣṭamī* and *Caturdaśī*. According to Manu, he who avoids women on the six forbidden nights and on eight others, is equal in chastity to a student (*brahmacārī*), in whichever order he may live.[18] Also, according to him, by having coition with the wife on the even nights sons are conceived and daughters are conceived by doing so on the uneven ones; hence a man who desires to have sons should approach his wife in due season on the even nights.[19]

Again, delivering girl children in succession is considered to be one of the many inadequacies of the wife, giving the husband the option to resort to polygamy.[20] Nārada also says that let not a husband show love to a barren woman, or to one who gives birth to only female children, and if he does have intercourse with her, he becomes liable to be censured.[21] It is said that the wife should be served and well-maintained and protected because she is the one who provides the man with a son.[22]

Why is that in the society the birth of a daughter was unwelcome, while the birth of a son was considered to be great fortune, an occasion to celebrate and sanctify with the chanting of *mantraṣ?* The reason behind such discrimination was rooted in the beliefs which originated out of the patriarchal mindset. It was only through the birth of a son that the continuity of the line of a household could be maintained, since the girls had to make an exit from the household at the time of their marriage. Thus, patrilocality, characteristic of patriarchy, was one of the major reasons that made birth of a son indispensable. Further it were the son, grandson and great grandson who were believed to perpetuate the tradition of the family and great deeds performed by whom lead to a man's attainment to heaven; and not the daughter.[23] Also, it was the son on seeing whom being born alive, the father is freed from the debt he owes to his ancestors *(pitṛ-ṛṇa)* and attains to immortality.[24] More so that the son liberates him from the hell.[25] Similar sentiments are voiced in the following verses.[26] While the son was the one to maintain the family line, to offer oblations to the departed manes, and to save the ancestors from hell; the daughter was to be married off before reaching a certain stage. Thus, apart from the non-utility of the daughter, there was the problem of getting her married. Altekar points towards this when he writes, "Child marriage came into vogue from about the beginning of the Christian era, and soon thereafter both levirate (*niyoga*) and widow remarriage were prohibited. Inter-caste marriages began to be disapproved by society; and there came into existence hundreds of sub-castes all insisting upon mutual exogamy. The field of choice for the selection of a suitable son-in-law thus became very narrow, intensifying thereby the anxiety of the daughter's father about the selection of a proper bridegroom."[27] However, Altekar seems to consider *niyoga* as conducive to the betterment of the women in the society, which may be contested on the grounds that it left no choice for the women, as also, considering them as mere vehicles of reproduction. Further, to safeguard the virginity of the girl till the time of marriage was an exacting task. Unlike celibacy in males which symbolizes their own self-control, virginity of girls implies control over her behaviour by her kinsmen. Loss of virginity is therefore, a loss of prestige for them.[28] Dowry might have been another reason why daughters were considered to be a burden. The birth of a daughter must have been unwelcome even for the mother who was herself a female. This is evident from the verses, as mentioned previously, which indicate that women who bore female children only could be superseded by another wife. Actually, in a patrilineal/patrilocal household if women were to bear only girls (who are only transitory members) then they are under threat of being marginalized, and their emasculation from any kind of authority is complete. For as mother-in-law (of their son's wives) they would have in course of time assumed a sub-dominant role. In a set-up like this girls cannot be a guarantee against their alienation the way boys are.[29]

There is no evidence to support that there was the prevalence of the practice of exposure of girl children. Scholars such as Chaudhuri[30] and Altekar[31] have refuted the evidence of exposure of female child in the ancient society. While sons born out of adultery or *niyoga* find mention in the texts in the form of their recognition in the various categories of sons or in case of adulterous sons, their censure from some religious rites; sinister silence of all the *dharmaśāstrakāras* without exception marks the birth of daughters born out of such relationships. Whether they were allowed to remain alive or not is a query, and what was their fate even if they lived to grow up? Given that marriage, which was considered to be the sole aim of a woman's existence, would have been difficult for such girls; what would have actually happened to them?

The discrimination that the girl child met with upon her very birth followed through the entire course of her life, which will become evident from the discussion to follow.

Marriage

Marriage being the other, and perhaps more important point of entry in the family of the in-laws in the case of girls. This was the first occasion in their lives when the ceremonies were performed with the recitation of the mantras. As mentioned earlier, marriage was considered to be initiation for women.[32]

Qualifications for Marriage

The details of qualities to be looked for in a maiden to be chosen as the bride are laid down by the *dharmaśāstrakāras*. Marrying a damsel of equal caste is recommended by all of them implicitly, and barring a few, others have specified this explicitly as one of the qualities indispensable to be found in the prospective bride.[33] However, as will be discussed later, in practice this restriction could not be much effective, also because of the prevalence of polygamy, and so this prescription was then limited to the case of first marriage. While propounding *varṇa* endogamy, it is laid down that the girl should not be a *sapiṇḍa,* i.e., related from the mother's or the father's side.[34] In this regard, Yājñavalkya adds that she should be at a distance of five and seven generations from the family of the *brahmacārī's* mother and father respectively.[35] Gautama and Śankha have laid down the same indictment.[36] However, Vasiṣṭha makes a slight relaxation in the degrees of relation on the mother's and the father's sides. According to him, the maiden should not be related within four degrees on the mother's side and six degrees on the father's side.[37] Besides *piṇḍa* exogamy, *gotra* and *pravara* exogamy is also propounded by the *dharmaśāstrakāras*.[38] Now mentioning *gotra, pravara* exogamy is propounded by Gautama too.[39]

Manu is particularly concerned about the auspiciousness of bodily marks of the maiden.[40] According to him, a maiden having no or too much or thick hair on the body, or having reddish hair and red eyes should not be married to.[41] A female who has the gait of a *hamsa* or an elephant, moderate hair on the body and the head, small teeth and soft limbs should be married to.[42] It seems that beauty was not or at least not the only concern of Manu here. Perhaps he wants to avoid the maidens belonging to the aboriginal race or foreign origin by laying down such qualifications. This concern becomes further pronounced when he says that women named after a constellation, tree, river, mountain, bird, snake or a slave, or bearing the name of a low caste should not be married to.[43] Perhaps he wished to avoid the tribal women or the women outside the *Āryan* fold as they were named in the aforementioned manner. However, regarding the appearance of the girl, Yājñavalkya merely says that she should be good in appearance and have a slim body.[44] Nārada also merely says that she should be free from physical deformity.[45] Like Manu, Viṣṇu also lays down that one should not marry a maiden whose hair are decidedly red.[46] He adds that one should not marry one 'with a limb too much'[47] or 'a limb too little'[48]. Vyāsa precisely says that she should be slender, carrying auspicious signs and clad in silken garments.[49] Kātyāyana lays down that one should not marry a woman who does not have auspicious marks and has profuse hair on her body.[50] Hārita is also concerned regarding the presence of auspicious marks on the maiden's body.[51] However, it is to be noticed that the details of physical characteristics that Manu has explained at length, are absent in *Yājñavalkya Smṛti* and many other *smṛtis.* Vasiṣṭha is among those who are silent on this issue. This has to be seen in the light of one of his statements that the male offspring of outcasts are (also) outcasts, but not the females[52], as they enter the family of a stranger[53]. He lays down that he may marry such a female without dowry.[54] However, this is also in contradiction with what Vasiṣṭha laid down earlier while saying that the maiden of same caste should be married to.[55]

The *dharmaśāstrakāras* are generally unanimous on the point that the maiden to be married should be free from contagious or hereditary diseases.[56] Yājñavalkya goes to the extent of saying that even if the girl belongs to a family renowned for the last ten generations, she should be disqualified if she is suffering from communicable diseases.[57]

The family to which the maiden belongs is also of concern to the lawgivers. Details of ten families to be carefully avoided, even if they be great or prosperous, are given by Manu.[58] This includes one which neglects the sacred rites, one in which no male children are born, one in which the *Veda* is not studied, one the members of which have thick hair on the body, those which are subject to haemorrhoids, phthisis, weakness of digestion, epilepsy, or white or black leprosy. By rejecting the sacred rites and not studying the *Veda,* the family might have lost the respectable *Āryan* status or it may not have been *Āryan* at any time. Along with the things already discussed, the only important issue that remains is that of the rejection of a family with no male heir. Other *dharmaśāstrakāras* also uphold this view of Manu. Yājñavalkya opines that the maiden to be married to should have brothers.[59] Kātyāyana lays down that one should not marry a woman who is born of a woman giving birth to a single child.[60] What Manu and Yājñavalkya have said explicitly is laid down implicitly by Kātyāyana. Hārita also mentions having a brother as one of the requisites in a maiden to be selected as bride.[61] Likhita omits all the other details of the girl to be married, and only says that a wise man should not wed a girl without a uterine (or step brother) of her own, apprehending lest she might have been previously given away as a *putrikā*.[62] In the following two verses, he explains the reason behind this. This was because the *putrikā* is given away by the father saying that the male child begotten on her person shall be his son.[63] The son begotten on a *putrikā* daughter should first offer oblations to his mother, then to his mother's father and then to his father's father.[64] Nothing is said regarding the offering of oblations to his biological father. As will be discussed later in detail, the major aim behind marrying was procreation of male offspring. Further, male offspring was needed as it was believed that he would relieve the ancestors from hell by offering them oblations after death. Hence, if the son begotten on a girl would not be eligible to offer oblations to his father after death, such a marriage would be fruitless to that man. Thus, the prohibition on marrying one who does not have a brother or is a single child certainly owed its origin to the fear of her being the appointed daughter, i.e., the *putrikā*.

The criteria laid down by Manu regarding the family of the prospective bride has to be seen in contrast with another statement of Manu where he says that an excellent wife may be taken from anybody, even from a base family.[65] This verse makes it clear that excellence of the wives was not judged on the basis of caste. It seems that excellence was considered as an individual characteristic, which anybody can possess, even one who belongs to a base family. However, as will be discussed later, excellence was not the criteria for determining the status or seniority of wives belonging to different castes. A better status is accorded to wives belonging to higher castes throughout the document. So, caste remained superior to excellence in that sense.

Yājñavalkya further says that the girl should not be from a higher status than that of the bridegroom's family.[66] This was important to maintain the superiority of the groom's family. Vasiṣṭha also emphasizes upon the superiority of family in this regard. He quotes a verse saying that lost learning comes back; but when the family is lost all is lost. Even a horse becomes estimable on account of its pedigree; therefore men marry wives descended from an unblemished family.[67] Vyāsa also has laid emphasis on the family of the maiden to be chosen. Unlike Manu, who has listed the families to be rejected, Vyāsa gives details of families to be chosen. He says that a twice-born, wishing to become a householder, should seek the hands of a girl of unimpeachable birth and family[68], and that she should be the daughter of an erudite father of good conduct, and born of a family free from any blemishes.[69] Again he says that a girl whose paternal ancestors to the tenth degree in the ascending line were all men of renown; should be solemnly wedded by the twice-born[70]. Viṣṇu also says that one should not marry woman of a low family.[71]

Chastity and virginity also became concerns of some *dharmaśāstrakāras*. While Manu gave considerable importance to virginity, as indirect references to it indicate, he did not specify virginity as one of the attributes of a girl to be chosen as the bride. He lays down that he, who gives a damsel in marriage after having openly declared her blemishes, is not liable to punishment.[72] This verse also, while citing examples of the blemishes, makes it clear that loss of virginity was a considered a blemish on the woman. This is in continuation of what has been said in the context of commodities. Similarly, it is laid down that the king shall himself impose a fine of ninety-six *paṇas* on him who gives a blemished damsel without informing the suitor of the blemish.[73] Also, it is notable that blemishes have been talked about only in the case of woman. In a patriarchal set-up, the woman is given to the man in marriage, and since it is considered as a transfer of possession, only her blemishes need to be taken into account. The man is the one to possess, and so he is left free from the consideration of blemishes. Again, this follows the laws concerning the breach of an agreement in the context of other things and matters. Further, he says that the man, who, out of malice, blames a maiden for not being a maiden falsely, shall be fined one hundred *paṇas* on failing to prove the blemish.[74] Nārada has repeated this indictment.[75] This shows how baneful a loss of virginity was considered. Again, one finds the indictment that nuptial texts are applied solely to virgins, for females who have lost virginity are excluded from the religious ceremonies.[76] Virginity was considered so important by Manu that he lays down that only those sons shall be considered as belonging to the same caste as their fathers, who are begotten on wedded wives who are equal in caste and were married as virgins.[77] Nārada also considers loss of virginity and proven intercourse with another man as one of faults of a maiden.[78]

Yājñavalkya explicitly states that among other qualities that the girl to be chosen as the bride should possess is virginity. She should be 'intact till the time of marriage'.[79] He further says that a virgin should be accepted with a record of ten earlier generations.[80] Later in the text, he states that a person, who performs *śrāddha* from the first day of the dark fortnight and engages himself daily in *śrāddha*, leaving off the fourteenth day, is blessed with a virgin along with many other things.[81] While this verse speaks of the importance attributed to virginity, it also makes few other things clear. One, that perhaps it was not always possible to find a virgin for marriage. Secondly, that in spite of the indictment laid down by Yājñavalkya, people were not always marrying virgins only. Like Manu, Viṣṇu also only lays down the imposition of fine for giving a blemished girl in marriage, without indicating her blemish.[82] Again, like Manu, he also lays down punishment for one who blames an unblemished damsel for being blemished.[83] Later in the text, one finds references to the son of an unmarried damsel[84] son received with the bride[85] and pregnant bride[86]. These instances prove that in reality, virginity was not an indispensable condition for being accepted by the men for marriage. Vasiṣṭha emphasizes upon virginity explicitly, and lays down that one should marry a maiden who has not had intercourse with another man.[87] However, later he says that if a damsel has been abducted by force, and not been wedded with sacred texts, she may lawfully be given to another man; and that she is like a maiden only.[88] This indicates that though virginity was considered important, the girl was not be punished for a forced loss of virginity. His liberal attitude in this regard further becomes pronounced when he says that if a damsel at the death of her husband had been merely wedded by the recitation of sacred texts, and if the marriage had not been consummated, she may be married again.[89] Vyāsa remains silent on the issue of virginity and merely states that she should not be plighted to anybody for money before.[90] Gautama only lays down that she should not have been wedded to another man previously, and remains silent on the issue of virginity.[91]

Dexter puts forward an interesting theory as to why virginity was considered so important. She says that virginity has a significant function within a "male-centered society". It is treated as a stage which renders a woman a "store-house" of untapped energy, energy which she will in the next stage (as a matron) transmit to man.[92]

Many of the lawgivers have specifically mentioned that the girl to be chosen should be younger in age.[93] That they needed to specify it might be reflective of the fact that sometimes the age of girls might have superseded that of the groom's. Again, according to the law codes, the girls had to be married off before puberty, as will be discussed subsequently, while the boys had to marry after the completion of their education. This must have left no room for such an apprehension. To keep the wife in complete obedience and subservience to the husband, her being younger must have been essential. To the aforementioned criteria, Viṣṇu adds that one should not marry one talking idly.[94]

Unlike Manu, Yājñavalkya also defines the eligibility of the bridegroom.[95] According to him, he should be from comparatively higher strata of society and regular in the study of *Vedas* and scriptures. His industry (potency) should be well-tried and he should be wise, popular and youthful. Nārada considers virility as the most important characteristic a man should possess in order to qualify as a groom. So he has laid down that an impotent should not obtain a maiden. Among the other faults of a suitor, he includes affliction with a chronic or hateful disease, deformity, madness, loss of caste, misery, to have forsaken his relatives.[96]

It is obvious that the qualifications laid down for the prospective bride are far more elaborate than those laid down for the prospective bridegroom. Even when Nārada lays down virility as the prerequisite, it seems to be a measure to ensure progeny out of a marriage relation, which was the most important purpose of marriage, as shall be discussed later.

Age of Marriage

The age at which the girls were expected to be married off was quite low, while the boys were expected to marry after their education was complete. According to Manu, a man of thirty years shall marry a maiden of twelve, or a man of twenty-four a girl of eight years of age.[97] The difference in the age prescribed for the marriage of girls and boys is astonishingly high. But the reasons behind this are quite obvious. The age for men is higher as they had to finish their education before marrying, while no education was considered necessary for the girls. The nuptial ceremony was considered to be the same as initiation for the women, serving the husband was considered equivalent to residing in the house of the teacher, and performance of the household duties was considered as the worship of daily fire.[98]

All the *dharmaśāstrakāras* advocated the marriage of girls before they attained puberty. Yājñavalkya lays down that if the person entitled to perform *kanyādāna*, does not solemnize the marriage in time, then he is accused of womb killing at each menstrual cycle of that girl. In case, there is no person as described above available for solemnizing marriage, the maiden herself is entitled to select an eligible bridegroom for her.[99] Pārāśara classified girls according to their age. An eight years old is a *Gaurī,* a nine years old is a *Rohiṇī,* and a girl of ten years or above is a *rajaswalā.* If a girl is not married off till the age of twelve years, the ancestors drink her menstrual blood and her parents and elder brother go to hell. Also, if a *brāhmaṇa* marries such a maiden, he loses the right to sit in the sanctified row during ceremonies.[100] Similarly, Bṛhaspati also says that a father who does not give his daughter in marriage in a proper time i.e., before she has reached maturity deserves contempt and shall be punished as ordained.[101] Vasiṣṭha also holds similar views. He says that if through a father's negligence a maiden is given away after the suitable age has passed, she destroys him just as the fee which is paid too late to the teacher destroys the pupil.[102] So he advises that the father should marry the daughter while she still runs naked, for if she stays in his house after the age of puberty, sin falls on him.[103] According to him, as often as the course of a maiden, who is filled with desire, and demanded in marriage by men of equal caste, recur, so often her father and mother are guilty of the crime of slaying an embryo.[104] Nārada and Vyāsa also hold similar views.[105] Like Yājñavalkya, Vasiṣṭha and Gautama also ordained that if the maiden is not married off till the time she reaches puberty, she may chose a husband for herself; the only difference being that they laid down that she shall wait for three years after attaining puberty.[106] Gautama further says that the guardians of the girl commit sin by not marrying her before the time she menstruates.[107] The tone of Yama goes sterner as he says that the father, who does not give away his maiden daughter in marriage after she has attained the twelfth year, drinks her menstrual blood, month after month.[108] According to him and Samvarta, by beholding a maiden in her menses, her mother, father, and her eldest brother go to hell.[109] Samvarta lays down the age of eight years for the marriage of a maiden.[110] Further, he eulogizes the giving of a maiden daughter in marriage by saying that such a father attains to celestial region[111], and that the fruit of the gift of an eight years old maiden follows seven births.[112]

In the perceived social order, women were expected to remain subservient to their husbands and to spend their lives in the performance of domestic activities. A low age of girls at the time marriage might have very well facilitated these twin objectives. Girls at a tender age could have been mentally conditioned and habituated of domesticity and subjugation before they could grow up to offer resistance to the intentions of the upholders of the patriarchal social order, or could have their minds opened up to other possible aims of life. Altekar guesses the joining of heretical sects by the girls as the possible cause for the lowering of the age of marriage, as 'if a girl is married before her personality is fully developed, there was no danger of her joining a nunnery'.[113] Though it may be one of the causes, Altekar seems to justify this in the favour of the 'parents' when he writes, "The institution of nunnery in Jainism and Buddhism and the instances of several grown up maidens taking holy orders against their parents' desire and *some of them later falling from their high spiritual ideal* (emphasis added) must also have strengthened the view of those who favoured marriages at about the time of puberty."[114]

Again, however, the few verses where it is categorically mentioned that the maiden to be chosen for marriage should be younger in age to the prospective groom,[115] may indicate that there might have been cases where the age of the girls superseded that of the male. Thus, the social reality, even if manifested only in sporadic instances, might have been away from the prescription of the lawgivers.

Forms of Marriage

Most of the *dharmaśāstrakāras* gave the various forms of marriage and laid down those which are lawful and unlawful for different *varṇas*. A few of them were considered unlawful for all the *varṇas*, still they were recognized as falling within the category of marriage. Eight forms of marriage were laid down, viz., *Brāhma*, *Ārṣa*, *Prājāpatya*, *Daiva*, *Gāndharva*, *Āsura*, *Rākśasa* and *Paiśāca*.[116] *Vasiṣṭha* laid down six forms of marriage, in which he included *Brāhma*, *Ārṣa*, *Daiva*, *Gāndharva*, *Kśātra*, *Mānava*.[117] The forms of marriage vary in the way they were been conducted. The gift of a damsel to a fit bridegroom, who has been invited by the father of the maiden, is called a *Brāhma* marriage. The gift of a daughter to a priest who is officiating at a sacrifice is called the *Daiva* marriage. When the father gives away his daughter after receiving one or two pairs of kine, it is called the *Ārṣa* marriage. Some of the *dharmaśāstrakāras* have defined the *Prājāpatya* marriage as the gift of a daughter by her father after having addressed the couple with the text, 'May both of you perform together your duties'.[118] Others consider that marriage as *Prājāpatya* where the father gives the maiden to the bridegroom who makes a demand for her hand.[119] A voluntary union between two lovers out of love is considered as *Gāndharva* marriage. When the bridegroom receives the maiden after having given wealth to the father or kinsmen of the bride, then it is called the *Āsura* marriage. Earlier the amount of money or wealth that was given by the bridegroom would have depended on his capacity or will,[120] however, later it might have taken the form of a purchase of the bride by bargain.[121] Vasiṣṭha named this type of marriage as *Mānuṣa* instead of *Āsura*. The forcible abduction of a maiden after destroying her relatives is considered as *Rākśasa* marriage. Vasiṣṭha has named this type of marriage as *Kśātra* marriage.[122] When a man, by stratagem, ravishes or seduces a girl who is sleeping, intoxicated, or disordered in intellect, then that is considered as the *Paiśāca* marriage.

According to Manu, the first six, i.e., *Brāhma*, *Daiva*, *Ārṣa*, *Prājāpatya, Āsura* and *Gāndharva* are lawful for a *brāhmaṇa*, the last four for a *kśatriya*, and the same four, excepting the *Rākśasa* rite, for a *vaiśya* and a *śūdra*.[123] In the next verse, however, he recognizes that the sages state that the first four are approved in the case of a *brāhmaṇa*, the *Rākśasa* rite is recognized in the case of a *kśatriya, and the Āsura* marriage in that of a *vaiśya* and of a *śūdra*.[124] Again, in the following verse, he changes his stand and says that three of the last five are declared to be lawful and two unlawful; the *Paiśāca* and the *Āsura* rites must never obtain.[125] According to him, *Gāndharva* and *Rākśasa* forms are permitted for the *kśatriyas* by the sacred tradition.[126] Nārada merely says that the first four, beginning with the *Brāhma* form, are declared to be lawful; the *Gāndharva* form is common to all castes; the three forms, which come after it, are unlawful.[127] According to Viṣṇu, the first four forms are legitimate for a *brāhmaṇa*, and the *Gāndharva* form is legitimate for a *kśatriya*.[128] Śankha is of similar opinion except that he permits *Rākśasa* form also in respect of *kśatriyas*.[129] Gautama merely states that the first four forms of marriage are based on virtue, while certain authorities hold the first six forms to be so.[130]

The various forms of marriage have been ascribed different qualities. In this way, while some of them are encouraged, the others are discouraged. Manu says that the son of a wife wedded according to the *Brāhma* rite, if he performs meritorious acts, liberates from sin ten ancestors, ten descendants and himself as the twenty-first.[131] Further, the son born of a wife, wedded according to the *Daiva* rite saves seven ancestors and seven descendants, the son of a wife married by the *Ārṣa* rite three in the ascending and descending lines, and the son of a wife married by the rite of *Kā* (*Prajāpati*) six in either line.[132] Viṣṇu also says that sons procreated out of *Brāhma*, *Daiva*, *Ārṣa* and *Prājāpatya* marriages liberate twenty-one, fourteen, seven and four men in the ascending and descending line respectively.[133] The first four marriages are thus encouraged. Further, Manu says that from these four forms of marriages spring sons who are radiant with the knowledge of the *Veda* and are honoured by the *Śiṣṭas*.[134] Also, he says that they would be endowed with the qualities of beauty and goodness, and would possess wealth and fame, obtain as many enjoyments as they desire and would live for a hundred years.[135] But from the remaining four blameable marriages spring sons who are cruel and speakers of untruth, who hate the *Veda* and the sacred law.[136] In the blameless marriages blameless children are born to men, in blameable marriages blameable offspring is born, so one should avoid the blameable forms of marriage.[137] Vyāsa also says that a daughter should be given in marriage to a suitable bridegroom according to the rites of a *Brāhma* marriage.[138] According to Samvarta, he, who gives a maiden to a suitable bridegroom according to the *Brāhma* mode of marriage, enjoys extraordinary prosperity, acquires the applause of the pious and unending fame, and attains the fruits of hundreds of *Jyotiṣṭoma* sacrifices.[139] Atri discouraged *Āsura* form of marriage by saying that a maiden, who is bought, should never be taken as a wife as the sons begotten on her are not qualified to offer funeral cakes to their departed manes.[140]

A careful analysis of the marriage forms is necessary with regard to women's position apropos of the institution of marriage. Perhaps marriage was considered a transfer of possession from the father to the husband. This may be the reason why *Brāhma* form of marriage where the father chooses the bridegroom is applauded. Also, in the *Daiva* form, the father could gift the daughter to a priest officiating in a sacrifice, just as he might receive other gifts which are material commodities. Again, in the *Ārṣa* form, the daughter could be given for getting a pair of kine. While selling the daughter according to the *Āsura* form was condemned by at least some of the *dharmaśāstrakāras*, giving her away for kine was not considered wrong by any. Regarding the *Āsura* form of marriage, Altekar comments, "The *Āsura* marriage is undoubtedly better than the *Kshātra* one, for it presupposes a recognition by society of the fact that woman has a value and has to be paid for. It therefore helped the improvement of the lot of the wife. The average husband became naturally unwilling to ill-treat his wife out of mere frivolity; very often she used to cost him dearly and to find another substitute for her was not always an easy economic proposition."[141] Altekar seems to have overlooked the fact that in the entire transaction, the girl is being treated as a commodity who could be sold and bought at the will of the males. In none of the forms except *Gāndharva*, the girl's choice for getting married or not to the bridegroom was heeded to. Surprisingly, though *Rākśasa* form is discouraged, it is considered lawful for the *kśatriyas*. Again, Altekar attributes the inclusion of this form among the recognized forms of marriage to the fact that in the pre-historic times, the victor carried the woman away and married her.[142] Though it may be true that the lawgivers might have included this form as it might have been one of the forms in practice; yet the inclusion of such ignominy in the name of marriage poses a question on the justice as viewed by the lawgivers. Manu's description of *Rākśasa* form of marriage is itself heart-rending: "The forcible abduction of a maiden from her home, while she cries out and weeps, after (her kinsmen) have been slain or wounded and (their houses) broken open, is called the *Rākśasa* rite".[143] What could have made a society to accept such an act is a query? Again, *Paiśāca* form of marriage was nothing but accepting a rapist as the husband. Though Manu and others condemn it, it seems unfortunate that even this was considered as a form of marriage. Altekar seems to justify the lawgivers for having recognized it as one of the forms of marriage, on the ground that since virginity was becoming a grave concern in those times, there was no other option, but to marry the girl to the one who blemished her, in order to preserve her welfare.[144] He says that, "They (the lawgivers) seem to have subscribed to the modern view that a culprit should not be allowed to be benefited by his wrong."[145] It seems that in the view of Altekar, the welfare of women consists in getting married only, and by remaining unmarried, their welfare is affected badly. In his view, strangely, the welfare of a girl lies in getting married to a rapist rather than remaining unmarried.

Inter-varṇa Marriages

Varṇa endogamy was advocated by all the *dharmaśāstrakāras* in general. Manu says that the father should give his daughter to a handsome suitor of the same caste, even though she has not attained the proper age.[146] However it could not have been possible to practically prohibit inter-*varṇa* marriages completely. Therefore, for the first marriage, a wife of equal *varṇa* was recommended by Manu.[147] But for those who were desirous of more wives, rules were being prescribed for choosing the females according to the direct order of the castes. Accordingly, it is laid down by him that 'a *śūdra* woman alone can be the wife of a *śūdra,* she and one of his own caste (the wives) of a *vaiśya*, those two and one of his own caste (the wives) of a *kśatriya*, those three and one of his own caste (the wives) of a *brāhmaṇa'*.[148] However, other *dharmaśāstrakāras* have laid down that a *brāhmaṇa* can have a *brāhmaṇa*, *kśatriya* and *vaiśya* wives, a *kśatriya* can marry a *kśatriya* and a *vaiśya* girl, and a *vaiśya* and a *śūdra* can marry only one of their own caste.[149] All of these have tried to prohibit the marriage of a twice-born with a *śūdra* girl.[150] Manu has discouraged the marriage of twice-born men with *śūdra* women by giving the testimony of various authorities in support of this. He further says that great families sink low by low marriages.[151] Vasiṣṭha acknowledged that some *dharmaśāstrakāras* have declared that the twice-born men may marry even a female of *śūdra* caste without the recitation of Vedic texts,[152] however, he advises one not to act in this manner as such a marriage results in the degradation of his family and loss of heaven after death.[153] Further, he quotes that 'the gods do not eat the offerings of a man whose wife is a *śūdra.*[154] Śankha says that even in distress a twice born one should not wed a *śūdra* girl, since a son begotten by him on her will never find his salvation.[155]

Like Manu, Nārada and Viṣṇu have permitted the marriage of twice-born ones with *śūdra* females. According to them, a *brāhmaṇa* may take four wives in the direct order of the four castes, a *kśatriya*, *vaiśya* and *śūdra* may take three, two and one wives respectively.[156] However, later Viṣṇu also discourages marriage with a *śūdra* girl by saying that no twice-born man shall ever perform religious duties with a *śūdra* wife,[157] as a union of a twice-born man with a *śūdra* wife can never produce religious merit; it is from carnal desire only that he marries her, being blinded by lust.[158] He further says that men of the three first castes, who through folly marry a woman of the last caste, quickly degrade their families and progeny to the state of *śūdras,*[159] and that if oblations to the gods and manes and hospitality to guests are offered principally through her hands, the gods and manes and the guests will not eat such offerings and he will not go to heaven.[160] Vyāsa has permitted a *vaiśya* to marry a *śūdra* girl besides one of his own caste.[161] He says that the gods and the *pitṛs* desert the *brāhmaṇa*, who takes a *śūdra* wife or partakes of boiled rice cooked by her, and he is consigned to the pangs of *Raurava* hell, after death.[162] Unlike others, Uśanā has completely discouraged inter-*varṇa* marriages. He says that twenty four penances are to be performed for having married a maiden of different caste; half of those, for living with her and there is no penance which can atone for procreating a son on her.[163] While inter-*varṇa* marriages were not completely prohibited, the status of the wives of a man remained dependent on *varṇa*. According to Manu, the seniority of the wives of a man is to be decided on the basis of their *varṇa*.[164] Yājñavalkya says that if a wife of same caste be there, the husband should not engage a wife of another caste in the performance of religious rites.[165] Viṣṇu also says that if a man has several wives of diverse castes, he shall perform the religious duties with the wife of the same caste, even though she may be the youngest of all.[166]

It is to be noted here that the marriage of a higher *varṇa* male was discouraged with a female of lower *varṇa* (*anuloma vivāha)*, but not altogether prohibited. But the reverse of it, i.e., the marriage of a lower *varṇa* male with a female of higher *varṇa* was prohibited (*pratiloma vivāha*). However, it can not be denied that both *anuloma* and *pratiloma* marriages were occurring in practice. Manu says that only those children who are begotten in direct order from wedded wives, equal in caste and married as virgins, are considered as belonging to the same caste as their fathers.[167] Even the sons born out of *anuloma* marriages were said to be forming different mixed castes, arisen out of a confusion of the castes and were placed on a lower rung on the social ladder.[168] Still lower was the degree of those mixed castes which arose out of a *pratiloma* marriage.[169] From further intermixture rose several other lower castes. Thus inter-caste and particularly *pratiloma vivāha* was discouraged by assigning a very low position to the progeny born out of such marriages. Similar views were expressed by other *dharmaśāstrakāras*. Yājñavalkya also says that the son born from the womb of a *śūdra* woman as a result of marriage solemnized by a *vaiśya* is called *karaṇa*.[170] He further says that *anuloma* is considered good and *pratiloma* is considered mean.[171] Vasiṣṭha also names the mixed castes to which sons born out of *pratiloma* and *anuloma* marriages would belong.[172] He further quotes that one may know them by their deeds who are born of *pratiloma* marriages, since they are destitute of virtue and good conduct.[173] Also, he says that a *pāraśava* (the son of a *brāhmaṇa* and a *śūdra* woman), is as impure as a corpse.[174] Viṣṇu says that sons born of mothers belonging to castes higher than their husbands are despised by the twice-born.[175] Then he names the mixed castes that arise out of *pratiloma* marriages.[176] He further says that besides these, there are innumerable other mixed castes produced by further intermixture between the abovementioned.[177] Vyāsa explicitly says that the member of an inferior caste cannot wed a girl of superior caste.[178] He further says that a son begotten by a man of inferior caste on a woman of superior caste is worse than a *śūdra*.[179] In the next verse he says that a son begotten by a *śūdra* on a *brāhmaṇa* girl should be considered as a *cāṇḍāla*.[180] Next he gives the names of other castes along with *cāṇḍāla*, who have arisen out of such marriages and says that even a conversation with a person of these castes should be expiated by an ablution and looking at the sun.[181] A milder treatment is given by him to the sons born of *anuloma* marriages. He merely lays down that the religious rites and ceremonies for sons born out of females lower in *varṇa* to their husbands should be carried out in the manner of the order to which the mother belongs.[182]

There was also a difference in the performance of ceremonies for marriage in case of *anuloma* marriages. It was laid down by the *dharmaśāstrakāras*, with slight variations in details, that if the marriage is being solemnized with the bride of uniform *varṇa*, then the groom should hold the hand of the bride, if a *brāhmaṇa* is marrying a woman of *kśatriya* caste, then she should catch an arrow held by the *brāhmaṇa*. In case the bride is a *vaiśya* getting married to *brāhmaṇa*, she should catch the goad carried by the groom and if the marriage is being solemnized with *śūdra*, she should take the border of his cloth.[183] No such details were given for *pratiloma* marriages, perhaps because they were considered unlawful.

What becomes clear from the aforementioned statements or injunctions of the *dharmaśāstrakāras* is that *varṇa* is inextricably linked with gender. Though this will be further discussed in the chapter from various angles, the observation of Chakravarti is interesting in this regard, where we can read 'caste' as *varṇa*. She writes, "Endogamous marriages ensure the perpetuation of bounded groups reproducing a closed structure of land, women and ritual purity in which the central figure is the woman: without total control over her sexuality, neither land nor ritual purity can be passed on with any certainty. The normative family, within what I have conceptualized elsewhere as Brāhmanical patriarchy, was thus designed to reproduce both itself and the caste hierarchy."[184] Elsewhere she has observed that, "The anxiety about polluting the ritual order and the quality of the blood through women is best demonstrated in the horror of miscegeny, as we shall show. In the theoretical explanations for the proliferation of caste, the most polluting and low castes are attributed to miscegeny, that is, the mixing of castes (*varṇasamkara*). The most polluting castes are those that are the product of reprehensible unions between women of a higher castes and men of a lower caste. The ideologues of the system had a particular horror of hypogamy – *pratiloma,* or against the grain, as it was described – and reserved for it the severest condemnation and the highest punishment … . Safeguarding the caste structure is achieved through the highly, restricted movement of women or even through female seclusion"[185]. In the words of Ganesh and Das, "Women are regarded as gateways – literally points of entrance – to the caste system. The lower-caste male whose sexuality is a threat to upper-caste purity has to be institutionally prevented from having sexual access to women of the higher castes, so women must be carefully guarded."[186] "Further, Chakravarti writes that, "When the structure to prevent miscegeny breaks down, the Brahmanical texts consider the whole elaborate edifice of social order built upon them to have collapsed. The *kaliyuga* of the future is such a time, when women of the high castes and men of the low castes regress from their duties."[187]

Aims of Marriage

Procreation was so important an aim of marriage that sometimes it seems that perhaps it was the sole objective behind it. Manu lays down that the *Brāhmaṇa* who wishes to marry for the sake of having offspring, should be considered as a *snātaka*, begging in order to fulfil the sacred law.[188] According to him, women were created to be mothers, and men were created to be fathers.[189] Nārada goes further to say that women have been created for the sake of procreation, the wife being the field, and the husband the giver of the seed. The field must be given to him who has the seed. He who has no seed is unworthy to possess the field. He even gives the right to remarry to a woman whose husband's semen lacks strength.[190]

Further, procreating a son was of utmost importance. This is voiced in a verse by Yājñavalkya where he says that the wife should be served and well-maintained and protected because it is the wife only who provides the man with a son, and the son, grandson and great grandson maintain a perpetual tradition of the family and the man attains heaven as a result of great deeds performed by them.[191] One of reasons why impurity was attached to menstruation in women might have been that sex during menstruation could not be expected to yield any fruit. Manu lays down rules giving details of days when the husband should approach the wife and when he should not with reference to the monthly courses of the wife.[192] In the following two verses, an attempt has been made to explain the birth of a daughter or a son. It is said that he who avoids the women on the six forbidden nights and on eight others, is equal in chastity to a student, in whichever order he may live.[193] Yājñavalkya also says that women have sixteen nights during menstruation cycle and one should enjoy coition with them on even nights. A person observing this rule is considered a *brahmacārī*.[194] He further says that for copulating with his wife during her menstrual period, a person attains purity by drinking clarified butter after the expiration of three nights.[195] Vasiṣṭha also prohibited the husband to cohabit with a woman during courses,[196] and lays down that he should approach her in 'proper season'.[197] Proper season denotes the time when the chances for conception are maximum. Further he says that for killing a woman of *brāhmaṇa* caste who is an *ātreyī*, i.e., one who has bathed after temporary uncleanness, the same penance must be performed as for killing a learned *brāhmaṇa*;[198] for if the husband approaches her at that time, he will have offspring.[199] While for killing a female of the *brāhmaṇa* caste who is not an *ātreyī*, the penance prescribed for the murder of a *kśatriya* must be performed.[200] It is obvious that the life of a woman ready for procreation of a son was considered to be much more important than the others. Viṣṇu lays down that if a man does not have connection with his wife in the natural season, unless there be some valid reason, he must fast for three days.[201] Natural season again denotes the time when chances for conception are highest. Vyāsa clearly says that the sixteen successive nights from the first appearance of the flow in women are called the menstrual period and healthy male seeds cast into healthy fields during this period are found to sprout leading to conception.[202] So the husband should visit his wife on any of these even nights whereby he would get a son.[203] He further says that even the vow of a *brahmacārī*, who visits his wife during her menstrual period, is not vitiated by doing so.[204] Again, he says that a husband not visiting his wife in her menstrual period is guilty of foeticide.[205] Similar indictment is laid down by Pārāśara, who also says that a woman who does not approach her husband during proper season goes to hell after death and attains to widowhood again and again.[206] Such views may be taken to indicate that *brahmacarya* only meant abstinence from sex from pleasure, and not from sex for procreation. Again, he says that a husband who does not visit his wife during her menstrual period is guilty of foeticide.[207] Samvarta also says that a man, who commits culpable deeds, but knows the wife in the time of *ṛtu*, attains to an excellent condition.[208] Again, this shows that how important the task of procreation was considered. He further says that a highly distressing penance is laid down for the expiation of his sin, who cohabits with a woman in her menses.[209] According to Uśanā, those *brāhmaṇas* who visit their wives at the proper time after menses, are among those who are considered as *pangtipāvanas* (i.e., entitled to seats of honour at dinner parties).[210] Like others, Sankha also says that one should visit one's wife on any day during the menstrual period from the fourth to the fifteenth day.[211] Āpastamba laid down that on the advent of the fourth night of her flow, a woman should ask her lord to procreate progeny on her person.[212] Yama defines a woman as *vṛṣalī* if she is barren, or gives birth to a dead child, is a *śūdra* woman or is in menses.[213] It is to be noted that all these are the woman who have faltered with the function of procreation. Even in the case of *śūdra* woman, the son born of her is not entitled to offering oblations to the departed ancestors. Yama says that if any *brāhmaṇa* marries such a maiden out of lust, then he should not be spoken to, nor should he be admitted into a row for the purpose of taking meals.[214] That the position of barren woman was low in society is testified by verses from other texts also. Āpastamba lays down that boiled rice should not be partaken of in the house of a barren woman. He, who unknowingly eats at such a house, is consigned to the hell of *Pūyasam*, after death.[215] Nārada goes to the extent of forbidding a man to have intercourse with his barren wife, lest he becomes liable to be censured.[216] Angiras gave a similar statement.[217] Atri goes a step ahead and forbids even the woman's father to take meals at her house.[218] Dakśa's statement speaks well about the thought process of the lawgivers. He says that if one performs a rite in the evening which should be performed in the evening, he reaps no fruit thereby, just as sexual intercourse with a barren woman yields no fruit.[219] A woman was valued only when she could procreate and that too when she gives birth to a male offspring.

In a similar move, there are several references which indicate that the *dharmaśāstrakāras* wanted the girls to be married off before puberty, as menstruation before marriage was considered as destruction of the embryo.[220] Procreation of male offspring was considered so important that sons begotten by others on one's wife were given acceptance. In some cases, where the husband would have failed to procure sons on his wife, other male might be even deputed for that purpose. Manu recognizes two kinds of sons born on wives of other men, i.e., a *kuṇḍa* (born while the husband lives) and a *golaka* (born after his death).[221] However, there were varying opinions regarding the ownership of such a son. Manu says that according to all the great ancient sages, the male offspring of a woman belongs to the lord, but they differ in the meaning implied by the term lord, according to some, it refers to the begetter of the child, while others say it refers to the owner of the soil.[222] As is clarified by the next verse, the woman is declared to be the soil and the man (the begetter of the child) is declared to be the seed. The husband is referred to as the owner of the soil. Later an attempt is made to resolve the issue by drawing an analogy. Manu says that as in the case of those who have no property in the field, but sow seed in another's soil do not receive the grain of the crop; as in the case of one man whose bull may beget a hundred calves on another man's cows, they would belong to the owner of the cows only; similarly, the men who have no marital property in women, but sow their seed 'in the soil of others', reaps no advantage out of it.[223] It is then said that if the field is made over to another for sowing by some special contract, then the owner of the seed and the owner of the soil are both considered as sharers of the crop.[224] However, verse 55 tells that such is the law concerning the offspring of cows, mares, slave girls, female camels, she-goats and ewes, as well as females of birds and buffaloes. It seems that this law of contract was not applicable to wives of men, as the list does not include them. But, in the previous verses, one notices that to explain the rule, an analogy is drawn by telling it in the case of animals, as well as crop. These signified the property of the owner. That wife was also considered as the property of the husband, is quite evident from these verses. Again, it follows that according to Manu if the seed is sown without any special contract, then only the owner of the field, i.e., the husband is the owner of offspring, however, in case there is a contract, the offspring shall belong to both the begetter and the husband of the woman. Also, in this case, one finds an acceptance of sons procreated by adulterous relationship (where there is no contract). Vasiṣṭha and Nārada also say similar things and refer to the contrary views regarding the ownership of the male offspring in such cases.[225] Vasiṣṭha also refers to a son received with the bride who was married while pregnant,[226] and says that such a son is kinsman but not heir. That such marriages were happening and that such sons were accepted, again shows that male progeny was held valuable. Uśanṛ also discusses this issue and opines that such a son should offer *piṇḍa* to both, the begetter and the husband of the woman in cases of a religious appointment for such procreation.[227] The birth of a male child was considered important for it was believed that the son, grandson and great grandson maintain the perpetual tradition of the family and man attains heaven as a result of great deeds performed by them.[228] In the same nerve, it is said that on seeing the face of a living son born, the father is freed from the debt (he owes to his ancestors) and attains to immortality.[229] Further, the son liberates him from the hell.[230] Similar sentiments are voiced in the following verses.[231] The son was the one to maintain the family line, to offer oblations to the departed manes, and to save the ancestors from hell. Marriage was placed within the framework of such a line of thinking. Procreation of the male offspring was the major objective behind marriage. Gender relations in that society need to be studied in this backdrop.

Choice Regarding the Decision to Get Married

It was considered obligatory for both the male and the female to get married and enter the *gṛhasthāśrama*. This was deemed necessary from the point of fulfilment of certain duties and obligations, which would remain impossible otherwise.

Choice of the Bride and the Groom

Even a cursory glance at the recognized forms of marriage reveals that except in the case of *Gāndharva* marriage, the girl had no choice or say in the decision as to whom to get married to. The decision regarding the selection of the groom rested with the father or guardian, in the cases of *Brāhma*, *Daiva*, *Prājāpatya*, *Ārṣa* and *Āsura* marriages. Out of these the first four mark the 'gift' of the daughter by the father, while *Āsura* form marks the sale of the daughter implicitly or explicitly. The last two forms of marriage, often condemned by the lawgivers, viz., the *Rākśasa* and *Paiśāca* forms marked forced abduction and rape, where no question of choice arises. Rather, a recognition, even if not approval, of abduction and rape as forms of marriage, implies a tacit acceptance of these heinous acts and grants the abductor and rapist the status of the victim's husband; further cutting down upon her choice. There is no denying the fact that it would have been mighty difficult or even torturous for the girl to accept such a person as her husband.

That the daughter was considered the possession or the property of the father is implicit in his right to give away the daughter as gift or to sell her for a price. Though there are verses in the texts which speak of the son also as the property of the father, there are no verses where the father is given the right to make choices regarding his marriage or vocation. In fact, *kanyādāna* was highly eulogized in the texts. It was considered the highest form of *dāna*. It is said that both the giver and taker of the bride stand exonerated from all penalties if the father gives the bride in this way.[232] Trautmann says about the *kanyādāna* complex that marriage by gift begins by presuming the superiority of the groom's people vis-à-vis the bride's. Bride is given by her guardian into the groom's keeping, utterly severing the connection between the bride and her family and transforms her into an extension of the groom and his family. Thus, marriage by gift is also a rite of initiation (into another family) for the woman and a sacrament that creates an indissoluble bond between husband and wife and makes any break impossible.[233] In a marriage like this, alienation of woman from her own family is so complete that she is unable to turn to them at any point in her life.[234] Kapoor provides the justification for *kanyādāna* in these words: "Here, an answer is possible. In a culture that puts greatest premium on renouncing, the giving away of the dearest, most precious object is regarded as the highest sacrifice. A daughter is generally very tenderly regarded by her parents; hence, as a kind of renunciation, *Kanya-dana* is given special importance."[235] However, Kapoor remains unable to bring the *daughter* out of the identification of an 'object' by way of providing this explanation, rather his explanation reinforces the fact of considering the daughter as an object, even though she may be regarded as 'the most precious one'.

It is notable that while in all the aforementioned forms of marriage, the father is making the choice regarding the groom of the girl, the man to be married is asked by the *dharmaśāstrakāras* to look for a suitable maiden for himself after *samāvartana* taking the blessings of his preceptor.[236]

It was only the *Gāndharva* form of marriage which accorded some space to the girl's choice. However, the *Manusmṛti* denied such a girl the right to take anything from her father, mother, or brother, regarding her, who violated the provision, aṣ a thief.[237] Another instance where the girl was given a choice was when her relatives failed to find a suitable husband for her even after her reaching the stage of puberty. Manu has given the right to the girls that if after the attainment of puberty, they do not get married for three years, then they can select their own husbands.[238] Yājñavalkya also lays down that if the person entitled to perform *kanyādāna*, does not solemnize the marriage in time, and there is no person as described above available for solemnizing marriage, the maiden herself is entitled to select an eligible bridegroom for herself.[239] Likewise, Vasiṣṭha, Viṣṇu and Gautama also ordained that if the maiden is not married off till the time she reaches puberty, she may chose a husband for herself.[240] Gautama and Viṣṇu have ordained that she should wait for three successive monthly periods, and Vasiṣṭha laid down this period to be three years after attaining puberty. Vyāsa laid down that the maiden's father, grand-father, brother, uncle, cognates and mother are successively entitled to give away a girl in marriage. In the absence of any of these, the bride can herself give her away.[241] It is to be noted that the fear of missing the age of marriage of the girl is so great in the minds of the lawgivers that it led them to concede the right of choice to the maiden herself. However, how far this was followed in practice is again a query.

Dowry

Reference to dowry comes in Bṛhaspati, where he recognizes it as one of the seven ways of acquiring immovable property.[242] Vasiṣṭha says that the male offspring of outcasts are also outcasts, but not the females,[243] and hence one may marry such a female without a dowry.[244] According to Viṣṇu the property of householders is of three kinds- white, mottled and black,[245] and recognizes dowry as one of the forms of white property.[246] Nārada also recognized wealth received with the bride as one of the forms of white property.[247] Thus, though there are relatively fewer references to dowry, those which are there, are sufficient to say that it might have existed and also must have found acceptance.

It is important to explore the nature of dowry. In Goody and Tambaih's terminology, dowry is an example of diverging devolution (i.e., women's property complex). Dowry in such circumstances cannot be treated as *pre-mortem inheritances,* but has a specific intention of linking the daughter, hence her family with a particularly desirable son-in-law.[248] Thus, where the girl chooses the groom herself, says Manu, she is not allowed to take with her any ornaments given to her by her parents and if she carried them away, it will be regarded a theft.[249]

It is true that in most other forms of marriages (other than perhaps *gāndharva*) brides themselves must have been given gifts, ornaments in particular, exclusively for their own use. There is reference to daughters alone inheriting their mother's *strīdhana* – the term used for dowry is *yautakam,* which means separate property. However, it will be discussed later if it remained an exclusive property for girls. Behind the apparent economic power that women got from dowry is the practice of depriving them of it by controlling their right to its use.[250]

Bride Price

There are many references to gratuity being taken by the father of the bride. In fact, such a marriage was recognized as one of the forms of marriage. When the bridegroom received the maiden after having given wealth to the father or kinsmen of the bride, then it was called the *Āsura* marriage. Earlier, the amount of money or wealth that was given by the bridegroom would have depended on his capacity or will,[251] however, later it might have taken the form of a purchase of the bride by bargain.[252] Vasiṣṭha named this type of marriage as *Mānuṣa* instead of *Āsura*.[253] Though recognized as a form of marriage, it was considered lawful for some *varṇas* while unlawful for others. According to Manu, this form of marriage was considered to be lawful for a *kśatriya*, *vaiśya* and *śūdra*, but not a *brāhmaṇa*.[254] In the next verse, however, he recognizes that the sages state that the *Āsura* marriage is lawful in the case of a *vaiśya* and of a *śūdra*.[255] Again, in the following verse, he changes his stand and says that three of the last five forms of marriage are declared to be lawful and two unlawful; the *Paiśāca* and the *Āsura* (rites) must never be used.[256] He further says that no father should take a gratuity for his daughter, otherwise he would be considered a seller of the daughter.[257] Again in verse 53, view similar to that in 51 is expressed. However, a concession is given to the relatives who do not appropriate the gratuity for their use.[258] There, as it is said, it is not sale but a token of respect and kindness towards the maidens. Again, later in the text, Manu laid down that if, after one damsel has been shown, another be given to the bridegroom, he may marry them both for the same price.[259] First notable thing is that this verse (and other two verses) follows the three verses on the sale and purchase of chattel and commodities. This may be indicative of the fact that marriage with a damsel was considered equivalent to the sale and purchase of chattel and commodities. This is corroborated by what is said in the verse itself, that both can be married 'for the same price'. Earlier in some verses, marriage by purchase was condemned; the father who accepts price for his daughter in any form is condemned. Again, it is said that if the giver of the nuptial fee for a maiden dies after such a payment, she should be given to his brother with her consent.[260] Once the nuptial fee is paid, the girl is considered to have been sold, so if the man dies, she should be given to his brother. A concession is that at least her consent is sought. Further, in the next verse, it is repeated that not even a *śūdra* shall accept a nuptial fee for the daughter, as it is considered as the sale of the daughter. It seems that marriage was considered a kind of deal or at best, an agreement between the two parties where the woman was transferred as a commodity without having any role to play in the decision-making.

It is also evident from the above discussion that even though this form of marriage was recognized, it was discouraged by Manu. Āpastamba says that a father, accepting any amount of money, however small, from the husband of a daughter on the occasion of her marriage is doomed to eat and drink excrements in the hell of *Raurava*, for many years, after death.[261] Atri also discourages this form of marriage, however, with a different argument. He says that a maiden who is bought should never be taken as a wife as the sons begotten on her are not qualified to offer funeral cakes to the departed manes.[262]

The analysis of bride-wealth arrangement in which women are exchanged for wealth is seen as women being treated as objects.[263] Tambiah says, "While dowry gives property rights to women, bride wealth does not give it to woman but to her family and kin (male) for loss of female to her family, while simultaneously transferring rights in the woman's reproductive potential (i.e., in any child she may bear) from her kin group to that of her husband."[264] Jack Goody, however, points out that while gifts from groom sometimes first go to the girl's father/brother who may take the cut (from bride-wealth) but the bulk goes to the bride herself.[265] Goody, therefore, concludes that the right term for this would be 'indirect dowry' rather than bride-price.

As discussed earlier, such a marriage was discouraged. However, as Shalini Shah says, this was not because woman does not remain an object (for didactic writers) but she is an object under control of her natal family rather than husband's family.[266] Perhaps dowry marriage or bride-wealth marriage does not reflect woman's status but rather the status of the males whether coming from her natal family or family by marriage. In either type of marriage, it is the male authority which triumphs and woman remains without subjective status. Anthropological data from the 'Bride

Wealth' societies clearly underline the element of control to which women are subjected in such a form of marriage.[267] Collier and Rosaldo point out that men establish claim (over wives) not by providing for them and children but rather by distributing produce to senior-in-laws, so as to win support and commitment from those who influence/control wives. This transaction which occurs between man and his wife's kin prevents such a marriage from being perceived as egalitarian. Woman in such a set-up is more of a prize to be achieved by man.[268]

Remarriage

Remarriage was another point of entry, this time, actually re-entry, to the household. However, it was not sanctioned by the lawgivers in general. Manu rejects a second husband for virtuous women. He says that she who cohabits with a man of higher caste forsaking her own husband who belongs to a lower one, will become contemptible in this world, and is called a remarried woman (*parapūrvā*). By violating her duty towards her husband, a wife is disgraced in this world, after death she enters the womb of a jackal, and is tormented by diseases, which is the punishment for her sin.[269] A virtuous wife is defined as one who, controlling her thoughts, words and deeds, never slights her lord and thus resides with her husband in heaven.[270] The reward for such a wife is that she gains the highest renown in this life and a place near her husband in the next world.[271]

At another place, he perhaps becomes ambiguous and so says that if the future husband of a maiden dies after betrothal, then her brother-in-law shall marry her according to the rule mentioned.[272] However, again, he says that he should approach her only till an issue be had.[273] Thus, this might actually be a reference to *niyoga* and not remarriage.

Yājñavalkya also says that a maiden is offered only once throughout her lifetime, whereby, the person reoffering her to another man thereafter is liable for punishment not less than that of a thief. However, the maiden can be offered to another person, if he comes forward and it is proved that he is more qualified and meritorious than the earlier person with whom the ring ceremony was celebrated.[274] He again says that a woman who has either enjoyed coition or is intact is called *punarbhū* on remarriage and one who divorces her husband for another person voluntarily is called *svairinī*.[275] Again, he includes the husband of remarried woman in the list of people to be censured in *śrāddha*.[276] Thus, where there is scriptural sanction the entry is marked with rites, while where there is no sanction, it is marked by exclusion from some other rituals besides the non-performance of rites to mark the occasion. Vasiṣṭha defines remarried woman as one who leaving the husband of her youth, and having lived with others, re-enters his family, and one who leaving an impotent, outcast or mad husband, or after the death of her husband takes another lord.[277] It is notable that there might have been cases where the woman, after having chosen to live with others forsaking her husband, was allowed to re-enter the household of the previous husband, if she chose to do so. That women were not entirely choice less, may be the fact this verse is pointing towards; though the authors of the texts under study sought to render them in that state. Vasiṣṭha permits marrying a damsel who had been abducted by force, and not been wedded with sacred texts, as also in case where a damsel at the death of her husband had been merely wedded by the recitation of sacred texts, but the marriage had not been consummated.[278] Though this proved the liberal attitude of Vasiṣṭha, these cases were not treated as remarriage by him. However, Viṣṇu, while defining *punarbhū* includes one who being still a virgin is married for the second time, and one, who, though not legally married more than once, had lived with another man before her lawful marriage.[279] The tone of Angiras goes stricter and he defines *punarbhū* as one who after having been promised to be given away in marriage to one, is given to another. He prohibits the acceptance of food from such a maiden.[280] However, it seems that more than the remarriage, it was the breaking of the promise, that was the reason behind such a censure. Uśanā also included those who marry widows and the son of a widow or remarried woman among those who are disqualified to be present at a *śrāddha* ceremony.[281]

Nārada's attitude seems to be milder in this regard. He says that if a man is potent with another woman but impotent with his own wife, his wife shall take another husband.[282] Again, he says that when a bridegroom goes abroad after having espoused a maiden, let the maiden wait till her menses have passed three times, and then choose another bridegroom.[283] Later, he laid down the period of waiting to be eight, six and four years respectively for *brāhmaṇa, kśatriya* and *vaiśya* woman; and half of the respective periods mentioned above in case she is issueless. After the lapse of the stipulated time, she was permitted to remarry, without incurring any guilt of offence. No specific period is laid down for a *śūdra* woman.[284] He reiterates this by saying that a woman may be justified in taking another husband in five cases of legal necessity: when her husband is lost or dead, when he has become a religious ascetic, when he is impotent, and when he has been expelled from caste.[285] Pārāśara also mentions impotence of the husband as one of the five conditions when the wife is permitted to remarry.[286]

Death

In case of performance of *śrāddha* ceremony, which marked the occasion of death, the ideal invitees were those who were considered as socially, ritually, and physically unblemished.[287] Gautama also gives a long list of people who shall not be invited to the *śrāddha* ceremony.[288] It includes men who act in the capacity of priests to women only, keepers of concubines, persons who have wilfully known interdicted women, among others. While food was meant primarily for *brāhmaṇas*, it could also be offered to kinsfolk.[289] Besides, the ritually sanctified middle *piṇḍa* or lump of grain offered to the patrilineal ancestor could be consumed by the wife who was a *pativratā*, i.e., devoted to her husband, and desirous of progeny.[290] The *śrāddha* thus provided an occasion for distinguishing between participants and non-participants on the one hand, and amongst participants on the other.[291]

Also to be noticed is that not much is said regarding performance of the ceremony for the women. Vyāsa says that the dead bodies of deceased and well born wives, who leave behind them sons, grandsons, and great grandsons, etc., should be duly cremated. They attain to the same region with their husbands, who had performed and are hence entitled to spiritual emancipation, after death.[292] The statement defines the criterion for the *wife* to receive ceremonial exit from the household, that *she leaves behind sons, grandsons and great grandsons etc.*, as also *her being 'well born'*, implying perhaps her caste at birth. Next, it is the due performance of *Pitṛ Yajñas* in her life which entitles her to reach the same region with their husbands and gain spiritual emancipation after death.

As a Part of the Household

Upbringing of Children

Differential Access to Resources

As far as caring and nurturing is concerned, there is nothing leading to the inference that the girl child was not cared for. Manu says that one's daughter is the highest object of tenderness.[293] However, no education was considered necessary for the women. The nuptial ceremony is considered to be the same as initiation for the women, serving the husband is considered equivalent to residing in the house of the teacher, and the household duties are considered as the worship of daily fire.[294] Similar view is voiced in Viṣṇu.[295] Yama has prohibited the shaving of heads and recitation of Vedic mantras by women.[296] Atri also says that recitation (of the *Gāyatrī*) and practice of mantras bring about the fall of women and *śūdras*.[297] In Dakśa, women are compared with illiterates.[298]

Deprivation from getting educated was quite in line with the dominant ideology of the *dharmaśāstra* texts, in which womanhood was recognized and given importance only in the role of the wife, whereby she is expected to procreate, serve the husband and be an appendage to him in some of the religious functions; none of which required her to be educated. Rather, a sharpening of the critical faculties of the woman, which is a natural concomitant of education, shall be detrimental to the purpose of the *dharmaśāstrakāras.* Only an illiterate and uneducated woman could be schooled in and made to internalize the patriarchal ideology. In the words of Shalini Shah, "Women's education is one of the criteria for understanding the nature of social set-up. Educational deprivation is tantamount to depriving women of the knowledge of her 'self'. Woman's lack of education and, therefore her lack of self-awareness is often found to be used by men to 'mould' her to his will. It is true that mere availability of education, need not necessarily engender a 'sense of self' that would actually depend on the nature of education imparted. Nonetheless, education by itself does have the effect of sharpening critical faculties and nurturing awareness which in itself is significant … . It is quite apparent that education, i.e., knowledge which could develop critical faculty and therefore, had a subversive potential could not possibly be encouraged or seen with any degree of equanimity by patriarchs."[299] Max Müller cited Megasthenes' quotation of women in India which says "Indians did not communicate their metaphysical doctrines to women, thinking that if their wives understood these doctrines and learned to be indifferent to pleasure and pain, and to consider life and death as the same *they would no longer continue to be the slaves of others.* Or if they failed to understand them they would be talkative and communicate their knowledge to those who had no right to it."[300] Altekar also comments, "The prohibition of *upanayana* amounted to spiritual disenfranchisement of women and produced a disastrous effect upon their general position in society. It reduced them to the status of *Śūdras*."[301]

It has to be noted that women were required to keep the record of income and expenditure of the household, for which some informal education must have been imparted. However, it was only to serve the goal of the authors of the *dharmaśāstras*. In fact, an education which was meant for socialization of the female in service role, played a significant part in determining women's social definition as a sex.[302]

Further, marriage, and that too at an early age made it impossible for them to get education in the house of the teacher, as also the only role that women were expected to play in the household swallowed all inspiration of the woman themselves to get educated. The stage was set for the women to remain immersed in ignorance for centuries to come.

While discussing the differential access to resources that the girl child had, it is to be noted that she was herself treated as a resource, possessed by the father, accessibility to and possession over whom could be transferred at his will in order to get material or spiritual benefits. Women's right to property as a resource will be discussed in detail in the next chapter.

Power of Decision-Making

The daughter had almost no right over her life and the decisions related to it. Manu's oft-quoted statement makes it amply clear.[303] This maxim was repeated by many other lawgivers if not all,[304] and even those who did not mention it specifically, adhered to it implicitly. As already laid down, no provision for education was deemed to be necessary for her. So no question of choice could arise here. Also, no options were available to her as far as vocation was concerned. Her life was meant to be moulded into the cast of the ideal wifehood- the *pativratā* as laid down by the *dharmaśāstrakāras*. The only functions that she was expected to perform were that of serving the husband and in-laws untiringly, taking care of household affairs and procreating children. Even when few of the girls chose to live a life away from the domestic mode, the choice was not left upon them. Father's permission was a must prior to the permission from the *sreṇī-pramukh*. Thus whether to get married or not was a decision not in her own hands. As has been discussed earlier, whom and how to get married to were issues where again her will carried no significance, barring the exception of *Gṛndharva* marriage.

Conjugal Relations

The wife was central to the existence of the household – *gṛha.* As would become clear subsequently, a woman's existence was recognized only in the role of a wife. However, the weaving together of a range of concerns within the household was accompanied by an insistence on the complete subordination and instrumentality of the wife,[305] and the *dharmaśāstras* are replete with prescriptions regarding this.

Role and Duties of the Wife

Manu says that the nuptial ceremony is considered to be the same as initiation for the women, serving the husband is considered equivalent to residing in the house of the teacher, and the household duties are considered as the worship of daily fire.[306] This sentence precisely defines the duties of the wife.

The Ideology of the Pativratā: Devotion or Subjection?

The most powerful tool in the hands of the *dharmaśāstrakāras* was the ideology of *pativratā*, in which women were thoroughly schooled, nullifying all the possibilities of attempts at inversion of the social order sought to be perpetuated by them. Accordingly, this is one of the most pervasive concepts associated with womanhood in the *dharmaśāstras.* It will not be an exaggeration to say that this ideology was the pillar which helped to support the entire edifice of the rigid patriarchal organization perceived by the lawgivers. Quite successfully, it attempted at subsuming all the critical faculty of women and muted them outwardly as well as inwardly. To quote Shah, "It was an ingenious ideology which eschewed the necessity of applying physical coercion over women in an oppressive patriarchal household, which would have been more difficult to establish and maintain. Instead this ideology was used to elicit conformity with the oppressive norms on a psychological plane."[307]

Jayal has commented on the transition of the concept of the wife from *sahadharmiṇī,* one who is true friend and confidante of her husband – who reserves for herself the right to independent judgement – to *pativratā* who is but a mere devotee of that exalted, all wise and all powerful God called *pati* (husband) for he is the Lord.[308] Not a few number of times, the husband and the wife were considered to be two parts of one organic whole, each one incomplete without the other. Bṛhaspati cites the testimony of all the three sources of *dharma* (the revealed texts i.e., the *Veda*, the traditional law i.e., the *Smṛtis* and popular usage), and says that the wife is declared by all these to be half the body of the husband, equally sharing the outcome of good and evil acts.[309] Vyāsa also said that according to *Śruti* (revealed texts), the god Brahmā cleft his body in two parts, out of which the husbands and the wives sprang respectively.[310] A man is half incomplete being till he doesn't take a wife, since he cannot beget (children) without her.[311] Atri similarly says that a woman is the left limb and the husband the right one.[312] Though believed to be two parts of one whole, the husband and wife were not placed on an equal footing. Often it is said that they were considered to be complementary beings, and so there is no place for question of competing equality between them. However, a closer analysis points to the contrary.

What *pativratā* symbolizes so well is really the 'service role' of women. Servility and complete subjection to the husband is prescribed for the wives by all the *Smṛti*-writers in general. While describing the duties of women further, Manu writes that she should obey her husband as long as he lives, and should not insult his memory when he is dead.[313] Again, it is told that the betrothal by the father or guardian is the cause of husband's dominion over his wife.[314] Yājñavalkya also says that the best religion of the wives is to observe the suggestions given by their husbands,[315] and that she reaps glory in this world and incomparable bliss in heaven, if she is always devoted to her husband, thinks good for him, is sociable and has a good control on her senses.[316] Nārada says that a husband, though feeble, must be constantly worshipped by his wives, in the same way a ruler though worthless must be constantly worshipped by his subjects.[317] Bṛhaspati laid down that the wife who is afflicted when he is afflicted, pleased when he is happy, squalid and languid when he is absent and who dies when he dies, is declared to be devoted to her husband.[318] Viṣṇu considers it the duty of the wife to live in harmony with her husband,[319] not to act by herself in any matter, to remain subject to her husband during his lifetime and to preserve her chastity, or to ascend the funeral pyre after his death.[320] To pay obedience to her lord (husband) is considered to be the only means for a woman to obtain bliss in heaven.[321] Vyāsa says that a woman has no separate existence from her lord in matters of piety, gain and desire. The *śāstras* have laid down this dependency of love.[322] Pure in her thought, speech and action and obedient to the dictates of her lord, she should follow him in life like his own shadow, seek his good like a trusted friend, and minister to his desires like a servant.[323] She should not speak too loudly, nor harshly, or unpleasantly to her lord and thus avoid all quarrels and confrontation.[324] According to Śankha, a true wife is one who bears the sacred fire, is faithful to her lord, is one in spirit with her husband and has borne children.[325]

Moreover, *pātivratya* demanded was an unquestioning and unconditional service from the wife, where there was no scope for any dissatisfaction or doubt. Manu further says that a faithful wife should worship the husband as a god, even though he may be destitute of virtue, or is seeking pleasure elsewhere, or is devoid of qualities.[326] So a faithful wife, who desires to dwell in heaven, should never do anything that might displease her husband, whether he is alive or dead.[327] Pārāśara also says that a wife who insults a husband who is poor, diseased or cunning, attains to the life of a bitch in the next birth.[328] Vyāsa says that she should not speak too loudly, nor harshly, or unpleasantly to her lord and thus avoid all quarrels and confrontation.[329] Dakśa says that a wife who is obedient, unsullied by harsh speech, chaste and devoted to her husband is a goddess personified,[330] and this world is like a heaven for one who has such a wife.[331] Otherwise, he becomes miserable and disappointed, as if the wife always goes against him, disagreement of the mind takes place between the two.[332] He further says that the domestic mode of life is for happiness, and happiness is dependent on the wife in the house. She who is humble and under the control of her husband is the real wife.[333] It is ironical that if a wife is disliked by the husband even though she may bend low with humility, then also the blame is rested with her only. Kātyāyana says that it must be the punishment for the woman for having disregarded her husband, Umā and the sacred fire in the previous birth.[334]

The ideology of *pativratā* negated the very identity of a woman, as well as her choice even in the matters completely personal to her. Bṛhaspati further lays down that a woman must avoid decorating herself, dancing, singing, attending public festivities, eating meat and drinking intoxicating drinks when the husband is absent.[335] Even her religious obligations were subordinated to her husband. According to Manu, no sacrifice, vow, or fast must be performed by women apart from their husbands, and if a woman obeys her husband, she will be exalted in heaven for that reason alone.[336] Viṣṇu laid down the same, and, further said that a woman who keeps a fast or performs a penance in the lifetime of her lord, deprives her husband of his life, and will go to hell.[337] Since the husband was considered to be the object of a woman's worship, no other mode of worship was deemed necessary for her. Śankha writes that a woman can ascend to heaven only by worshipping her husband and not by fasting or bearing penances.[338] Atri goes a step ahead and says that a woman, who desires of bathing in sacred water, should drink the water washing the feet of her husband and she would thereby attain to the most excellent station.[339] Gautama says that a wife is subservient to the husband even with respect to the performance of religious acts, and should never try to supersede him in these matters.[340] Since the woman was constantly required for her services, she could never be allowed to have the choice of renunciation for acquiring religious merit.

Unlike any code of conduct to govern the life of the husband, a specific code of conduct is prescribed for the wife. Manu gives a list of actions which cause the ruin of women. These include drinking spirituous liquor, associating with wicked people, separation from the husband, rambling abroad, sleeping at unreasonable hours, and dwelling in other men's houses.[341] Later, it is said that a wife who drinks spirituous liquor, is of bad conduct, rebellious, diseased, mischievous, or wasteful may be superseded by another wife.[342] Similarly, Vasiṣṭha is of the opinion that a *brāhmaṇa* woman who drinks spiritual liquor loses all spiritual merit and wanders about in this world during her lifetime, and after death is born as a leech or a pearl-oyster. She is also forbidden by the gods from being admitted to the same abode with her husband.[343] Since wife is considered as half the body of her husband, it is said that half the body of the husband falls if his wife drinks spirituous liquor and that no purification is prescribed for this fallen half.[344] Nārada laid down that a wife who utters unkind words, or eats before her husband shall be quickly expelled from his house by the husband.[345] Vyāsa also says that she should not be prodigal in her purse, not hostile to the spirit of piety or gain. Carelessness, fickleness of mind, anger, envy, deception, vanity, rivalry, mischievousness, cruelty, inordinate pride, cunningness, atheism, daringness, discontent, and dissimulation are the fifteen vices which a chaste wife should always try to renounce.[346]

In order to facilitate unquestioned and complete internalization of this ideology, rewards were said to have accrued to the conformist women, and punishments to those who were deviant or non-conformist. Those who propounded the norm of *pativratā* were fully aware that this *dharma* was nothing short of penance for women. Hence, great rewards were promised to the women in the form of gaining supernatural powers. What was expected from of this was that the women would behave according to the set ideal not only for the sake of *dharma*, but also for the fruits that they were made to believe to attain for practicing it. Manu says that if she does not violate the duty towards her lord, she dwells with him in heaven after death and is called faithful in this world by the virtuous.[347] Further, it is told that for disloyalty to her husband, a wife is censured among men, and is punished for her sin in next birth.[348] In a similar move Vasiṣṭha opines that faithful wives who are constantly pure and truthful reside in the same abodes with their husbands after death, while those who are unfaithful are born as jackals.[349] A chaste wife, who worships her lord, acquires fame and blessings in this life, and lives in the same region with him, after death.[350] Kātyāyana finds the woman who follows the commands of her husband comparable to Umā.[351] Like others, Kātyāyana also believes that a woman attains to hell on death and sorrows upon rebirth if she disregards her husband.[352]

When the temptation to attain heaven as well as fear of sinking into hell also failed to make the woman conform, coercion was used. Viṣṇu says that let the king put to death a woman who violates the duty which she owes to her lord, the latter being unable to restrain her.[353] This was not the only form of violence done to women. Manu lays down that a wife, a son, a slave, a pupil and a younger brother of full blood can be beaten by with a rope or a split bamboo on committing faults, though on the back part of the body only and never on the noble part.[354]

All that has been said about *pativratā* is in fact symbolic of a society in which patriarchy has struck deep roots. In such a society, women started to find themselves as dependents of men. Lerner says, "What we see here is the emergence of a set of power relationships in which some men acquired power over other men and over all women. Women, even the most secure, high born and self-confident, thought of themselves as persons depending on the protection of a man. This is the female world of the social contract".[355]

Also linked up with the notion of *pativratā* is the issue of chastity which will be discussed elsewhere. As will be seen, chastity was a virtue women needed to maintain even after the death of the husband and thus were disallowed from going for remarriage.

The *pativratā* was thus, a woman stripped of her individuality and reduced to a mere glorified appendage of the husband, who could not even dare to think of any existence without or away from him. Depriving women of any choice, agency, justice and resourcefulness; the *pativratā* ideology was designed as an effective tool towards the social exclusion of women.

Settlement of Domestic Chores

Settlement of domestic chores was considered to be another foremost duty of the women. Manu considers fulfilment of household duties by women as equivalent to the worship of daily fire by the men.[356] Further, he says that she must always be cheerful, clever in the management of household affairs, careful in cleaning utensils, and economical in expenditure.[357] Later in the text he indicates the reason for limiting the sphere of women's activities to the household. It is admitted that no man can completely guard women by force.[358] So to be able to exercise a control over women, in the following verse some ways are suggested. It says that let the husband engage his wife in looking after the savings and expenses of his money, in keeping everything clean, in the fulfilment of religious duties, in cooking his food, and in looking after the household utensils. Bṛhaspati also expresses similar views and says that employing a woman in the receipt and expenses of money, in the preparation of food, in the preservation of domestic utensils, in purification, and in the care of the sacred household fire, is declared to be the best way of guarding women.[359] Thus, keeping women busy in the performance of mundane activities was an effective way in excluding women from the public arena, and depriving them of any active agency or resourcefulness. He further says that the duties of women have been declared as getting up from bed before the others, paying reverence to the elders of the family, preparing food, and using a low seat and bed.[360] Yājñavalkya also says that a woman should be efficient in carrying out the domestic chores, humorous, economical and obedient to her husband. Also, she should touch the feet of her in-laws with keen obeisance.[361] Viṣṇu declares keeping household articles in good array, maintaining saving habits and being careful with the domestic utensils to be among the general duties of women.[362] Vyāsa lays down the household duties of the wife in minute details.[363] These include quitting the bed before her husband, bathing, folding up the beds, cleaning the house, washing and plastering the floor and the yard, washing the vessels of oil and butter with warm water, keeping the vessels at proper places, cleaning and refilling them, repairing and plastering of the oven, lighting the fire, allotment of work to different workers, looking after the daily expenditure of the household, making obeisance to the elders of the family etc. Among the other qualities of a true wife, Dakśa mentions one who is acquainted with the security and number of household articles.[364]

Giving Birth to Progeny

Fertility was one of the most essential qualifications for a wife in patriarchy. The barren wife was considered to be worthless.[365] Nārada says that a wife who gets abortion shall be banished from the town by the husband.[366] Pārāśara also laid down the desertion of a wife who undergoes abortion.[367] Giving birth to progeny, more specifically, the sons, was considered to be one of the most important duties of the wife. This is testified by some of the verses where it is said that the wife should be cared for and nurtured because she is the one to give birth to the sons. It is declared by Manu that there is no difference between the wife and the goddess of fortune who reside in the house of women.[368] While in the earlier verses, a control over woman is said to be necessary, here it is said that the wife is worthy of worship. Perhaps because, as is expressed in verse 28, offspring, the due performance of religious rites, faithful service, highest conjugal happiness and heavenly bliss for the ancestors and for oneself depend on the wife only. It is clear that it is for the function of producing children, (and thus help in the securing of bliss for the men) that women are accorded a high position as that of a goddess. Yājñavalkya also lays down that the wife should be served and well-maintained and protected since it is the wife only who provides the man with a son and the son, grandson and great grandson maintain a perpetual tradition of the family and the man attains the heaven as a result of great deeds performed by them.[369] Āpastamba laid down that on the advent of the fourth night of her flow, a woman should ask her lord to procreate progeny on her person.[370] Pārāśara also laid down that a wife who does not approach her husband in proper season goes to hell and is subsequently born as a widow again and again.[371]

Duties of the Husband/Householder

Performance of Pañcamahāyajñas and Other Duties of the Gṛhastha

It is said that there are five places in the household where the animals are liable to be destroyed – the hearth, the grinding-stone, the broom, the pestle and mortar, the water-vessel.[372] For the expiation of the sin of the destruction of lives in this manner, it was enjoined upon the *gṛhastha* to perform the five great sacrifices, *pañcamahāyajña* with the sacred fire kindled at his wedding. These five religious sacrifices are called *Brahma-yajña,* addressed to the *brāhmaṇa*; *Devayajña*, addressed to the gods; *Bhūta-yajña,* addressed to the goblins; *Pitṛ- yajña,* addressed to the manes and *Nṛ- yajña,* addressed to men.[373] Teaching and studying (or reciting) the *Vedas* is the sacrifice offered to the *brāhmaṇa,* the burnt oblation is the sacrifice to the gods, the offerings of water and food (*pitṛ-tarpaṇa*) is the sacrifice to the manes, the *bali* offering is the sacrifice offered to the goblins, and the hospitable reception of guests the offering to men.[374] Further, it is said that he who does not offer their share to these five, the gods, his guests, his wife and children and others, whom he is bound to maintain, his manes, and himself, is not alive, though he breathes.[375] Pārāśara also laid down the performance of the five sacrifices.[376] The duties of the householder included giving alms to the ascetic and the student, thus supporting the remaining three orders.[377] Manu says that by giving alms, a twice-born householder gains the same reward for his meritorious act which a student obtains for presenting, in accordance with the rule, a cow to his teacher.[378] It is also enjoined upon the householder to take care of the *poṣyas* i.e., the dependents upon him, which includes the women, children, old and sick of the family. Gautama says that a householder should first feed the infants, old men, pregnant women, sick-folks and married girls residing in his house (*suvásinī)*, as well as those who cannot be persuaded to take their meals a little after, residing in his house.[379] Dakśa goes to the extent of saying that to support the *poṣyas*, is the most excellent expedient for attaining to the celestial region, and by oppressing them, one goes to hell.[380] Thus, the householder was viewed as the one supporting the entire creation. The wife was the one to assist him in the discharge of such duties. However, being included in the list of dependents, she is accorded a status below the householder at the very beginning. Also implicit in this regard is the fact that he was the one who was the wielder of authority in all matters regarding the process of production and distribution. Vyāsa's statement makes it clear. He says that the householder should "acquire that which has not been already acquired, and having obtained it distribute it as soon as possible".[381]

Extending Hospitality: Extra-domestic Connections

Extending hospitality was considered to be one of the important functions of the householder. However, hospitality was viewed as a two-way transaction, and criteria were also laid down for excluding at least some households from the distributive network.[382] Thus, food could not be accepted from households where women performed sacrifices,[383] from those where husbands and sons were absent and from the house of a man who was either dominated by his wife or tolerated her having a lover.[384] Once again, the households which were excluded from participating in hospitality were those where gender relations were relatively loosely structured. Nevertheless, the need to take into account such households, even in order to condemn them and debar them from what were viewed or portrayed as prestigious forms of social intercourse, points to their existence.[385] Again, it is to be noted that all the extra-domestic connections were also managed through the householder.

Duties as a Husband

Viṣṇu laid down that the king should punish a husband who forsakes his blameless wife like a thief.[386] Kātyāyana also interestingly says that if a wife, worthy of respect, being insulted by her husband, dies before, she attains to manhood for three births, and the man becomes born as a woman.[387] Of course, Kātyāyana intends to protect the right of a deserving wife to be honoured and respected by her husband in this verse; however; what makes it interesting is the punishment laid down for a husband who does not do so. Few can disagree with the fact that an acceptance of the superiority of male birth and life over the female is very obviously implicit in this statement. Dakśa has mentioned the wife as one of the *poṣya* i.e., those who should be supported by the householder,[388] and says that to support the *poṣyas*, is the most excellent expedient for attaining to the celestial region and by oppressing them, one goes to hell.[389] Hārita also says that a king who is endued with righteous understanding should, among other things, be devoted to his wife and self restrained, and avoid other people's wives.[390] These are the few verses which lay down the husband's duties towards supporting the wife. However, the most important of all his duties towards her were to keep her guarded and procreating progeny on her person, which are discussed subsequently.

Control over Women's Sexuality

Keeping the women under guard was a constant preoccupation with the *dharmaśāstrakāras.* A constant fear of transgression of boundaries set by the lawgivers for women is evident throughout the texts. This apprehension is so deep-rooted in the psyche of the authors of *dharmaśāstras* that keeping the wife under control is laid down as one of the foremost duties of the husband. While declaring the eternal laws for the husband and wife who keep to the path of duty, Manu says that even the weak husbands must strive to guard their wives, considering it their highest duty.[391] He further says that a woman should be guarded by her father during adolescence/childhood, by her husband in married life and by her son in old age. The women are therefore, never independent.[392] Similar intention was expressed previously, where Manu laid down that nothing must be done independently by a girl, by a young woman, or even by an aged one even in her own house, and that she must remain subject to her father, husband and son respectively during different stages of her life.[393]

Other lawgivers reiterate the view of Manu.[394] To this Yājñavalkya adds, that in case, all these are absent, it is the duty of the siblings to protect her. Again he says that a woman should not live without her father, mother, children, brothers-in-law or maternal uncle, if her husband is absent. If she lives alone, it is certain that the society will criticize her.[395] Nārada also says that it is through independence that women go to ruin, therefore, the Lord of creatures has assigned a dependent status to them.[396] Bṛhaspati declares that a woman must be restrained from slightest transgressions by her relations and that day and night she must be watched by her mother-in-law and other wives belonging to the family.[397] Notable here is the employment of women for keeping guard over women. Sowing the seeds of differences among the women and preventing any kind of solidarity amongst the women was one of the means adopted for the sustenance of patriarchy. Viṣṇu mentions the following among the duties of a woman; not to act by herself in any manner, and to remain subject to her father in infancy, to her husband in youth and to her sons in old age.[398] Similarly, Vasiṣṭha also says that a woman is not independent, the males are her masters. Their fathers protect them in youth, and their sons protect them in age; a woman is never fit for independence.[399] Angiras declares that the food of a woman, who, disregarding the command of her husband, acts at her will, should never be taken.[400] Dakśa says that if a wife is under the control of her husband, there is no other mode of life better than the domestic mode of life.[401] This world is like a celestial region for such a husband[402] and such a wife is goddess personified.[403] But, if she follows her own will and is not curbed by her husband out of love, then later she becomes uncontrollable like a neglected disease.[404]

The eagerness to control women has to be seen in the light of several misogynist statements found in the texts regarding what is considered to be the natural disposition of women- *strīsvabhāva.* Manu says that women give themselves to the handsome and to the ugly, and without any consideration for age or beauty; for them it is enough that he is a man.[405] Again, he says that however carefully women are guarded by their husbands; they become disloyal to their husbands because of their passion for men, their mutable temper and their natural heartlessness.[406] Similarly, later he says that that knowing their disposition, man should most strenuously exert himself to guard her.[407] It further says, that when creating them, Manu[408] allotted to them a love of their bed, seat and ornament, impure desires, wrath, dishonesty, malice and bad conduct.[409] An attempt is made to derive authority for these statements by citing from the *Veda* in the next two verses. Pārāśara also refers to the onset of *kaliyuga* which is characterized by women dominating over men and conception by unmarried females.[410]

Verses which describe women as faithlessly adulterous might be reminiscent of an age of promiscuity, long before the time of composition of the *dharmaśāstras*, an age when the notions of chastity, faithfulness and sexual restraint were non-existent. Frequent references to the term *jāra*, meaning paramour, can be found in the *Ṛgveda.* In this context, Sarkar observes "It is presumed by a domestic ritual formula in the *Ṛgveda* that every married woman might have a *jāra.*"[411] Later, with the establishment of patriarchal social order, the notion of chastity took roots but only for women. It will be later discussed that though adultery was punishable even for the males, it was considered a serious offence only when (1) it was committed with other's wife, and (2) it was committed with women belonging to higher *varṇa*.

Again, men might have had not forgotten that earlier period, it was the memory of that age together with the fear that women may not actually be taking kindly to the new restrictions placed on them, which resulted in vituperative attack on 'deviant' (sexually adventurous) women.[412]

While the above inference may satisfy the primary query, what gave rise to the need for control of women's sexuality is yet to be answered. This is made clear by a statement of Manu himself, where he says that it was necessary to preserve the purity of the offspring *(prasūti)*, virtuous conduct, his family *(kula)*, himself (*ātman)* and his means of acquiring merit (*dharma)*.[413] That women needed to be controlled in order to maintain the purity of offspring and thus lineage, also becomes clear from similar verses by other *dharmaśāstra* writers. Again, preserving the purity of the offspring was central to the successful perpetuation of patriarchy. Scholars like Lubbock and McLennan were of the view that in the early stages of human race and in a promiscuous society with no established institution of marriage, there was no way of identifying the paternity of the child, only motherhood was a fact and descent was therefore, reckoned through the mother.[414] In an earlier stage, children of individual mothers were also not identified, rather all the women of a group were jointly mothers of all children. Words like *dvaimātura, sānmātura, saptamātura* are indicative of this situation.[415] With the creation of patriarchy reckoning came into being.[416] This is further explained by Shalini Shah in the following words –"In patrilocality the tenuous bond between wife and husband will be undermined by liaisons with other men. Actually one of the basic dilemma of the agnatic group is to deal with the anomalous presence of women who are in the group (husband's family) but not of it. It is only as mother that wife in a patrilocal/patrilineal set-up secures a place in the group, bound to it through a blood tie. To ensure that this child was indeed of the same blood as the agnatic group, it was essential that woman's sexuality be controlled".[417] Roy gives a deeper explanation of the control that was sought to be exercised over women. She says, "The need to control the wife was intrinsically related to the definition of procreation which was sought to be established, a definition in which the woman was viewed as the field or passive recipient of the male seed.[418] However, male control over the produce of the field, progeny, rested not only on claims to contribute and sow the seed, but also, and more basically, on the ownership of the field, i.e., his role as *kśetrasvāmin*[419]."[420]

That in spite of all the efforts made by the husband, it would not have been possible to guard the women completely, is attested to by some other verses by Manu. At one place, he says that however carefully women be guarded by their husbands, they become disloyal to their husbands because of their passion for men, their mutable temper and their natural heartlessness.[421] Later, one finds one finds Dakśa saying dejectedly that in childhood, she always remains afraid, in youth, she becomes disobedient; and afterwards in old age, she considers her own husband as a servant.[422]

Manu also admits that no man can completely guard women by force.[423] So to be able to exercise a control over women, he suggests that the husband should employ his wife in the maintenance of his accounts, in keeping everything clean, in the fulfilment of religious duties, in the preparation of his food, and in looking after the household utensils.[424] Verse no. 12 goes further to say that women confined in the house under trustworthy and obedient servants are not well guarded, but those who of their own accord keep guard over themselves, are well guarded. Same as Manu, Bṛhaspati also says that employing a woman in the receipt and expenditure of wealth, preparation of food, preservation of domestic utensils, purification, and the care of the sacred household fire, is the best way of guarding women.[425]

Control was also imposed upon women by adopting other means. Manu gives a list of actions which cause the ruin of women. These include drinking spirituous liquor, associating with wicked people, separation from the husband, rambling abroad, sleeping at unseasonable hours, and dwelling in other men's houses.[426] Yājñavalkya has laid down that a woman whose husband is not at home, should not involve in games, additional make-up, gatherings, visit at marriage etc., festivities, places for recreation and in the houses of other people.[427] He further says that a woman should not live without her father, mother, children, brother-in-laws or maternal uncle, if her husband is absent. If she lives alone, it is certain that the society will criticize her.[428] Viṣṇu goes a step ahead, and what was mentioned as the duty of the males, the onus of it got shifted to the women themselves. Among the duties of a woman, he mentions not to act by herself in any manner, and to remain subject to her father in infancy, to her husband in youth and to her sons in old age.[429] Angiras declares that the food of a woman, who, disregarding the command of her husband, acts at her will, should never be taken.[430] Dakśa says that if a wife is under the control of her husband, there is no other mode of life better than the domestic mode of life.[431] This world is a like a celestial region for such a husband[432] and such a wife is a goddess personified.[433]

Thus, by various means such as prescription, threat of ruin or social criticism, disapprobation and reward of being attributed the status of a goddess personified; women's identity and freedom of movement were curbed with the aim of avoiding any opportunity for transgression of the control over their sexuality.

Whether or no should there be a control over women's sexual freedom and choice? Indian scholars with adherence to feminist ideology have been criticized by some scholars for advocating complete sexual freedom for women following the Western feminists. Kapoor writes, "Feminist critiques of Indian social reality are flawed in that they assume an absolute, universalist Hindu code. They are also asymmetrical with the given Indian reality in that they are derived from the reality of, for want of a better word, western social system which in its history of unbridled sexuality and in it progressive weakening for the institutions of family and marriage and a general ethical collapse is foundationally different."[434] He points towards the fact that sexuality has been handled differently in India and the West and writes:

> "As in other areas of knowledge, in women studies also, we have tried to fit the Indian reality to a borrowed western framework … . Western social condition has been and is very different from ours. Three facts stand out. First of all, the societal attitude to sexuality, both male and female, has been different. Both homosexuality and lesbianism have some kind of legitimacy ever since Plato (*Symposium*) and Sappho, the poetess of Lesbos. Add to this the Old Testament narrative of the two cities of Sodom and Gomorrah and you have a picture of unbridled sexuality – a sexuality not governed by any societal institution or ethical framework. There is a sanction, in Genesis, in the roots of western civilization, for self indulgence and for the gratification of one's appetites and desires. No ethics of restraint governs these. Secondly, as we have already noted, there is an ethical vacuum … . In any case, there never was anything analogous to the Indian system of *sanyam* (restraint) and *niyama* (the right way) … . India has handled sexuality differently. Its reality and its power have been more explicitly recognized than in any other culture (no other culture has a whole *sastra* devoted to it) and no other culture has honoured sexual union as our culture has done (witness its place in temple sculpture). But from the raw reality of a basic urge to an honoured fact of disciplined life, there is an orderly upward passage in the form of a rigorous ethical framework, both institutional and general."[435]

The question demands some serious thinking. Feminists do seem to advocate sexual freedom for women. Does sexual freedom amount to women's emancipation? Seen solely on the physical plane, the right to choice and freedom cannot be denied. But human beings are not merely physical beings. They are also emotional, mental and spiritual beings. Again, they are also social beings having social identities beyond an atomistic individual existence. This fact cannot be overlooked while dealing with any question related to human life. Sexual freedom may be advocated if sex merely remains a physical act. However, even if the West denies it to be a spiritual act, even they have to acquiesce in the emotional and mental bearing of the act. Excessive indulgence leads to emotional and mental deterioration, is a fact recognized by Western psychology itself. Further, Indian philosophy rightly points towards spiritual degradation of an individual as a consequence of sexual excess. As Kapoor rightly comments, "Sex is an appetite; and its gratification, like that of other appetites such as hunger, has to be regulated as is required by the general philosophy of self-imposed restraint and abstemiousness (*sanyama*)."[436] Equally important is the fact that excessive sexual freedom has significant social implications. Kapoor writes, "But we may note, quite unlike other appetites, its gratification has social, beyond-the-individual consequences. Therefore, apart from the merely personal, there is the need for its social regulation."[437] Excessive sexual freedom may actually result in women and men being identified as sex objects more than as mental, emotional or spiritual beings. This stands truer in case of women, whose identity may, as Kapoor comments, be reduced to the existence as a "Baby-doll with the Marilyn Monroe image."[438] Also, the institutions of marriage and family would be weakened, leading to chaos. Marriage and family have to be there until some superior social arrangement is suggested. So far as the *dharmaśāstras* would have advocated sexual abstinence or regulation for both men and women, it would not have been derogatory to the women's lives. However, even though adultery was considered a crime both in case of men and women, men were permitted polygamy. It may be argued that gradually the lawgivers went in disfavour of polygamy. But again, even if it is agreed that sexual control was advocated for both men and women, the distinction lies in the fact that while for women, it was control by the husband and other agnatic relations, for the men it implied self-control of the impulse. There is a difference between sexual control and sexual abstinence. While abstinence implies self-control, sexual control by others implies the use of force and suppression by them. While men were expected to exhibit self-control as a measure to guard against adultery, females were to be guarded by the male members, and even at times, *other female members* of the household. This is evident from a number of verses which emphasize upon the need to keep women guarded. To quote Shalini Shah in this regard: "What was affirmed through this conception of 'mastery' (over one's self) as ensuring freedom was the virile character of this mastery. Just as in the household it was man, who ruled, it was only right that he alone should exercise self-restraint. Self-mastery was a way of being a man with respect to oneself. This does not mean that women were not expected to be moderate. But moderation in this case was imposed on them by their condition of dependence, in relation to their families, their husbands. *For what was symbolized in woman's chastity was not her own self control as in the male celibacy but the control of her kinsmen over her behaviour* (emphasis added)."[439] It is here that the inequality in gender relations as sought to be established by the *dharmaśāstrakāras* lies. The sexuality of a woman was not a matter of self-control by her, but the possession of the husband and agnates. This control over her sexuality becomes further pronounced in control over her procreative power by the agnates, undeniably expressed in the practice of *niyoga*, to be discussed in detail later in this chapter.

Procreating Progeny on the Wife's Person

While Manu only mentions guarding the wife as the duty of the husband, Yājñavalkya goes a step ahead and directs him to take care of the desires of his wife. Religious sanction is drawn for such a dictum by telling that Lord Indra had once blessed the woman that the man not taking care of her passion in menstrual period will fall in hell.[440] In the same verse, it is further said that it is the supreme religion to give the best protection cover to his woman. It is already discussed that the need for both protection and control of wife originated out of a sense of necessity for the protection of one's progeny and as such, the lineage. The dictum of Yājñavalkya also emanated out of a sense of indispensability for the procreation and protection of one's progeny. The desire of the wife had to be catered to for two reasons, one, in order to actually be able to stop her from looking towards other options and thus, to control her, one needed to satiate her desires; and second, procreation was considered the most important cause for marriage and hence, one should unite with one's wife. It is reiterated a number of times at other places that it is the duty of the husband to unite with his wife in her season, otherwise he shall incur guilt.[441] Thus what is apparently mentioned as the duty of the husband, has actually little to do with the welfare or rights of the wife, but was only meant to serve as one of the measures in the intended scheme of preserving the social order.

Further important it is to notice what is said regarding a husband who was impotent. What is significant is that while the barren wife was looked down upon, almost nothing is said in case the husband was impotent. Bhattacharji points out that as an agricultural people ancient Indians must have known that a dead seed (sperm) would not germinate in a fully fertile field (womb) but they observed a sinister silence on this aspect of childlessness.[442] However, Nārada and Pārāśara present a strong exception to this, proving the statement of Bhattacharji to be flawed. Nārada says that another husband must be procured for the wife of one who spills his semen, or whose semen is devoid of strength, after she has waited for half a year.[443] He further says that women have been created for the sake of propagation, the wife being the field, and the husband the giver of the seed. The field must be given to him who has seed. He who has no seed is unworthy to possess the field.[444] Pārāśara mentions impotence of the husband as one of the conditions when the wife is permitted to remarry.[445]

Even a cursory glance at the roles ascribed to and duties prescribed for the wife and the husband is enough to reveal the inherent gender bias in them. While the wife remains the *bhāryā* or the *poṣyā*, meaning one to be nurtured and supported, the role of the husband was that of *bhartā*. Thus a woman was dependent on man for her existence. The dependence and subjection of women was completed with the propagation of the ideology of the *pativratā*, whereby she was expected to worship even an unjust or undeserving husband, while for the men it was enough to respect, and if possible, not to transgress, a wife who fulfils all the requirements of a *pativratā*. Since the husband was the sole object of worship for the wife, no religious penances or vow were rightful for her apart from the husband. She was to be merely an appendage of the husband in fulfilling religious obligations. The husband was her lord, and also of the household, which she was expected to take complete care of. While she was the one to provide all the domestic services, the husband wielded the entire power regarding any decisions to be made. Procreating sons was obligatory for her, not a matter of choice. The husband wielded complete rights and control over her reproductive potential. The authority over the progeny was also ensured to be given to the husband by establishing the superiority of the seed, i.e., the male sperm over the field, i.e., the womb. The *Manusmṛti* states, "Of the seed and the womb, the seed is superior. All creatures of life assume the qualities of the seed. The qualities of the womb are never shared by the seed".[446] Again, it is the bounden duty of the husband to keep her guarded so as to protect the purity of the lineage. It is also the duty of the husband to procreate progeny on the wife's person, which has nothing to do with the welfare of the wife, but merely a fulfilment of religious and social obligation. In such a scheme of things, the husband was the one who was resourceful and powerful, while the wife was resourceless and powerless. The mechanisms envisaged for maintaining or enforcing the definition of the *gṛha* included empowering the *gṛhapati*.[447] Besides control over the woman's reproductive potential and sexuality, there were other means to ensure the empowerment of the *gṛhapati*. He was the one who was expected to maintain harmony within the household by avoiding quarrels.[448] He was given the right to beat the wife, son, servant, brother and slave with a rope or a cane in case they commit faults.[449] He was also the one expected to administer punishment in cases of adultery, as shall be discussed subsequently in the section on adultery. Thus the role of the wife was; even though being central to the existence of the household; subordinated to the husband, and she was expected to live a life of complete dependence, subjection and acceptance of everything that the husband uttered or did.

Polygamy

Polygamy was permitted, rather accepted in general by all the *dharmaśāstrakāras*. An indirect acceptance of polygamy is found in the form of the acceptance of inter-*varṇa* marriages. For the first marriage, a wife of equal caste is recommended, but for those who are desirous of more wives, rules are being prescribed for choosing the females according to the direct order of the castes.[450] However, there were other reasons which were accepted for resorting to polygamy. Some of the *dharmaśāstrakāras* have laid down conditions when a wife can be superseded by another. Manu says that a wife, who drinks spirituous liquor, is of bad conduct, rebellious, diseased, mischievous, or wasteful, may be superseded by another wife.[451] Yājñavalkya has added the attributes shrewd, barren, bitter mouth, delivering girl children and envying her husband continuously to this list.[452] It is to be noted that giving birth to girl children was not appreciated and the blame lay on the women instead of the men. Manu is somewhat lenient in the case of a diseased wife, and says that if a sick wife is kind to her husband, and virtuous in conduct, then she should be superseded only with her consent and must never be disgraced.[453] Yājñavalkya grants no such respite to such a wife. However, Yājñavalkya lays down the provision for maintenance for a wife who is superseded by another. He says that a man should provide proper maintenance to the aforesaid first wife, if the husband resorts to polygamy while the first wife is living. If the husband makes any negligence, he falls prey to evils.[454] In the same verse, it is further said that where husband and wife are living under mutual harmony, the threefold objects, i.e., *Artha*, *Dharma* and *Kāma* always multiply there. Dakśa also says that disagreement of the mind always takes place when a person has a wife always going against him, and especially when she has two wives thus accepting that polygamy gives rise to problems.[455] Atri gives a list of persons who should not be fed. Among others, he mentions one who has taken two wives.[456] Kātyāyana goes a step ahead and says that no *homa* is laid down for that person for maintaining his Sacred Fire, who having a living wife wishes for other wives, for some reason or other.[457] It is obvious that the attitude of later *dharmaśāstrakāras* gradually became negative towards polygamy. There are no references to testify the acceptance of polyandry.

Respective Status of Wives in a Polygamous Household

What needs to be examined is the life of a woman in a polygamous household. The polygamous household generated hierarchy among the wives. One of the wives was more exalted than the others, being the chief or the most senior wife. Thus she might be having a better position than the rest in some matters. However, in other matters, some other wife may supersede her, for example, in the case of one who might be the dearest and closest to the husband. Again, the position of the wives might have depended on whether they have sons or daughters. There is no doubt that plurality of wives tended to strengthen man's domination over women more often and with greater ease than either polyandrous or monogamous marriage. Thus, women's constant sense of insecurity was the characteristic feature of a polygynous household. A woman with a co-wife was generally seen as having a tough time. To make it worse, a constant sense of enmity must have been a characteristic feature amongst the co-wives, who, instead of blaming the husband, tended to blame each other for their plight. The sense of insecurity prevented any kind of solidarity among the women in a polygamous household.

The seniority of the wives of a man is to be decided on the basis of their *varṇa*.[458] Yājñavalkya also testifies this by laying down that if a wife of same caste exists, the husband should not engage a wife of another caste perform the religious rites. In case there are many wives of one's own caste, the first-married one is entitled to perform the religious rites.[459] Most of the other *dharmaśāstrakāras* hold similar views.[460] Since performance of religious rites was of utmost importance, it may be inferred that the wife of the same *varṇa* was placed the highest in the hierarchy of wives belonging to different *varṇas*. Even while dividing the property among sons born of wives belonging to different *varṇas*, greater share was prescribed for the son born of the wife of same *varṇa*.[461]

Being treated as the one to be the partner of the husband in the performance of religious rites, the wife of same caste must have got a position far superior to those of other wives. Her position must have been further strengthened with her son receiving greater share in the property of her husband. This might have well been the reason why the *dharmaśāstrakāras* advocated a wife of equal caste for the first marriage. At the first place, the older wife of other caste must have resented the superior position of a younger wife whose caste be the same of the husband. This must have given rise to further tensions in an already tense polygamous household. Again, the first wife being of the same caste, her son must have been the eldest, and greater share could have been given to him without disturbing the law of primogeniture.

However, Manu laid down that an excellent wife may be taken from anywhere, even from a base family.[462] While a better status is accorded to the wife belonging to higher *varṇa* throughout the text, these verses make it clear that excellence of the wives is not judged on the basis of caste. It seems that excellence is considered as an individual characteristic, which anybody can possess, even one who belongs to a base family.

Menstrual Taboos

Menstrual taboos have been common to all ancient societies and find place in some of the societies even to this date. These mark the customs prevalent in society that publicly restrict the behaviour of woman at the time of menstruation and apply throughout most of a woman's life. They found easy entry into the minds of the *dharmaśāstrakāras,* already excessively preoccupied with the concepts of purity and pollution. Vasiṣṭha explained menstruation in women in the terms of a sin committed by Indra (having slain Vṛtra, who was a learned *brāhmaṇa*), third part of the guilt being taken over by the woman upon herself. In return for this favour, Indra granted them a boon, whereby they would obtain offspring in the proper season. He attributed this explanation as a declaration in the *Veda*.[463] The *Veda* being attributed a divine origin; divine sanction was obtained for these taboos.

Women were considered to be impure during the period of menstrual flow. Even talking to a menstruating woman is forbidden.[464] The impurity associated with miscarriage and menstruation is repeatedly asserted throughout *Manusmṛti*.[465] Similar sentiments are voiced out when it is said that if a man has touched a menstruating woman or a woman in childbed, he becomes pure by bathing.[466] In the same verse similar rule is laid down in case he touches a *cāṇḍāla* or a corpse. Yājñavalkya lists the food touched by a woman in menses among other types of food which should not be accepted.[467] He further says that one should take a bath and chant *apohiṣṭha* hymn thrice and *gāyatrī* once, if he happens to touch women in their menstrual cycle, corpse or *cāṇḍālas*.[468] Vasiṣṭha also says that a woman in her courses is impure during three days and nights and during that period, she shall not apply collyrium to her eyes, nor anoint her body, nor bathe in water; she shall sleep on the ground; she shall not sleep in the daytime, nor touch the fire, nor make a rope, nor clean her teeth, nor eat meat, nor look at the planets, nor smile, nor busy herself with household affairs, nor run and shall drink out of a large vessel, or out of her joined hands, or out of a copper vessel.[469] He further says that among others, those *brāhmaṇas* in whose house menstruating women sit, are equal to *śūdras*.[470] According to Āpastamba, on the first day of the menses, she is like a *cāṇḍāla* women; on the second day, she is the murderess of a *brāhmaṇa*; on the third day, she is called a washer-women; and on the fourth day, she becomes purified.[471] This is reiterated by Pārāśara and Angiras.[472] He prescribes fasting for a night followed by the performance of *pañcagavya* for a *brāhmaṇa* who is touched by a woman in her menses.[473] Yama says that being touched by a woman in her menses or by a woman of degraded caste in the night, a *vipra* should bathe with the water brought during the daytime.[474] Earlier, Āpastamba prescribed performance of *krichchhra* penance for a *brāhmaṇa* before washing his mouth after a meal, having touched a woman in her menses.[475] According to Atri, a *brāhmaṇa*, who unknowingly partakes of cooked food touched by outcastes or by woman in their menses, should perform half a *Prājāpatya*.[476] Further he lays down that if one touches a woman in her menses, he should fast for three nights to obtain purity.[477] The degree of obsession with the impurity of menses was so high that penances were laid down even for two menstruating women if they happen to touch each other.[478] Also, the penances varied with the *varṇa* of the two women. According to Viṣṇu, having touched a woman in her courses, a woman in her courses becomes pure after four days by bathing.[479] Further, if a man unawares eats the food of a woman in her courses, he must fast for seven days.[480] Similar indictments are laid down by Pārāśara, who also told the ways of purification from the impurity incurred in this way.[481] Samvarta also says that by being touched by a dog or by another woman in menses, a woman in menses should fast for the remaining days of the menstrual period and get herself purified by drinking clarified butter after bathing at the end of the menstrual period.[482] Also, by taking food from the vessel of a degraded caste, or from that of a woman in menses, one would become purified, in half-a-month, by living upon barley and the urine of a cow.[483] Yama lists menstruating woman in the category of woman called *vṛṣalī*, which included barren woman, one who gave birth to dead child, a *śūdra* woman, one who desires the company of other men forsaking her own husband, besides menstruating woman.[484] He further says that the sin that a twice born person commits by associating with a *vṛṣalī* for a night, is dissipated in three years by living upon food acquired by begging and reciting the *Gāyatrī* daily.[485]

A specific code of conduct is being laid down for a woman in her menses. Vyāsa, while laying down the specific duties of the wives, says that a wife, on the appearance of her flow, should renounce all the general duties prescribed for her, as she becomes unclean. Bashfully she should reside in a lonely chamber, avoiding the eyes of her friends and relations and clad in a single sheet of cloth, and forsaking ornaments and ablution, she should sit silent with her eyes cast downward. Avoiding all listless movements of her eyes and extremities, she should take boiled rice at night alone during her periods. Having passed three nights in such a staid condition of mind, she should wash her clothes, and bathe, on the morning of the fourth day. Then having seen the face of her husband she would be clean again, whereupon she should resume her usual household duties as before.[486] In fact, Viṣṇu goes to the extent of saying that if a woman in her courses touches a person, she shall be lashed with a whip.[487]

Any physical contact or intercourse between the husband and the wife is prohibited during the period when the wife is menstruating. Manu lays down rules giving details of days when the husband should approach the wife and when he should not with reference to the monthly courses of the wife are given.[488] It is said that he who avoids the women on the six forbidden nights and on eight others, is equal in chastity to a student, in whichever order he may live.[489] He further enjoins that the *brāhmaṇa* husband should not approach the wife during the monthly courses.[490] It is said that his wisdom, energy, strength, vitality and sight will perish if he does so, and otherwise they will increase.[491] Yājñavalkya says that for meeting his wife during her menstrual period, a person attains purity by drinking clarified butter after the expiration of three nights.[492] Vasiṣṭha also says that one should not cohabit with a woman during her courses.[493] According to Angiras too, a woman does not become of pure conduct so long as the menstrual flow continues. When the menses is stopped, she may be employed in domestic works and known for sexual purpose.[494] After this, it is considered the bounden duty of the husband and wife to copulate during the 'season' of the wife. Apastamba lays down that on the advent of the fourth night of her flow, a woman should ask her lord to procreate progeny on her person.[495] Vasiṣṭha also says that let him approach his wife in the proper season.[496] Vyāsa says that a husband not visiting his wife in her menstrual period is guilty of foeticide.[497]

In fact, menstruation is considered as an unequalled means of purification for women, which removes her sins.[498] Immediately after the disappearance of the flow, she is considered to have regained purity. Āpastamba says that a woman remains unclean as long as the flow continues in her each month and becomes clean again on the suppression of the discharge, thus becoming fit for the purposes of domestic or conjugal duties.[499] Vasiṣṭha lays down that a woman is purified by her monthly discharge just as a river by its current, brass by being scoured with ashes, and an earthen pot by another burning.[500] Angiras also says that a woman is purified by her menses like a river is purified by its current.[501] A woman is considered to have regained purity in menstruation even if she has made an illicit relation with another man. Yājñavalkya has written the same thing and says that the wife should be renounced only if she has conceived out of such a relation.[502] Vasiṣṭha voices similar sentiment when he says that the wife on being unfaithful to her husband, can expiate the sin by performing penances prescribed for her, as month by month the menstrual excretion takes away her sins.[503] Again, he says that a wife, even though she be tainted by sin, be quarrelsome, or have left the house, or have suffered criminal force, or have fallen into the hands of thieves; must not be abandoned. To forsake her is not prescribed by the sacred law. Let him wait for the time of her courses; by her temporary uncleanness she becomes pure.[504] Similar indictment is laid down by Vyāsa and Atri.[505] Pārāśara also voices similarly, except for the case when the woman had an association with one belonging to one of the lowest castes.[506]

As noted earlier, such a preoccupation with menstrual taboos is not a feature that marks the ancient Indian society alone, rather it was common to all ancient societies of the world. The preponderance of such strict norms regarding something which constitutes nothing more than bodily function of women, raises questions regarding the origin and existence of these. Menstrual taboos have been interpreted as 'institutionalized ways in which males in primitive society discriminate against females'.[507] Douglas believes that pollution beliefs such as menstrual taboos serve as analogies for the social order. She says, "We cannot possibly interpret rituals concerning bodily emissions unless we are prepared to see in the body a symbol of society and to see the powers and dangers credited to social structure reproduced in small on the human body" (usually the female body).[508] Godelier argues, "Sex related differences between bodies are continually summoned as testimony to social relations and phenomena that have nothing to do with sexuality. Not only as testimony to, but also testimony for legitimization."[509] It seems that what is attempted at is to make the woman feel less and degraded because of her natural bodily function.

The only probable way in which such taboos can be explained is the duality of perceptions regarding this peculiar biological phenomenon. The life giving power of the menstrual blood was recognized, and as such, it was considered sacred. Being sacred and carrying potency, it was dreaded. On the other hand, it was considered polluting. Thomson thus explains these conflicting views- "Its potency makes it something to be dreaded … . From one aspect the woman who may not be approached is inviolable, holy; from another aspect she is polluted, unclean. She is what the Romans called sacra, sacred and accursed. And hence in patriarchal society, after woman has lost her control of religion, it is the negative aspect that prevails."[510] This has been further explained by some other scholars on the basis of their studies of matriarchal and patriarchal societies. While in the matriarchal societies, menstrual blood is considered to be life giving and hence received with joy and gratitude when it comes to the girl for the first time; in patriarchal societies, which lay emphasis on fecundity, it becomes unclean. Sanday on the basis of her study[511] of such male dominant societies like, Hausa, Mundurucu, Yanomamo and Papagoes says that in such societies men attempt to neutralize power (sexual and reproductive – which in turn is linked with menstrual blood) which they think is inherent in women by stealing it, nullifying it or banishing it to invisibility. It is this which explains the menstrual taboos in societies.

The notion that woman should be secluded during menstruation and that sexual intercourse with such a woman is polluting for men, results in the physical separation of the sexes. Again, such a seclusion in everyday affairs plays a crucial role in the rise of male dominance and is a means for the exclusion of women.

It may be inferred that menstrual taboos play a significant role in the construction of a gendered society. Since the *dharmaśāstrakāras* were advocates of a patriarchal social order, and worked towards the firm establishment and institutionalization of patriarchy, menstrual taboos were mechanisms devised to serve these ends.

Women as the Daughter-in-Law

Not much is said in this regard directly. However, reverence to the elders is prescribed in general. Also, while the household duties of the wife are defined, they indirectly imply taking over of the responsibilities of the elderly ladies of the household including the mother-in-law. Viṣṇu explicitly mentions it to be the duty of the daughter-in-law to pay reverence to the father-in-law and the mother-in-law.[512]

Motherhood

As discussed earlier, motherhood was considered to be imperative. However, it was only procreation of children, more specifically, male children, that was deemed to be essential. Nothing is said beyond bearing children. Rearing up of children, though a task of enormous significance from the point of view of building up of a healthy society, received no attention from the *dharmaśāstrakāras* surprisingly. While providing lengthy details regarding the role and duties of a wife, duties of a woman as a mother are conspicuous by their absence in these texts. The upbringing of the children was considered an unimportant subject by the authors of the texts. In the words of Roy, "Clearly, even the prescriptive literature, despite its claim to be all-pervasive, had its limits. It is important to remember that the areas which were thus relatively autonomous, in the sense that they were implicitly recognized as outside the purview of the shastras, were nonetheless significant in terms of socialization and generating resources. As such, the inability to encompass them within the scope of prescriptions meant in effect, recognising the existence of space which could threaten the order which was sought to be imposed."[513] Perhaps the lawgivers were less concerned about the sustained health of the society; but only the sustenance of patriarchal social order, to which women's role as wife was far more important.

Again, there is another argument that serves as an answer for the question as to why child bearing, or 'bearing a son' was considered so important. Boserup has argued that in regions of female farming women were valued both as workers and as child bearers; on the other hand where women do little agricultural work (productive work) they are valued as mothers only and the status of a barren woman is particularly vulnerable in such communities.[514] Furthermore, emphasis on motherhood particularly on the birth of a son in a patriarchy is also conditioned by the fact of patrilocality, severed from her own natal group in which she has no further rights, the bride joins a household consisting of a husband who is a virtual stranger, his male agnates, other in-married women with whom she has no consanguine connections (prevented by exogamic prescriptions) and unmarried girls who are transitory members. Where males are born into a situation in which loyalty to the group (agnatic) coincides with their own interests as heirs and property holders, women marry into a group to which they have no equivalent basis for loyalty. And yet the survival of the household depends on the one half of adult membership that is composed of such women. The basic dilemma of the agnatic group is to deal with the anomalous presence of those people who are in the group but not of it. It is only as the mother, above all of a son, that a wife in a patrilocal/patrilineal set-up secures a place in the group, bound to it through a blood tie.[515]

The mother is considered to be the foremost of all the ones to be respected. Viṣṇu considered the mother to be one of the three *Atigurus* (or specially venerable superiors); to whom he must always pay obedience and do what is agreeable and serviceable to them.[516] He further says that those three are equal to the three *Vedas* (the mother being the *Sāma Veda*), they are equal to the three gods (the mother being Viṣṇu), the three worlds (the mother equal to the world of gods), and the three fires (the mother equal to the *Dakśiṇa* or ceremonial fire).[517] By showing respect to these three, one pays regard to all his duties; while he who shows no regard to them, derives no benefit from any religious observance.[518] By honouring his mother, a man gains the present world.[519] Gautama and Atri also consider the mother as the highest of all superiors.[520] Similar treatment to mother is found in other *Dharmaśāstras*.[521]

A high degree of respect was accorded to the mother, is obvious from the aforementioned statements. Altekar says "The apotheosis of motherhood had reached a greater height in India than anywhere else".[522] However, whatever was the degree of respect accorded to the mother, it seems improbable that she was at any time given the right to or even consulted while decision-making. The male being the head of the family, she was accorded with no authority by the *dharmaśāstrakāras*. Even though it is said that the mother was more worthy of respectful than the father, the father actually was granted the authority and a greater claim over the children. At times, the son is considered to be the property or possession of the father. Even the daughter was father's property to be gifted or sold to anyone at his will as is evident from the laws governing forms of marriage. The greater claim of the father over the child was legitimized by the giving the oft-mentioned theory of the seed and the womb. The *Manusmṛti* states, "Of the seed and the womb, the seed is superior. All creatures of life assume the qualities of the seed. The qualities of the womb are never shared by the seed".[523] Thus was the superiority of the seed, i.e., male sperm, established over the womb.

Other Women as Relatives

Rules to show respect for the women related to a man in different ways; as the wife of another man, a maternal aunt, mother-in-law, wife of one's brother, wives of other paternal and maternal relatives, sister of one's father and mother and one's own elder sister are laid down in *Manusmṛti*.[524] It is further stated that women must be honoured and adorned by the male relations, if they desire their own welfare, as gods are pleased where women are honoured, but where they are not, even the sacred rites do not yield rewards. Gifts are recommended for women on holidays and festivals to honour them.[525] According to Yājñavalkya, one who accuses a woman is prohibited to offer oblation to manes.[526] Bṛhaspati declares the mother's sister, the wife of a maternal uncle, a paternal uncle's wife, a father's sister, a mother-in-law, and an elder brother's wife to be equal to a mother.[527] Uśanā also declares the mother, the maternal grandmother, the preceptor's wife, paternal and maternal aunts, the mother-in-law, the paternal grandmother and the eldest sister as elderly women,[528] who should be followed by one with mind, words and deed.[529] He further adds that seeing an elderly person, one should get up and salute him or her with folded palms. One should not sit with the elders nor should one quarrel with them on any account.[530] Also, women, among others, should be provided the way while travelling.[531] These are few of the well-meaning verses which indicate that women as female relations were to be held in great regard.

Exclusion from the Household

Adultery

Adultery was considered extremely baneful and every attempt was made by the *dharmaśāstrakāras* to prevent adulterous relationships. However, in spite of all the restrictions placed by them, it would not have been possible to completely stop the occurrence of the cases of adultery, which becomes obvious from many verses. Adultery or incest formed a reason for exclusion from the household, sometimes only temporarily and at other times, permanently; both for the male and the female. Again, death was the penalty for some kinds of adultery and incest, and as such, resulted in forced exclusion from the household. The following discussion will throw light on occasions considered fit for temporary or permanent exclusion, and the role of kinship, *varṇa* and gender in such decisions.

Several verses indicate that adultery and lasciviousness was considered to be the 'basic nature' of women – *strīsvabhāva.* This was also the reason why women were to be guarded by their male relations. Manu says that women give themselves to the handsome and to the ugly, and without any consideration for age or beauty; for them it is enough that he is a man.[532] Again, he says that however carefully women are guarded by their husbands; they become disloyal to their husbands because of their passion for men, their mutable temper and their natural heartlessness.[533] In the following verse, it is said that knowing their disposition, man should most strenuously exert himself to guard her.[534] An effort is made to assert that such a disposition is rooted in the nature of women, by saying that it was laid in them by the lord of creatures at the time of creation only. It further says that when creating them, Manu allotted to them a love of their bed, seat and ornament, impure desires, wrath, dishonesty, malice and bad conduct.[535] An attempt is made to derive authority for these statements by citing from the *Veda* in the next two verses.

Incest also would not have been very uncommon is evident from a number of verses prescribing punishments for incestuous relationships. Sexual intercourse with sibling sisters, with the wives of a friend or a son, is considered to be equal to the violation of a guru's bed.[536] Adultery with the guru's wife is again declared to be one of the *mahāpātakas*.[537] Yājñavalkya also considers one who commits incest as the sinner of the worst kind and prescribes as severe a punishment for such a person as the multilating of his penis.[538] In case, consent was given by the woman, she should be slaughtered too. Thus, incest and adultery with preceptor's wife were considered to be punishable in the form of expulsion from the household by Yājñavalkya. Nārada also laid down that if a man commits adultery with any of the twenty listed female relatives, he shall be considered to have committed incest, for which no other punishment than excision of the organ is a sufficient atonement.[539] Viṣṇu's attitude is milder. Like Manu, he also considers commission of incest equal to sexual connection with guru's wife, however, according to him such offenders are minor offenders and they become pure by a horse sacrifice and visiting *tīrthas*.[540] According to Pārāśara, a man committing incest with his mother or sister, can get expiated from his sin only by multilating of his sexual organ. However, for having incestuous relationships with other female relatives, penances are prescribed by him.[541] Atri is silent about all other forms of incest, but keeps cohabitation with the step mother in the category of five heinous crimes.[542] Samvarta prescribes various penances for incestuous relationships like *cāndrāyaṇa*, *paraka*, *krichchhra* and *atikrichchhra*.[543] However, no atonement is laid down for one who knows his own mother, daughter, or his own sister.[544] There is a marked change in attitude of Śātātapa. Instead of laying down punishments for incestuous relationships, he merely tries to prevent them by instilling fear in the minds of people. He says that the generative organ of a person who knows his mother disappears.[545] The sin of incest can be expiated by some mild ritual performances addressed to different deities depending on with whom incest was committed.[546] However, the attempt made by Śātātapa to prevent adultery by instilling fear of ordained punishments was not something new. Gautama had already said that a person who carnally knows a courtesan or a woman of his own *gotra*, as well as he who holds incest with his own father's or mother's sister, is successively reborn as a haunch back, dwarf, insane, diseased, deformed, indigent, short-lived, foolish, irascible, worthless, thievish, carrying out other men's behests, bald, and miscreant person in low and vulgar families. Hence according to him, one should atone for one's sin. Atonement preserves one's virtues intact and helps one to be reborn with commendable attributes and physical traits.[547] Again, his tone gets stricter in some worse cases. A man, who has defiled the bed of his elder or preceptor, should lie down on a red hot bed of iron, or he should be made to embrace a hot iron image of a female, or he should cut his genital, and holding them in his united palms, should walk towards the south west quarter, until he drops down dead from bleeding. Such a death absolves him of his sin. Similar penance is prescribed for knowing the wife of one's son, friend, disciple or cognate, or having held incest with a cow.[548]

Uśanā also says that by lustfully knowing a step mother, a *brāhmaṇa* should embrace a heated female form, made of black iron after his heart, or having himself cut off his generative organ and testes and taken them in his palms, he should proceed straight on to the south or to the west till the destruction of his body, or for expiation, he should meet with death for his preceptor, or he should practice the *Brāhma* vow for twelve years. In a year he may be purified by embracing the branch of a tree full of thorns.[549] He further says that by willingly knowing his daughter, sister or daughter-in-law, a *vipra* should enter into a burning fire.[550] However, for incest with other related females, he prescribes penances.[551]

Adultery vs *Varṇa* Identity

There is a connection between adultery and the *varṇa* structure. Manu explicitly says that adultery is condemned and punishment is prescribed to men who commit adultery with others' wives,[552] as by adultery is caused the mixture of *varṇa* among men, from which sin follows and cuts up the roots, causing the destruction of everything.[553] This statement of Manu is quite telling as far as the cause for condemnation of adultery is concerned. It was not morality in the contemporary sense of the term that bothered the *dharmaśāstrakāras*, but the sustenance and maintenance of the social order, while condemning and making tireless attempts at preventing adultery. This will further be shown by subsequent discussion.

Punishment and atonement for adultery varied with difference in *varṇa*. For commission of adultery with one's preceptor's wife, which is considered a *mahāpātaka*, the punishment is milder in the case of *brāhmaṇa*.[554] In fact, it was the respective status of the one who committed and another, with whom adultery was committed; on the social ladder, that determined the degree of severity of the crime. According to Yājñavalkya, the highest form of pecuniary punishment is the penalty when adultery is committed with a woman of the same caste, the second form is the punishment when adultery is committed with a woman of lower caste; and death is the penalty when it is committed with a woman of a higher caste.[555] This was repeated by Nārada and Viṣṇu.[556] However, later Nārada prescribes middling fine for one who commits adultery with a woman of low caste which is the same as the one when he has sexual connection with a cow.[557] The severity of the crime was considered to be the highest in the case of the woman of higher *varṇa*, and lowest in the case of woman of lower *varṇa*. This 'rule' is the same as in the case of inter-*varṇa* marriages. Any kind of association between men of comparatively lower status and women of higher status is feared, and so is impermissible and is tantamount to exclusion from the household. This can be explained in the terms of attempted watertight compartmentalization of *varṇa* structure, preventing any occasion for social mobility and maintaining the hegemony of the higher *varṇa* over the lower, thus strengthening the *varṇa* hierarchy. Since women were considered to be the possession or property of men, men belonging to lower *varṇa* should not be allowed to attempt at having any connection with the women belonging to men of higher *varṇa*, also thus preventing any chances for upward social mobility for males. Yājñavalkya's comment makes it clear. According to him, affliction with the people below their caste is one of the main activities that tarnish the image of women.[558] This has to be seen in contrast with the view of Manu, previously quoted, where he prevents all sorts of adultery, not only with lower caste males, since adultery was believed to cause admixture of castes. Thus Yājñavalkya's statement makes it one step clearer. He further says that knowing a virgin of higher *varṇa* is as evil as violating the preceptor's bed.[559] Vasiṣṭha goes a step ahead and gives meticulous details of the way in which punishment is to be inflicted upon the adulterer and the adulteress, depending on how many grades higher is the *varṇa* of the female as compared to the male.[560] The male is to be tied up in different types of grasses depending on his *varṇa* and the *varṇa* of the female he approached, and thrown into fire; and the female was to be punished by shaving her head and having anointed her body with butter, she was to be placed on a donkey, whose colour varied according to the respective *varṇas*, and then caused to be conducted along the highroad. The punishment, as is obvious, is very harsh, and the degree of harshness is the same for all inter-*varṇa* adultery cases. But the use of different types of grass and colours of donkeys must have been resorted to in order to symbolically indicate the severity of the crime, and the degree of social indignation and disapproval might have rested upon this. Gautama's stand was also extreme in case of adultery with a man of lower caste. According to him, a woman of a superior caste, having been found guilty of illicit intercourse with a man of an inferior caste, the king of the country shall cause her to be torn alive by dogs at a public place, or the guilty man should de dealt with in the same manner.[561] Atri prescribes penances for knowing women of low castes, which also included women of lower origins as *cāṇḍāla*, *mlechchha* and *śvapākas*, if such cohabitation was done unknowingly;[562] however, if one knows them willingly, and procreates children, he is degraded to the same caste.[563] Samvarta is milder and lays down the performance of some penances, varying with the degree of sin.[564] Pārāśara only speaks of men committing adultery with *cāṇḍālī* or *śvapākī* women and prescribes only penances for expiation, thus exhibiting a milder attitude in this regard.[565] However, for women committing adultery with a *cāṇḍāla,* the penance was much harder.[566]

Adultery and Gender Identity

Adultery by Female

It is important to study the comparative degrees of punishment for and social stigma attached to adultery when committed by the male and the female, thus finding if gender played a role here too. Manu says that a *brāhmaṇa* should shun at sacrifices these lowest of the twice born, whose conduct is reprehensible and who are unworthy to sit in the company at a repast.[567] Among many others are mentioned, one in whose house resides the paramour of his wife, the son of an adulteress, he who eats the food given by the son of an adulteress, he who lasciviously dallies with a brother's widow. The prescription against one in whose house the paramour of his wife resides, may be indicative of such cases happening in the society. This has to be seen with reference to the term *jāra*, which occurs a number of times in the *Vedas*, and which meant the paramour of the wife. Traces of this practice might have remained till these times, and hence the prohibition. Again, adultery by a woman is so much discouraged that even her son is mentioned in this category. The fact that nothing is said about an adulterer cannot be overlooked. However, a man who has adulterous relations with a deceased brother's wife is included in this list. But it seems that it was because *niyoga* is disfavoured in this document.

In spite of Manu's prescription against adulterous women and sons born to them, two kinds of sons borne by wives of other men are recognized.[568] A *kuṇḍa* is born while the husband lives, and a *golaka* is born after his death. It is curious that the birth of such sons is not criticized being an outcome of adulterous relationships, rather in the next verse it is stated that those who are born of wives of other men, cause a loss to the giver (begetter), both in this life and after death. This is said perhaps because the offspring does not belong to him, and so he gains not when he is alive and neither when he dies, for the food sacred to the manes is not given to him by this son. This is significant as it indicates the importance of birth of son in the patriarchal set up. Again, silence marks the birth of girl child as a result of adulterous relationship.

A further attempt to discourage adultery is made by saying that she who cohabits with a man of higher caste forsaking her own husband who belongs to a lower one, will become contemptible in this world, and is called a remarried woman (*parapūrvā*).[569] However, in this case, cohabitation with a man of higher caste is discouraged and nothing is said regarding one of a lower caste, indicating that only *varṇa* consciousness was instrumental behind this statement. Adultery was considered a low task, but still lower was committing adultery with men of lower caste. Later he says that an exceedingly corrupt wife should be confined to one apartment, and compelled by her husband to perform the penance which is prescribed for males in cases of adultery.[570] Thus, in this case temporary expulsion from the household formed the punishment for the adulterous wife. It is to be noticed that the penance prescribed for male adulterers is prescribed for the female only when she becomes exceedingly corrupt. This may point towards milder treatment being accorded to the adulteress. This might have been rooted in the belief that a woman gets purified in menstruation even if she has made an illicit physical relation with another man.[571] Accordingly, he suggests that the woman should not be expelled from home, instead her rights should be denied, restrictions should be imposed on her dressing and cleaning, should be frequently reprimanded for the evil committed, allowed food only to the extent she can survive, and should be made to sleep on ground.[572] Later he reiterates this and lays down the provision for separate accommodation near their homes for the debauch woman as well as her protection.[573] However, if she has conceived, then it is considered good to renounce her.[574] Thus permanent expulsion from the household formed the punishment for adultery resulting in conception. Nārada also laid down that when a married woman commits adultery, her hair shall be shaved, she shall have to lie on a low couch, receive bad food and bad clothing, and the removal of the sweepings shall be assigned to her as her occupation.[575]

Again, chastity is encouraged by saying that a woman acquires fame in this world and enjoys the company of goddess Pārvatī after her death if she does not make any relation with any person either at a stage when her husband is living or even when he is dead.[576] He further stigmatizes adultery by laying down that among others, a husband's murderer and a corrupt woman are not worth getting the water of *aśauca* (*jalāñjali*) from the people.[577] These are also considered to be the main activities that tarnish the image of women in society.[578] Bṛhaspati assumes a stricter tone in matters pertaining to adultery. According to him, a woman should be paraded in the streets and plunged into water; or she shall be torn to pieces by dogs in a public place frequented by many persons; her nose, lips and ears having been cut off beforehand for entering a man's house and seducing him. Half of this punishment should be inflicted upon the man.[579] Vasiṣṭha also advocates stringent punishments like that of tying the adulterer with grass and throwing in fire; while the adulteress to be conducted along the highroad in a naked state, her head being shaven.[580] He also lays down that food given by a woman of bad character, the paramour of a married woman, husband of such a woman should not be taken.[581] Penances are prescribed by him for woman who has been mentally unfaithful to her husband, or has held improper conversation with another man.[582] If she has actually committed adultery, a stricter penance is prescribed for one year after which she is considered to have regained purity.[583] Adultery with the preceptor is considered a grave misdemeanour and such a wife is devoid of her role as the co-performer of religious sacrifices with her husband.[584] However, he lays down abandonment, and thus permanent expulsion from the household as the punishment for those wives who yield themselves to the husbands' pupil or preceptor, or a man of degraded caste, or one who attempts the life of her lord.[585] Again, the wife of a *brāhmana*, *kśatriya* or *vaiśya* may be purified by penance if no child is born out of adulterous relationship with a *śūdra*, not otherwise.[586] Finally, he says that faithful wives who are constantly pure and truthful reside after death in the same abodes with their husbands, those who are unfaithful are born as jackals.[587] As also discussed earlier, Gautama's stand was extreme in case of adultery with a man of lower caste. According to him, a woman of a superior caste, having been found guilty of illicit intercourse with a man of an inferior caste, the king of the country shall cause her to be torn alive by dogs at a public place, or the guilty man should de dealt with in the same manner.[588] Viṣṇu remains very precise on the issue of adultery and merely says that a woman who has committed adultery once, must perform that penance which has been prescribed for an adulterer.[589] Vyāsa is ambiguous about the treatment to be meted out to a faithless wife. At one place he says that the infidel wife, who gets herself impregnated by another man is fit to be abandoned by her lord and should be banished in a distant country after a good censuring.[590] Again, he says that a faithless wife may be again entrusted with the wifely duties by her lord after her next menstrual ablution after the act of infidelity, and treat her as before.[591] Following this he again includes a faithless and deceitful wife in the list of those who may be forsaken and abandoned.[592] Yama calls a woman who renounces her own husband for the company of another man as *vṛṣalī*, and lays down that no redemption for a person who has procreated a son upon her person.[593] Again, he says that on seeing the husband of a *vṛṣalī*, the departed manes go back disappointed.[594] Thus no punishment was explicitly prescribed for *vṛṣalī* herself by Yama. While the previous *dharmaśāstrakāras* believed that no means of purification was there for an adulteress once she has given birth to the child out of such a relationship, Atri lays down that she becomes pure after giving birth to the child.[595] Again, while earlier, an adulterous relationship of a *brāhmaṇa* woman with a *śūdra* male was considered unpardonable, Samvarta lays down the performance of the *cāndrāyaṇa* penance for its expiation.[596]

Adultery by Male

Adultery with the wife of one's preceptor is considered to be a *mahāpātaka* by Manu.[597] Corporal punishment is prescribed for those who do not perform a penance for such a sin.[598] Further, it is said that for such a sin, the mark of a female organ shall be impressed on the forehead with hot iron[599], and then the sinner shall be excluded from all fellowship at meals, sacrifices, instruction, matrimonial alliances and religious duties.[600] They must be cast off by all their relations, and shall receive neither salutation nor compassion.[601] On performance of penances, they must be given respite from being branded on the forehead.[602] Again, as discussed earlier, sexual intercourse with sisters by the same mother, with (unmarried) maidens, with females of the lowest castes, with the wives of a friend, or of a son, are declared to be equal to the violation of a guru's bed.[603]

Yājñavalkya gives a list of actions which may be considered as indicative of adultery and says that if a woman does the forbidden act, she should be made to pay a fine of hundred *paṇas*, while for the man the fine is double this amount.[604] As already mentioned, the degree of punishment was higher for adultery with woman of higher caste.[605] He tries to prevent adultery by saying that one who knows another's wife is born among stable objects[606] and a person who knows the wife of a teacher, receives the *yonīs* of a star, creeper and tree respectively.[607] To know the wife of one's friend, a virgin of higher *varṇa*, a sister, a *cāṇḍālī*, a homogeneous and daughter-in-law is described as evil as violating a preceptor's bed.[608] Later, for violation of preceptor's bed, he prescribes sleeping with the idol of woman on bed, both made of iron blazed to the extent that it look like embers, or cutting of his testicles, giving them in his palm and made to walk until death in the south-west direction.[609] Still later, a penance is also prescribed which involves recitation of the *puruṣa sūkta*, consisting of eighteen *ṛcās*.[610] Incest was considered extremely baneful by Yājñavalkya too, and he lays down a severe punishment for this. According to him, the genital of such a person should be cut and then he should be slaughtered for such a heinous crime. In case, consent was given on the part of the woman, she should be slaughtered too.[611] Similar indictment with a slight variation is laid down by other lawgivers.[612] Another possible punishment is embracing heated iron image of a woman having shaved all his hair and smearing his body with clarified butter.[613] The same expiation is prescribed if the offence was committed with the wife of the teacher, of a son, and of a pupil.[614] Gautama also made an attempt to prevent adultery by laying down that he who holds incest with his own father's or mother's sister, is successively reborn as a haunch back, dwarf, insane, diseased, deformed, indigent, short-lived, foolish, irascible, worthless, thievish, carrying out other men's behests, bald-headed, and miscreant person in low and vulgar families. Hence one should atone for one's sin.[615] However, knowing another's wife is considered as a minor sin by Yājñavalkya.[616] For having intercourse with a female who is considered venerable in the family, with a female friend, with the female friend of a Guru, with an *apapātrā* female, or with an outcast, performance of *krichchhra* penance is prescribed during three months by Vasiṣṭha.[617] However, again, Vasiṣṭha is strict when it comes to inter-*varṇa* adultery, where the woman is of a higher caste than the man. The punishment in such cases was tying the man with grass and throwing him in fire.[618]

Nārada and Bṛhaspati also give a list of actions to be treated adulterous in varying degrees[619] and accordingly prescribes fines for such acts. However, when a woman seduces a man coming to his house, severe punishment is prescribed for her which includes cutting of her nose, lips and ears, and then after being paraded in the streets and plunged into water, torn to pieces by dogs in a place frequented by visitors. Only half of this punishment is prescribed for the man.[620] Nārada and Viṣṇu also lays down death as the penalty for committing adultery with a woman of one of the lowest castes, while second amercement for one of a lower caste, and highest for one of one's own caste.[621] Incest was considered to be the same as sexual connection with the wife of one's preceptor, however, according to him such minor offenders become pure by a horse sacrifice and visiting *tīrthas*.[622] Atri lays down performance of *paraka* penance for knowing women of lower or lowest castes unknowingly, but for knowing them knowingly and having procreated children, one was considered to be degraded to the same caste as hers.[623] For lying on the bed of a step-mother, Samvarta prescribed lying down on an iron bed, or performance of three to four *cāndrāyaṇas*.[624] Penance prescribed for knowing *cāṇḍāla* woman is *Prājāpatya* and three *krichchhras*; for knowing *pukkasa* woman, an actress, a dancing girl, a washer woman, cobbler woman, or one who makes her living by bamboo-made articles, again *cāndrāyaṇa*; for knowing *kśatriya* or *vaiśya* woman, *sāntāpanam*; and so on.[625] No redemption is there for knowing one's own mother, daughter, or sister or even the wife of a paternal uncle, or a brother's wife.[626] Śātātapa gives a long list of different women with whom adultery could be committed, and then prescribes the atonement for such sins, which include giving away of gifts to *brāhmaṇa* with the recitation of mantras and making prayers to different gods.[627] It is obvious that he frightens the adulterer of dire consequences of adultery on the one hand, and then makes way for *brāhmaṇa's* earning by way of various ritual centered ways of making gifts to him. Here, the fear for mixture of castes, as noticed in the other texts, seems to be resolved, only that the general condemnation of adultery is used for filling the bags of the *brāhmaṇas* with gold. The surprising addition of a female ascetic and one's wife who is initiated is unique to Śātātapa in this list.[628] More surprising is his inclusion of a dead wife in this list.[629] Unique to Nārada is the indictment that a man is not punishable as an adulterer for having intercourse with the wife of one who has left his wife without her fault, or of one impotent or consumptive, if the woman herself consents to it.[630]

Like the others, Uśanā also considers violation of a preceptor's bed as one of the great sins.[631] For knowing one's step mother, he prescribes embracing a female form made of black iron and heated, or cutting off of his genitals and running with them in hands till he dies.[632] Practice of severe vows is prescribed as an alternative.[633] For willingly knowing one's daughter, sister or daughter-in-law, a *brāhmaṇa* is prescribed to enter into burning fire.[634] For other incestuous relationships, penances are prescribed.[635]

The following observations may be made on the basis of the survey of the texts.

There must have been a period characterized by promiscuity. This is testified by the verses regarding the *strīsvabhāva.* The established order of the time must have been matriarchal organization. Later, with the establishment of patriarchy, women's sexuality needed to be controlled in order to preserve the purity of line of the offspring, which was central to the sustenance of patriarchy. Hence there was a need to prevent adultery in the society. Scholars like Lubbock and McLennan were of the view that in the early stages of human race and in a promiscuous society with no established institution of marriage, there was no way of identifying the paternity of the child, only motherhood was a fact and descent was therefore, reckoned through the mother.[636] With the creation of patriarchy reckoning came into being. Wife's sexual transgression in patriarchal societies could have meant falsification of descent, and this was precisely the reason for the eagerness to keep her under the guard of males. A detailed discussion on this is undertaken elsewhere.

Again, it has to be noted that severe punishments as death, and thus forced permanent exclusion from the household, was inflicted upon both the male and the female in cases of incest and adultery between a woman of higher and man of lower caste or adultery with the wife of one's *guru*, or in case of female, adultery with husband's guru or pupil. Penances have been prescribed by some of the *dharmaśāstrakāras* for preventing such exclusion. However, for women, adulterous relationship even with a man of higher caste caused temporary expulsion from household, mild punishment is inflicted upon men conducting adultery with women of lower castes. Again, in case of women having conceived or procreated out of adulterous relationship too, permanent abandonment, i.e., exclusion from the household was the punishment. However, for men, nothing is said in case a child is born out of adultery.

Also, since a man was permitted to marry any number of wives, chances of adultery in his case would have been less. He could have taken any woman as a wife, provided she belonged to a higher *varṇa* and was unmarried. So, in the case of the male only cases where the woman was either married, or of a higher *varṇa,* could be considered as adultery. This was not so in the case of a woman. There was yet another aspect of the control over female sexuality. Since patrilocal/patriarchal society was not only about domination of men over all women but also domination of some men over others, one way in which this domination was ensured was by denying access to women or withholding women from junior men by their superiors.[637] This practice would have been threatened by women's free sexual choice. In such societies male competition for resources and labour came to be expressed in control over female sexuality and reproduction.[638]

Another significant observation in this regard is that while men were expected to exhibit self-control as a measure to guard against adultery, females were to be guarded by he male members, and even at times, *other female members* of the household. This is evident from a number of verses which emphasize upon the need to keep women guarded. To quote Shalini Shah in this regard: "What was affirmed through this conception of 'mastery' (over one's self) as ensuring freedom was the virile character of this mastery. Just as in the household it was man, who ruled, it was only right that he alone should exercise self-restraint. Self-mastery was a way of being a man with respect to oneself. This does not mean that women were not expected to be moderate. But moderation in this case was imposed on them by their condition of dependence, in relation to their families, their husbands. *For what was symbolized in woman's chastity was not her own self control as in the male celibacy but the control of her kinsmen over her behaviour* (emphasis added)."[639]

Rape

Manu considers defiling a woman as one of the minor offences causing only a loss of the caste.[640] However, Yājñavalkya lays down death as the penalty when a woman of higher caste is ravished against her will.[641] Again, cutting of finger is the only penalty for having ravished a female of lower caste. Thus, forced exclusion from the household is the penalty for the rapist only when the crime is committed with a woman of higher caste. It is surprising that a concern for the sustenance of the perceived social order was a matter of graver concern for the *dharmaśāstrakāras* than the misery and pain experienced by the victim, which will be the same irrespective of the *varṇa* to which a woman may belong. Thus, in the view of Yājñavalkya, it was basically a violation of the *varṇa* norms that caused the exclusion from the household.

However, Bṛhaspati lays down the confiscation of the entire wealth of the violator of an unwilling woman, cutting of his penis and scrotum and being paraded on an ass; as the punishment.[642] In the case of enjoyment of a woman by fraud, the punishment remains the same except for the cutting of penis and scrotum, instead of which he prescribes branding with the mark of a female part and banishment from the town.[643] Cutting of the penis and scrotum must have resulted in the death of the violator, hence it may be inferred that death was the punishment in the previous case. Thus, permanent exclusion from the household, irrespective of the *varṇa* of violator or the victim, was the punishment for the rapist in the opinion of Bṛhaspati. However, while Manu and Yājñavalkya remained silent regarding the treatment to be meted out to the victimized female, Bṛhaspati lays down punishment for her too.

According to him, when a woman has been enjoyed against her will, she shall be kept in the house well guarded, smeared with ashes, lying on a low couch, and receiving a bare maintenance only.[644] This might have well been equivalent to exclusion from the household. However, this might have been temporary as performance of penances is prescribed as atonement for the sin in case she has been enjoyed by one of equal caste. Again, if she had been enjoyed by a man of inferior caste, abandonment and death is the penalty prescribed for her.[645] Thus again the influence of *varṇa* identity comes into play. Pārāśara says nothing about the treatment to be meted out to the rapist; instead only prescribes penances for the victim to regain purity.[646] Irrespective of the fact that the woman held no responsibility for the happening, which must have rather left her torn and miserable, she was to be punished for it, and the punishment was stringent in case of violation of the *varṇa* norm.

Atri's tone gets milder on the issue and he says that if a woman is known deceitfully, forcibly or stealthily despite her complete unwillingness, she should remain unaffected by any sin, and as such, should not be renounced; for she has not done so willingly. Her husband may hold congress with her at the time of the menses, for a woman becomes pure at the flowering time.[647] Again, he prescribes penances for the women violated by the *mlechchhas*, or perpetrators of crimes, or known by being forcibly taken away.[648] Thus while Atri also lays down performance of penances for the victim, he is milder in that he does not prescribe penalty or punishment for the women.

Husband's Death: Widowhood, *Niyoga* and *Sati*

Stripped of her individuality, reduced to a mere glorified appendage of her husband, the *pativratā* lost their very *raison d'etre* if their god (husband) died. Unfortunately for the *pativratās* their gods were mortal and to make their relationship immortal the onus was on woman to sacrifice her life and thereby gain immortality for her husband and herself.[649] Widowhood is the most miserable state of a woman in patriarchy. A woman's identity was given recognition, approval and significance only as a wife. Her role as the wife was considered to be the one to lend importance to her life. In roles other than this, her identity and existence was reduced to insignificance. Among her wifely duties, serving the husband and procreation were the most important. Death of the husband ended the possibility as well as requirement of the performance of both of these functions. The very objective of a woman's existence was considered to have been lost. A widow is, thus, of 'no use' to such a society, rather her existence and presence was a kind of disturbance. The death of the husband, therefore, was considered to be an occasion for exclusion of the woman from the household life, or even at times, life at all in the patriarchal set up.

Chakravarti presents a thoughtful analysis of the condition of a widow in her recent work.[650] In her words, "The problem posed by Brahmanical patriarchy therefore is: since the wife has no social existence outside of her husband's house, then, as a widow, who or what is she? The texts and rituals attempt to work the problem out. The problem itself is simply that although the widow is socially dead, she remains an element in society; the question then is how to incorporate her. One way could be to constitute a separate community of widows, a non-sexual community, such as that of female ascetics. Another could be to retain her in society but place her on its margins and then institutionalize her marginality. This is what Brahmanical patriarchy did with the widow. The widow's institutionalized marginality, a liminal state between being physically alive and being socially dead, was the ultimate cultural outcome of the deprivation of her sexuality as well as of her personhood. The widow's marginal state meant that she was, in a manner of speaking, functionally incorporated into the household while being considered an outsider."[651] Thus, a specific code of conduct for the widow was laid down by the *dharmaśāstrakāras.* Manu lays down that she should at her pleasure emaciate the body by living on pure flowers, fruits and roots, but never mention the name of other man after her husband has died.[652] She is recommended to live an austere life with patience and strive to fulfil that most excellent duty which is recommended for wives who have one husband only. Bṛhaspati also says that she shall recite the *Dhūmavasanika* prayer in the evening, bathe frequently, and pay no regard to dwelling, food, or clothing after her husband's death.[653] It is obvious that she was permitted a petty and meagre existence only once the husband was dead. Pārāśara says that a widow who observes celibacy all through her life after the death of her husband, attains to heaven after death just like the *brahmacārīs.*[654] According to Vyṛsa, the widow of a *brāhmaṇa* should either immolate herself in fire with the corpse of her husband or observe a vow of lifelong continence from that date, shaving the hair of her head, and foregoing all articles of luxury.[655] In line with the above indictments,

Vasiṣṭha also lays down that the widow of a deceased person shall sleep on the ground during six months, practicing religious vows and abstaining from pungent condiments and salt,[656] and after the completion of six months, she shall bathe, and offer a funeral oblation to her husband. Then her father or brother shall assemble the gurus who had taught or sacrificed for the deceased and his relatives, and shall appoint her to raise an issue to her deceased husband.[657] *Niyoga* or levirate was laid down as one of the duties of the widow by most of the *dharmaśāstrakāras*. Vasiṣṭha further lays down conditions when the widow was considered unfit for such an appointment, which included one who is mad, ill conducted, diseased or aged.[658] An appointment shall also not be made if the male entitled to approach the widow is sickly.[659] A code of conduct for the performance of *niyoga* is laid down which includes visiting the widow in a *muhurta* (hour) sacred to Prajāpati, and behaving like a husband without amorously dallying with or abusing or ill treating her.[660] A son born out of such a union belongs to both the begetter and the diseased husband of the widow.[661] No appointment shall be made through a desire to obtain the estate, or out of covetousness.[662] Gautama laid down *niyoga* as the duty of the widow, and says that under no circumstance, she should let her menstrual period pass unfruitful.[663] He says that controlled in her speech, mind and senses, during her menstrual period, she should evince her desire to be the mother of a male child by her husband's younger brother. In the absence of such and uterine brother of her deceased husband, she should get herself impregnated, for giving birth to a male child, by a *sapiṇḍa* or a cognate relation, standing in the same category even through ties of spiritual clanship (*Ṛṣis*), or bearing her the same relationship through the female line. Although he accepts that the birth of a male child in the womb of a widow by any one other than her husband's younger brother (or cousin), is rejected by certain authorities, further, he says that a widow shall not get herself impregnated more than twice by her dead husband's brother. In the absence of any express stipulation, sons, begotten on her person, shall belong to their progenitor.[664] Yājñavalkya also says that a woman left barren by her husband can conceive through her brother-in-law or sibling after obtaining due permission from the preceptor. He should enjoy coition with her during menstruation cycle (*ṛtukāla*) and prior to coition, he should put ghee on his body. Such coition should be made until insemination. On excessive or additional coition by him, his character will be blamed. The son so obtained will be called *kśetraja* of his father.[665] Later, he lays down that a person indulged in coition with his brother's wife without *niyoga* should observe *cāndrāyaṇa* fast for regrettal and purity.[666] Nārada also lays down such a performance of *niyoga* upon the death of a woman's husband.[667]

Manu has disfavoured the practice of *niyoga.* He includes the son of a widow and one who lasciviously dallies with the brother's widow in the list of those who should be carefully avoided,[668] and should be shunned at sacrifices by the *brāhmaṇa.*[669] Such a man, even though she is appointed to bear a child by him in accordance with the sacred law, must be known to be a *didhiśupati.*[670] Later, to answer the question what will happen to the woman after death if she does not have a son, the analogy is drawn from the case of chaste *brāhmaṇas*, who reach heaven even though they may have no son.[671] The women who violate their duty towards their husband, out of a desire for an offspring, are threatened that they lose their place in this world and also the place with her husband in the heaven.[672] In the following verse an attempt is made to justify this by saying that offspring begotten by other man is not considered lawful and nor does such an offspring belong to the begetter. Though Manu is against it, he recognizes the practice of *niyoga.* He says that a brother-in-law or some other *sapiṇḍa* of the husband is appointed to cohabit in a prescribed manner with the widow for begetting a son.[673] Once the purpose has been attained, the two shall behave with each other like a father and a daughter-in-law. If they deviate from the rule and act with carnal desire, they will become outcastes.[674] Later the practice of *niyoga* is condemned for having caused the confusion of castes.[675] If the future husband of a maiden dies after betrothal, then her brother-in-law shall marry her according to the rule mentioned.[676] However, it is further said that he should approach her only till an issue be had.[677] Bṛhaspati also cites the opinion of Manu and says that *niyoga* has been declared by Manu, and again prohibited by the same; on account of the successive deterioration of the four ages of the world. So it must not be practised by mortals according to law.[678]

Thus it is clear that the stand of the lawgivers on the practice of levirate union was ambiguous at best. While some of them favoured it, others rejected or at least denounced the idea. A careful analysis of *niyoga* is important in determining the position of the widow. Some of the historians have favoured *niyoga* as one of the ameliorative measures for the plight of the widow in ancient Indian society. One of these is Altekar, who while accepting that the 'leaders of Hindu society took a step in the right direction in stamping out the custom of *Niyoga*, as it was a relic of barbarism and was quite incongruous and incompatible with higher ideas and ideals of marriage, that were held before society'[679]; opines that, "*Niyoga* served a useful purpose in its own days. Men are disinclined to marry widows, though they expect virgins to marry widowers. The custom of *niyoga* solved the widow's difficulty to some extent by permitting the brother-in-law to raise issues on his sister-in-law under certain circumstances. *Niyoga* served as a halfway house between a formal remarriage and an absolute celibacy, especially in earlier days when three sons were allowed to be raised under it .... It also helped in improving the economic condition of the widow. When she had no son, she could get no share in the family property. When she got a son by *niyoga*, she could get a share, *if not as an heiress, at least as the guardian of her minor son* (emphasis added)."[680] Again, Altekar seems to believe that marriage is the only resort for the women, and that small concessions can do good for their lot.

However, it has to be borne in mind at the first place that it was not the welfare of the widow but the welfare of the deceased husband of the widow, who died sonless; that was the primary concern of the lawgivers while declaring *niyoga* as the duty of the widow. The procreation of a son was considered so important that even if one died, he needed to get a son by way of his surviving wife. The begetting of son in this way might have lent a support to the otherwise shattered and miserable widow in a patriarchal set up. However, surprising is the fact that deep silence marks the birth of daughter by levirate. Further, *niyoga* was not a matter of choice for the widow. She might have been further subjected to misery on account of males taking advantage of the practice. *Niyoga* did not actually lead to the inclusion of women into the household.

Thus *niyoga* was the temporary deputation of a husband's conjugal rights in his brother or kinsmen or to a man considered equal or superior to him. R.S. Sharma sees levirate as a remnant of matrilineal practices.[681] The purpose of *niyoga* was to beget sons. The practice only underlines the procreative role of women to the exclusion of any other and in this sense, this practice represents degradation of women's position. Woman was the property of the family for producing progeny. After the death of the husband, the rights in the reproductive potential of the woman were transferred to the husband's agnatic heirs. Thus *niyoga* is an expression of ownership of the woman by the husband and his family. As women were treated as an instrument for producing heir for men in their lives, their own desire was not of much consequence. *Niyoga* under such circumstances was a task not a pleasure, the woman and the man she had intercourse with had to perform it without least bit of desire or lust. It is evident then that women were treated as property.

However, there is one more question. Why was *niyoga* discouraged by some of the *dharmaśāstrakāras*? This might be because it might have given rise to several controversies and conflicts of self-interest among the agnatic heirs of the deceased husband. In the words of Kumkum Roy, "*Niyoga* certainly did not imply, theoretically at least, any control by the woman over her own procreative powers or progeny. However, it was evidently perceived as potentially threatening or possibly disruptive as far as the unity of the patrilineage was concerned. The problem of regulating sexual contact between the widow and her brother-in-law, for instance, was frequently viewed as being as serious as the problem of the absence of male progeny. The relationship was perceived as problematic as the woman would have been superior to the man in status if not in age, deriving her position from her husband's seniority. The man, in turn, could be seen as usurping his elder brother's position. As such, it posed an implicit challenge to the notion of hierarchy between genders on the one hand and between senior and junior kinsmen on the other."[682] Also, it might have resulted in a sexual exploitation of the woman by them. This was also against the norms of patriarchy where the younger male members of the family are also subordinated to the male patriarch. This superiority might have been undermined by the younger brother's getting the right to cohabit with the wife of the deceased brother. Again, a widow with children might have found their upbringing an uphill task.

Remarriage of a widow was considered to be baneful. Among the people to be carefully avoided are the son and husband of a remarried woman.[683] Then it is said that a *brāhmaṇa* should shun at sacrifices these lowest of the twice born, whose conduct is reprehensible and who are unworthy to sit in the company at a repast.[684] This is the first reference to remarriage of a woman in the document. Later, while mentioning the duties of a widow, the remarriage of a widow is rejected.[685] It is also said that a second husband is nowhere prescribed for virtuous women. By violating her duty towards her husband, a wife is disgraced in this world, after death she enters the womb of a jackal, and is tormented by diseases, which is the punishment for her sin.[686] A virtuous wife is defined as one who, controlling her thoughts, words and deeds, never slights her lord and thus resides with her husband in heaven.[687] The reward for such a wife is that she gains the highest renown in this life and a place near her husband in the next world.[688] However, he tries to make a concession by laying down that if the future husband of a maiden dies after betrothal, then her brother-in-law shall marry her according to the rule mentioned.[689] But he might have become ambiguous and so further says that he should approach her only till an issue be had.[690] Uśanā also mentions those who marry widows, son of a remarried woman among the list of those who are disqualified to be present at a *śrāddha* ceremony.[691] However, an exception is presented by Nārada when he mentions the death of the husband as one of the conditions in which a woman is justified in taking another husband.[692] Pārāśara also mentions death of the husband after betrothal, but before marriage as one of the five conditions when a woman shall be remarried.[693]

While forbidding the remarriage of a widow, Manu permits a man to remarry after having burnt the wife of equal caste.[694] Yājñavalkya also says that having burnt a wife of good conduct with *agnihotra*, a husband should, duly and without delay, marry again and bring fire.[695]

It is obvious that the death of a husband lead to an exclusion of the wife from the household life, while the husband was required to remarry at the earliest for maintaining the fire; i.e.; for maintaining the due performance of the functions of the household. The misery that the life of a widow must have been fraught with, might have led some of them to die with their husbands. Even if the practice of *sati* did not find its origins in the *dharmaśāstras*, it cannot be denied that the misery to which the widow was to be subjected, must have worked towards an increase in the instances of *sati*. There are sporadic references to this practice in some of the texts. Viṣṇu says that it is the duty of the wife to preserve her chastity after her husband's death or to ascend the pyre after him.[696] According to Vyāsa, the widow of a *brāhmaṇa* should either immolate herself in fire with the corpse of her deceased husband or observe a vow of lifelong continence from that date, shaving the hair of her head, and foregoing all articles of luxury.[697]

Bṛhaspati alludes to this practice when he says that a wife is considered half of the body of her husband, equally sharing the result of his good or wicked deeds and that whether she ascends the pyre after him, or chooses to survive him leading a virtuous life, she promotes the welfare of her husband.[698] According to Atri, the woman, who falls down from the funeral pyre of her husband becomes purified by a *Prājāpatya* and feeding ten *brāhmaṇas.*[699] Pārāśara eulogizes the practice by saying that the wife who immolates herself upon the death of her husband rescues her husband from hell just as a snake charmer forcibly takes out a snake from a hole, and thereafter resides with him in heaven.[700] Dakśa also says the same.[701] Again, he says that a woman who ascends the funeral pyre after her husband's demise, becomes of good conduct and lives gloriously in the celestial region.[702] Uśanā also supports *sati* by laying down that the anniversary day of the death of the lady, devoted to her husband, who ascends the same funeral pyre with him should be celebrated by offering two separate funeral balls (*piṇḍas*).[703]

Varying explanations have been given regarding the origin of the practice of *sati.* D.D. Kosambi explaining the *sati* system came up with the argument that widow burning could only have developed from suppression of matriarchal tradition, presumable it was a warning or precaution against its surreptitious revival.[704] He believes that in the early period the word 'husband' denoted some chieftain or sacred king who gained his title to sovereignty primarily by formal marriage to some local high priestess or queen. If, then the husband died, there was ample grounds for suspicion that it was the wife's doing, a reversion to the old ritual. The *sati* custom would not only discourage this but act like a curious inversion of the older sacrifice [of husband] and count further as provision for the departed leader in the next world.[705]

However, there is nothing that can deny that *sati* system has to be directly linked to the socio-economic realities of widow's life under patriarchy. It was also a natural concomitant of her psychological conditioning and indoctrination in the ideology of the *pativratā* in such a society which egged her on to the path of self-destruction. A historian who has worked on *sati* system during the late first millennium AD has argued that there seems to be some kind of co-relation between decline of *niyoga* and the rise of *sati.*[706]

Whatever be the reasons behind the origin of the practice of *sati*, it is clear that the prescriptive texts clearly outline only two models of widowhood: that of the dying sati who mounts the pyre, rejects widowhood and proves herself to be the best follower of '*strīdharma*', and that of the living sati who becomes an ascetic within the home, remaining a celibate, steadfastly devoted to her husband till she dies.

There is no third model, certainly not of the true renunciate, at least in the Brāhmanical prescriptive texts.[707]

Desertion

Desertion by the husband was another instance of exclusion from the household. However, desertion or abandonment of the wife was in general disfavoured by the *dharmaśāstrakāras*. According to Vasiṣṭha, a wife who is defiled by sinful deeds must first be reproved and if she does not amend, be cast off. He who forsakes her in any other way, himself becomes an outcaste.[708] Sons and pupils are also included in the same category. Viṣṇu also says that a husband who forsakes a blameless wife shall be punished as thief.[709] Pārāśara laid down that a deserted or widowed wife shall be left in another region, if she conceives adulterously.[710] Again, he says that if a *brāhmaṇa* woman goes away with another man, she shall be considered to have died, and never again allowed to come back to the home.[711] Further, he lays down that if a woman returns back after leaving her husband, without having gone to another man, and the time lapsed is less than ten days, then she can be accepted back after performance of penances. However, if she has spent more than ten days, or had connection with any other man, then she shall be abandoned.[712] However, he mentions husband's migrating to a far-off region as one of the five conditions when the betrothed is permitted to be remarried.[713] According to Vyāsa, a husband by unjustly deserting his own innocent wife, becomes a spiritual out-caste.[714] Dakśa also lays down that he, who renounces his youthful wife who is free from any fault and is not degraded, will attain to womanhood after death and become barren.[715] It is obvious from this verse that the position of a woman was worse as compared to the male, and that is why attaining to womanhood is frightening for a man; more so if one remains barren. The verse defines the position of women in the then society. Uśanā includes one who renounces his wife in the list of people to be avoided.[716] However, Nārada says that one who wastes the entire property of her husband under the pretence that it is her own *strīdhana*, or who procures abortion, or who makes an attempt on her husband's life, shall be banished from the town by her husband.[717] Again, one who always shows malice to him, or who makes unkind speeches, or eats before her husband, he shall quickly expel from his house.[718]

Again, in case of the husband having emigrated and not returned till a long time, the wife should wait for five years, after which she may go to seek her husband.[719] Vasiṣṭha lays down that if she does not want to leave the home for some reasons, then she should act as if the husband were dead, and after waiting for one to five years depending on the *varṇa* and where she is issueless or not, should go for *niyoga*.[720] Pārāśara mentions husband's migrating to far-off region as one of the five conditions when the betrothed is permitted to be remarried.[721] It is obvious that a life as that of widow is prescribed for a deserted wife, which is close to expulsion from the household.

However, Nārada says that when a bridegroom goes abroad after having espoused a maiden, let the maiden wait till her menses have passed three times, and then choose another bridegroom.[722] Again, he denounces a man who leaves his wife who is obedient, soft-spoken, skilful, virtuous, and the mother of male issue, and says that the king shall make him mindful of his duty by inflicting severe punishment on him.[723] Then he laid down the period of waiting to be eight, six and four years respectively for *brāhmaṇa, kśatriya* and *vaiśya* woman; and half of the respective periods mentioned above in case she is childless. After the lapse of the stipulated time, she was permitted to remarry, without incurring any guilt of offence. No specific period is laid down for a *śūdra* woman.[724]

Opting-out of the Household

Life within the household offered little or no scope for choices for women. The urge to find choices and freedom, or self expression, must have far superseded the bounds of norms, and become instrumental in providing requisite move to the women to 'choose' to 'opt-out of the household'. Such cases, though few, were not completely non-existent, is evident from some of the verses found in the texts. One such instance was divorcing or abandoning the husband. In this case, it was not complete opting-out of the household life, as the woman may at times choose to remarry. However, the other case, i.e., adoption of nunhood or heretical life, was marked by a complete and permanent opting-out of the household life. It is important from the point of view of our study to find out the attitude of *dharmaśāstrakāras* towards such women.

Divorce/Abandonment of the Husband

Manu says that she who cohabits with a man of higher caste forsaking her own husband who belongs to a lower one, will become contemptible in this world, and is called a remarried woman (*parapūrvā*).[725] By violating her duty towards her husband, a wife is disgraced in this world, after death she enters the womb of a jackal, and is tormented by diseases, which is the punishment for her sin.[726] A virtuous wife is defined as one who, controlling her thoughts, words and deeds, never slights her lord and thus resides with her husband in heaven.[727] The reward for such a wife is that she gains the highest renown in this life and a place near her husband in the next world.[728] These verses make it clear that there were women who left their husbands, thus opting out of their marriages and chose other men, thus re-entering married life. Yājñavalkya says that a woman who divorces her husband for another person voluntarily is called *svairiṇī*.[729] Nārada repeats this.[730] Vasiṣṭha defines a remarried woman as one who leaving the husband of her youth, and having lived with others, re-enters his family; and one who leaving an impotent, outcast or mad husband, or after the death of her husband takes another lord.[731] Nārada also speaks of a woman who, after having left the husband of her youth and betaken herself to another man, returns into the house of her husband, while giving the details of different types of *punarbhū*.[732] The verses are significant as they point towards cases of abandonment of husband by the woman, exhibiting an element of choice; and more so; as the previous one points towards 're-entry' of a woman to the husband of her young age after having lived with others. This might not have been sanctioned, but this verse makes it clear that there might have been sporadic instances where women were accepted by their previous husbands providing them a re-entry to the household if they chose to do so. One may infer that women were not completely 'choiceless', though the *dharmaśāstrakāras* sought to render them in that state. This is further clear from the indictment of Vyāsa which says that a chaste wife should not renounce her lord, even if he be guilty of a *Mahāpātaka*m, praying that his sin might be extinguished in no distant time.[733] Dakśa also says that a woman, who forsakes her poor or diseased husband, is repeatedly born either as a bitch, a vulture, or a shark.[734] Nārada also denounces divorce by laying down that when husband and wife leave one another, from mutual dislike, it is a sin, except when a woman, who is kept under supervision, commits adultery.[735] Pārāśara says that if a *brāhmaṇa* woman goes away with another man, she shall be considered to have died, and never again allowed to come back to the home.[736] However, both Nārada and Pārāśara have mentioned five cases of legal necessity in which a woman may be justified in taking another husband, i.e., when her husband is lost or dead, when he has become a religious ascetic, when he is impotent, and when he has been expelled from caste.[737] The permission to remarry may be taken to imply a permission to divorce a husband in the five cases enumerated above.

Adoption of Nunhood/Heretical Life

Women who chose to join the heretical sects, and thus, opt out of the social organization envisaged by the lawgivers, received little attention of the authors of these texts. Their silence over this issue might have been a conscious choice too. For wherever this silence is broken; directly or indirectly such women have been disapproved of. However, it is to be borne in mind that the lawgivers were non-appreciative of men joining heretical orders too, for easily comprehensible reasons. Manu says that libations of water shall not be offered to those women who have joined a heretical sect.[738] To further digress women from any such manoeuvres, he lays down that no sacrifice, no vow, no fast must be performed by women apart from their husbands; if a wife obeys her husband, she will be exalted in heaven for that reason alone.[739] Viṣṇu also says that the women should not recite incantations with roots, nor is any sacrifice, no penance, and no fasting is allowed to women apart from their husbands; and that to pay obedience to her lord is the only means for a woman to obtain bliss in heaven.[740] Similar indictments are laid down by other lawgivers.[741]

To summarize, the following inferences can be drawn from the entire discussion:

The structure of the family kept on changing with time, and the matriarchal society in the initial phase of civilization gradually gave way to a patriarchal social organization. Though often taken to be a protective umbrella for individuals, family is often a ground of conflict and contending claims by the members. Thus, power is as much in play in determining relationships and place of different members within the hierarchy, as in any other institution. With the emergence of patriarchy, the power equation became skewed towards the interests of the male, according him a position of dominance within the family as well as the society as a whole. Within the scope of the ideology expressed in the *dharmaśāstra* texts, the *gṛha* or the household is conceived to be the upholder of all the rest of the orders directed towards attainment of differing goals of life. The head of the household, the male patriarch, *gṛhapati*, held dominance over not only the female members of the family, but also the other males, who remained junior to him. Quite in consonance with the importance ascribed to the *gṛha,* the points of entry to and exit from the household were attributed a high degree of significance. The chapter has devoted space to study the position of the female vis-à-vis the males at the crucial points of entry to and exit from the household, as also while remaining a part of the household, as well as on instances when she is made to face exclusion from the household. A significant point is that while the male remains the member of a household throughout the life, the female has to make exit from one set-up and become the part of an alien set-up within the initial span of her life. The fact of patrilocality has a defining influence in shaping women's destiny, as the discussion amply demonstrates. Accordingly, the birth of a daughter was not a welcome and there were no recitation of mantras and other ritual performances for the girl child. This was so because only the son would remain a part of the family to be able to perform for the emancipation of the ancestors. Thus the daughter's entry to and inclusion in the family of her birth was partial till the point of her exit. In such a social arrangement, marriage becomes the turning point in the life of a woman. Taking an exit from the natal family, she enters another household, unbound to her by natural ties of affection and identification. The *dharmaśāstrakāras* do not impart any agency to women at this critical juncture of their lives and define their identity as mere possession of the father and the natal family, rights over whom are to be transferred to the groom's family at the father's will. This transfer of authority over the woman may be in the form of a gift, or a transaction or exchange between the father and the groom. Among the other forms of marriage were those where the girl was subjected to fraud or force. Only the *Gāndharva* form imparts some choice to the woman, but this was approved for the *kśatriyas* only. The qualifications for a girl to be chosen as the bride were far more elaborate than the boy, and virginity was ascribed a high importance, in contrast to the male, who was permitted polygamy. In order to ensure virginity as well as the subjection of the female to the male, the age of marriage for the girls was very low, in fact, they had to be married off before the onset of puberty. Also, the difference in the age of the groom and the bride was large. Marrying the girl even before puberty might also be to ensure the fullest use of her reproductive years, procreation being considered as the sole objective of marriage. Procreation was important for the perpetuation of the family line, and more so because it was believed that only a son could save the man from sinking into hell after death. Perhaps the fear of death, and more so, the life after death, dominated the minds of the lawgivers. Along with the perpetuation of the male line, and ensuring the attainment of heaven after death, the other dominant concern of the authors of the *dharmaśāstras* was the preservation of the *varṇa* order. That *varṇa* identity was inextricably linked with the issue of gender, becomes obvious from the promotion of *varṇa* endogamy, and discouragement of *varṇa* exogamy, particularly prohibiting the marriages 'against the grain' or hypogamy (*pratiloma*).

In accordance with the thinking of the *dharmaśāstrakāras*, who considered women merely as means of reproduction, no education was considered to be necessary for them. Marriage was the only ceremony in a woman's life, which was performed with due recitation of mantras and was thus, ritually sanctified. The girls were not initiated, and ideologically lacked identity in the *varṇa* order before marriage, marriage ceremony itself considered to be the initiation for women. The sole important identification of women in the order perceived by the *dharmaśāstrakāras* was wifehood. An elaborate list of the duties of and code of conduct for the wife is prescribed. While criticizing the critiques of *dharmaśāstras*, Kapoor has referred to the multiple identities imparted to women in the form of multiple bio-social roles.[742] Though this may be true in the contemporary society, in the society envisaged by the *dharmaśāstrakāras*, no duties are laid down for women as a mother or sister or daughter, or aunt. As a mother she is to be revered, and while child bearing is given extreme importance, no mention could be found of a woman's duties towards her children. Rearing up of the child or nurturing the child, which is a matter of great significance, lacked the attention or concern of the authors of *dharma* texts. In fact, such a silence stands in sharp contrast in a society where in order to qualify as a wife, a woman necessarily had to be fertile.

The role envisaged for the woman was mainly the service role. She had to serve the husband unconditionally, and also his agnatic line by procreating progeny. The role of the homemaker envisaged for the women, left no scope for the need for any education for women, rather their deprivation from self-awareness became imperative. The ideology of the *pativratā* was devised as a means to ensure an unquestioning and unconditional service, that brook no dissatisfaction or doubt. Much in contrast, no set of duties was prescribed for the husband, except for exercising control over the wife's sexuality and procreating progeny on her person during her season. Though this is not to say that unbridled sexuality was permitted to the male, in his case it was self-control which was expected to be exercised, and vent was given to the male yearning by permitting polygamy, even though discouraging it. It is explicitly acknowledged that women needed to be controlled in order to maintain the purity of offspring and thus the lineage. Procreation was an important duty of the man, not as a husband actually, but as the upholder of the social order. Further, the definition of procreation, as enunciated by the *dharmaśāstras* ensured the control of the male over both the 'field' as well as the 'produce', i.e., the woman as well as the offspring, both of whom were considered to be the man's property or possessions. The only other duties of the male were in his capacity as a householder, where he was expected to function as a sustainer of the remaining three orders. This further confined the women to the 'private' sphere of activity, while rendering the 'public' space open wide for the men. Thus the woman in the form of a wife, is accorded a position of subjection and dependence, leading to uneven and unequal relations between the male and the female. An important role was played by the menstrual taboos in the creation of a society divided across gender lines, and these helped in ascribing to the women a position inferior to the men.

Adultery was considered to be baneful both for the man and the woman in a society which was attempting towards establishment of an order. However, the difference lies in the facts that firstly, adultery was considered to be *intrinsic* to the women's nature; secondly, while men were expected to exhibit self-control in this regard, women needed to be 'controlled' by the males, and thirdly, men might not have felt inclined towards committing adultery except in case they were attracted towards married women, as they were permitted polygamy.

Within the patriarchal order, if women remained subjected and 'devoted' to the sustenance of the order perceived by the *dharmaśāstrakāras*, they were given a mild treatment. This accounts for those verses where respect is demanded to be shown to the women. A women bound by the norms of patriarchy, was the one to be worshipped!

Though punishment is prescribed for crimes such as rape, one of the marriage forms itself is tantamount to inclusion of rape as a form of marriage. Further, *varṇa* comes into play even here, and it was the *varṇa* position of the victim and the criminal within the hierarchical ladder, that determined the degree of the stringency of punishment.

Widowhood was the most miserable stage in the life of a woman in patriarchy. Marriage and procreation being considered as the sole objectives of the life of a woman, the reason for her existence seemed to be lost with the husband's death. Rather, her existence became a source of disturbance, creating a need for her marginalization within or rather, exclusion from the household. The life of an ascetic was prescribed for a widow by the *dharmaśāstrakāras*, and yet there was a grave difference between her life and that of an ascetic. It was the seclusion and utter lack of freedom of movement and expression that the widow was subjected to, unlike the mendicant who could roam about at his or her will. *Niyoga* was another instrument of patriarchal order to ensure the control over the reproductive potential of the woman by her husband's relations even after his death. In case of not having a son who could liberate the deceased husband from hell, the wife had to complete her duty towards her lord by procreating a son through levirate, even if it be against her choice. Remarriage of the widow was in general rejected by the lawgivers with the exception of Nārada. Thus, though *sati* is not prescribed for women (though it is upheld by some), widows might have felt that as the only satisfactory path open to them.

Desertion or abandonment of the wife was generally disfavoured, and some lawgivers have even permitted such a wife to remarry, remarriage of women is discouraged by the *dharmaśāstrakāras* in general. There was no possibility of a woman leaving her husband, except in case he himself had left her before. Thus it was not considered good for the women to opt out of the household, even as an ascetic. The ethos of the *dharmaśāstras* was actually not in the favour of even men adopting the ascetic mode of life without or before fulfilling the duties of a householder. Thus, both men and women were ascribed roles conducive to the upholding of the patriarchy and *varṇa* order of the society. However, the problem lies in the fact that the burden was far greater on women than on men. Kapoor also recognizes this while being an upholder of the *dharmaśāstra* tradition.[743]

It can be further inferred that the existence of the household life was deemed to be necessary for the perpetuation of the social order perceived and sought to be maintained by the *dharmaśāstrakāras*. Again, an attempt was made to enforce a specific definition of the *gṛha*. A particular form of the family is represented as normative, while the others are categorised as deviant. As Chakravarti pointed out, "The domestic ideology outlined here encapsulates within itself codes of duties and responsibilities, love and nurture, control over property, and work and labour, but the hierarchy of power and of exclusions is quite clear."[744] However, that alternative forms of household organization existed is obvious from the fact that an attempt to enforce a specific definition of the *gṛha* was made. This and other such questions, answers to which will bring to the fore the dichotomy between prescription and practice, will form the field of inquiry for one of the following chapters. Another inference that can be drawn out of the discussion in this chapter is that even the authors of the *dharmaśāstras* held varying opinions with regard to various issues, though their ethos matched. Thus, instead of being strict law codes, the texts were constantly under revision, which must have been a response to differing conditions as discussed in previous chapter, and in that they might reflect a society that was in a state of flux.

Notes

1. Chakravarti, Uma, *Everyday Lives, Everyday Histories: Beyond the Kings and Brahmanas of 'Ancient' India*, Tulika Books, New Delhi, 2006, p. 253.
2. Lerner, Gerda, *Creation of Patriarchy,* OUP, New York, 1986, p. 239.
3. Chakravarti, Uma, op. cit., p. 253.
4. Roy, Kumkum, "Defining the Household: Some Aspects of Prescription and Practice in Early India", *Social Scientist*, Vol. 22, No. 248–249, Jan-Feb. 1994, p. 3.
5. *Manu*.III.77,78, *Manu*.VI.89.
6. *Manu*.VI.87.
7. *Manu*.VI.90.
8. *Vasiṣṭha*.VIII.14–16, *Viṣṇu*. LIX.27–29, *Śankha*.V.6.
9. *Vyāsa*.III.5.
10. This has to be distinguished from the entry to the life of a householder, which is possible only after marriage.
11. *Yāj*.I.2.13 and *Viṣṇu*.XXVII.13.

12. *Yāj*.I.2.13 and *Viṣṇu*.XXVII.14.
13. *Manu*.II.67.
14. Roy, Kumkum, op. cit., p. 11.
15. *Manu*.IV.185.
16. *Manu*.III.45–47.
17. *Yāj*.I.3.79
18. *Manu*.III.50
19. *Manu*.III.48
20. *Manu*.IX.81 and *Yāj*.I.3.73
21. *Nārada*.XII.94
22. *Yāj*.I.3.78.
23. *Yāj*.I.3.78.
24. *Atri*.53, *Viṣṇu*.XV.45.
25. *Atri*.54, *Viṣṇu*.XV.44.
26. *Atri*.55, 56 and *Viṣṇu*.XV.46.
27. Altekar, A.S., *The Position of Women in Hindu Civilization,* Motilal Banarsidass, 2nd ed., Fifth reprint, Delhi, 1987, p. 4.
28. Shah, Shalini, *The Making of Womanhood: Gender Relations in the Mahābhārata*, Manohar, New Delhi, 1995, p. 63.
29. Ibid., p. 65.
30. Chaudhuri, J.B., *Position of Women in the Vedic Ritual*, The Author, Calcutta, 2nd ed., 1956, pp. 46–49.
31. Altekar, A.S., op. cit., pp. 7–8.
32. *Manu*.II.67.
33. *Manu*.III.4, *Vasiṣṭha*.VIII.1, *Vyāsa*.II.3–4, *Gautama*.IV, *Samvarta*.35.
34. *Manu*.III.5, *Yāj*.I.3.52, *Vasiṣṭha*.VIII.2, *Vyāsa*.II.4, *Viṣṇu*.XXIV.9, *Śankha*.IV.
35. *Yāj*.I.3.53.
36. *Gautama*.IV, *Śankha*.IV.
37. *Vasiṣṭha*.VIII.2.
38. *Viṣṇu*.XXIV.9, *Vasiṣṭha*.VIII.1, *Vyāsa*.II.3–4, *Śankha*.IV.
39. *Gautama*.IV.
40. *Manu*.III.4.
41. *Manu*.III.7, 8.
42. *Manu*.III.10.
43. *Manu*.III.9.
44. *Yāj*.I.3.52.
45. *Nārada*.XII.36.
46. *Viṣṇu*.XXIV.15.
47. *Viṣṇu*.XXIV.13.
48. *Viṣṇu*.XXIV.14.
49. *Vyāsa*.II.4.
50. *Kātyāyana*.XXVIII.4.

51. *Hārita*.IV.1–2.
52. *Vasiṣṭha*.XIII.51.
53. *Vasiṣṭha*.XIII.52.
54. *Vasiṣṭha*.XIII.53.
55. *Vasiṣṭha*.VIII.1.
56. *Manu*.III.7–8, *Yāj*.I.3.53, *Viṣṇu*.XXIV.12, *Vyāsa*.II.2, *Nārada*.XII.36.
57. *Yāj*.I.3.54.
58. *Manu*.III.6–7.
59. *Yāj*.I.3.53.
60. *Kātyāyana*.XXVIII.4.
61. *Hārita*.IV.1–2.
62. *Likhita*.51.
63. *Likhita*.52.
64. *Likhita*.53.
65. *Manu*.II.238, 240.
66. *Yāj*.I.3.53.
67. *Vasiṣṭha*.I.38.
68. *Vyāsa*. II.1.
69. *Vyāsa*.II.2.
70. *Vyāsa*.II.4.
71. *Viṣṇu*.XXIV.11.
72. *Manu*.VIII.205.
73. *Manu*.VIII.224.
74. *Manu*.VIII.225.
75. *Nārada*.XII.34.
76. *Manu*.VIII.226.
77. *Manu*.X.5.
78. *Nārada*.XII.36.
79. *Yāj*.I.3.52.
80. *Yāj*.I.3.54.
81. *Yāj*.I. 10.264.
82. *Viṣṇu*.V.45.
83. *Viṣṇu*.V.47.
84. *Viṣṇu*.XV.10,11.
85. *Viṣṇu*.XV.15.
86. *Viṣṇu*.XV.16,17.
87. *Vasiṣṭha*.VIII.1.
88. *Vasiṣṭha*.XVII.73.
89. *Vasiṣṭha*.XVII.74.
90. *Vyāsa*.II.3.
91. *Gautama*.IV.

92. Dexter, M.A., *Whence the Goddesses,* Pergamon Press, New York, 1990, p. 161.
93. *Yāj.*I.3.52, *Gautama.*IV.
94. *Viṣṇu.*XXIV.16.
95. *Yāj.*I.3.55.
96. *Nārada.*XII.8,9,37.
97. *Manu.*IX.94.
98. *Manu.*II.67.
99. *Yāj.*I.3.64.
100. *Pārāśara.*VII.6–10.
101. *Bṛhas.*XXIV.3.
102. *Vasiṣṭha.*XVII.69.
103. *Vasiṣṭha.*XVII.70.
104. *Vasiṣṭha.*XVII.71.
105. *Nārada.*XII.25–27, *Vyāsa.*II.7.
106. *Vasiṣṭha.*XVII.67–68 and *Gautama.*XVIII.
107. *Gautama.*XVIII.
108. *Yama.*22.
109. *Yama.*23 and *Samvarta.*67.
110. *Samvarta.*68.
111. *Samvarta.*64.
112. *Samvarta.*76.
113. Altekar, A.S., op. cit., pp. 54–55.
114. Ibid.
115. *Yāj.*I.3.52, *Gautama.*IV.
116. *Manu.*III.27–34, *Viṣṇu.*XXIV.17–24, *Gautama.*IV, *Nārada.*XII.38–39, *Śankha.*IV.2–6.
117. *Vasiṣṭha.*I.28–35.
118. *Manu.*III.30, *Gautama.*IV, *Nārada.*XII.40.
119. *Vasiṣṭha.*I.32, *Viṣṇu.*XXIV.22.
120. *Manu.*III.31.
121. *Vasiṣṭha.* I.35, *Viṣṇu.*XXIV.24, *Śankha.*IV.5, *Gautama.*IV.
122. *Vasiṣṭha.*I.34.
123. *Manu.* III.23.
124. *Manu.*III.24.
125. *Manu.*III.25.
126. *Manu.*III.26.
127. *Nārada.*XII.44.
128. *Viṣṇu.*XXIV.27–28.
129. *Śankha.*IV.3.
130. *Gautama.*IV.
131. *Manu.*III.37.

132. *Manu*.III.38.
133. *Viṣṇu*.XXIV.29–32.
134. *Manu*.III.39.
135. *Manu*.III.40.
136. *Manu*.III.41.
137. *Manu*.III.42.
138. *Vyāsa*.II.5.
139. *Samvarta*.61–63.
140. *Atri*.380.
141. Altekar, A.S., op. cit., p. 39.
142. Ibid., p. 37–38.
143. *Manu*.III.33.
144. Altekar, A.S., op. cit., p. 37.
145. Ibid.
146. *Manu*.IX. 88.
147. *Manu*.III.12.
148. *Manu*.III.13.
149. *Yāj*.I.3.57, *Vasiṣṭha*.I.24, *Śankha*.IV.7–8.
150. *Yāj*.I.3.56–57, *Vasiṣṭha*.I.25–27, *Śankha*.IV.9.
151. *Manu*.III.63.
152. *Vasiṣṭha*.I.25.
153. *Vasiṣṭha*.I.26–27.
154. *Vasiṣṭha*.XIV.11.
155. *Śankha*.IV.9.
156. *Nārada*.XII.5,6 and *Viṣṇu*.XXIV.1–4.
157. *Viṣṇu*.XXVI.4.
158. *Viṣṇu*.XXVI.5.
159. *Viṣṇu*.XXVI.6.
160. *Viṣṇu*.XXVI.7.
161. *Vyāsa*.II.11.
162. *Vyāsa*.IV.68.
163. *Uśanā*.IX.52.
164. *Manu*.IX. 85.
165. *Yāj*.I.3.88.
166. *Viṣṇu*.XXVI.2.
167. *Manu*.X.5.
168. *Manu*.X.6–10.
169. *Manu*.X.13,14.
170. *Yāj*.I.4.92.
171. *Yāj*.I.4.95.
172. *Vasiṣṭha*.XVIII.1–6,8–9.
173. *Vasiṣṭha*.XVIII.7.

174. *Vasiṣṭha*.XVIII.10.
175. *Viṣṇu*.XVI.3.
176. *Viṣṇu*.XVI.4–6.
177. *Viṣṇu*.XVI.7.
178. *Vyāsa*.II.11.
179. *Vyāsa*.I.8.
180. *Vyāsa*.I.9.
181. *Vyāsa*.I.10–12.
182. *Vyāsa*.I.7–8.
183. *Manu*.III.43–44, *Yāj*.I.3.62, *Viṣṇu*.XXIV.5–8, *Śankha*.IV.14.
184. Chakravarti, Uma, op. cit., p. 254.
185. Ibid., pp. 139–140.
186. Cited in Chakravarti, Uma, op. cit., pp. 139–140.
187. Chakravarti, Uma, op. cit., pp. 139–140.
188. *Manu*.XI.1–2.
189. *Manu*.IX.96.
190. *Nārada*.XII.18,19.
191. *Yāj*.I.3.78.
192. *Manu*.III.45–47.
193. *Manu*.III.50.
194. *Yāj*.I.3.79.
195. *Yāj*.III.5.287.
196. *Vasiṣṭha*.XII.6.
197. *Vasiṣṭha*.XII.21.
198. *Vasiṣṭha*.XX.34–35.
199. *Vasiṣṭha*.XX.36.
200. *Vasiṣṭha*.XX.37.
201. *Viṣṇu*.LIV.8.
202. *Vyāsa*.II.42.
203. *Vyāsa*.II.44.
204. *Vyāsa*.II.45.
205. *Vyāsa*.II.46.
206. *Pārāśara*.IV.14–15.
207. *Vyāsa*.II.46.
208. *Samvarta*.96.
209. *Samvarta*.163.
210. *Uśanā*.IV.3–7.
211. *Śankha*.V.
212. *Āpas.Dh.S.*VII.6.
213. *Yama*.25.
214. *Yama*.24.
215. *Āpas.Dh.S.*IX.24.

216. *Nārada*.XII.94.
217. *Angiras*.I.70.
218. *Atri*.299.
219. *Dakśa*.I.24.
220. *Yāj*.I.3.64, *Nārada*.XII.25–27, *Bṛhas*.XXIV.3, *Vasiṣṭha*.XVII.69–71, *Vyāsa*.II.7.
221. *Manu*.III.174.
222. *Manu*.IX. 32.
223. *Manu*.IX.48–51.
224. *Manu*.IX.53.
225. *Vasiṣṭha*.XVII.6–9, *Nārada*.XII.55–58.
226. *Vasiṣṭha*.XVII.26–27.
227. *Uśanā*.V.89–90.
228. *Yāj*.I.3.78.
229. *Atri*.53, *Viṣṇu*.XV.45.
230. *Atri*.54, *Viṣṇu*.XV.44.
231. *Atri*.55, 56 and *Viṣṇu*.XV.46.
232. *Vyāsa*.II.8.
233. Trautmann, T.R., *Dravidian Kinship*, CUP, Cambridge, 1981, p. 26.
234. Shah, Shalini, op. cit., p. 25.
235. Kapoor, Kapil, "Hindu Women, Traditions and Modernity", in Padia, Chandrakala (ed.), *Feminism, Tradition and Modernity*, IIAS, Shimla, 2002, p. 40.
236. *Manu*.III.4, *Yāj*.I.3.52, *Vyāsa*.II.1, *Śankha*.IV.1.
237. *Manu*.IX.92.
238. *Manu*.IX.90–81.
239. *Yāj*.I.3.64.
240. *Vasiṣṭha*.XVII.67–68, *Viṣṇu*.XXIV.40, *Gautama*.XVIII.
241. *Vyāsa*.II.6.
242. *Bṛhas*.X.2.
243. *Vasiṣṭha*.XIII.51.
244. *Vasiṣṭha*.XIII.53.
245. *Viṣṇu*.LVIII.1–2.
246. *Viṣṇu*.LVIII.9.
247. *Nārada*.I.45,51.
248. Goody, Jack and Tambiah, S.J., *Bride Wealth and Dowry*, CUP, Cambridge, 1973, p. 17.
249. *Manu*.IX.92.
250. Shah, Shalini, op. cit., p. 33.
251. *Manu*.III.31
252. *Vasiṣṭha*. I.35, *Viṣṇu*.XXIV.24, *Śankha*.IV.5, *Gautama*.IV.
253. *Vasiṣṭha*.I.35.
254. *Manu*. III.23.

255. *Manu*.III.24.
256. *Manu*.III.25.
257. *Manu*.III.51.
258. *Manu*.III.54.
259. *Manu*.VIII.204.
260. *Manu*.IX. 97.
261. *Āpas.Dh.S*.IX.25.
262. *Atri*.380.
263. Shah, Shalini, op. cit., p. 34.
264. Goody, Jack and Tambiah, S.J., op. cit., pp. 61–62.
265. Ibid., p. 2.
266. Shah, Shalini, op. cit., p. 35.
267. Ibid.
268. See Ortner, Sherry and Whitehead, Harriet (eds.), *Sexual Meanings: The Cultural Construction of Gender and Sexuality,* CUP, Cambridge, 1981, p. 285.
269. *Manu*.V.164.
270. *Manu*.V.165.
271. *Manu*.V.166.
272. *Manu*.IX.69.
273. *Manu*.IX.70.
274. *Yāj*.I.3.65.
275. *Yāj*.I.3.67.
276. *Yāj*.I.10.224.
277. *Vasiṣṭha*.XVII.19–20.
278. *Vasiṣṭha*.XVII.73–74.
279. *Viṣṇu*.XV.8–9.
280. *Angiras*.I.66.
281. *Uśanā*.IV.23–30.
282. *Nārada*.XII.18.
283. *Nārada*.XII.24.
284. *Nārada*.XII.97–101.
285. *Nārada*.XII.97.
286. *Pārāśara*.IV.30.
287. *Manu*.III.140,144,145,146,161,162.
288. *Gautama*.XV.
289. *Manu*.III.262.
290. *Manu*.III.262.
291. Roy, Kumkum, op. cit., p. 11.
292. *Vyāsa*.II.55–56.
293. *Manu*.IV.185.
294. *Manu*.II.67.

295. *Viṣṇu*.XXII.32.
296. *Yama*.73.
297. *Atri* 135.
298. *Dakśa*.VII.26.
299. Shah, Shalini, op. cit., p. 140.
300. Cited in Sangari, K. and Vaid, S. (eds.), *Recasting Women: Essays in Colonial History*, Kali for Women, Delhi, 1990, p. 41.
301. Altekar, A.S., op. cit., p. 204.
302. Shah, Shalini, op. cit., p. 144.
303. *Manu*.IX.3.
304. *Yāj*.I.3.85, *Nārada*.XIII.31, *Vyāsa*.II.54, *Viṣṇu*.XXIV.13.
305. Roy, Kumkum, op. cit., p. 5.
306. *Manu*.II.67.
307. Shah, Shalini, op. cit., p. 82–83.
308. Jayal, Shakambari, *The Status of Women in the Epics*, Motilal Banarsidass, Delhi, 1966, pp. 101–103.
309. *Bṛhas*.XXV.46.
310. *Vyāsa*.II.13.
311. *Vyāsa*.II.15.
312. *Atri*.138.
313. *Manu*.V.151.
314. *Manu*.V.152.
315. *Yāj*.I.3.77.
316. *Yāj*.I.3.87.
317. *Nārada*.XVIII.22.
318. *Bṛhas*.XXIV.8.
319. *Viṣṇu*.XV.2.
320. *Viṣṇu*.XV.12–14.
321. *Viṣṇu*.XV.15.
322. *Vyāsa*.II.19.
323. *Vyāsa*.II.26–27.
324. *Vyāsa*.II.33.
325. *Śankha*.IV.15.
326. *Manu*.V.154.
327. *Manu*.V.156.
328. *Pārāśara*.V.20.
329. *Vyāsa*.II.33.
330. *Dakśa*.IV.4,12.
331. *Dakśa*.IV.5.
332. *Dakśa*.IV.8.
333. *Dakśa*.IV.7.
334. *Kātyāyana*.XVIV.8.

335. *Bṛhas.*XXIV.9.
336. *Manu.*V.157–162.
337. *Viṣṇu.*XV.15–16.
338. *Śankha.*V.8.
339. *Atri.*137.
340. *Gautama.*XVIII.
341. *Manu.*IX.13.
342. *Manu.*IX.80.
343. *Vasiṣṭha.*XXI.11.
344. *Vasiṣṭha.*XXI.15.
345. *Nārada.*XII.93.
346. *Vasiṣṭha.*XXI.15.
347. *Manu.*IX.29.
348. *Manu.*IX.30.
349. *Vasiṣṭha.*XXI.14.
350. *Vyāsa.*II.36.
351. *Kātyāyana.*XVIV.7.
352. *Kātyāyana.*XVIV.11–12.
353. *Viṣṇu.*V.18.
354. *Manu.*VIII.299,300.
355. Lerner, Gerda, *The Creation of Patriarchy*, OUP, New York, 1986, p. 75.
356. *Manu.*II.67.
357. *Manu.*V.150.
358. *Manu.*IX.10.
359. *Bṛhas.*XXIV.4.
360. *Bṛhas.*XXIV.6.
361. *Yāj.*I.3.83.
362. *Viṣṇu.*XXV.4–6.
363. *Vyāsa.*II.20–25, 28–32.
364. *Dakśa.*IV.13.
365. *Nārada.*XII.94, *Āpas.Dh.S.*IX.24, *Angiras.*I.70, *Atri.*299, *Dakśa.*I.24, *Yama.*24,25.
366. *Nārada.*XII.92.
367. *Pārāśara.*V.20.
368. *Manu.*IX.26.
369. *Yāj.*I.3.78.
370. *Āpas.Dh.S.*VII.6.
371. *Pārāśara.*IV.14.
372. *Manu.*III.67,68, *Viṣṇu.*LIX.19, *Śankha.*V.1.
373. *Manu.*III.69–71, *Viṣṇu.*LIX.20, *Śankha.*V.2–4, *Gautama.*V, *Vasiṣṭha.*VIII.11–17.
374. *Manu.*III.70, *Viṣṇu.* LIX. 21–25, *Vyāsa.*III.11–44.
375. *Manu.*III.72, *Viṣṇu.*LIX.26.

376. *Pārāśara*.II.5–6.
377. *Manu*.III.94, *Vyāsa*.III.44, *Gautama*.V.
378. *Manu*.III.95.
379. *Gautama*.V.
380. *Dakśa*.I.31.
381. *Vyāsa*.III.5.
382. Roy, Kumkum, op. cit., p. 8.
383. *Manu*.IV.205.
384. *Manu*.IV.213–214, 217.
385. Roy, Kumkum, op. cit., p 8.
386. *Viṣṇu*.V.163.
387. *Kātyāyana*.XX.13.
388. *Dakśa*.I.29.
389. *Dakśa*.I.31.
390. *Hārita*.II.3.
391. *Manu*.IX.6.
392. *Manu*.IX.3.
393. *Manu*.V.147, 148.
394. *Yāj*.I.3.85, *Nārada*.XIII.31, *Viṣṇu*.XXIV.13, *Vyāsa*.II.54.
395. *Yāj*.I.3.86.
396. *Nārada*.XIII.30.
397. *Bṛhas*.XXIV.2.
398. *Viṣṇu*.XXV.12–13.
399. *Vasiṣṭha*.V.1–2
400. *Angiras*.I.69.
401. *Dakśa*.IV.1,7.
402. *Dakśa*.IV.5.
403. *Dakśa*.IV.4, 12.
404. *Dakśa*.IV.3.
405. *Manu*.IX.14.
406. *Manu*.IX.15.
407. *Manu*.IX.16.
408. Perhaps the reference here is to *Svayambhu Manu,* who is said to have instilled such qualities in women at the time of creation itself.
409. *Manu*.IX.17.
410. *Pārāśara*.I.30–31.
411. Sarkar, S.C., *Some Aspects of the Earliest Social History of India,* Humphrey Milford, London, 1928, p. 85.
412. Shah, Shalini, op. cit., p. 55.
413. *Manu*.IX.7.
414. Engels, Frederick, *The Origin of the Family, Private Property and the State*, Foreign Languages Publishing House, Moscow, 1948, p. 52.

415. Rajvade, Vishvanath Kashinath, *Bhārtīya Vivāha Samsthā kā Itihāsa,* Peoples Publishing House, New Delhi, 1986, p. 95.
416. Shah, Shalini, op. cit., p. 19.
417. Ibid., p. 53.
418. *Manu*.IX.33–44.
419. *Manu*.IX.43.
420. Roy, Kumkum, op. cit., p. 5.
421. *Manu*.IX.15.
422. *Dakśa*.IV.11.
423. *Manu*.IX.10.
424. *Manu*.IX.11.
425. *Bṛhas*.XXIV.4.
426. *Manu*.IX.13.
427. *Yāj*.I.3.84.
428. *Yāj*.I.3.86.
429. *Viṣṇu*.XXV.12–13.
430. *Angiras*.I.69.
431. *Dakśa*.IV.1,7.
432. *Dakśa*.IV.5.
433. *Dakśa*.IV.4, 12.
434. Kapoor, Kapil, op. cit., p 27
435. Ibid., pp. 28–34
436. Ibid., p 34
437. Ibid.
438. Ibid., p 32
439. Shah, Shalini, op. cit., p. 57.
440. *Yāj*.I.3.81.
441. *Vyāsa*.II.46.
442. Bhattacharji, Sukumari, "Motherhood in Ancient India", in *Economic and Political Weekly*, Vol.25, No. 40, October 20–27, 1990, p. WS–51.
443. *Nārada*.XII.16.
444. *Nārada*.XII.19.
445. *Pārāśara*.IV.30.
446. *Manu*.IX.35.37.
447. Roy, Kumkum, op. cit., p. 9.
448. *Manu*.IV.179–181.
449. *Manu*.VIII.299,300.
450. *Manu*.III.12, *Yāj*.I.3.57, *Nārada*.XII.6, *Vasiṣṭha*.I.24, *Viṣṇu*.XXIV.1–4, *Vyāsa*.II.10–11, *Śankha*.IV.7–8.
451. *Manu*.IX.80.
452. *Yāj*.I.3.73.
453. *Manu*.IX.82.

454. *Yāj*.I.3.74.
455. *Dakśa*.IV.8.
456. *Atri*.339–340.
457. *Kātyāyana*.XIX.13.
458. *Manu*.IX.85.
459. *Yāj*.I.3.88.
460. *Viṣṇu*.XXVI.1,2, *Vyāsa*.II.12, *KātYāyana*.VIII.6,7.
461. *Vasiṣṭha*.XVII.47–50.
462. *Manu*.II.238, 240.
463. *Vasiṣṭha*.V.7.
464. *Manu*.IV.57.
465. *Manu*.V.66.
466. *Manu*.V.85.
467. *Yāj*.I.7.167–68.
468. *Yāj*.III.1.30.
469. *Vasiṣṭha*.V.5–6
470. *Vasiṣṭha*.V.9.
471. *Āpas.Dh.S*.VII.4
472. *Pārāśara*.VII.20, *Angiras*.I.38.
473. *Angiras*.I.39.
474. *Yama*.63.
475. *Āpas.Dh.S*.VII.12.
476. *Atri*.171.
477. *Atri*.269.
478. *Āpas.Dh.S*.VII.19–21, *Atri*.275–279, *Yama*.56–60.
479. *Viṣṇu*.XXII.69,72.
480. *Viṣṇu*.LI.6,16.
481. *Pārāśara*.VII.13–16.
482. *Samvarta*.181.
483. *Samvarta*.194.
484. *Yama*.25.
485. *Yama*.26.
486. *Vyāsa*.II.37–41.
487. *Viṣṇu*.V.105.
488. *Manu*.III.45–47.
489. *Manu*.III.50.
490. *Manu*.IV.40.
491. *Manu*.IV.41,42.
492. *Yāj*.III.5.287.
493. *Vasiṣṭha*.XII.6.
494. *Angiras*.I.37.
495. *Āpas.Dh.S*.VII.6.

496. *Vasiṣṭha*.XII.21.
497. *Vyāsa*.II.46.
498. *Vasiṣṭha*.XXVIII.4.
499. *Āpas.Dh.S.*VII.3.
500. *Vasiṣṭha*.III.58.
501. *Angiras*.I.42.
502. *Yāj*.I.3.72.
503. *Vasiṣṭha*.V.3,4.
504. *Vasiṣṭha*.XXVIII.2–3.
505. *Vyāsa*.II.46, 49, 52–53 and *Atri*.189,193–194.
506. *Pārāśara*.VII.4.
507. Young, F.W. and Bacdayan, A.A., "Menstrual Taboos and Social Rigidity", *Ethnology*, Vol. 4, No. 2, April, 1965, p. 230.
508. Cited in Sanday, P.R., *Female Power and Male Dominance: On the Origin of Sexual Inequality,* CUP, Cambridge, 1981, p. 92.
509. Godelier, Maurice, "The Origin of Male Domination", *New Left Review*, I/127, May-June, 1981, p. 17.
510. Bhattacharyya, N.N., *The Indian Mother Goddess,* 2nd revised ed., Manohar, New Delhi, 1977, p. 286.
511. Sanday, P.R., *Female Power and Male Dominance: On the Origins of Sexual Inequality*, CUP, Cambridge, 1981.
512. *Viṣṇu*.XXIV.3.
513. Roy, Kumkum, op. cit., p. 9.
514. Boserup, Ester, *Women's Role in Economic Development,* St. Martin's Press, New York, 1970, p. 51.
515. Rosaldo, M.Z. and Lamphere, L. (eds.), *Women, Culture and Society*, Stanford University Press, California, 1974, p. 251.
516. *Viṣṇu*.XXXI.1–6.
517. *Viṣṇu*.XXXI.7–8.
518. *Viṣṇu*.XXXI.9.
519. *Viṣṇu*.XXXI.10.
520. *Gautama*.II and *Atri*.149.
521. *Vasiṣṭha*.XIII.47,48; *Hārita*.III.10,11; *Uśanā*.I.30,33–37.
522. Altekar, A.S., op. cit., p. 101.
523. *Manu*.IX.35.37.
524. *Manu*.II.129–133.
525. *Manu*.III.55–59.
526. *Yāj*.I.10.223.
527. *Bṛhas*.XXV.88.
528. *Uśanā* I.26.
529. *Uśanā*.I.27.
530. *Vasiṣṭha*.XIII.58 and *Viṣṇu*.LXIII.51.

531. *Manu*.II.138, *Vasiṣṭha*.XIII.58 and *Viṣṇu*.LXIII.51.
532. *Manu*.IX.14.
533. *Manu*.IX.15.
534. *Manu*.IX.16.
535. *Manu*.IX.17.
536. *Manu*.XI. 59.
537. *Manu*.XI.55.
538. *Yāj*.III.5.232–3.
539. *Nārada*.XII.73–75.
540. *Viṣṇu*.XXXVI.4, 5, 8.
541. *Pārāśara*.X.12–15.
542. *Atri*.164.
543. *Saṁvarta*.123, 156–159, 162.
544. *Samvarta*.160.
544. *Śātātapa*.V.1.
545. *Śātātapa*.V.2–32.
547. *Gautama*.XX.
548. *Gautama*.XXIV.
549. *Uśanā*.VIII.23–26.
550. *Uśanā*.IX.1.
551. *Uśanā*.IX.2–5.
552. *Manu*.VIII.352.
553. *Manu*.VIII.353.
554. *Manu*.IX.241.
555. *Yāj*.II.24.286.
556. *Nārada*.XII.70, *Viṣṇu*.V.40–43.
557. *Nārada*.XII.76.
558. *Yāj*.III.5.297.
559. *Yāj*.III.5.231.
560. *Vasiṣṭha*.XXI.1–5.
561. *Gautama*.XXIV.
562. *Atri*.169, 183.
563. *Atri*.184.
564. *Samvarta*.149, 150, 153, 154, 165–168.
565. *Pārāśara*.X.6–9.
566. *Pārāśara*.X.19–24.
567. *Manu*.III.167.
568. *Manu*.III.174.
569. *Manu*.V.163.
570. *Manu*.XI.177.
571. *Yāj*.I.3.72, *Vasiṣṭha*.XXVIII.1–4.
572. *Yāj*.I.3.70.

573. *Yāj*.III.5.296.
574. *Yāj*.I.3.72.
575. *Nārada*.XII.91.
576. *Yāj*.III.3.75.
577. *Yāj*.III.1.6.
578. *Yāj*.III.5.297.
579. *Bṛhas*.XXIII.15–16.
580. *Vasiṣṭha*.XXI.1–5.
581. *Vasiṣṭha*.XIV.2, 6.
582. *Vasiṣṭha*.XXI.6–7.
583. *Vasiṣṭha*.XXI.8.
584. *Vasiṣṭha*.XXI.9.
585. *Vasiṣṭha*.XXI.10.
586. *Vasiṣṭha*.XXI.11.
587. *Vasiṣṭha*.XXI.14.
588. *Gautama*.XXIV.
589. *Viṣṇu*.LIII.8.
590. *Vyāsa*.II.46, 49.
591. *Vyāsa*.II.52.
592. *Vyāsa*.II.53.
593. *Yama*.27–28.
594. *Yama*.35.
595. *Atri*.189, 191–192.
596. *Samvarta*.164.
597. *Manu*.IX.235 and XI.55.
598. *Manu*.IX.236.
599. *Manu*.IX. 237.
600. *Manu*.IX. 238.
601. *Manu*.IX. 239.
602. *Manu*.IX.240.
603. *Manu*.XI. 59.
604. *Yāj*.II.24, 283–285.
605. *Yāj*.II.24.286.
606. *Yāj*.III.4.136.
607. *Yāj*.III.5.208.
608. *Yāj*.III.5.231.
609. *Yāj*.III.5.259.
610. *Yāj*.III.5.304.
611. *Yāj*.III.5.232–233.
612. *Nārada*.XII.73–75, *Vasiṣṭha*.XX.13, *Gautama*.XXIV, Pārāśara.X.10–11.
613. *Vasiṣṭha*.XX.14, *Gautama*.XXIV.
614. *Vasiṣṭha*.XX.15.

615. *Gautama*.XX.
616. *Yāj*.III.5.234–242.
617. *Vasiṣṭha*.XX.16.
618. *Vasiṣṭha*.XXI.1–5.
619. *Nārada*.XII.62–69, *Bṛhas*.XXIII.5–9.
620. *Bṛhas*.XXIII.15–16.
621. *Nārada*.XII.70, *Viṣṇu*.V.40–43.
622. *Viṣṇu*.XXXVI.4–8.
623. *Atri*.169, 183, 184.
624. *Samvarta*.123.
625. *Samvarta*.149–157.
626. *Samvarta*.158, 160.
627. *Śātātapa*.V.1–38.
628. *Śātātapa*.26, 33, 34.
629. *Śātātapa*.V.31.
630. *Nārada*.XII.61.
631. *Uśanā*.VIII.1.
632. *Uśanā*.VIII.23–24.
633. *Uśanā*.VIII.25–29.
634. *Uśanā*.IX.1.
635. *Uśanā*.IX.2–5.
636. Engels, Frederick, *The Origin of the Family, Private Property and the State*, Foreign Languages Publishing House, Moscow, 1948, p. 52.
637. Coontz, Stephanie and Henderson, Peta (eds.), *Women's Work, Men's Property: The Origin of Gender and Class*, Verso, London, 1986, pp. 141–142.
638. Shah, Shalini, op. cit., p. 53.
639. Ibid., p. 57.
640. *Manu*.XI.62–67.
641. *Yāj*.II.24.288.
642. *Bṛhas*.XXIII.10.
643. *Bṛhas*.XXIII.11.
644. *Bṛhas*.XXIII.13.
645. *Bṛhas*.XXIII.14.
646. *Pārāśara*.X.26–27.
647. *Atri*.193–194.
648. *Atri*.197–198.
649. Shah, Shalini, op. cit., p. 85.
650. Chakravarti, Uma, op. cit.
651. Ibid., p. 157.
652. *Manu*.V.157.
653. *Bṛhas*.XXV.71.
654. *Pārāśara*.IV.31–32.

655. *Vyāsa*.II.50–51.
656. *Vasiṣṭha*.XVII.55.
657. *Vasiṣṭha*.XVII.56.
658. *Vasiṣṭha*.XVII.57–59.
659. *Vasiṣṭha*.XVII.60.
660. *Vasiṣṭha*.XVII.61.
661. *Vasiṣṭha*.XVII.64.
662. *Vasiṣṭha*.XVII.65–66.
663. *Gautama*.XVIII.
664. *Gautama*.XVIII.
665. *Yāj*.I.3.68–69.
666. *Yāj*.III.5.286.
667. *Nārada*.XII.81–88.
668. *Manu*.III.166.
669. *Manu*.III.67.
670. *Manu*.III.173.
671. *Manu*.III.159.
672. *Manu*.V.161.
673. *Manu*.IX.59, 60.
674. *Manu*.IX.62,63.
675. *Manu*.IX.66–68.
676. *Manu*.IX.69.
677. *Manu*.IX.70.
678. *Bṛhas*.XXIV.12.
679. Altekar, A.S., op. cit., p. 149.
680. Ibid.
681. Sharma, R.S. (ed.), *Perspectives in Social and Economic History of Early India*, Munshiram Manoharlal, New Delhi, 1983, p. 136.
682. Roy, Kumkum, op. cit., pp. 6–7.
683. *Manu*.III.166.
684. *Manu*.III.167.
685. *Manu*.V.157–162.
686. *Manu*.V.164.
687. *Manu*.V.165.
688. *Manu*.V.166.
689. *Manu*.IX.69.
690. *Manu*.IX.70.
691. *Uśanā*.IV.
692. *Nārada*.XII.97.
693. *Pārāśara*.IV.30.
694. *Manu*.V.167–168.

695. *Yāj.*I.3.89.
696. *Viṣṇu.*XXV.1.14.
697. *Vyāsa.*II.50–51.
698. *Bṛhas.*XXIV.11.
699. *Atri.*209.
700. *Pārāśara.*IV.33.
701. *Dakśa.*IV.20.
702. *Dakśa.*IV.19.
703. *Uśanā.*III.119.
704. Kosambi, D.D., *Myth and Reality*, Popular Prakashan, Bombay, 1962, p. 80.
705. Shah, Shalini, op. cit., p. 92.
706. Cited in Thapar, Romila, "Tradition versus Misconceptions", in *Manushi*, Nos.42–43, 1987, p. 8.
707. Chakravarti, Uma, op. cit., p 164.
708. *Vasiṣṭha.*XIII.49.
709. *Viṣṇu.*V.163.
710. *Pārāśara.*X.31.
711. *Pārāśara.*X.32–33.
712. *Pārāśara.*X.34–36.
713. *Pārāśara.*IV.30.
714. *Vyāsa.*II.47.
715. *Dakśa.*IV.17.
716. *Uśanā.*IV.32.
717. *Nārada.*XII.92.
718. *Nārada.*XII.93.
719. *Vasiṣṭha.*XVII.75–76.
720. *Vasiṣṭha.*XVII.77–80.
721. *Pārāśara.*IV.30.
722. *Nārada.*XII.24.
723. *Nārada.*XII95.
724. *Nārada.*XII.97–101.
725. *Manu.*V.163.
726. *Manu.*V.164.
727. *Manu.*V.165.
728. *Manu.*V.166.
729. *Yāj.*I.3.67.
730. *Nārada.*XII.49.
731. *Vasiṣṭha.*XVII.19–20.
732. *Nārada.*XII.47.
733. *Vyāsa.*II.48.
734. *Dakśa.*IV.18.

735. *Nārada*.XII.90.
736. *Pārāśara*.X.32–33.
737. *Nārada*.XII.97, *Pārāśara*.IV.30.
738. *Manu*.V.89–90.
739. *Manu*.V.155.
740. *Viṣṇu*.XXIV.7,15.
741. *Pārāśara*.IV.20, *Śankha*.V.8.
742. Kapoor, Kapil, op. cit., p 33–34.
743. Kapoor, Kapil, op. cit., p. 47.
744. Chakravarti, Uma, op. cit., p. 258.

3

Property and Legal Rights

While one could be sceptical with regard to complete economic determinism as the only truth, it has to be acknowledged that the role of economics has been definitive in human history in more ways than one. When and how economics started wielding a defining influence on human life? Human life is based on exchange, give and take, for it is impossible for anyone to remain completely independent or self-dependent. This exchange is the basic component of the economics involved in life. Where one is stationed in such processes involving exchange economics determines the power relationships. It is also important to consider what one has to offer and what one wants in exchange. Therefore, power relationships are also dictated by one's necessities as well as desires. For example, the fact whether one has the right to property or not will determine the position of only those who are within the frame of reference where ownership or entitlement carries weight. For a renunciate, male or female, the degree of independence or power of decision-making does not rest upon economic independence. Empowerment on the *external* plane has to be accompanied by an empowerment from within, an empowerment on the *inner* plane. All talks about gender equity and women's empowerment need to be cognizant of this point.

Before discussing the issues of property and legal rights granted to women, it should be necessary to define some of the terms involved.

Rights

The general notion of "right" applies both in legal and moral contexts. It is in the legal context that it is used here. Right in the legal context entails the claims or entitlements of an individual. Rights are characterized as being possessed, exercised and enjoyed. It is not the same as grant of a privilege, the receipt of a favour, or permission. How far this definition of rights applies in the ancient Indian context, has to be looked into. Coming to defining property rights, it is important to trace the definition of property and ownership in ancient India, which must have varied with variations in time and space. Subsequent to the attempt at discussing ownership and property in ancient Indian context, a discussion on the concept of "law" in ancient India will be crucial in order to understand the implications of the term "legal rights".

Ownership and Property in Ancient India

In the hunting gathering stage of economy, there must have hardly been any concept of property. Whatever might have existed is a sense of possession of the implements used in hunting, and that too not in the very initial phase. The sense of possession and ownership must have originated and strengthened only with the beginning of pastoralism and agriculture. The concept of individual ownership must have taken still longer to come into existence. The internal evidence of the *Ṛgveda* indicates that the concept of individual ownership had not taken shape in the early Vedic age. However, many references to 'common wealth' or 'collective ownership' can be found in the text.[1] Since the early Vedic society was characterized by the tribal bond of kinship, whatever was recognized as tribal wealth, was divided among the constituting clans and subclans. The vedic people were mostly pastoral warring tribes, the tribal wealth was counted in terms of cattle. The pastoral societies have, however, greater scope to develop the sense of property and individual ownership, since cattle could be preserved and multiplied, used as the best medium of exchange, increased by wars and raids, and divided among clans, families, even individuals. Evidence of some kind of individual possession is found in the later books of the *Ṛgveda.* That in the later period of the *Ṛgveda* even women were entitled to have some share of cattle wealth as marriage gift is suggested in the 'wedding hymn'.[2] The term mentioned there is *vahatu* which has been explained by Sāyaṇa as 'cow and other gifts' given for pleasing the girl.[3] Agriculture was introduced only in the later Vedic age, and even then, land was subjected to joint or corporate holding. So no question of individual ownership or inheritance could arise then. During this period, tribes must have exercised control over the areas they had taken possession of. This right of the conqueror must have been the initial form of land right. The tribes allotted land to the individual families for their utilization. The jungle which covered a large expanse of land, although economically useless, led to another form of land right, namely, the right of the first clearer. The one who had cleared a plot in the jungle also had the right to use it. However, this individual right of utilization was only valid as long as the land was actually cultivated. As soon as it was abandoned, the power of disposition over it reverted to the tribe. The strenuous work of clearing, the necessity of mutual help, small-scale defence measures, and the expansion of the families led, in the course of time, to the formation of villages which in turn led to the regulation of land rights. Two different forms developed in course of time. The village which had individual land rights consisted of a group of families which had rights to the land on the basis of having cleared it. The claims of the families were limited to the cleared land. The uncultivable land in the vicinity of the village was jointly utilized, but no claims were made to it. It belonged to the ruler who, in later epochs, also granted permission to cultivate the land. In the case of villages which held land rights jointly, the village community claimed the right to all land within the village boundaries and allotted it to individual families for utilization. Thus, both individual and joint land rights took shape at quite an early period. However, landed property, as known in Western terms, did not exist at all. The rights were a privilege granting inheritable utilization rights and included social obligations. With the subsequent formation of state, the ruler assumed the supreme position in all matters. Costs of governing were covered, at first, with gifts. Soon, however, it became obligatory to deliver a share of the grain yield, in other words, a tax was introduced. The king was thus only given a right to a share of the yield, but no rights to the land and its utilization. However, he was entitled to all the uncultivated land that lay between the villages. Again, it became necessary to establish an official hierarchy to collect the taxes. While the Mauryas had vast state-administered farms, during the post-Mauryan period, the Sātavāhanas started the practice of donating land with fiscal and administrative immunities to *brāhmaṇas* and Buddhist monks. Ostensibly, the land grants were made on religious grounds, however, the underlying idea was to extend the area under cultivation through private efforts. The investment of physical labour in a piece of unclaimed land made the individual its owner. According to Manu, a field belonged to him who first cleared it and a deer to him who first wounded it.[4] During the Gupta period, however, the land grants paved the way for the growth of feudal society. Women's entitlement to property also has to be seen in this light. At the first place, the introduction of the iron ploughshare increased the importance of male labour as far as agriculture was concerned. Accordingly, land came to be the entitlement of the male who cleared the forest and cultivated the land. Again, when land was donated, it was donated to the *brāhmaṇas* and Buddhist monks who were males. Initially, it was the right to utilization, and land was utilized by the males who tilled it. Later, with the emergence of hereditary rights, males must have become the inheritors too. Also, the society being patriarchal, males must have been the recognized heirs.

Concept of Law in Ancient India

To the modern mind, law is essentially a human institution. The underlying assumption is that law is nothing but the order of the State, and that there can be no law apart from the State. However, the ancient Indians ascribed a divine origin to law, and thus viewed it not merely as the order of the king, rather as superior to and binding upon him. It differs from the Austinian conception of law according to which the state or sovereign may only be bound by law at will. Contrary to this, for the ancient Indians, obedience to the law implied only obedience to the divine will. However, this is not to say that adherence to the legal injunctions laid down by the lawgivers was complete. There always were temporal and spatial variations based on custom. Also, how far the injunctions could be enforced is also a query.

One peculiar thing about the ancient Indian law is that in it, the moral and the legal injunctions are inextricably mixed together. The entire body of rules regulating the life of man, from prescribing the general code of conduct to regulating the performance of religious sacrifices, is discussed under the general name of *dharmaśāstra.* Though some lawgivers like Yājñavalkya attempted to divide the subjects as *Ācāra, Vyavahāra,* and *Prāyaścitta*; yet they failed in making a clear distinction between the moral and legal injunctions. It is in this light that the legal rights granted to women in ancient India need to be studied.

Property Rights

The Vedic society was essentially patriarchal. Though women were not entitled to partition and inheritance directly, in practice it would not have been possible to suppress all their property rights. The term *pārināhya* has been used in the *Taittirīya Samhitā*[5] indicating the authority of the wife on family resources.[6] Again, it has to be noted that as mentioned earlier, during this period, there must have existed a natural contradiction between the social and individual ownership. Perhaps owing to the community ownership of land, women were not invested with the rights to immovable property, which would have remained unchanged even with the growth of private ownership. In accordance with this, the *dharmasūtras* advocated an extremely patrilineal form of inheritance, in which in the absence of sons, the property will rather go to the near and remote agnates of the property holder than to his own daughters. However, it was laid down that the ornaments and such wealth as bestowed upon her by her relations, both agnate and cognate, should be absolutely owned by her.[7] Thus, women's right to property varied for the immovable and movable property. Again, the *dharmaśāstras* or the *smṛtis* were the first documents which provided a distinct codification of rules relating to ownership, inheritance and partition. The following section will discuss the rights of women with respect to immovable and movable property as given in these texts.

Inheritance and Partition of Immovable Property

Daughter's Right to Father's Property

In consonance with the norms and requirements of patriarchy, the daughter was not recognized as the natural heir to father's property. However, some rights to property were conceded to her. To quote Bhattacharyya:

> Manu made the *Dharmasūtra* traditions up to date. But while dealing with the *Dharmasūtra* injunctions regarding the property-rights of women, he faced two apparently contradictory principles. The first is that *Dharmasūtra* allow women to become exclusive owners of such wealth as is obtained by them as gifts from their relations. This formed the basis of his famous formulation of the sixfold concept of *strīdhana* (IX.194). The second principle of the *Dharmasūtras* was rather difficult for him to accept. The *Dharmasūtras* categorically say that property should be transmitted only through the male line and that women have no right to inherit their paternal property by themselves. Manu was no less patriarchal than the authors of the *Dharmasutras*, but as the first universal law-giver he had to take into consideration the existing laws belonging to other popular

> traditions, apart from the Vedic sources, which speak of women's right to inherit their ancestral property. So he had to make a compromise. Thus, on the one hand, nowhere in his codes he says that sisters are equally entitled to the patrimony as their brothers but, on the other, he says that for the purpose of the marriage of their sisters the brothers should forego one-fourth of their own shares in favour of the sisters (IX.118).[8]

Though after the death of the father and the mother, the sons are directed to divide the paternal and maternal estate in equal shares among themselves,[9] or the eldest must take the whole estate and rest of the sons shall live under him as under the father;[10] they are asked to give one-fourth each out of their shares to the sisters, lest they would become outcastes[11]. It is obvious that the daughter is not granted a direct share in the inheritance. Yājñavalkaya also laid down that upon the death of both the father and the mother, all the sons should distribute the property and liability of their father equally. However, if the sisters are not married at the time of partition, each brother should give one-fourth part of his share or money equal to the value of one-fourth part of his share for their marriage.[12] Again, he says that in case a person dies without leaving any of the twelve kinds of sons, then his wife, daughters, parents, brothers, nephews, siblings, near and dears, disciples and the *brahmacārīs* are entitled to his property in seriatim. This rule is applicable to all *varṇas*.[13] This implies that in the wake of the absence of any of the twelve kinds of sons and the wife of the deceased, the daughter is the next legitimate heir to his property. However, as Bhattacharya points out, "Like Manu, Yājñavalkya does not make any clear statement whether this one-fourth share, enjoyed by the sisters, is owing to a natural succession or to a moral obligation for which the brothers should forego their one-fourth."[14] Viṣṇu also says that the wealth of a man who dies without male issue goes to his wife, and in the absence of the wife also, goes to his daughter.[15]

Besides the cases when the daughter was entitled to a limited share in father's property herself, there are references to the appointed daughter, i.e., the *putrikā*. According to Manu, a man who does not have any son, may appoint his daughter, *putrikā*, whose son shall perform his funeral rites.[16] The husband of the daughter had to be informed of the girl's *putrikā* status before marriage, precisely because begetting a son was considered to be one of the main aims behind marrying as the son was considered to be the one to liberate the father from hell. In the case of the appointed daughter, however, the son begotten would rather liberate the girl's father. It would have been certainly difficult for the appointed daughter to get a husband, also in the wake of the fact that the lawgivers themselves discouraged men from marrying such girls. Further, Manu says that a son is like one's own self, and a daughter is equal to the son, so in the presence of his daughter, who is identical to one's self; who else shall take the estate.[17] However, it has to be noted that the daughter is only indirectly identified with the father, and accordingly, the estate is not given to her, but to her son. The son of one's daughter and one's own son are both equal because both of them save him in the next world.[18] Yājñavalkya makes a passing reference to *putrikā* where he says that the son born of an appointed daughter is to be treated the same as the *aurasa* son (son born from a lawful wife).[19] According to Bṛhaspati, a daughter springs from a man's person just as a son, and so no one else shall inherit the father's property (in the absence of sons and wife), whether she be expressly appointed or not. The necessary precondition, however, is that she should be equal in caste to her father and married to a man of same caste. Ultimately her son becomes the owner of this property.[20] Vasiṣṭha also regards the son of a *putrikā* among the six kinds of sons who are regarded as both kinsmen and heirs. Again, it has to be declared to the man beforehand with whom the girl is going to be married.[21] Viṣṇu repeats the injunction with the only difference that he declares a brotherless maiden to be *putrikā* even if she has not been expressly appointed.[22] Gautama says that a sonless father shall give away his daughter in marriage saying "her sons shall be my sons". Several authorities hold that mere entertainment of such a thought by a father in his mind will create the right of *putrikā*. Hence, there is a prohibition regarding marrying a brotherless bride, in as much as the existence of Putrikaship in such a case may not be easily discovered.[23] Likhita also laid down that a wise man should not wed a girl without a brother, apprehending lest she might have been given away as a *putrikā*. Subsequently, he defines an appointed daughter.[24] The case of an appointed daughter is actually not a property right granted to the daughter. It is her son who got the entitlement to the maternal grandfather's property in this way. In fact, the status of an appointed daughter reduced her chances of getting a suitable husband to a considerable extent. This would have made her life miserable in a patriarchy where marriage and procreation were considered to be the sole aim of female existence.

Wife's Right to Husband's Property

According to Yājñavalkya, in case of a dead person who had no sons out of the twelve kinds, then his wife, daughters, parents, brothers, nephews, siblings, near and dears, disciples and the *brahmacārīs* are entitled to his property in seriatim. This rule is applicable to all *varṇas*.[25] Bṛhaspati also opined similarly, however, he tries to derive support for this by saying that the wife is declared to be half the body of her husband in the *Vedas*, *Smṛtis* and in popular usage, equally sharing the outcome of good and evil acts. Hence one whose wife is not dead, half his body survives. So, even though *sakulyas* (kinsmen), parents, or uterine brothers be living, the wife of one who dies without leaving male issue shall succeed to the share.[26] Again, he says that a wife deceased before her husband takes away his consecrated fire (*Agnihotra*); but if the husband dies before the wife, she takes his property, if she has been faithful to him.[27] However, in case the husband was separated from his coparceners, the wife shall take a pledge after his death and whatever else is recognized as property, excepting the immovable wealth. Bṛhaspati again appears to be in a state of confusion when he says that a wife is unworthy to obtain immovable property, even if she has preserved her character, and if partition had already been made she only needed to be given food or a portion of arable land for support.[29] Immediately in the next verse, he again says that the wife is declared to succeed to the husband's property, and in her absence, the daughter.[30] Gautama also says that the estates of a childless person shall go to his wife after his death, or she shall seek for a son from his uterine brother. However, a son begotten on such a widow by any one except her deceased husband's brother shall not be competent to inherit the property of his mother's deceased husband.[31] It is quite surprising to note that Manu is completely silent regarding the rights of the widow to husband's property. However, it has to be noted that the right of the widow to husband's property could not be rejected completely by all the lawgivers, and some of them rather granted her the right to get the husband's property. However, the wife's right was recognized only in the absence of any of the recognized sons.

Mother's Right to Son's Property

According to Manu, a mother shall obtain the inheritance of a son who dies without leaving any issue, and if mother be dead, the paternal grandmother shall take the estate.[32] It is notable that it is the son who has the first right to inherit the property of his father, and then his heirs, only when none of them is there, does the mother receive the property. Bṛhaspati also entitled the mother to inherit a son's property who died without leaving any male issue or wife. The brothers may be given a share if the mother chooses so.[33]

Women's Right to Movable Property: *Strīdhana* (Women's Property)

It was with reference to the immovable property that the Hindu society was for a long time unwilling to invest the wife with full or exclusive ownership. The main reason for it, perhaps, was the ownership of the community on the land. Also, society being patriarchal, the daughter had to become a part of another clan, so in order to keep the ownership with the same tribe, it would not have been feasible to invest the daughter with the same rights on property as the son. But in case of movable property viz., ornaments, jewellery, costly apparels etc., women's rights on their possession were recognized at quite an early stage. Later on, this particular part of movable property was formally labelled as *strīdhana.*

Definition and Scope of Strīdhana

Though some terms like *vahatu* and *pāriṇṛhya,* as referred to above, are indicative of women possessing some forms of movable property even during the age preceding that of the *dharmaśāstras*; it is the *dharmaśāstra* literature which dealt with the subject of *strīdhana* at length for the first time. Literally, the term *strīdhana* denotes women's property. However, in the *dharmaśāstras,* the term has been used in a technical sense, rather than carrying only the etymological meaning. It has to be studied whether it denoted the possessions of women, which were so only in name or whether they were completely owned by her in the sense that she exercised complete rights to use or dispose of them at her will. But before getting into that discussion, the varying definitions given by the *dharmśāstrakāras* deserve consideration. This shall be helpful in giving a conceptual understanding of *strīdhana.*

Manu refers to six kinds of *strīdhana,* viz., the property given before the nuptial fire; given at the bridal procession; given to a woman through affection; given by a brother; given by mother and given by the father.[34] Viṣṇu adds few more kinds of property in the *strīdhana.* According to him, what has been given to a woman by her father, her mother, her son, her brother, what has been received by her before the nuptial fire, what has been presented to her on her husband's espousal of another wife (*adhivedanika*), what has been given to her by kindred, as well as her fee (*śulka*), and a gift subsequent are called *strīdhana*.[35] Yājñavalkya also enumerates six kinds of *strīdhana* including property given by the father, mother, husband or brother, that given before the nuptial fire; that given by the husband on superseding the wife by marrying another women etcetera.[36] *Nārada's* description of *strīdhana* is very close to that of Manu. The only difference is that he mentions 'husband's donation' in the place of 'what was given before the nuptial fire.[37] He further declares that what has been given to a wife by her loving husband, that she may spend or give away, as she likes, even after her death excepting immovable property.[38]

The most detailed description of *strīdhana* has been given in the *Kātyāyana Smṛti*. Kātyāyana makes the most elaborate treatment of *strīdhana* making improvement upon what was suggested by Manu and Yājñavalkya and his version has been accepted by all digests including the *Dāyabhāga*. Kātyāyana discusses the topic of *strīdhana* in about twenty seven verses. He says that what is given before the nuptial fire, what is given during the bridal procession, what is given for love and what is received from mother, brother or father; these are the six fold property of a woman. He is quoted in the *Dāyabhāga* thus: "What is given to a woman at the time of her marriage, near the nuptial fire, is celebrated by the wise as the woman's peculiar property bestowed before the nuptial fire. That again, which a woman receives while she is conducted from the paternal (abode to her husband's dwelling) is instanced as the separate property of a woman under the name of gift presented in the bridal procession."[39] He is further quoted in *Mitākśarā* thus: "Whatever has been offered to her as a token of respect, is denominated an affectionate present (*prītidatta*). That which is received by a married woman or by a maiden in the house of her husband or of father, from her brother, from her parents is termed gift of affectionate kindred (*saudāyika*)."[40] Explaining the term perquisite he says: "Whatever has been received as a price of workmen on houses, furniture, beasts of burden, milch animals and ornaments is denominated a fee or perquisite."[41] Vyāsa defines perquisite as "the property which is given to bring the bride to the family of her husband, or which is given as a bribe or the like, that she may cheerfully go to the mansion of her lord."[42] Explaining those kinds of property which do not constitute the *strīdhana*, he is quoted in the *Smṛticandrikā* as follows: "Whatever has been given conditionally or with a fraudulent design by the father, brother or husband is declared not to be *strīdhana*".[43]

Referring to the kind of *strīdhana* over which women enjoy absolute right, Vyāsa says that whatever is presented at the time of nuptials to the bridegroom, intending [the benefit of the bride] belongs entirely to the bride and shall not be shared by kinsmen.[44] Āpastamba maintains that ornaments are the exclusive property of a wife and so is wealth given to her by kinsmen or friends according to some legislatures.[45] Manu and Viṣṇu ordain that such ornamental apparel as women wear during the lives of their husbands, the heirs of those husbands shall not divide among themselves, they who divide it among themselves fall deep (into sin).[46] Medhātithī in his commentary upon *Manusmṛti* recommends that all the ornaments worn by a wife with the assent of her husband is her own property, although they were not given by the husband.[47] But the ornaments or the like given to woman on condition that they are to be worn only on occasions of festivals, as well as property given with a defraudulent desire will not constitute *strīdhana* or separate property of a woman.[48] Kātyāyana while discussing what does not constitute *strīdhana* writes: "The wealth which is earned by mechanical arts, or which is received through affection from others is always subject to her husband's dominion. The rest is pronounced to be the woman' property."[49] In his digest on Hindu law, S.C. Sarkar argues that the above text of Kātyāyana must be interpreted as follows: "Wealth which is earned by mechanical arts, or received through affection from others is subject to the husband's control but still it constitutes *strīdhana* though not uncontrolled or absolute as the rest is."[50] On the question whether the immovable property constitutes women's peculiar property, Sarkar opines that the property purchased by a woman with her *strīdhana* as well as the income thereof her *strīdhana* constitutes *strīdhana* only, because the property so purchased, though in a different shape represents the *strīdhana* with which it was bought.[51] However, in the opinion of some other writers, the immovable property given to a woman by her husband does not constitute her *strīdhana*, for she is not regarded competent to alienate it without the consent of her husband during his lifetime, and even after his death. Again, Sarkar observes that although such property cannot, for the above reason, be held to be the woman's absolute *strīdhana* yet when it does not cease to belong to the woman and its course of decent is the same as that of any *strīdhana*, it cannot be excluded from the category of such property, but is to be regarded as *strīdhana* with restrictions.[52] As Bṛhaspati provides, any immovable and other property that has been given to women by their father in law can never be taken away by the coparceners.[53]

It becomes clear from the above discussion that no one definition of *strīdhana* is given by the *dharmaśāstrakāras*. Initially, six kinds of *strīdhana* were enumerated and the list got longer with time. However, broadly the following forms of property are considered by the lawgivers to fall within the scope of *strīdhana*:

1. *Adhyāgni* – gifts given before the nuptial fire.
2. *Adhyavāhanika* – gifts given by the time of bride's departure from the house of her parents to the house of her husband.
3. *Bhrātṛdatta*, *Mātṛdatta* and *Pitṛdatta* – gifts received from brother, mother and father respectively.
4. *Prītidatta* – gifts given as a token of love by father-in-law, mother-in-law and others at the time of her making obeisance at their feet.
5. *Anvādheya* – property given to a woman after her marriage by her husband, father and mother out of affection.
6. *Adhivedanika* – gifts given by her husband when he takes another wife.
7. *Bandhudatta* – gifts received from any relation.
8. *Śulka* – the property given to a female as consideration of marriage.

It can be inferred that the term *strīdhana* might not have been inclusive of all the properties that might have belonged to the women. In fact, if the meaning of *strīdhana* would have been 'all the properties which belong to women', there would not have been any need for the enumeration of particular descriptions of property. Sir Gooroodas Banerjee's observation seems to carry meaning in this regard:

> It may, therefore, be deduced from the texts quoted above that as rule, it is only gifts obtained by a woman from her relations, and her ornaments and apparel, that constitute her *strīdhana*, and that the only sorts of gifts from strangers which come under that denomination are, presents before the nuptial fire, and (according to some) presents made at the bridal procession. But neither gifts obtained from strangers at any other time, nor her acquisition by labour and skill would constitute her *strīdhana*. These limitations may appear to you unreasonable; and judged according to advanced notions

> about individual rights, so, no doubt, they really are. But you have seen that in the Hindu law the position of women is one of absolute dependence. Their time, therefore, is deemed to be absolutely at the disposal of their husbands; and consequently whatever is acquired by them at the expense of that time is deemed to belong to their husbands. As for the distinction between gifts from relations and those from strangers, that appears to be based upon the idea that outside the circle of her near relations, the social existence of a married woman is completely merged in that of her husband, so that she cannot be the recipient of a gift from any one but her relations, without making her husband a participator in it.[54]

Banerjee's observation should not be taken as a justification for narrowing the scope of *strīdhana*. It is significant in that it provides an insight into as to why the scope of *strīdhana* was limited.

All talks about the scope of *strīdhana* would remain incomplete without the interpretations given by different commentators upon it. However, it has to be borne in mind that the interpretations given by different commentators might have been influenced by the developments during the period when these commentators wrote. Again, it is also to be noted that the commentators' interpretations are referred to here only to facilitate a better understanding of the concept and scope of *strīdhana*, and not with an objective of analysing them as the study of commentaries actually falls out of the scope of the present research.

In fact, from the tenth century onwards there was a qualitative change in the approach towards property and property relations. It was possible after the advent of Jimūtavāhana (circa AD 1100–50) and Vijñaneśvara (circa AD 1080–1100). The *Dāyabhāga* of Jimūtavāhana and the *Mitākśarā* of Vijñṛneśvara became so important that throughout the successive ages these two works and their legal interpretations came to be regarded as almost the sole source of the Hindu laws relating to ownership, partition and inheritance.[55]

Vijñaneśwara, the author of *Mitākśarā,* to whom the credit to broaden the scope of *strīdhana* goes, observes that the term *strīdhana* (woman's property) conforms in its import with its etymology, and is not technical; for, if the literal sense be admissible, a technical acceptation is improper.[56] Accordingly, for him, *strīdhana* includes property of any description which belongs to women. This includes, that given by the father, mother, husband or brother, that which was presented by the maternal uncles and the rest at the time of wedding before the nuptial fire, and a gift on a second marriage or gratuity on account of supersession; as also the property which she may have acquired by inheritance, purchase, partition, acceptance or finding. He says that all this is *strīdhana* according to Manu and the rest.[57] He has deduced this 'unlimited' sense of *strīdhana* on the basis of the term 'ādya', in the text of Yājñavalkya. While some scholars agree with this interpretation of the term *ādya* by Vijñaneśwara, some others reject it outrightly. In fact, this interpretation got into a lot of controversy. Among those of the commentators who accepted or followed it, the prominent ones are Aparārka, Nanda Pandit, Mitramiśra and Kamalākara. Those who refuted it include: Jimūtvāhana, Devaṇṇabhaṭṭa, Śrikṛṣṇa and Viśvarūpa. Among the more recent writers, Altekar refuses to accept the interpretation of Vijñaneśwara. He argues that there can not be any doubt that the original verses in *Yājñavalkya Smṛti* (II. 143–44) did not contemplate the inclusion of any of the categories mentioned by Vijñaneśwara within the scope of *strīdhana*. Even it cannot be said with certainty that the term *'ādyam'* which has been used by Vijñaneśwara expending the scope of *strīdhana,* really occurred in the original verse of Yājñavalkya or not.[58] He further writes, "But even supposing that the reading of Vijñṛneswara is the genuine one, we have to concede that Yājñavalkya could hardly have intended to include items like inheritance and share at partition under the term 'etcetera'. These were very important items which not only increased extensively the woman's rights, but circumscribed those of the coparceners. Yājñavalkya would surely have specifically and prominently mentioned them in his description of *strīdhana*, instead of smuggling them surreptitiously under the term 'etcetera'. The word etcetera, if at all used by him, must have been obviously intended to include items like bride-price, gifts from grandfather and other relations, and presents received after the marriage, which are mentioned in the immediately following line."[59]

The interpretation of the verse of Yājñavalkya also is the point where the *Dāyabhāga* is in direct conflict with the *Mitākśarā*. Jimutavāhana, the author of *Dāyabhāga* completely rejects *Mitākśarā's* unlimited interpretation of the term *strīdhana*. He adopts reading of Yājñavalkya's text different from the ordinary one substituting the expletive *eva* for the suppletory term *Ādya* (and the rest) which forms the basis of that interpretation. He rather restricts the application of the term *strīdhana* to certain descriptions of property belonging to a woman. Quoting the text of Viṣṇu, he says, "What has been given to a woman by her father, her mother, her son or her brother, what has been presented to her on her husband's espousal of another wife, what has been given to her by kindred, as well as her perquisite, and a gift subsequent are a woman's separate property."[60] Explaining the term 'kindred' in the above quote, he says that it must be intended at including maternal uncle and others, for the father and the rest are specified by the appropriate terms.[61]

However, *Dāyabhāga,* like *Mitākśarā* opines that enumeration of six kinds of property of a woman is not aimed at restricting a greater number of it. It says: "Since the various sorts of separate property of a woman have been thus propounded without any restriction of number, the number of six (as specified by Manu and other) is not definitely meant. But the texts of the sages merely intend an explanation of woman's separate property."[62]

Referring to Kātyāyana's text regarding the term 'a gift subsequent', Jimutvāhana says that Kātyāyana includes following kinds of property under the term: "What has been received by a woman from the family of her husband at a time posterior to her marriage, is called a gift subsequent, and so is that which is similarly received by a woman after her nuptials, either from her husband or from her parents, through the affection of the giver, Bhṛgu pronounces to be a gift subsequent."[63] Further, he explains the term 'kindred' used in the above text of Kātyāyana as follows: "By the word 'kindred' her father and mother are denoted. Hence, the meaning is this: any thing received subsequently to the marriage, from (maternal or paternal uncle or other) persons who are related through the father or the mother, or from those two parents themselves, or so received from the husband, or from those two parents themselves, or so received from the husband, or from his family, namely her father-in-law and rest; is a gift subsequent."[64] Again, while defining *adhyāgni* and *adhyāvāhnika* kinds of *strīdhana*, he refers to Kātyāyana's text which runs thus: "What is given to women at the time of their marriage, near the nuptial fire, is celebrated by the wise as the woman's peculiar property bestowed before the nuptial fire. That again which a woman receives while she is conducted from the paternal abode to her husband's dwelling is instanced as the separate property of a woman, under the name of gift presented in the bridal procession."[65] Explaining the *adhivedanika*, he says that the wealth which is given to gratify a first wife by a man desirous of marrying a second, is a gift on a second marriage, for its object is to obtain another wife.[66] Further, elaborating upon the term 'husband's donation', he writes, "Her 'husband's donation' (*dāya*) is wealth given (*datta*) to her by her husband. For Manu and others notice that which is given (*datta*) to her by him, without mentioning his donation (*dāya*) and Nārada specifies donation (*dāya*) without any separate notice of what is given (*datta*)."67 Later, he says that "husband's donation" is used for wealth given by the husband. Thus, Kātyāyana, says: "Let the woman enjoy her husband's donation as she pleases, when he is dead but while he lives, she should carefully preserve it or else commit it to the family."[68] Explaining the above text of Kātyāyana, the author of *Dāyabhāga* writes: "The meaning of the passage is this: wealth given to her by her husband, she may dispose of, as she pleases, when he is dead; but while he is alive she should carefully preserve it. This is intended as a caution against extravagance."[69]

He refers to the views of Devala regarding the definition of *śulka*, "Her subsistence, her ornaments, her perquisite, and her gains are the separate property of a woman. She herself exclusively enjoys it, and her husband has no right to use it, unless in distress."[70] The text quoted here in the *Dāyabhāga* establishes woman's exclusive right of enjoyment over the perquisite of a woman but her husband can take it from her in case of distress. But, the word 'distress' has not been properly explained, hence woman's absolute power of disposal on such sort of property has been in question.

According to Jimutavāhana, the main characteristic of *strīdhana* is that woman shall enjoy absolute right over this kind of property. "That alone is her peculiar property over which she has power to give, sell or use, independently of her husband's control."[71] In support of his view, he quotes Kātyāyana: "The wealth which is earned by mechanical arts or which is received through affection from any other, is always subject to her husband's dominion. The rest is pronounced to be the woman's property."[72] The property which she acquires through mechanical arts or receives from strangers can be taken by the husband even though there is no distress. Hence, though the wealth is seemingly hers, it does not constitute woman's property; because she has no independent power over it.

Thus, the commentators differ on the question as to what constitutes *strīdhana*. They are further divided on the issue as to if inherited property constitutes *strīdhana* or not. While *Mitākśarā* includes inherited property in the *strīdhana*, *Dāyabhāga* totally rejects the view that inherited property constitutes *strīdhana*. Sir Banerjee opines that the property which women get through the means of inheritance can be divided into two kinds: (a) a woman may inherit the ordinary property of a male owner, and (b) she may also inherit the *strīdhana* of a female.[73] He says that these two cases are distinct, and should be separately considered. In the former case, the relations from whom a woman may inherit are her husband, her father, her son, grandson or other male lineal descendants and her brother and *sagotra* kinsmen of her husband; in the latter case, they are her mother, her mother's mother and her daughter.[74] Again, *Mitākśarā* recognizes widow's right to inherit her husband's property only if he be separated and not otherwise. But Jimūtavāhana recognizes her right to inherit her husband's property even if her deceased husband is not separated. However, though Jimūtavāhana allows woman to inherit her issueless husband's property, he does not invest her with the absolute right over it. He limits her interest to mere enjoyment with moderation, and declares that on her death, the estate should devolve not on the heirs who inherit her *strīdhana*, but on the next heirs of her husband. Regarding daughter's right to inherit her father's property, Jimūtavāhana says, "In like manner, if the succession have devolved on a daughter, those persons, who would have been heirs of her father's property in her default, take the succession on her death; not the heirs of the daughter's property."[75] Thus, according to *Dāyabhāga*, the property which a woman obtains through the means of inheritance does not constitute her *strīdhana* because of the two reasons: first, woman lack absolute right over the inherited property; second, the property which a woman obtains through the means of inheritance, after her demise does not go to those who are entitled to inherit her peculiar property, rather it goes to the inheritors of paternal property.

In contrast to the opinion of Jimūtavāhana, Vijñaneśwara regards the share which a woman gets at the time of partition as *strīdhana,* and thus includes inherited property within the scope of *strīdhana*. He says, "... and also property which she may have acquired by inheritance, purchase, partition, seizure or finding are denominated by Manu and the rest 'woman's property."[76]

It may be concluded from the above discussion that to define as well as to find the scope of *strīdhana* is a complicated task. Since the views of both the lawgivers and commentators, who have interpreted the *dharmaśāstras,* have given varying definitions and scope of *strīdhana.*

Succession to *Strīdhana*

Strīdhana had a character different from that of the ordinary property of the family. Accordingly, special laws were formulated regarding its succession and inheritance. These laws were complex and based on the mode of acquiring *strīdhana*. Also, the type of marriage had a bearing on the order of succession to *strīdhana*. At one place, Manu says that the property of the mother is the share of the unmarried daughter alone.[77] However, later he says that when the mother has died, all the uterine brothers and sisters shall equally divide the mother's estate.[78] This seems to contradict the previous statement. Again, he says that something should be given on the score of affection even to the daughters of these daughters out of the estate of their maternal grandmother.[79] Still later, after describing what constitutes *strīdhana,* Manu said that it is ordained that such property shall go to the offspring of the woman on her death.[80] In case of her having died issueless, the property should go to the husband in case of unblamable marriages and to the parents of the woman in case of blamable marriages.[81] It is further said that the ornaments worn by women during their husbands' lifetime should not be divided by his heirs, otherwise they become outcastes.[82] Thus, Manu's stand remains unclear regarding the succession to *strīdhana*. It seems that both the sons and daughters were entitled to such property, in the absence of whom it shall be divided as already mentioned. Yājñavalkya sounds clearer in this regard. According to him, the wealth belonging to the mother should be distributed by daughters among themselves, after clearing out her liability during lifetime. In case, there are no daughters, the sons are entitled to distribute that wealth among them.[83]

In case of the woman dying issueless, her money shall go to the husband if she had been married according to the first four forms of marriage (*Brāhma*, *Daiva*, *Ārṣa* and *Prājāpatya*). Having been married according to any of the remaining forms of marriage, her property shall go to her father.[84] Viṣṇu also stated similarly as Yājñavalkya except that he does not specify that in the absence of daughters, sons are entitled to *strīdhana.*[85] Like Manu, he also says that the ornaments worn by women when their husbands were alive shall not be divided by the heirs, lest they shall become outcasts.[86] Bṛhaspati provides a share to the daughter in the *strīdhana* only if she is not betrothed. If she is married, she shall receive only an honorary trifle.[87] Vasiṣṭha only says that the nuptial present of the mother shall be divided by the daughters amongst themselves.[88] Gautama gives the right to inheritance of *strīdhana* to only those daughters of a woman who are unmarried and not well settled in life.[89] Thus though daughters have been a party to the inheritance of *strīdhana*, not all the lawgivers have recognized them as the first and sole owners. Also, not much is said to clarify the stands of individual lawgivers. Hence, it becomes imperative to refer to the commentaries regarding the rules of succession of *strīdhana*. However, even the commentaries do not give any general rule of succession to woman's property as different schools of Hindu law have propounded different rules in this regard.

Mitākśarā on Succession to Strīdhana

Vijñaneśwara gives the following order of succession to *strīdhana*:

> "If a woman dies 'without issue' (that is, leaving no progeny i.e., having no daughter, nor daughter's son, nor son, nor son's son), the woman's property, as above described, shall be taken by her kinsmen; namely her husband and the rest, as will be explained."[90] Thus, according to Vijñaneśwara, the kinsmen have been declared to be competent to succeed to a woman's property. The author now distinguishes different heirs according to the differences in the forms of marriage.[91] Of a woman dying without issue, and who had become a wife by any of the four modes of marriage viz: *Brāhma*, *Daiva*, *Ārṣa* and *Prājāpatya*, the property belongs, in the first place, to her husband. On failure of him, it goes to his nearest kinsmen (*sapiṇḍas*). But, in the other forms of marriage (*Āsura* to *Paiśāca*), the property of childless woman goes to her parents, that is, to her father and mother. The succession devolves first on the mother, and then to the father. On failure of them, their next of kin takes the succession.[92] In all forms of marriage, if the woman has issue, her property devolves on her daughters. In this place, by the term 'daughters', grand daughters are signified; for the immediate female descendants are expressly mentioned in a preceding passage: 'the daughters share the residue of their mother's property.[93] Hence, if the mother be dead, daughters take her property in the first instance and where both married and unmarried daughters exist, the unmarried daughters take the succession; but, on failure of them, the married daughter; and where there exist both daughters who are provided for and those who are unendowed, the unendowed take the succession first; but on failure of them, those who are endowed. In support of this, he cites Gautama, according to whom, a woman's property goes to her daughters 'unmarried or unprovided', as already mentioned. 'Unprovided' are such as are destitute of wealth or without issue.'[94] But this applies to wealth other than the fee or gratuity. For that goes to brothers of the whole blood, conformably with the text of Gautama: 'The sister's fee belongs to the uterine brothers after the mother.'[95] On failure of all daughters, the grand daughters in the female line take the succession under this text: 'If she leaves progeny, it goes to her (daughter's) daughters'.[96]

If there be a multitude of these (granddaughters) children of different mothers, and unequal in number, share should be allotted to them through their mothers, as directed by Gautama: 'Or the partition may be according to the mothers; and particular distribution may be made in the respective sets.'[97] But if there be daughters as well as daughters' daughters, a trifle only is to be given to the granddaughters as declared by Manu.[98] On failure also of daughter's daughters, the daughter's sons are entitled to the succession. Thus Nārada says: 'Let daughters divide their mother's wealth; or on failure of daughters, their male issue.'[99]

If there be no grandsons in the female line, sons take the property, as declared by Manu.[100] But though springing from a different mother, the daughter of a rival wife, being superior by class shall take the property of a childless woman who belongs to an inferior class. Or, on failure of the stepdaughter, her issue shall succeed. On failure of sons, grandsons inherit their paternal grandmother's wealth. For Gautama says: They who share the inheritance must pay the 'debt' (*Gautama.* XII.40); and the grandsons are bound to discharge the debts of their paternal grandmother; for the text expresses, 'Debts must be paid by sons and sons' sons. (*Yāj.*II.40).[101] On failure of grandsons also, the husband and other relatives above mentioned are successors to the wealth.[102]

If a betrothed girl dies, the bridegroom shall take the rings and other presents, or the nuptial gratuity which had been previously given by him (to the bride). Paying, however, the charges of both sides; that is, clearing or discharging the expense which has been incurred both by the person who gave the girl and by himself, he may take the residue. But her uterine brothers shall have the ornaments and other gifts, which may have been presented to the maiden by her maternal grandfather, or other relations; as well as the property which may have been regularly inherited by her.[103]

Dāyabhāga on Succession to Strīdhana

Dāyabhāga, cites Manu on the subject of succession to the peculiar property of woman,[104] and on its basis, suggests the participation of both the brother and the sister in the inheritance. According to the author of *Dāyabhāga,* it should be interpreted as implying the share of sisters and brothers of the whole blood.[105] He further cites Bṛhaspati[106] and others to support his contention. On failure of both of them, the succession devolves with equal right on the married daughter who has a son, and on her who may have male issue. For, by means of their sons, they may present oblations at solemn obsequies.[107] Neither a barren, nor a widowed daughter inherits; for these present no oblations at solemn obsequies, either in person or by means of their offspring. Accordingly Nārada says: "On failure of the son, the daughter inherits; for she equally continues the lineage."[108] But if there be a son's and a daughter's son claiming the succession, the son has the exclusive title; since the married daughter is debarred from the inheritance by the son, therefore, the son of the debarred daughter shall be excluded by the son of the person who bars her claim.[109] On failure of all these above mentioned, including the daughter's son, the barren and the widowed daughters both succeed to their mother's property; for they also are her offspring; and the right of others to inherit is declared to be on failure of issue.[110]

However, as far as the nuptial presents of the mother are concerned, in case of *Brāhma* marriage, what has been received by a woman at the nuptial fire goes, after her death, first to her daughters. Again the right devolves first on the maiden daughter; if there be none, it descends to the betrothed daughter; or for want of such, it goes to a married daughter; or, on failure of all daughters, it devolves on the son. For the husband's right of succession is relative to property of a wife who leaves no issue whatever.[111] However, further complex interpretations are given by the author of *Dāyabhāga,* the details of these seem to fall out of the scope of the present research.

It is clear that there were no fixed rules of succession to *strīdhana* and both the lawgivers and commentators have given varying interpretations. However, what could be deduced with a measure of certainty is that the succession to *strīdhana* depends, first on the marital status of the deceased women, and secondly, on the form on her marriage, whether it was approved or unapproved; thirdly, on the nature of the *strīdhana* i.e., the source from which the *strīdhana* had come; and lastly, on the schools of Hindu Law she was governed by.

Women's Dominion over *Strīdhana*

Though women were vested with rights to some form of property in the limited sense of the term, it is important to find the extent of the power which women really possessed over their *strīdhana.* This has to be seen in the light of two aspects, one, that to what extent it was regarded as exclusive possession of women, and two, what was the extent of the power of alienation that women had over such property. The early *smṛtikāras* were quite reluctant to invest women with absolute and exclusive right over the *strīdhana.* Manu declares that a wife ought not to alienate even her own property without her husband's sanction.[112] However, he also provides that a husband could not deprive the wife of her *strīdhana.* According to him, a husband can temporarily take his wife's *strīdhana,* if she is inimical to him. He further states that her other relatives had no right to use her *strīdhana,* no matter how direly they needed it and that on doing so, they shall be punished like thieves.[113] He further says that those relations who live on the property of women commit sin and sink into hell.[114] They shall be treated as outcastes, if they divided the ornaments of a widow she wore during her husband's life-time.[115] Later, *strīdhana* was divided into two categories, *saudāyika* and *asaudāyika. Saudāyika strīdhana* included free gifts given by relations like the father, the mother, or the husband out of affection. Women were apparently accorded complete control over this category. The rest of the *strīdhana* was *asaudāyika strīdhana* which can only be enjoyed by the woman during her lifetime but can not be disposed of. To quote *Kātyāyana*: "Whatever is obtained by the married or unmarried girl, at her husband's house or at her father's house, from the brother or parents is called *saudāyika* (dowry). After having obtained the *saudāyika* property, women are free to do what they like with it, since it has been given to them through kindness as a means of livelihood. With regard to the *saudāyika* property, women have been declared to be free to do what they like, as to selling it or giving it away, even in case of immovable property."[116] Nārada, excluding the immovable property from this category, says that what has been given to the woman by her husband through love, she may, on his death, enjoy it as she likes, or give it away except the immovable property.[117]

Again, Kātyāyana proclaims: "Neither husband, nor son, nor father, nor brothers have the right to take away or spend *strīdhana.* If anyone of them forcibly spends the *strīdhana*, he should be made to repay it with interest, and should also suffer punishment for having done so. If, however, he spends it with her consent, and in a conciliatory manner, he should be made to repay only the principal, if he has the requisite means."[118] So long as a woman is alive, her husband, sons, brother-in-law or paternal relation have no right over her *strīdhana*; if they misappropriate it, they should be punished.[119] Kātyāyana mentions the following restriction to the rule: "What a woman has received as a gift from her husband she may dispose it of at pleasure after his death, if it be movable; but as long as he lives let her preserve it with frugality, or she may commit to his family."[120] Manu also says that so long as a woman is alive, her husband, sons, brother-in-law or paternal relation have no right over her *strīdhana*, if they misappropriate it, they should be punished.[121] In consonance with such indictments, Viṣṇu also said that the heirs shall not divide among themselves the ornaments worn by women when their husbands were alive; by doing so, they shall become outcastes.[122] Āpastamba also tries to protect women's property by laying down the dictum that those relations of a woman, who live by selling carts, clothes, and golden ornaments which have become her *strīdhana*, commit sin; and they come by a worse fate in the next world.[123]

Women's absolute right over her *strīdhana* is recognized by Bṛhaspati also. He says that such property, whether immovable or other, as has been given to women by their father in law, can never be taken away from them by the co-heirs. Such a property, whether immovable or not, as has been given to woman by her father-in-law, can never be taken away from her by her co-heirs.[124]

Thus most of the *smṛtikāras* lay down that woman has absolute and independent ownership over her *saudāyika strīdhana* (gifts from affectionate relations), except the gifts received from her husband. However, she had absolute power to dispose them of only after his death, in case it did not consist of immovable property.

However, some of the *smṛtikāras* have recognized husband's right to use his wife's *strīdhana* under exceptional circumstances, when the family is in distress, for religious ceremonies, during illness or in times when some great calamity has befallen. Again, while according to some of them, the *strīdhana* utilized by the husband under the pressure of any of such circumstances should be returned; others, including Yājñavalkya, are rather lenient regarding its repayment. According to him, if a husband utilizes the *strīdhana* for discharging any great deed, to cope with famine, or for treatment and for avoiding the imprisonment, he needn't return it to his wife again.[125] Like all the other issues associated with women's property, Kātyāyana has written elaborately on this subject. He says that husband must not take his wife's *strīdhana* without her consent but if he takes it with her consent, he shall pay back the principal amount only and that too when he has enough wealth to restore it.[126] Whatever she has put amicably into the hands of her husband afflicted by disease, suffering from distress, or sorely pressed by creditors, he should repay that by his own free will. Still Kātyāyana, protecting the wife's right, writes: "Yet more, if he has taken a second wife, and no longer gives his wife the honour due to her, the king shall compel him, even by violence, to restore her property, though it was put amicably into his hands." 'In case he fails to repay', instructs Kātyāyana, 'the husband is about to give some part of her property as *strīdhana* to his wife; if he dies without fulfilling this condition his heirs are required to do so.'[127] Emphasizing woman's absolute right over her *strīdhana,* Nārada says that no adverse possession could not deprive a woman of her title to *strīdhana.*[128] It is clear that according to most of the lawgivers, wife's *strīdhana* (except the *saudāyika*) can be used by the husband. But the husband is invested with this right with the condition that he would be liable to return it. If the husband used it for some other purposes, besides the ones enumerated above, without the consent of his wife, he was considered to be guilty.

It may be inferred that gifts as a gesture of affection from the kindred, called in technical terms *saudāyika strīdhana,* alone constitutes a woman's absolute property over which she had at all times an independent power of alienation. Her husband had only a qualified right over it, namely, the right of using it in times of distress. Again, however, it needs to be tested whether this right was only theoretical or could be exercise by women practically also. Thus, there is little doubt that though women were granted rights to property, they were more in theory, and were limited by various other indictments even in theory by the lawgivers. Also, how much they wielded these rights in practice, is another query. Again, this is quite in line with the existing social order which was largely patriarchal, which was characterized by patrilocality for the girls, and as such, a right of girls over immovable property would have meant transfer of property to another clan to which the girl went after marriage. Hence only movable property was considered to be woman's exclusive property. Again, even after marriage, the hold over the *asaudāyika strīdhana* of the woman was maintained by the males, not to give her complete authority over immovable property.

Legal Rights

Besides the property rights, some other rights were conceded to the women by the lawgivers. However, it needs to be analysed if they were rights in real sense of the term or merely privileges.

General Rights to All the Women

Right to the Protection of Property

Certain norms were laid down for the protection of the property belonging to women. Yājñavalkya declares the loss of ownership of land to one who possesses it for twenty years, and loss of elephant, horse, gem etc. to one who has taken these things in possession for ten years. However, he adds that these limitations of twenty and ten years do not hold good in cases of the properties of women.[129] Viṣṇu also enjoins upon the king to protect the property of minors, helpless persons and of women.[130]

Right against being Raped

Rape was considered a serious offence and punishments were laid down for the guilty. Manu says that he who violates an unwilling maiden shall suffer corporal punishment, but a man who enjoys a willing maiden shall not suffer corporal punishment, if his caste be the same as hers.[131] Again, he says that if any man forcibly contaminates a maiden, two of his fingers shall be instantly cut off, and he shall pay a fine of six hundred *paṇas*.[132] Manu's stand as to what should be the punishment in such a case is not clear. Later he considers defiling a girl as one of the minor offences causing only a loss of the caste.[133] However, Yājñavalkya is clearer in this regard. According to him, no offence is committed, if a maiden of an inferior caste, is lustfully disposed; but if she is ravished against her will, the cutting off of the fingers is the penalty. Death is the penalty, if a similar offence is committed with a woman of a higher caste.[134] *Varṇa* of the female determined the degree of punishment. It is obvious that surpassing the *varṇa* norms was considered a more serious crime than a heinous crime like rape. Further, Yājñavalkya says that for committing rape on female servants who are prevented by their husbands to visit other people, one shall have to pay a fine of ten *paṇas*, according to law. If many persons know a woman against her will, each of them should be fined twenty-four *paṇas*.[135] Again, instead of the enormity of sorrow that a crime like rape would have brought on the victimized female, what bothered the lawgiver more was whether the rape had husband's sanction or not. A crime like rape is sure to bring same misery to a woman irrespective of her *varṇa* status or her being a servant. Again, the injury done to a woman by his kind of a deplorable deed cannot be undone by the payment of few *paṇas*. In fact, to call these as rights of the victim of rape is itself ridiculous. It is discussed here only with an intention to pose a question to all those who uphold the lawbooks as representing the Hindu way of life, and even more, at times, representative texts of Indian culture.

Bṛhaspati also imposed a fine of fifty *paṇas* on sexually reviling a sister or other relation of another man.[136] It is to be note that the victim is addressed as a man's sister or other relation. It seems to indicate that the fine was to be paid to the man, as if the injury is done to him more than the victim herself. However, later Bṛhaspati lays down the confiscation of the entire wealth of the violator of an unwilling woman, cutting of his penis and scrotum and being paraded on an ass; as the punishment.[137] In the case of enjoyment of a woman by fraud, the punishment remains the same except for the cutting of penis and scrotum, instead of which he prescribes branding with the mark of a female organ and banishment from the town.[138] Cutting of the penis and scrotum must have resulted in the death of the violator, hence it may be inferred that death was the punishment in the previous case. Again, Bṛhaspati lays down punishment for the victimized female too. According to him, when a woman has been ravished against her will, she shall be kept in the house well guarded, smeared with ashes, lying on a low couch, and receiving a bare maintenance only.[139] Pārāśara says nothing about the treatment to be meted out to the rapist; instead only prescribes penances for the victim to regain purity.[140] Irrespective of the fact that the woman held no responsibility for the happening, which must have rather left her torn within and miserable, she was to be punished for it, and the punishment was stringent in case of violation of the *varṇa* norm. Likhita omits all the other details and only says that there is atonement for the guilt of an abettor or accomplice of a ravisher of female chastity, but the ravisher alone should be regarded as *brahmāghātī*.[141]

Right against being Carried away by Force

According to Yājñavalkya, the king should inflict the highest form of pecuniary punishment upon a person who carries away a maiden of the same caste who was adorned for marriage. In ordinary cases, the lowest form of pecuniary punishment should be his penalty. In case of carrying away of a maiden of higher caste, death is the penalty.[142] Again, *varṇa* of the victim determines the degree of punishment.

Right against Abandonment before Marriage

Yājñavalkya lays down that a person who conceals the apparent defects of a maiden and offers her to the bridegroom, is liable for pecuniary punishment for such adventure and the person who abandons a meritorious maiden, is also liable for the same punishment.[143] Viṣṇu also says that one who abandons a faultless girl shall be punished as a thief.[144]

Right against Publicizing actual Blemishes and False declaration of Blemishes

A person who falsely accuses a woman of having blemishes, is to be fined. Yājñavalkya says that one who accuses falsely, a number of defects in the maiden prior to marriage, is liable for a punishment of one hundred *paṇas*.[145] On exposing deficiencies like carrying ailments or having committed debauchery, falsely, a fine no less than two hundred *paṇas* was prescribed by him. Again, a fine no less than one hundred *paṇas* is prescribed for publicizing such defects of a maiden, even though it may be true.[146] According to Viṣṇu also, he who falsely accuses a girl of having blemishes, shall pay the highest amercement.[147]

Rights of the Wife

Right to Maintenance

Maintenance had to be secured to the wife in cases where one was leaving for business, or in case of desertion, divorce or resorting to polygamy. According to Manu, a man should go abroad for business only after securing maintenance for the wife, as the virtuous wife may also go corrupt in the wake of lack of arrangements for subsistence.[148] It has to be noted that to prevent the wife from going astray is the major concern here. After mentioning the conditions when a man can resort to polygamy,[149] Yājñavalkya says that he should provide the aforesaid wife with proper maintenance if polygamy has been resorted to while she is living. Upon neglecting this, the husband shall become prey to evils.[150] While the wife is said to deserve maintenance from the husband in spite of her being carrying blemishes or defects, later Yājñavalkya lays down the provision of one-third of earnings to be given to the wife in case she is meritorious. He says that a king has an absolute right to order a man to give one-third of his earnings to the wife divorced by that man provided that she should be obedient, efficient, mother of a son and humble and in case such a man is poor, the king can order him to provide food grains and apparels from his earnings.[151] Again, he says that if someone's wife is surviving, but he remarries, he will have to pay an amount equal to the expense incurred on such second marriage to his first wife. In case, the first wife has already received *strīdhana*, only half of the expense so incurred on second marriage is to be paid.[152]

Right against Abandonment

Abandonment of the wife is denounced in any condition. According to Vasiṣṭha, a wife, even though tainted by sin, or being quarrelsome, having left the house, having suffered criminal force, or have fallen into the hands of thieves; must not be abandoned; to forsake her is not prescribed by the sacred law. Let him wait for the time of her courses; by her temporary uncleanness she becomes pure.[153] Atri also holds similar views.[154] Viṣṇu also says that he, who forsakes his blameless wife, shall be punished as a thief.[155]

Right to Remarry

Remarriage was not sanctioned by the lawgivers in general. Manu rejects a second husband for virtuous women. He says that she who cohabits with a man of higher caste forsaking her own husband who belongs to a lower one, will become contemptible in this world, and is called a remarried woman (*parapūrvā*). By violating her duty towards her husband, a wife is disgraced in this world, after death she enters the womb of a jackal, and is tormented by diseases, which is the punishment for her sin.[156] A virtuous wife is defined as one who, controlling her thoughts, words and deeds, never slights her lord and thus resides with her husband in heaven.[157] The reward for such a wife is that she gains the highest renown in this life and a place near her husband in the next world.[158]

At another place, Manu perhaps becomes ambiguous and so says that if the future husband of a maiden dies after betrothal, then her brother-in-law shall marry her according to the rule mentioned.[159] However, again, he says that he should approach her only till an issue be had.[160] Thus this might actually be a reference to *niyoga* and not remarriage. Again, it is laid down by Manu for the wife to wait for the husband to return for eight, six or three years depending on the reason for his departure.[161] It seems that a remarriage is permitted to the wife after the lapse of the prescribed period. If this is true, then it is curious that remarriage is permitted to a woman on desertion, but not on the death of the husband. It seems to imply that death can not dissolve the tie of marriage; however, the husband's action (by not returning) can lead to dissolution of the tie.

Yājñavalkya also says that a maiden is offered only once throughout her lifetime, whereby, the person reoffering her to another man thereafter is liable for punishment not less than that of a thief. However, the maiden can be offered to another person, if he comes forward and it is proved that he is more qualified and meritorious than the earlier with whom the ring ceremony was celebrated.[162] He again says that a woman who has either enjoyed coition or is intact is called *punarbhū* on remarriage and one who divorces her husband for another person voluntarily is called *svairiṇī*.[163] Again, he includes the husband of remarried woman in the list of people to be censured in *śrāddha*.[164] Thus, where there is scriptural sanction the entry is marked with rites, while where there is no sanction, it is marked by exclusion from some other rituals besides the non-performance of rites to mark the occasion. Vasiṣṭha defines remarried woman as one who leaving the husband of her youth, and having lived with others, re-enters his family, and one who leaving an impotent, outcast or mad husband, or after the death of her husband takes another lord.[165] It is notable that there might have been cases where the woman, after having chosen to live with others forsaking her husband, was allowed to re-enter the household of the previous husband, if she chose to do so. That women were not entirely choiceless, may be it is this fact the verse is pointing towards; though the authors of the texts under study sought to render them in that state. Vasiṣṭha permits marrying a girl who had been abducted by force, and not been wedded according to the sacred texts, as also in case where a girl at the death of her husband had been merely wedded by the recitation of sacred texts, but the marriage had not been consummated.[166] Though this shows the liberal attitude of Vasiṣṭha, these cases were not treated as remarriage by him. However, Viṣṇu, while defining *punarbhū* includes one who being still a virgin is married for the second time, and one, who, though not legally married more than once, had lived with another man before her lawful marriage.[167] The tone of Angiras goes stricter and he defines *punarbhū* as one who after having been promised to be given away in marriage to one, is given to another. He prohibits the acceptance of food from such a maiden.[168] However, it seems that more than the remarriage, it was the breaking of the promise, that was the reason behind such a censure. Uśanā also included those who marry widows and the son of a widow or remarried woman among those who are disqualified to be present at a *śrāddha* ceremony.[169]

Nārada's attitude seems to be milder in this regard. He says that if a man is potent with another woman but impotent with his own wife, his wife shall take another husband.[170] Again, he says that when a bridegroom goes abroad after having espoused a maiden, let the maiden wait till her menses have passed three times, and then choose another bridegroom.[171] Later, he laid down the period of waiting to be eight, six and four years respectively for *brāhmaṇa, kśatriya* and *vaiśya* woman; and half of the respective periods mentioned above in case she is issueless. After the lapse of the stipulated time, she was permitted to remarry, without incurring any guilt of offence. No specific period is laid down for a *śūdra* woman.[172] He reiterates this by saying that a woman may be justified in taking another husband in five cases of legal necessity: when her husband is lost or dead, when he has become a religious ascetic, when he is impotent, and when he has been expelled from caste.[173] Pārāśara also mentions impotence of the husband as one of the five conditions when the wife is permitted to remarry.[174]

Right against Repayment of Debt

A woman was expected to pay only that debt which she had promised to repay, that which she had contracted along with her husband, and what she had done herself.[175] According to Viṣṇu also, a woman shall not be compelled to pay the debt of her husband or son.[176]

Right against Unnatural Intercourse

Yājñavalkya lays down a fine of twenty four *paṇas* on a person holding intercourse with the wife at any other place but the sexual organ.[177] In a similar nerve, Vasiṣṭha also says that let him not commit a crime against nature with her. The ancestors of a man who commits an unnatural crime with a wedded wife, feed during that month on his semen, All unnatural intercourse is against the sacred law.[178] It can be inferred from the above discussion that though they may seem insufficient, some legal rights were granted to the women. They may seem to be more in the shape of privileges seen from the point of view of contemporary definition of rights. Also, as has been observed, some of these were indirectly directed towards upholding the order only. However, this does not seem to hold true for all the cases in general.

Notes

1. *Ṛ V.*I.141.1; III.2.12; VI.26.1; VII.76.5; VIII.99.8.
2. *Ṛ V.*X.85.13–38.
3. Bhattacharyya, N.N., "Proprietary Rights of Women in Ancient India", in Roy, Kumkum (ed.), *Women in Early Indian Societies*, Manohar, New Delhi, 1999, p. 117.
4. *Manu*.IX.44.
5. *T.S.*VI.2.1.1.
6. Bhattacharyya, N.N., op. cit., p. 117.
7. *Āpas.Dh.S.*II.6.14.19, *Baudh.Dh.S.*II.2.49 and *Vasiṣṭha*.XVII.48–9.
8. Bhattacharyya, N.N., op. cit., p. 118.
9. *Manu*.IX.104.
10. *Manu*.IX.105.
11. *Manu*.IX.118.
12. *Yāj*.II.8.117,124.
13. *Yāj*.II.8.135,136.
14. Bhattacharyya, N.N., op. cit., p. 119.
15. *Viṣṇu*.XVII.4–5.
16. *Manu*.IX.127.
17. *Manu*.IX.130.
18. *Manu*.IX.139.
19. *Yāj*. I.8.128.
20. *Bṛhas*.XXV.56–58.
21. *Vasiṣṭha*.XVII.15–17.
22. *Viṣṇu*.XV.4–6.
23. *Gautama*.XXIX.
24. *Likhita*.51–53.
25. *Yāj*.II.8.135–136.
26. *Bṛhas*.XXV.46–48.
27. *Bṛhas*.XXV.49.
28. *Bṛhas*.XXV.53.
29. *Bṛhas*.XXV.54.
30. *Bṛhas*.XXV.55.
31. *Gautama*.XXIX.
32. *Manu*.IX.217.
33. *Bṛhas*.XXV.63–64.
34. *Manu*.IX.194.
35. *Viṣṇu*.XVII.18.
36. *Yāj*.II.143–144.
37. *Nārada*.XIII.8.
38. *Nārada*.I.28.

39. Quoted in *Dāyabhāga*. IV.I. 5, 6, 13.
40. Quoted in *Mitāksarā*, Ch. II, Sec. XI.5.
41. *Vyavasthā Darpaṇa: A Digest of Hindu Law* by Sarkar, S.C., Pt. I, 3rd ed., Vidya Bhushan, Calcutta, 1883, p. 212.
42. Colebrook, H.T., *A Digest of Hindu Law on Contracts and Succession*, Vol. III, Calcutta, 1797–88, p. 570.
43. See *Smṛti Chandrikā*.IX.I, CI.II; *Vyavahāra Mayūkha* IV.X.6.
44. Quoted in *Dāyabhāga* IV.I.16.
45. Colebrook, H.T., op. cit., pp. 570–71.
46. Colebrook, H.T., op. cit., pp. 570–71.
47. Medhātithī cited by Raghunandana – See *Dāyatattva of Raghunandana*: *text and translation*, Sastri, G.C. Sarkar, Calcutta, 1904, p. 41.
48. *Vyavasthā Darpaṇa: A Digest of Hindu Law* by Sarkar, S.C., op. cit., p. 218.
49. *Kātyāyana* cited in *Smṛti Chandrikā*.IX.I.16.
50. See *Vyavasthā Darpaṇa: A Digest of Hindu Law* by Sarkar, S.C., op. cit., p. 219.
51. Ibid., p. 218.
52. Ibid., p. 219.
53. Quoted in Jha, Ganganath, *Hindu Law in its Sources*, Patna University, Patna, 1931, p. 550.
54. Banerjee, G.D., *Hindu Law of Marriage and Strīdhana*, reprinted, Mittal Publications, Delhi, 1984, p. 297.
55. Bhattacharyya, N.N., op. cit., p. 120.
56. *Mitākśarā*.II.XI.2.
57. *Mitākśarā* on *Yāj*.II. 143.
58. Altekar, A.S., *The Position of Women in Hindu Civilization,* 2nd ed., Fifth reprint, Motilal Banarsidass, Delhi, 1987, p. 222.
59. Ibid., p. 222.
60. *Dāyabhāga*.IV.1.1.
61. *Dāyabhāga*.IV.1.3.
62. *Dāyabhāga*.IV.1.1.8.
63. *Dāyabhāga*.IV.1.2.
64. *Dāyabhāga*.IV.1.3.
65. *Kātyāyana* Quoted in *Dāyabhāga* IV.1.5.
66. *Kātyāyana* Quoted in *Dāyabhāga* IV.1.14.
67. *Kātyāyana* Quoted in *Dāyabhāga* IV.1.7.
68. *Kātyāyana* Quoted in *Dāyabhāga* IV.1.8.
69. *Kātyāyana* Quoted in *Dāyabhāga* IV.1.9.
70. *Kātyāyana* Quoted in *Dāyabhāga* IV.1.15.
71. *Kātyāyana* Quoted in *Dāyabhāga* IV.1.18.
72. *Kātyāyana* Quoted in *Dāyabhāga* IV.1.19.
73. Banerjee, G.D., op. cit., p. 310.

74 Ibid., p. 311.
75. *Dāyabhāga*. XI.1.65.
76. *Mitākśarā*.II.XI.2.
77. *Manu*.IX.131.
78. *Manu*.IX.192.
79. *Manu*.IX.193.
80. *Manu*.IX.195.
81. *Manu*.IX.196, 197.
82. *Manu*.IX.200.
83. *Yāj*.II.8.117.
84. Yaj.II.8.145.
85. *Viṣṇu*.XVII.19–21.
86. *Viṣṇu*.XVII.22.
87. *Bṛhas*.XXV.87.
88. *Vasiṣṭha*.XVII.46.
89. *Gautama*.XXIX.
90. *Mitākśarā*. II. XI.9.
91. *Mitākśarā*. II.XI.10.
92. *Mitākśarā*. II.XI.11.
93. *Mitākśarā*. II.XI.12.
94. *Mitākśarā*. II.XI.13.
95. *Mitākśarā*. II.XI.14.
96. *Yāj*.II.146 cited in *Mitākśarā*. II.XI.15.
97. *Mitākśarā*. II.XI.16.
98. *Mitākśarā*. II.XI.17.
99. *Nārada*.XII.2 cited in *Mitākśarā*. II.XI.18.
100. *Manu*.IX.92 cited in *Mitākśarā*. II.XI.19.
101. *Manu*.II.XI.24.
102. *Manu*.II.XI.25.
103. *Manu*.II.XI.24.
104. *Manu*.IX.192 cited in *Dāyabhāga*, IV.II.1.
105. *Manu*.IV.II.2.
106. *Bṛhas*.XXV.87.
107. *Bṛhas*.IV.II.9.
108. *Nārada*.XII.50 cited in *Bṛhas*. IV.II.10.
109. *Nārada*.IV.II.11.
110. *Nārada*.IV.II.12.
111. *Nārada*.IV.II.24.
112. *Manu*. IX. 299.
113. *Manu*. IX.77.
114. *Manu*. III. 32.
115. *Manu*. IX 200.

116. *Kātyāyana* Quoted in *Aparārka*, pp. 751–52.
117. *Nārada* Quoted in *Aparārka*, p. 752.
118. *Kātyāyana* Quoted in *Aparārka*, pp. 752–5.
119. *Kātyāyana* Quoted in *Aparārka*, p. 752.
120. *Kātyāyana* Quoted in *Dāyabhāga*, p. 76.
121. *Kātyāyana* Quoted in *Aparārka*, p. 752.
122. *Viṣṇu*.XVII.22.
123. *Āpas.Dh.S*.IX.26.
124. *Bṛhas*.XXV.86.
125. *Yāj*.II.147.
126. *Kātyāyana* Quoted in *Aparārka*, p.755.
127. Ibid.
128. *Nārada*.III.83.
129. *Yāj*.II.2.24–25.
130. *Viṣṇu*.III.65.
131. *Manu*.VIII.364.
132. *Manu*.VIII.367.
133. *Manu*.XI.62–67.
134. *Yāj*.II.24.288.
135. *Yāj*.II.24.291.
136. *Bṛhas*.XX.13.
137. *Bṛhas*.XXIII.10.
138. *Bṛhas*.XXIII.11.
139. *Bṛhas*.XXIII.13.
140. *Pārāśara*.X.26–27.
141. *Likhita*.69.
142. *Yāj*.II.24.287.
143. *Yāj*.I.3.66.
144. *Viṣṇu*.V.162.
145. *Yāj*.I.3.66.
146. *Yāj*.II.24.289.
147. *Viṣṇu*.V.47.
148. *Manu*.IX.74.
149. *Yāj*.I.3.73.
150. *Yāj*.I.3.74.
151. *Yāj*.I.3.76.
152. *Yāj*.II.8.148.
153. *Vasiṣṭha*.XXVIII.2–3.
154. *Atri*.193–194.
155. *Viṣṇu*.V.163.
156. *Manu*.V.164.
157. *Manu*.V.165.

158. *Manu*.V.166.
159. *Manu*.IX.69.
160. *Manu*.IX.70.
161. *Manu*.IX.76.
162. *Yāj*.I.3.65.
163. *Yāj*.I.3.67.
164. *Yāj*.I.10.224.
165. *Vasiṣṭha*.XVII.19–20.
166. *Vasiṣṭha*.XVII.73–74.
167. *Viṣṇu*.XV.8–9.
168. *Angiras*.I.66.
169. Uśanā.IV.23–30.
170. *Nārada*.XII.18.
171. *Nārada*.XII.24.
172. *Nārada*.XII.97–101.
173. *Nārada*.XII.97.
174. Pārāśara.IV.30.
175. *Yāj*.II.2.49.
176. *Viṣṇu*.VI.31.
177. *Yāj*.II.24.293.
178. Vasiṣṭha.XII.22–23.

4

The Ideal and the Reality

In the two preceding chapters, the order of the society as perceived and sought to be established by the *dharmaśāstrakāras* was discussed in detail, woven around the question of gender in that order. It is clear that there was no uniform body of law, which laid down fixed rules, and though the different *dharmaśāstras* sought to establish and perpetuate norms directed towards similar ends, there were differences, both minor and major, in the opinions of their authors. The degree of stringency with which the norms were laid, also varied in accordance with the difference in the treatment of different issues by different lawgivers. Contradictions are not a rarity in one single text also. It seems that while an attempt was being made to establish a particular social order, there were issues where the rules were stringent, however, at other times, there were attempts at reconciliation and assimilation, without which bringing about uniformity of social structure would have been an impossibility. While the *dharmaśāstras* might have wielded considerable influence in shaping the Brahmanical society, it can not be said with certainty if the norms were carried to other societies too. The existence of diverse cultures following diverse ethos has been the characteristic of Indian society since the beginning. Thus, the sphere of influence of the dictates of the *dharmaśāstras* might have been limited, or might have started expanding or further limiting with time. Again, where the *dharmaśastras* wielded considerable influence, how much was actually followed is a question. Precisely, to consider the *dharmaśāstras* as the sole or most authoritative and defining texts may lead to false interpretations and conclusions. Thus, though it is of crucial importance to study the norms laid down for women by these texts, the actual position of women in the society of those times cannot be deduced solely on their basis. Here comes the problem of sifting reality out of myth. To quote Romila Thapar, "The relationship between law and society involves both the actual and the ideal. To the extent that particular laws are to a particular society they can be regarded as a reflection of its value system. But law (both customary and codified) is also seen as means of controlling societal function and, as such, an attempt is made to perfect the legal framework, which then becomes a reflection of the aspiration of that society … . The problem of sifting ideals from actuality becomes increasingly difficult when the period under study is considerably removed from the present. Both time and environment lead to changes in the concept of law. Even within a single tradition there can be apparently divergent and contradictory attitudes at various levels for which there is little or no precise explanation; in such cases one has to search for detailed, accurate information in order to understand the contradictions. Such information is difficult to establish if the society is one which existed two thousand years ago."[1] Keeping the aforesaid remarks in the mind, an attempt is made in the present chapter to find out the position of women from other important sources for the study of the then society. The Epics, forming the most crucial documents carrying reflection of the society, are taken up for study. Also, in order to mark regional variations, a study of *Śangam* texts is expected to provide glimpses into the realm of reality. Finally, the epigraphic records, the so-called records of 'silent voices of women', have been studied to dig deep into the layers of myth and uncover reality. The proposed study is expected to meet two objectives, the first, that the picture of the gender relations or the position of women which emerges out of a study of these sources may be different to the one attempted at in the *dharmaśāstras*, and second, there might be deviations from or variations of norms which may be marked out upon the a study of sources other than the *dharmaśāstras*. Such a comparative analysis may help in getting a picture closer to reality than the one solely based on a study of the *dharmaśāstras*.

Women in the Epics

Hardly any words are needed to establish the importance of epics as the mirrors of ancient Indian society. They provide a veritable repository of events, images, ideals, customs, morals, deviations from the norms, as well as impact of following norms and so on. The list can go endlessly long, so much so that they are at times considered to be encyclopaedia of life. The *Rāmāyaṇa* has been instrumental in generating role model stereotypes for the generations to follow, and delineating a path for them which is considered to be the path of virtue. Macdonell comments, "Probably no work of world literature, secular in origin, has ever produced so profound an influence on the life and thought of a people as the *Rāmāyaṇa*."[2] As for the *Mahābhārata,* Winternitz writes, "We find in this most remarkable of all products of literature war-like hero-songs with colourful descriptions of bloody battle-scenes, pious priestly poetry with frequent interesting discussions on philosophy, religion and law and gentle ascetic poetry full of serene wisdom and overflowing love towards man and beast, all these side by side of one another and intermixed with one another to a confusing degree. Therefore, the Indians themselves consider the *Mahābhārata* doubtless as an epic, as a work of poetry, but at the same time they consider it also as a textbook of morals, of law and philosophy based on ancient tradition and hence endowed with indisputable authority; and since more than 1500 years it has served the Indians as much for entertainment as for instruction and sublime edification."[3]

The *Mahābhārata* has been representing conflict, and the means and ways of its resolution. It is not the conflict between the Kauravas and the Paṇḍavas alone, but the conflict between right and wrong, *dharma* and *adharma,* that is dealt with. The *Mahābhārata* has been well-known for the moral dilemmas it explores. Arjuna's anxiety in pursuing the path of '*dharma',* which was his duty; while facing the call of affection towards his near and dear ones, whom he would have to kill in order to pursue the delineated path; is one of the most striking and thought-provoking moral dilemmas sought to be resolved in the epic. However, this is not the only one. The number of such questions confronted by different characters at different points of time abounds. Not surprisingly, the stories in the *Mahābhārata* are considered to be both, historical precedents as well as an ethical methodology. In fact, the frequency of these tales of moral choice suggests that these narratives function as exemplars of ethical problem-solving, providing in each instance a rationale for the choice made and ultimately correlating the separate rationales to a uniform underlying moral code.[4] While the *Mahābhārata* explores moral dilemmas by way of representing inner conflicts, the characters in the *Rāmāyaṇa*, as Goldman writes, 'lack the quality of inner conflict',[5] and that 'this very feature of monovalent characterization is at the heart of the epic's extraordinary success'.[6] Thus, while the *Rāmāyaṇa* presents an unambiguous definition of *dharma*, the *Mahābhārata* reflects over the implications of the term, and attributes to it varying interpretations by way of representing conflicts. Nevertheless, differences apart, the influence of the two epics in shaping the Indian psyche for ages to come cannot be underestimated. Again, what else makes the case for the study of epics in the context of our research is that they provide glimpses of deviations from the norms, as also regional variations in the influence of norms, along with providing insights into the results when the norms were followed.

Such narratives as talked about earlier are built around the lives of some of the important characters in both the epics. It is through the portrayal of questions and dilemmas in their lives, that answers are provided for. Thus, to study women characters in the epics, both the epics will hopefully provide valuable insight. Both the epics have provided numerous portrayals of women. Interestingly, while the female characters in the *Rāmāyaṇa* are more of stereotypes, those in the *Mahābhārata* are complex and unconventional in the sense that they are not passive; rather considerable degree of agency can be attributed to at least few of them with respect to incidents in their lives. Ironically, however, it is the image of woman as she appears in the *Rāmāyaṇa* which has formed the ideal for Indian woman, even though the women in *Mahābhārata* have shown dynamism and vigour.

In its extant form, the *Vālmīki Rāmāyaṇa* is epic poem woven in around 50,000 lines retelling the story of Rāma, a legendry prince of the ancient kingdom of Kośala. The text survives in several thousand partial and complete manuscripts,[7] the oldest of which appears to date from the eleventh century AD.[8] The poem is traditionally divided into seven major *kāṇḍas,* or books, that deal chronologically with the major events in the career of Rāma, from the circumstances surrounding his birth to his death.[9] The central body of the poem recounts his disinheritance and exile and the abduction and recovery of his wife. The text has come down to us in two major regional recensions, the northern and the southern, each of which has a number of versions defined generally by the scripts in which the manuscripts are written. The former has two regional sub-recensions belonging to the north-east and north-west respectively. The three major recensions and sub-recensions differ considerably among themselves. However, 'The numerous interesting and important textual differences that characterize the various recensions, subrecensions, and versions of the epic-differences that we shall discuss in detail below, are not, in fact, reflected in any significant variations in the major outlines of the story, its contents, tone, moral, or characterizations.'[10] There has been a lot of disagreement among the scholars regarding the date of the *Vālmīki Rāmāyaṇa.* There are numerous complex problems regarding dating the poem. As with most of the literary and philosophical documents of ancient India, there exists virtually no independent and objective testimony in the form of historical, archaeological, epigraphic, or similar survivals on the basis of which to establish the dates even roughly.[11] According to Goldman, the *Vālmīki Rāmāyaṇa* must have been composed sometime between 750 and 500 BC.[12] Kane believes that the core of the story may be only as old as 300–250 BC.[13] According to Winternitz, about the 2nd or 3rd century, the text came to acquire the present shape.[14] Further, Kane states that the *Rāmāyaṇa* in its present form cannot be placed later than 200 AD.[15]

Regarding the date of composition of *Mahābhārata,* according to Winternitz, the text as it is now known, was under composition for at least eight hundred years (4th century BC to 4th century AD) or perhaps even more.[16] According to Hopkins, the date of the composition of the epic is between 4th century BC to the 4th century AD.[17] Keith also believes that the transformation of the epic into the present collected work must have gradually occurred between 4th century BC and 4th century AD.[18] Kane also believes that the core of the *Mahābhārata* existed before 500 BC.[19] Since the epic tradition, unlike the *Vedas*, was not guarded by canonical authority or religious sanctions, no great care could have been lavished by its custodians to guard it against interpolations or corruptions.[20] Two stages in the development of the *Mahābhārata* text have been underlined:[21] (A) The *Jaya* stage of some 8,000 *ślokas*, (B) *Bhārata* stage of nearly 24,000 *ślokas*. Both the texts were prone to interpolations and depict existence of multiple societies and cultures.

Characters in the *Vālmīki Rāmāyaṇa*

Rāma vis-à-vis Sītā

Rāma and Sītā both present the ideal of manhood and womanhood in India. Rāma is considered to be the embodiment of virtues,[22] and Sītā is portrayed in the *Rāmāyaṇa* as the 'quintessence of wifely devotion'.[23] A stark difference is, however, reflected in the definitions that are sought to be established of ideal manhood and womanhood by setting both of them as role models. While Rāma is defined to be *puruśottama* more in terms of being an ideal son, brother and king; Sītā's definition of idealhood consists solely in being the ideal wife. Rāma's evaluation of being an ideal husband, though attempted at, could not be pushed beyond a point. The only point which could be used to push this idea forward was that he remained monogamous. However, to what extent this should be used to exalt the status of Rāma has to be judged keeping in view that the rest of his brothers were also monogamous. From the point of view of evaluating the position of women in the *Rāmāyaṇa,* therefore, the role models generated by Rāma and Sītā regarding the husband-wife relationship, and thus their impact in structuring gender relations, is of importance.

The story of Rāma and Sītā begins when Vishwṛmitra leads Rāma and Lakśmaṇa to the royal court of king Janaka where he asks king Janaka to show the celestial bow, lifting and stringing of which was the bride price set by Janaka for marrying his daughter Sītā.[24] Sītā was actually Janaka's adopted daughter.[25] He discovered her while tilling the soil.[26] There is a high possibility that this was an instance of female child exposure. However, Janaka's adoption of Sītā as his daughter proves that dislike towards the girl child must not have been a general or universal phenomenon. That marrying a daughter must have been a source of worry for the father is proven by Sītā's statement when she is later briefing Anasūyā about the story of her marriage, where she tells her that, "Now, when my father observed that I had reached the age of marriage, he began to worry, and he grew desolate, like a man impoverished by the loss of his wealth. The father of an unmarried girl, though he be equal of Indra on earth, finds himself humiliated by people, by his equals, and even his inferiors. When the king perceived how close he was coming to humiliation, he was launched upon a sea of worry, and like a man without a raft he could not make the shore."[27] Such a worry and humiliation as talked about for a daughter's father is characteristic of patriarchy. Also, the *dharmaśāstrakāras* denounced a father who failed to give his daughter in marriage at time.[28] A test of martial valour was to decide the fate of Sītā, as according to her father Janaka, only the one to display great strength by stringing the 'bow of Śiva', could only be her husband. Accordingly, he set this condition as the bride-price for her marriage.[29]

It has to be noted that among the forms of marriage recognized by the *dharmaśāstrakāras*, this kind of a marriage was not included. The eight forms of marriage recognized by the *dharmaśāstrakāras* included *Brāhma*, *Ārṣa*, *Prājāpatya*, *Daiva*, *Gāndharva*, *Āsura*, *Rākśasa* and *Paiśāca*.[30] None of these forms of marriage implies the winning over of the bride on the basis of martial test. Though Janaka calls this condition or test, as the bride price,[31] the *Āsura* form of marriage, which involved taking of bride price by the maiden's relatives, is defined by the *dharmaśāstrakāras* as 'the one where the bridegroom receives the maiden after having given wealth to the father or kinsmen of the bride'.[32] Clearly, a test of martial strength was not the condition enumerated and it amounted to only an exchange of money or wealth. Again, even though the *Āsura* form was recognized as one of the forms of marriage, it was not considered lawful by the *dharmaśāstrakāras*. Manu recognizes this form for a *vaiśya* and a *śūdra* at first,[33] but then in the following verse, says that the *Paiśāca* and the *Āsura* rites must never be used.[34] Other *dharmaśāstrakāras* also considered this form of marriage as one of the unlawful forms.[35] This marks the existence of forms other than specified by the *dharmaśāstrakāras*, as also ignorance of the disapproval of the *dharmaśāstrakāras*, in case it is considered a variant of *Āsura* form, and thus it was a case of variation or deviation from the norms. However, just as in all the other forms except *Gāndharva* form of marriage, the girl had no choice or power of decision making regarding the one to be her husband, here also Sītā did not have any choice in this regard. Two points need to be admitted here. One, that being a *kśatriya*, the father might have thought it to be in the best of the daughter's advantage to get married to a groom who had martial capabilities *par excellence*. Second, that while arguing 'for' choice of the girl, it is not to deny the fact that choice may not always result in the welfare of any individual. In spite of agreement with the aforementioned points, it has to be noted that in such cases, the fate of the girl was decided by factors that were beyond the capacity of determination of both the girl and the father. In fact, martial capability could not have been the sole determinant of a maiden's welfare in terms of getting married to a person. It still remained a matter of chance. Thus, such a deviation from the norm did not actually mark a deviation from the basic ethos of the *dharmaśāstras*.

Since all the kings who came to Mithilā to test their strength and get Sītā in marriage had failed,[36] Janaka told the sage Viśvāmitra that he would give Rāma his daughter if he can string the bow.[37] It was not difficult for Rāma to string the bow;[38] not only that; in an attempt to fit an arrow to it, he broke the celestial bow.[39] Janaka was glad and promised giving Sītā to Rāma in marriage at the earliest.[40] Subsequently, the two daughters of Janaka- Sītā and Urmilā, and the two daughters of Janaka's brother- Māṇḍavī and Śrutakīrti were married to Rāma and his three younger brothers respectively.[41] Gifts were given by Janaka to his daughters at this juncture, which included hundreds of thousands of cows, finest blankets, fine silk garments; as also beautifully adorned and godlike troops, including elephants, horses, chariots, and foot soldiers; an unsurpassed complement of male and female servants, and lots of silver, gold, pearls and coral.[42] This could have constituted the *strīdhana* of the princesses. This is in line with the injunctions of the *dharmaśāstras*, which mention the wealth given by the father at the time of wedding as the daughter's *strīdhana.*[43] Rāma and Sītā passed some time happily devoted to each other in Ayodhyā.[44] The real twist came when king Daśaratha expressed his wish to consecrate Rāma, his eldest son as the prince regent.[45] In the subsequent exile that Rāma was to face at the behest of queen Kaikeyī, Sītā resolved to accompany Rāma both out of intense love and devotion, and sense of duty, and refused steadfastly Rāma's contention of leaving her in Ayodhyā given the miseries of forest life.[46] Sītā's love stood tested, however, Rāma's love towards his devoted wife was yet to be tested. It was actually put to test when during the exile Sītā was abducted by Rāvaṇa.[47] Though Rāma laments for his wife,[48] and it seems that the reason for his fight with Rāvaṇa was to get her back; this intention does not get reflected in his attitude towards Sītā even when finally he conquers Rāvaṇa. Even before this, number of times, Rāma's love for Sītā is overshadowed by his love for his brothers. When Lakśmaṇa lay unconscious on the battlefield, Rāma says mourningly, "Of what use to me is the recovery of Sita or even life itself, since my brother, now lying before mine eyes, has been struck down in the fight. It were possible for me to find a consort equal to Sita in this world of mortals but not a brother, friend and comrade in arms such as Lakshmana!"[49] Once again when Lakśmaṇa was stunned unconscious by the Śakti arrow, Rāma repeats this. He addresses Suṣeṇa and says, "The valiant Lakshmana, struck down by the ruthless Ravana, is writhing like a serpent, filling me with anguish … . Wives may be found everywhere and everywhere one may meet with friends but I see no place where one could find so dear a brother. Without Lakshmana of what use will it be for me to rule over a kingdom, O invincible warrior."[50] It is evident that his love for the wife becomes subsidiary and insignificant in comparison with love for the brother. Also, his saying that a wife like Sītā may be found again in the world, and again, that wives are easily available; point towards lack of singular love and devotion towards Sītā in his heart. Bhattacharji comments, "It is evident that Rāma could think of 'other women' who are like Sītā. So he can think that a wife is easily available, she is also easily disposable as well."[51] This is in stark contrast with Sītā's love and devotion to her husband, which is singular and unconditional. Subsequently, the incidents after the battle was won do lend support to this contention.

After the battle was won, and Vibhīṣaṇa installed as the king of Lankā,[52] Rāma told Hanumāna to go to Sītā with his message, informing her regarding the happenings and the well-being of himself, Sugrīva and Lakśmaṇa, and return after receiving her commands.[53] Surprisingly, Rāma does not express any wish to meet his long separated wife, supposedly for getting back whom he fought such a great battle. It was Sītā who expressed her desire to meet 'her lord, the friend of his devotees' when Hanumāna carried the message of Rāma to Sītā, whom he found 'like an anguished Rohini, uncared for, sitting sorrowfully at the foot of a tree surrounded by female titans' in the Aśoka Vāṭikā.[54] Coming back to Rāma, Hanumāna told him about Sītā's desire to see him; which instantly evoked thoughts in him, causing him to shed tears.[55] Rāma's state indicates him to be in a dilemma regarding Sītā. He ordered Vibhīṣaṇa to bring Sītā 'anointed with celestial unguents, adorned with heavenly jewels, having laved her head'.[56] Once again, Sītā's eagerness to meet her husband becomes pronounced when she urges to go without taking a bath, upon which Vibhīṣaṇa requests her to follow the command of Rāma.[57] Sītā was brought before Rāma, not for a private meeting, but in the presence of a huge crowd consisting of warriors, bears, monkeys and titans, which needed to be dispersed in order to make room for the palanquin of Sītā to move. Upon seeing them dispersing, whilst confusion was created amongst themselves, Rāma told Vibhīṣaṇa in terms of reproach to let Sītā come on foot so that the dwellers in the woods may see her at his side. What he says deserves notice: "Why, disregarding me, dost thou harass them, are they not my people? Her conduct, not raiment, walls, seclusion or other royal prohibitions are a woman's shield. In times of calamity, peril, war, the *Swayamvara* or the nuptial ceremony, it is not forbidden to behold a woman unveiled. It is not prohibited to look upon a woman who has fallen into distress and difficulty, above all in my presence. Therefore, leaving the palanquin, let Vaidehī come on foot so that the dwellers in the woods may see her at my side."[58] It may be inferred that there were some royal prohibitions on women coming out in public view. Again, Rāma's feelings seem to be ambiguous here. Hearing these words of Rāma, Vibhīṣaṇa became thoughtful, and Lakśmaṇa, Sugrīva and Hanumāna were saddened.[59] Rāma's speech made to Sītā at this point is further revealing, as he thus expressed the 'feelings he had concealed in his heart':

> "O illustrious Princess, I have re-won thee and mine enemy has been defeated on the battlefield; I have accomplished all that fortitude could do; my wrath is appeased; the insult and the one who offered it have both been obliterated by me. Today my prowess has been manifested, today mine exertions have been crowned with success, today I have fulfilled my vow and am free … . What a man should do in order to wipe out an insult, I have done by slaying Rāvaṇa for I guard my honour zealously! Thou wert re-won as the southern region, inaccessible to man, was regained by the pure-souled Agastya through his austerities. Be happy and let it be known that this arduous campaign, so gloriously terminated through the support of my friends, was not undertaken wholly for thy sake. I was careful to wipe out the affront paid to me completely and to avenge the insult offered to mine illustrious house. A suspicion is arisen, however, with regard to thy conduct, and thy presence is as painful to me as a lamp to one whose eye is diseased! Henceforth go where it best pleaseth thee, I give thee leave, O daughter of Janaka. O Lovely One, the ten regions are at thy disposal; I can have nothing more to do with thee! What man of honour would give rein to his passion so far as to permit himself to take back a woman who has dwelt in the house of another. Thou hast been taken into Ravana's lap and he has cast lustful glances on thee; how can I reclaim thee, I who boast of belonging to an illustrious house? The end which I sought in re-conquering thee has been gained; I no longer have any attachment for thee; go where thou desirest! This is the outcome of my reflections, O lovely one! Turn to Lakshmana or Bharata, Shatrughna, Sugriva or the Titan Bibishana, make thy choice, O Sita, as pleases thee best. Assuredly Ravana, beholding thy ravishing and celestial beauty, will not have respected thy person during the time that thou didst dwell in his abode."[60]

Every sentence of this monologue of Rāma, 'who was apprehensive of public rumour'[61], is revelatory of the character of *puruṣottama* Rāma. At the first place, why was Rāma apprehensive about public opinion regarding events in which neither Sītā nor he himself was at any fault? Had Rāma been truthful and honest in his own feelings towards Sītā, he would not have been filled of fear of scandal mongering by anyone. This, and the following discussion, is not to criticize Rāma, but to analyse the mindset of a society which held, and still holds, Rāma to be the one to have presented an ideal of manhood in India. That the ideal man, the so-called embodiment of virtues; was actually a weakling is proven from his fear to face the truth and uphold justice. Rāma is also full of the pride, characteristic of a *kśatriya*, as he again and again repeats that he did what he did not only for Sītā's sake, but to avenge the insult done to him and his illustrious house. This, as he says, he did by slaying Rāvaṇa for 'he guards his *honour* zealously'. Repeatedly, Rāma uses the phrase - 're-won thee' for Sītā, instead of rejoicing on 'getting her beloved wife back'. In fact, he compares having 're-won her' with Agastya's having regained the southern region. Was Sītā Rāma's property that he lost to Rāvaṇa and 'won' back by defeating him in a battle? To add insult to injury, Rāma expresses his suspicion regarding Sītā's character. He earlier said that 'he undertook the arduous campaign, not wholly for her sake'; which implies that getting back Sītā was at least 'one of the motives' behind it. However, his words uttered to Sītā subsequently belie this; as he tells her that having avenged his insult, 'he has nothing more to do with her, and so she may go anywhere at her will, the ten regions lying at her disposal'. His utterances reach the basest level when he suggests her to choose anyone out of Lakśmaṇa, Bharata, Śatrughna, Sugrīva or Vibhīṣaṇa. Is this the character of Rāma, who is held as the ideal? Again, he doubted the character of Sītā, who herself never yielded before Rāvaṇa. Even if Rāvaṇa's lustful gaze besmirched her, or even if he would have not respected her person during the time of her dwelling in his abode, as doubted by Rāma, it was not her fault. It becomes clear from his statements that he was reminded of his vindicated pride on seeing her.

Rāma's non-acceptance of Sītā shall be seen in comparison with the opinions of different *dharmaśāstrakāras* on the question of treatment to be meted out to woman who is forcibly abducted or raped against her will. Manu and Yājñavalkya have remained silent regarding the treatment to be meted out to the victimized female, while laying down punishment for the wrong-doer. Manu considers defiling a woman as one of the minor offences causing only a loss of the caste.[62] However, Yājñavalkya lays down death as the penalty when a woman of higher caste is ravished against her will.[63] Again, cutting of finger is the only penalty for having ravished a female of lower caste. Bṛhaspati is the only one who lays down punishment for the victim too. According to him, when a woman has been ravished against her will, she shall be kept in the house well guarded, smeared with ashes, lying on a low couch, and receiving a bare maintenance only.[64] However, performance of penances is prescribed as atonement for the sin in case she has been enjoyed by one of equal caste. Again, if she had been enjoyed by a man of inferior caste, abandonment and death is the penalty prescribed for her.[65] Pārāśara says nothing about the treatment to be meted out to the rapist; instead only prescribes penances for the victim to regain purity.[66] Atri's tone gets milder on the issue and he says that if a woman is known deceitfully, forcibly or stealthily despite her complete unwillingness, she should remain unaffected by any sin, and as such, should not be renounced; for she has not done so willingly. Her husband may hold congress with her at the time of the menses, for a woman becomes pure at the flowering time.[67] Again, he prescribes penances for the women violated by the *mlechchhas*, or perpetrators of crimes, or known by being forcibly taken away.[68] It is obvious that except Bṛhaspati, the *dharmaśāstrakāras* have in general not prescribed the abandonment of the victimized wife, though some of them may have prescribed the performance of penances or a temporary exclusion from household activities. Thus, Rāma's abandonment of Sītā is actually in contrast with the general opinion of the *dharmaśāstrakāras*.

Sītā's reply to Rāma is also important to be analysed. Though she was overwhelmed with shame, and cried bitterly, her reply was mild to the harsh utterances of Rāma. She tries to prove herself free of guilt by swearing that her conduct is worthy of his respect. She further says that it is the behaviour of other women that has filled him with distrust.[69] By putting these words in Sītā's mouth, a justification is sought for Rāma's doubt on her character. She further tried to convince Rāma that although her limbs came in contact with another's, it was against her will, and not through any inclination on her part; it was brought about by fate. That which was under her control, her heart, had ever remained faithful to him. She says that her loss is irrevocable if she remains a stranger to him despite having given proofs of love that she gave to him while she lived with him.[70] She questions Rāma as to why did he not repudiate her when he sent Hanumāna to seek for her; as she would have given up her life then and there, thus saving the lives of a great number of people who died in the battle that ensued.[71] It is clear that she lived to face all the hardships only to unite with her husband one day, and repudiated by him, she found no reason to live. This is followed by the sole utterance where she seems to be rebuking Rāma as she says, "But thou, O Lion among men, by giving way to wrath and thus passing premature judgement on a woman, hast acted like a worthless man."[72] However, followed by this, she tells Lakśmaṇa, "Raise a pyre for me, O Saumitri, this is the only remedy for my misery! These unjust reproaches have destroyed me, I cannot go on living! Publicly renounced by mine husband, who is insensible to my virtue, there is only one redress for me, to undergo the ordeal by fire!"[73] Two things deserve to be noted here. One, that it does not become clear that whether Sītā wished to mount the pyre to bring an end to her life, or she wished to give the proof of her chastity by going through the fire ordeal. Secondly, though she considers Rāma to be insensitive to her virtue, she is ready to go through a terrible ordeal to give him the proof of the purity of his conduct. It is to be noted that here Rāma does not ask Sītā to undergo fire ordeal, his decision was to abandon her. However, when she leaps into fire in front of his eyes, he does not even stop her from doing so, while all the women assembled there cried out- 'Alas!' and 'a great and terrible cry rose from the titans and the monkeys'.[74] It is to be noted that this is the same public whom Rāma was feeling apprehensive about for scandal mongering or raising rumours; who now raised a cry when Sītā leaped into fire. Rāma's 'eyes get filled with tears and he becomes afflicted' only upon 'hearing the lamentation of masses'; and still Vālmīki uses the epithet 'righteous' for him.[75] Even when the Gods appear to declare the purity of the conduct of Sītā, upon hearing to their speech, the first reaction of Rāma is not to try for the restoration of Sītā out of fire, but he inquires the 'Grandsire of the World' to tell him his real identity.[76] Later when the God of Fire restores Sītā, Rāma disclosed to the Chief of the Gods that it was imperative for Sītā to pass through the trial by fire, on account of the people, and that it was always well-known to him that she was ever devoted to him.[77] Again, none of the *dharmaśāstrakāras* had ever laid down such an ordeal for a woman to prove her chastity. Was this not a scapegoat devised by Rāma for his heartless conduct? Rāma was reunited with Sītā.

Some time was spent blissfully followed by their return to Ayodhyā, during which period Sītā conceived.[78] However, based on aspersions by some of the people among his subjects, Rāma decided to abandon Sītā. Chakravarti's observation regarding the abandonment of Sītā is significant in this regard:

> In all the canonical *Ramayanas,* beginning with Valmiki, the '*praja*', a faceless and nameless aggregate whose social location is fuzzy at best, is the catalyst for Sita's abandonment. When Rama seeks information from his spies about what the people think of him as king, we are told that they extol him for his heroism but are critical of him for having accepted Sita back following her violation by Ravana, and installing her as queen. Rama regards this opinion as an indictment of his rule and immediately abandons Sita... .The abandonment is done *at the behest of the praja.* One of the Sanskrit versions defines what is meant by the people being protected as the king's subjects-brahmanas, women, old people and children,[79] among others, even if they are in the wrong. Significantly, this notion of the *praja* or *jana*-people-has been overlaid by a popular notion of the scandal around Sita originating with a dhobi, so a slide is made to the *praja* being the common, 'brutish' people. Two moves are made through such a portrayal: first, it is the common people who are responsible for Sita's sufferings; and second, Rama is exonerated of blame-in fact, he too is a victim of the cruel expectations of the 'people' who in reality govern the personal lives the king and the queen.[80]

Another observation may be added to Chakravarti's thoughtful observation. Who were those people who criticized Rāma, and what were the grounds of criticism? To quote the utterances: "... What pleasure can his heart experience in possessing Sita, whom Ravana formerly held in his lap, having borne her away by force? How is it that Rama was not filled with aversion for her after she had been taken to Lanka and conducted to the Ashoka Grove, where she was left to the mercy of the titans. *We shall now have to countenance the same state of affairs regarding our own wives, since what a king does, his subjects follow* (emphasis added)!"[81] It is obvious that the people who criticized Rāma included only the males, and hence, the criticism was not the reaction of the entire *prajā*, but only the males, and may be only a section of the males, to the total exclusion of the perspective of females regarding the acceptance of Sītā. Rāma then summoned all the three brothers, and ordered Lakśmaṇa to take Sītā with him and leave her on the confines of the kingdom, on the further side of the Ganges, where sage Vālmīki has his hermitage.[82] What made Rāma take such a harsh decision. In his own words spoken to his brothers: "… Whoever it may be, if his ill fame be current in the world, he falls to a lower state, so long as the defamatory rumours exist. Dishonour is condemned by the Gods; honour is revered in the world, and it is on account of fair repute, that great souls act. As for me, so greatly do I fear dishonour that I would renounce my life and you yourselves on its account, O Bulls among Men, how much more therefore is it incumbent on me to separate myself from the daughter of Janaka."[83] It does not even need to be specified that Rāma was much bothered about his reputation and feared infamy. Again, Rāma's sense of justice as well as his love for Sītā are overpowered by his desire to be honoured and always appreciated in the world. Again, the false pretence under which he asked Lakśmaṇa to take the pregnant Sītā away, also speaks of his heartlessness and lack of concern for both his wife as well as his progeny in her womb. That Lakśmaṇa found this decision unjust and only followed the dictates of Rāma out of the compulsion of authority, is evident from his crying upon reaching Ganges, and his admission that this act shall bring universal censure upon himself.[84] His statement also proves that Rāma's repudiation of Sītā would not be upheld by all in the society, and that there must be some who would censure this act. Yet at this point of disagreement with Rāma, Lakśmaṇa tells Sītā that- "It is by remaining faithful to thy Lord and practising devotion to Rama in thy heart that thou shalt, by thy conduct, acquire supreme felicity, O Goddess."[85] Indoctrinated in the ideology of the *pativratā* and the theory of the results of past *karma*, Sītā wept bitterly while addressing Lakśmaṇa, wondering what sin had she committed in the days gone by or whom did she separate from her husband, that she, even though being virtuous and chaste, should be cast off by the king.[86] Obviously, Sītā was trying to attribute the blame for her misery to some sin that she may have committed, thus exonerating Rāma of having committed any sin by renouncing her. At this point, one is reminded of the statement of Kātyāyana, where he says that if a wife is disliked by the husband even though she may bend low with humility, then it must be the punishment for the woman for having disregarded her husband, Umā and the sacred fire in the previous birth.[87]

Sītā tells Lakśmaṇa to 'say to the king who is established in righteousness', "As thou dost act in regard to thy brothers, so shouldst thou act in regard to thy subjects; this is pre-eminently thy duty and will bring thee immeasurable renown; by its observance thou wilt enjoy the fruits of the earth! As for me, I am not distressed on mine own account, O Prince of Raghu, it is for thee to keep thy name untarnished! The husband is as a God to the woman, he is her family, and her spiritual preceptor, therefore, even at the price of her life, she must seek to please her lord."[88] It is evident that the *Rāmāyaṇa* of Vālmīki seeks to provide a definition of *pativratā*, which lacks everything except complete subjection and subordination of the wife to the husband's desires or will; completely betraying the least sense of justice towards the woman.

Later, Rāma recognized his two sons, Lava and Kuśa, while they were singing the story of Rāma during an interval in the *Aśvamedha* sacrifice, which Rāma had undertaken.[89] Upon this, he 'reflected deeply' and summoned messengers to carry his message to Sītā, asking her to attest her purity on oath in his presence the day after before the assembly getting the approval from Vālmīki for doing so.[90] Valmiki swore that the twin belonged to Rama, he pledged all the merit he had accumulated through his penances.[91] Still Sītā had to prove her chastity. This time Sītā called upon the goddess earth to take her inside, and this was what happened. At this point the earth splits open and Sītā goes back to where she came from, the earth, her mother.[92] The daughter of the Earth wanted to go back to the earth itself, she refused the glory of the queen, of the mother of princess. A husband was supposed to protect the wife from all dishonour. Rāma, however, repeatedly dishonours his wife. He is stricken with grief at this unexpected move of Sītā, and is inflamed with anger on earth; whereupon he is consoled by Brahmā that he will be united with Sītā in the heaven.[93] To quote Chakravarti here:

> Thus ends the Sitayana. Throughout the last moments when Sita and Rama are face to face, Sita does not lift her tear-filled eyes and Rama does not address her directly. Neither does Sita; there is too much and too little to say. The tension around the person of Sita in the *Ramayana* remains unresolved. Valmiki may have ended the *Ramayana* on a satisfactory note as far as kingship, succession and male *dharma* is concerned, but that his resolution of the Sitayana is unacceptable to popular sentiment has been amply borne out over the centuries.[94]

Perhaps Sītā's returning back to the earth, thus espousing death, is symbolic in the sense that though spared out of the earth by Janaka, and thus saved to live; a woman's life was fated to end in misery. Only death could bring an end to her miseries.

It is evident from the above discussion that the gender relations were skewed towards the male to a very high degree. This is in line with what the *dharmaśāstrakāras* sought to establish. However, the *Rāmāyaṇa* may be presenting a stricter subjugation of women, as evidenced by the deviations from the norms. Some other important female characters in the *Rāmāyaṇa* may be studied in order to delve further into the issue.

Daśaratha's Wives

King Daśaratha, in accordance with the accepted customs, was polygamous. He was married to Kauśalyā, daughter of the mighty and powerful king of Kośala; Kaikeyī, daughter of the Kekeya region; and Sumitrā, daughter of the king of Magadha. As pointed out by Chakravarti, it was polygamy that proved to be the source of tension in the king's household, since primogeniture was contested only because there were sons from multiple wives.[95] The story of *Rāmāyaṇa* would not have moved in the direction as it went, had there been no polygamy. This stands true for *Mahābhārata* too, as will be discussed later. Polygamy was mostly used as a means to enhance political power by way of marriage alliances with powerful rulers. However, it also endangers smooth transitions of political power.[96] In a society where the interests and position of women within the household depended on male support, polygamy spelled dangers to the rights and interests of women. Among the many wives, the one to get the husband's favours automatically attained pre-eminence. Again, the power equation amongst the wives depended on whose son would be the successor to the throne. To quote Chakravarti, "That polygamy spells danger to women's rights and is a continuing source of insecurity to women both when the king/husband is alive and after he dies, is evident from the existence of structural means of enhancing women's material interests in the king's/husband's household in both epics, through negotiations on succession as part of the bride price. … Bride price is a factor in the Kaikeyī narrative too, although the Vālmīki text, the only *Ramayana* that mentions this, tries to sweep the fact under the carpet since it would put a totally different perspective on Rama's hastily manoeuvred coronation and on Kaikeyi's demands on her son's behalf."[97] That Bharata's succession to the throne was the condition, and thus, the bride price that Daśaratha had agreed to pay in order to get married to Kaikeyī is obvious from the statement of Rāma, telling Bharata that long ago, when their father was about to marry Kaikeyī, he made a bride price pledge to her father; the ultimate price; the kingship.[98] If this is true, then perhaps Kaikeyī has been falsely villainized. While the king's lust for power and more wives than one is nowhere held to be responsible, Kaikeyī's bid to protect her self-respect is villainized to the extreme. An ideal woman is always the one who compromises and sacrifices. Self-sacrifice is certainly a virtue, but only to an extent, after which it amounts to self-negation. Further, sacrifice should not be hailed as a feminine virtue, rather a virtue needed to be practised by both, men and women, in limited degrees. If Kaikeyī declined to relent, it was absolutely normal human behaviour. For that matter, even Kauśalyā wanted her son to succeed to the throne. If she was wronged, it was done by her husband, who firstly wronged her by bringing another wife, and secondly, accepting a condition detrimental to the interests of the first wife and her son. Again, the marriage of Daśaratha with Kaikeyī was the *Āsura* form of marriage, in which the groom received the maiden after having given wealth to the father or kinsmen of the bride. However, this form of marriage was denounced by the *dharmaśāstrakāras*, and was considered to be one of the blemished or unlawful forms of marriage.[99] Thus, this is a case of ignoring the norms laid down.

While the two pledges that Kaikeyī sought to be redeemed, have survived in the later versions of *Rāmāyaṇa*, the bride price issue has not been taken up. To quote Chakravarti further:

> It is fairly clear that this casual reference in the Valmiki *Ramayana* and the suppression of the pledge in later versions is an attempt to preserve the integrity of Dasharatha and erase his calculated, opportunistic political manoeuvre. Further, neither Rama's undisputed claim and therefore, his sacrifice and 'generosity', nor Dasharahtha's argument that Rama was the most qualified, nor the settled principle of primogeniture would come through in the way they have if Valmiki had frontally dealt with the issue of Kaikeyi's bride price. It would be difficult to villainize Kaikeyi so successfully as Valmiki has done; the negative image of the archetypal malevolent woman in mythology would have been badly dented if her claim had been recognized. It would have been less easy to consolidate patriarchal norms of kingship and primogeniture as facilitating uncontested patrilineal lineage rules within a king's household, if Kaikeyi was presented as a wronged woman.[100]

It is obvious that the king's unequal relations with the different wives was a source of tension. Kauśalyā could not get the status of being her husband's favourite queen in spite of being the chief queen, and endowed with goodness and virtuous conduct. Kaikeyī, until the point when the latent tension in the king's household burst open, might have been using her status as the king's favourite, to marginalize or even humiliate Kauśalyā. This becomes evident when Mantharā tells Kaikeyī, "Then too, because of your beauty's power you used to spurn your co-wife, Rāma's mother, so proudly. How could she fail to reply that enmity?"[101] So Kauśalyā must have been waiting for her son to succeed the throne and thus get respite. This is voiced in her statement where she says that, "The joy and comfort I had not found to be within my husband's power to give me, I cherished hopes I might find in a son."[102]

Sumtirā remains the less mentioned and focussed upon of the three queens. This might be attributed to her being away from the question of power. It seems that she had good relations with both the other queens. This must have been to ensure her place in the wake of any of the two becoming the queen mother. Whatever small amount of space Sumitrā has got in Indian psyche, is due to her being Lakśmaṇa's mother, and even for her sacrifice and pain involved in remaining away from her son for so many years, she has not been duly acknowledged.

The questions Chakravarti asks deserve to be quoted in this context: "Where do women figure in the realm of power? Are they to be mere conduits for reproduction and instruments of political alliances? How much agency do women have in directing the course of their own lives? Is power a monopoly of men? How will women secure their material interests in a polygamous household? How will the contests between women be settled? These are some of the issues that come up in the text through the voices of Kaikeyi and Kaushalya themselves, in the *Ayodhyakānda,* or the Ayodhya section of the *Rāmāyana,* which is deeply embedded in the 'domestic' politics of the royal household."[103]

As far as adherence to or deviation from the norms laid down by the lawgivers is concerned, at the first place, polygamy was accepted by the lawgivers in general,[104] though it was not favoured and there were conditions when a man could resort to polygamy.[105] Also, the later *dharmaśāstrakāras* held a negative opinion in this regard.[106] Thus resorting to polygamy had the sanction of the lawgivers, even though they disfavoured this practice. In fact, the disfavour of the *dharmaśāstrakāras* could have been a reaction to the problems that were found to arise because of polygamy. If *Rāmāyaṇa* is taken to antedate these texts, the authors of these texts might have taken lessons from the story of the epic, where the root of the entire problem lay in polygamy only. Again, as already discussed, the *Āsura* form of marriage, exemplified in the marriage of Daśaratha and Kaikeyī, was not favoured by the *dharmaśāstrakāras*.

Anasūyā

Anasūyā has been hailed in the Indian memory as one of the revered *pativratās*. An interesting account of the meeting between the two *pativratās*, Anasūyā and Sītā, is given in the three chapters at the end of the *Ayodhyākāṇḍa* in the *Vālmīki Rāmāyaṇa*.[107] The hermitage of sage Atri and his wife, Anasūyā, is the first stop after starting from Citrakūṭa. The conversation between Anasūyā, the veteran *pativratā,* and young Sītā, enunciated in six simple verses,[108] is revealing as far as the ideal of *pativratā* is sought to be established in the epic. Anasūyā tells Sītā that the woman who loves her husband; whether living in the city or in the forest, or being evil or inauspicious; attains the best regions. Whether he is of bad character, or is licentious or indignant, the husband is the supreme deity for a woman of noble nature. She further says that even upon giving it a critical thought, she is unable to find anyone among the kinsmen who is superior to him. Evil women whose hearts are dictated by passion and who behave as superior to their husbands do not understand the merits or demerits in this manner. Such women, who have been overpowered by wrong actions, indeed destroy their own code of conduct, and attain disrepute. But women like Sītā, who are well-qualified, and who can visualize the later regions, good or bad, shall attain to heaven just like the ones who have done meritorious deeds.

It is obvious that the ideal laid down in the epic is much the same as that given by the *dharmaśāstrakāras*. One is reminded of the words of Manu, upon reading the speech of Anasūyā, where he says that a faithful wife should worship the husband as a god, even though he may be destitute of virtue, or is seeking pleasure elsewhere, or is devoid of qualities.[109] It is required of a *pativratā* to go on loving even an evil or inauspicious husband, and he shall remain the supreme deity for her in spite of shortcomings. The ideology of the *pativratā* is echoed in the statements made by the other *dharmaśāstrakāras*.[110] Women whose hearts are dictated by passion are said to be evil. This conforms to the *dharmaśāstric* portrayal of women in categories of good and bad, conformist and deviant. While the husband who is evil, still ought to be loved by the wife; the wife's being evil shall amount to her destroying the code of conduct and earning disrepute. Women who behave as superior to their husbands are included in the same category. Only those women who shall not commit such acts of misconduct and misdemeanour, shall attain to heaven. Thus a woman shall worship a husband who is involved in mistakes, in order to attain heaven.

Such is the indoctrination, that Sītā agrees to the words of the elderly lady completely and says that she would have followed her husband even if he had been devoid of character.[111] This indoctrination of Sītā stopped her from raising her voice even when she was subjected to humiliation and abandonment by her husband later on, though she was taken aback. However, this was the time when she was enamoured by his virtues. She tells Anasūyā that, "How much more readily would I obey a man praised for his virtues, a compassionate, self-disciplined, and righteous man, who is constant in his love, who defers to his mother and holds his father dear. He behaves towards all the women of the king exactly as he does towards Kauśalyā."[112] Further, she praises Sāvitrī and Arundhatī as two women who have followed such a code of conduct and have secured their place in heaven.[113] Anasūyā is so pleased with the conduct of the young princess, that she gave her divine ornaments.[114]

However, it might not have been only faithfulness towards her husband or *pātivratya* alone that amounted to Anasūyā's greatness. When Rāma and Sītā met Atri, he appreciated Anasūyā for her creativity and immensity of penance. It is significant to note what he said:

Once when the world was utterly ravaged by drought for ten years, it was Anasūyā who created roots and fruit, and caused the Jāhnavī to flow, for the ascetic power she has acquired is awesome, and mortifications adorn her. She has practised intense asceticism for ten thousand years, and by her vows all obstacles have been removed. It was she who, to advance the cause of the gods, straightway reduced ten nights to one. Here she is, blameless prince; look on her as a mother. Now have Vaidehi approach her; she is a glorious woman worthy of every creature's adoration, an aged and ever amiable woman.[115]

This speech acquaints us with many positive qualities of the lady, who seems to be endowed with a high degree of creativity. Not only this, she has the intelligence and perseverance enabling her to adapt to difficult circumstances. From the passage, it seems that she pursued agriculture. Although the narration is exaggerated, there seems to be an element of truth in it, in a lesser degree. Another thing which is to be noted in Atri's praise for her having performed harsh penance, or *tapas*. This is in contrast with the indictments of the lawgivers who have generally laid restriction on the performance of penances by women.[116] Though the definition of *pātivratya* was the same in the epic and the *dharmaśāstras*; the characteristics of a *pativratā* as depicted in the epic carried some very positive and constructive notes. It is clear that both conformity and deviation from the norms could be found in the epic in the portrayal of women.

Women outside the Āryan Influence

Vālmīki's *Rāmāyaṇa* testifies to the existence of societies at different stages of economic and cultural development. While the inhabitants of Ayodhyā are in the phase of settled agriculture, the *Vānaras* and *Rākśasas* are in the pre-agricultural stage of economic development. The *Vānaras* occupy forestland and mountain tracts, and even Lankā shows no clear evidence of agriculture. It has been argued that the kernel of the *Rāmāyaṇa* represents the spread of agriculture and destruction of forest culture, ultimately making way for the establishment of an agricultural economy. According to Chakravarti, "An important aspect of the Valmiki *Ramayana's* portrayal of womanhood is the development of the image of women in the *Āryan* prototype, in contrast to women in tribal society."[117] Power must have been in play in determining the fate of the women even in the societies outside the *Āryan* influence, which is obvious from Rumā's abduction by Vāli, her husband Sugrīva's elder brother.[118] But the contrast between the two cultures lies in the unhesitant acceptance of Rumā by Sugrīva even after such abduction,[119] while Rāma's reservations in accepting Sītā went beyond all humane considerations and sense of justice. However, Sugrīva also acquires Tārā, widow of Vāli, after Vāli was killed,[120] who was devoted to him, and who might have disliked getting subjected to Sugrīva. Both Vāli and Sugrīva abduct or acquire each others wives when they come into power. Thus, though this is in contrast to the *Āryan* ideals, where the widow was not to be married to the brother of the deceased, it might not have actually meant independence for women.

Śūrpaṇakhā is the most significant non-*Āryan* female character. She displayed considerable independence in that she roamed about freely in the forest and could make sexual overtures to men. Rāvaṇa, his three brothers and Śūrpaṇakhā were children of the grandson of Brahmā, Pulastya, and a *rākśasī* named Kaikasī. This is another example of deviation from the norm where a *brāhmaṇa* was married to a *rākśasī.* While the *dharmaśāstrakāras* have expressed general disfavour, even though permitting them, with regard to inter-*varṇa* marriages,[121] and have particularly denounced the marriage of a *brāhmaṇa* marrying a *śūdra* woman.[122] A marriage with a *rākśasī* was not even mentioned, and it may be assumed with a degree of certainty that it must have been considered worse than marrying a *śūdra* female. Again, even though the father was a *brāhmaṇa,* the children were recognized as *rākśasas*. This also marks a deviation from the norm of patriarchy, and points towards existence of matrilineal organization. Śūrpaṇakhā's marital status is not very clear, however, in some versions such as the *Uttarakāṇḍa* of Vālmīki *Rāmāyaṇa,* she is a widow whose husband was killed by Rāvaṇa.[123] Again, her position stands in sharp contrast with those of the *Āryan* widow, who was marginalized. Facing rejection and mutilation at the hands of the two princes, upon expressing her desire to espouse either of the two, and trying to kill Sītā,[124] she went to her brothers Khara and then Rāvaṇa to persuade them to avenge the treatment meted out to her.[125] This also stands in contrast to the loneliness and helplessness of Sītā when she was abandoned by Rāma. The only place she could find to take refuge was the *āśrama* of a sage.

The existence of societies beyond the pale of *Āryan* influence, testify to the fact that the sphere of influence of the *dharmaśāstras* would have been limited to the *Āryan* elite. Even amongst these, there would have been only a partial adherence to the norms, as testified by the deviations marked out. Nevertheless, an attempt has been made in the *Rāmāyaṇa* to establish and strengthen the same patriarchal ideology as that attempted at by the *dharmaśāstrakāras*. Chakravarti's comment is worth quoting with regard to women's portrayal in the *Rāmāyaṇa*. She writes:

> The extension of the original story in the Valmiki *Ramayana* resulted in the story hinging upon three crucial incidents, each of which expresses stereotypical denigration of the female. The first is Kaikeyi's demand that Rama be exiled; the second is Surpanakha's overtures to Rama, her rebuff at his hands and her subsequent mutilation by Lakshmana; and the third is Sita's demand for the deer and her unjust accusation against Lakshmana

following his reluctance to leave her alone in the hermitage. This last results in her being left unprotected and facilitates her abduction. In fact, the Valmiki story conveys the idea that life would run smoothly but for the evil or whimsical nature of women. Apart from this, it also provides negative images of women by suggesting that women who display ambition or initiative, such as Kaikeyi and Surpanakha, are both evil and disgusting.[126]

Characters in the *Mahābhārata*

The *Mahābhārata* is lengthier and much more exhaustive than the *Rāmāyaṇa*. Its scope is wider as it covers a wider range of issues as well as contexts, acknowledges more variations in time and space, and encompasses varying perspectives as well as conventions. Accordingly, the *Mahābhārata* is much more complicated, and the number of characters far outnumber those that are in the *Rāmāyaṇa*. However, it is not only the number of the characters but also the nature of characterization that makes *Mahābhārata* unique. It is interesting as well as significant from the point of view of present research to go through the various characterizations of women, as well as various issues that rise in varying contexts.

Like the *Rāmāyaṇa*, the plot of the *Mahābhārata* also originates out of polygamy being resorted to by the king (or having wished to be resorted to in this case). Polygamy created the problem of contending interests in the inheritance of the kingdom, and lead to primogeniture being contested in both the cases. The main plot of the *Mahābhārata* story originated out of king Śāntanu's eagerness to marry Satyavatī, the adopted daughter of a fisherman.[127] Though Satyavatī's birth is shrouded in myths, it is clear that she was the daughter of king Uparicara Vasu, who had begotten two children on a fisherwoman; and while he accepted the son born of this union, declined to accept the daughter, who was brought up by a fisherman.[128] Firstly, Satyavatī's story testifies to the rejection of a girl child on the basis of her sex. Though there are examples in the epic where the male child is abandoned, like Kuntī herself abandoning Karṇa[129], in this case it was not the sex of the child which led to his abandonment, but the fear of being condemned for having borne a child before marriage. The only example of exposure of male child is after marriage is that of Gangā, Śāntanu's first wife who drowned seven of her sons, before Śāntanu finally stopped her from doing so upon the birth of Devavrata; which led to their final separation.[130]

Being rejected by her father, Satyavatī could not find a place in the royal household. Although known as the king of the fishers, her adoptive father was still a *dāsa*, which further distanced Satyavatī from the centre of *Āryan* power. Her only capital was her beauty. Satyavatī helped her father by ferrying people across the river.[131] It was while ferrying, that she met the two men who changed the course of her life radically, and brought her to the centre of power. The first of the two was the great sage Pārāśara, and the second was the king of Hastināpura, Śāntanu. Both of them were enamoured by her beauty and desired for her. The observation of Jayatri Ghosh is significant in this regard. She writes:

> The story of her compliance in both cases is one of transformation of social and sexual subordination into far-reaching personal and political advantage. Still more remarkable is that the matriarchal ascendancy she gained is recognized in the Mahabharata as a moral supremacy that lent to her political decisions unquestioned validity. Her story thus inverts the conventional power relationship: rejected by her father at birth and forced into the underclass, she became the arbiter of the fate of Kurujāngāl. Nor is her success fortuitous because the narrative is careful to mark the shaping intelligence that underwrote her progress.[132]

It is well known that Satyavatī yielded to the wishes of both the men desiring her. However, she displays remarkable intelligence in putting up conditions before both of them, and thus, while she gains from the sage knowledge suited to *Āryan* upbringing, as well as sweet odour, along with the retention of her virginity;[133] from the next suitor[134] she gets the promise of inheritance of kingdom for her future progeny as the bride price.[135] Even if the demand for bride price was the brain child of her father,[136] she seemed to show no great inclination to marry the king without such a promise. Again, in spite of being a *śūdrāṇī,* for all her life to come she commanded the respect of both her son from Pārāśara-Vyāsa, and Śāntanu's son from previous wife, Gangā- Devavrata, later came to be known as Bhīṣma, due to his terrible vow of not getting married in order to fulfil the condition laid down by Satyavatī's father for marrying her to Śāntanu.[137] The *Mahābhārata* presents many examples of pre-marital adulterous relationships of women. One of these is Satyavatī's case. But her case stands out in that she did not abandon her *kāṇīna* son, but affectionately acknowledges him to be her son; and when demanded by circumstances, also discloses his identity to Bhīṣma.[138] Though the *dharmaśāstrakāras* also recognized *kāṇīna* son as one of the twelve kinds of sons,[139] they disfavoured the birth of such sons. However, nowhere in the *Mahābhārata* Satyavatī is seen as being criticized for this. Her attitude towards Vyāsa stands in sharp contrast with that of Kuntī, who abandons her son, Karṇa.[140] Kuntī's higher degree of fear and sense of shame can be attributed to her being brought up in the *Āryan* surroundings. However, Ghosh does not consider this as a satisfactory explanation. According to her:

> The contrast between Kuntī and Satyavatī is not easy to explain. To see them, respectively, as representatives of the *Āryan* and non-*Āryan* cultures is tempting but not altogether persuasive. Even if we discount Satyavatī's biological origins, she was, after all co-opted into the *Āryan* ethos and recognized as one learned in the ways of *dharma*, an *Āryan* construct that is also the transcendent category in the *Mahābhārata* … . In that Satyavatī and Kuntī make opposite choices in identical circumstances, should we take their stories as illustrations, respectively, of what *dharma* does and does not mean. But Kuntī is not charged with violating *dharma* when she abandons her child, which seems to be regarded as a venial act because bearing an illegitimate child is recognized as a matter of shame; at the same time, if that is the norm, then that is precisely why it seems extraordinary that Satyavatī should receive such positive endorsement in the epic for rearing and acknowledging an illegitimate child. At the very least, then, the contrast between the two stories seems to turn *dharma* into an ambivalent if not inconsistent category.[141]

Satyavatī displays strength and calmness even at other points of time, when she was confronted with the crisis upon the death of her two sons, one after the other.[142] The latter left two young issueless queens behind, posing a threat to the kingdom in the wake of the absence of any successor. Śāntanu's line was faced with the threat of extinction. From this point onwards, she is the one to take strong decisions. To quote Ghosh again:

> With Bhīṣma's leadership precluded by his vow, an impasse had been reached, the resolution of which fell exclusively into the hands of Satyavatī, on whom alone the fate of Kurujāngāl depended. *This situation is unparalleled in the Mahābhārata both in the statement of the problem and, as we shall see, in its resolution. Equally unique is the narrative's choice of a woman as the singular cause both of the crisis and of its resolution* [emphasis added]. The problem was to carry on the male line. Satyavatī's solution was to bring about the birth of one or more *kśetraja* sons – that is,

> sons begotten in the wombs of her daughters-in-law by a man engaged solely for that purpose.[143]

First she asks Bhīṣma to either marry or procreate sons by *niyoga* on the young wives of Vicitravīrya;[144] and upon his refusal due to the vow;[145] she calls her *kāṇīna* son, the great Ṛṣi Kṛṣṇa Dvaipāyana Vyāsa for the resolution of the problem,[146] who obeys her command.[147] She thus manages to come out of the crisis. A few things deserve consideration at this juncture. First, Satyavatī is acting contrary to the norms when the conditions demand so. According to the *dharmaśāstras*, *niyoga* has to be performed only with the husband's brother or some other male from the agnatic kinship line.[148] Second, she is the decision-maker unlike any other male member of the lineage. This is again in contrast to the injunction in the *dharmaśāstras*, according to which after the completion of six months, the widow's father or brother shall assemble the gurus who taught or sacrificed for the deceased and his relatives, and they shall appoint her to raise issue to her deceased husband.[149] Thus, the males actually wielded the authority for appointing the women for *niyoga* according to the *dharmaśāstras.* Third, she reverses the customary ignominy of bearing a child out of wedlock and rather uses it to resolve the crisis; and lastly, she anchors the *dharma* of her decisions in a biological observation that lays claim to gender parity. All of these reversals of the norm have serious implications for the nature of the moral discourse in the *Mahābhārata* that demand attention.[150] Later, in the *Sabhā Parvan*, when Draupadī was dragged into the assembly of the Kauravas by force, following the defeat of Yudhiṣṭhira in the dice game, Bhīṣma tells the sorrowful Draupadī, "I have already said, O blessed one, that the course of morality is subtle. Even the illustrious and wise fail to understand it always. What in this world a strong man calls morality is regarded as such by others, however otherwise it may really be; but what a weak man calls morality is scarcely regarded as such even if it be the highest morality ..."[151] Bhīṣma explicitly admits the role of power in determining the definition of morality. This points towards Satyavatī having wielded power in that she could admit of what would otherwise have been considered immoral. Whether this 'power' that Satyavatī had; emanated out of her status as a married queen, or queen-mother, or was an inherent self-confidence; is a point worth asking. However, it needs to be noted that she does not abandon her illegitimate son even before having arrived at the centre of political authority. Again, it has to be admitted that though Satyavatī's coming into a commanding position was geared through her intelligence; it was also circumstantial to an extent. Further, what is important to note in this context is that the *Mahābhārata* carries such narratives, portraying women in an unconventional frame, and still upholding her as conformist. The ambiguity regarding the definition of *dharma* as admitted by Bhīṣma, is carried through all the threads of the epic. Ghosh comments:

> There seems to be little room for doubt that the *Mahābhārata* is using the Satyavatī story to support an alternative view not only of *dharma*, but also of the hierarchy of power. That it does so by electing for the central figure of the discourse an embodiment of powerlessness as an abandoned child, a woman-and a woman from the underclass at that, and an unwed mother underlines the departure from the norm. Satyavatī's rise from outcaste to revered matriarch is a unique transformation, but its significance is not so much a success story as a reversal of social relationships that sees the women's assumption of the role of the nation's saviour.[152]

Just like Satyavatī's story speaks of her acquiring power, the stories of her twin daughters-in-law, Ambikā and Ambālikā speak of the complete powerlessness of women with regard to the happenings in their lives. These were two of the three beautiful daughters of the king of Kāśī, the third being Ambā. All the three were dragged away forcibly by Bhīṣma for his younger brother Vicitravīrya,[153] as the king of Kāśī proclaimed the performance of *swayamvara* whereby the princesses were to choose their husbands.[154]. Bhīṣma, while dragging the three maidens away, also mentioned the eight kinds of marriages taken recourse to by people, and eulogized the eighth one saying that the learned always applaud the eighth form, and that the sages have said that, that wife is dearly to be prized who is taken away by force, after the slaughter of opponents, from amidst the concourse of princes and kings invited to a self-choice ceremony.[155] It is to be noted here that though the *Rākśasa* form of marriage is recognized by the *dharmaśāstrakāras* as one of the forms of marriage,[156] considered to be lawful only for the *kśatriyas.*[157] However, Nārada considers it among the three unlawful forms.[158] According to Viṣṇu also, only the *Gāndharva* form is legitimate for a *kśatriya.*[159] It is clear that though Bhīṣma's action does not mark a deviation from the norms, such an action was not hailed in the texts, as he asserted. However, this action of Bhīṣma is hailed in the *Mahābhārata* calling it 'an extra-ordinary feat' achieved by him.[160] Upon reaching

Hastināpura, while the eldest- Ambā, refused to get married to Satyavatī's son; the rest of the two were married to him.[161] Obviously, the other two had to do even if this would not have been their choice, which they could only have exhibited had Bhīṣma not obstructed their *Swyamvara* ceremony. However, as mentioned earlier, Vicitravīrya's untimely death left both of them without children, and the kingdom of Hastināpura, heirless.[162] In order to resolve the crisis and ensure the continuation of the male lineage of Śāntanu, Satyavatī first decided to give them in marriage to Bhīṣma, or else to procure sons by performing *niyoga,* both of which were declined by Bhīṣma.[163] Then she decided to ask her *kāṇīna* son, Vyāsa to procreate sons by *niyoga* upon both of the widows.[164] There was no question of choice for both the queens. Rather than being their choice, it was something that they feared or abhorred, becomes evident from the reactions of the two women when approached by Vyāsa.[165] Later, in spite of Ambikā's unwillingness, Satyavatī insisted that a healthy child be obtained and Ambikā afraid to say no to her, sent her *dāsi* instead.[166] In fact, Ambikā and Ambālikā producing sons through *niyoga* to ensure the survival of the Kuru clan is an example of women being treated as property. *Niyoga* was the deputation of husband's conjugal rights in his brother or kinsmen or to a man considered equal or superior to him, exclusively for the purpose of procreation. Women or their procreative capacity was treated as a private property of husband or his agnatic heirs. This becomes evident with Satyavatī's statement that "... that great ascetic will beget children upon Vicitravīrya's field"[167]. The woman's womb, or her reproductive potential, being symbolized by the field, was considered to be the property of the husband. As women were treated as an instrument for producing heir for men in their lives, their own desire was not of much consequence. *Niyoga* under such circumstances was a task not a pleasure, the woman and the man she had intercourse with had to perform it without least bit of desire or lust. This was in line with the injunctions of the *dharmaśāstrakāras*, according to whom it was the duty of the widow and her appointment was made by the male elders of the agnatic line.[168] Thus, the two women figure as completely helpless women devoid of any identity in a patriarchal set-up, only working at the commands of patriarchy to work towards its strengthening.

While Ambikā and Ambālikā carry no voice, and exhibit no identity, their elder sister Ambā figures as one who refuses to relent to the norms of patriarchy. On his way to Hastināpura after having won the three princesses, Bhīṣma was challenged by a young king, Śalya. In the ensuing fight, Bhīṣma defeated Śalya, who withdrew in shame and anger.[169] When Bhīṣma reached Hastināpura, the two younger princesses were duly married to Vicitravīrya but Ambā refused because she loved Śalya, whom she had mentally chosen as her husband and whom she was about to espouse at the *Swayamvara* ceremony had Bhīṣma not interrupted.[170] The refusal of a woman was not to be taken well in a patriarchy, and it amounted to Ambā's rejection from everyone, including the one she loved, the one for whom she was captured, and the one who captured.[171] Ambā tried to avenge for the misery wrought upon her due to abduction by Bhīṣma, with the help sage Paraṣurāma, but failed.[172] She grew more vengeful and determined at this and resorted to severe ascetic practices for several years to attain such prowess as to be able to destroy the invincible Bhīṣma.[173] A woman resorting to ascetic practices was against the ethos of the *dharmaśāstras*. However, the answer given by Ambā to ascetics enquiring about the reason for practising austerities is interestingly revealing. She said, "Expelled I have been by Bhīṣma, prevented by him from the virtue that would have been mine by living with a husband! My observance of this vow is for *his* destruction and not for the sake of regions of bliss… . He for whom mine hath been this state of continuous grief, he for whom I have been deprived of the region that would have been mine if I could obtain a husband, he for whom I have become neither woman nor man, without slaying in battle that son of Ganga I shall not desist … . As a woman, I have no longer any desire. I am, however, resolved to obtain manhood, for I will be revenged upon Bhīṣma. I should not, therefore, be dissuaded by you."[174] It is obvious that though Ambā resorted to ascetic practices, still the merit obtained by such practices was considered to be inferior to the merit that she must have obtained by living with a husband. Also, in spite of being a practitioner of penances hard to be practised by the male ascetics only, she considers herself neither a woman nor a man, by being devoid of a woman's fated societal function. She herself thinks that she would not be able to destroy Bhīṣma without attaining to manhood. This is in line with the ethos of the *dharmaśāstras* according to which a woman can attain to highest regions only by serving the husband and not by practising austerities.[175] Also, the importance of roles ascribed to woman and man is stressed upon in this way.

Pleased with her austerities, Śiva appeared before her and promised her that one day she would bring about the death of Bhīṣma- *but not in her present life and not as a woman.* She would have to be reborn as the daughter of King Drupada of Pāñcāla and *obtain manhood to fulfil her mission.* She was assured that her desire for revenge on Bhīṣma would be passed on to her new body and that she would remember everything.[176] In order to hurry the process, she set a fire and leaped into the flames on the bank of Yamunā.[177] Thus, though she left her mortal body, but her desire for revenge continued into her next birth. Subsequently she was born as a daughter to the eldest queen of king Drupada, who practised the most austere of penances earlier to procure a son who shall destroy Bhīṣma. Lord Śiva granted him a boon that he shall have a child, who shall be both a female first and then a male subsequently.[178] Though born as a daughter, her feminine identity was hidden and she was brought up as a son, all rites being performed for her as prescribed for a male child.[179] She was later married with a princess,[180] and was subsequently granted manhood by a *Yakśa.*[181]

The dream nurtured by Śikhanḍin-Ambā's was fulfilled on the battlefield of Kurukśetra. He took part in the battle against the Kauravas as an ally to the Pāṇḍavas. He was brought and placed before Arjuna's chariot on the tenth day of the battle, when Arjuna found it impossible to fight Bhīṣma any longer. It was known to Kṛṣṇa, that as a strict follower of *kśatriyadharma*, Bhīṣma would never lift his arms against a women or one who had been born female. Seeing Arjuna shooting his arrows from his chariot crouched behind Śikhanḍin, Bhīṣma put down his arms and stopped fighting.[182] Arjuna continued to strike Bhīṣma with his arrows until he fell to the ground. Bhīṣma awaited his death patiently, lying on his arrow bed, and died.[183]

Ambā's story is significant in that it points towards the destiny of a woman who dares to refuse and reject in a patriarchy. Not only that she had to face bitter rejection at the hands of everyone, but also that in order to take revenge, she had to take another birth. In the new birth, how could she be born as a male as she had done no great deed in previous birth, and how could she take the revenge as a woman. So she had to get manhood from a goblin in order to face the world of man. Still she is not given an opportunity to face in real terms, as in order to take her revenge, she had to become a mere puppet of Arjuna; the very name of Śikhanḍin has survived not as a model but as a common label for a powerless front man.

In spite of all her single-minded efforts, Ambā could not brook the satisfaction of having taken the revenge herself. Her story stands in sharp contrast with those of her sisters who followed the norms without questioning and displayed no eagerness to have a control over marriage or motherhood. They were treated as the conformist, and hence the model women. But in contrast to this, Amba's resistance disrupted the social norm, and this defiance brought her nothing but trouble and unhappiness. Her defiant assertion of individuality was never approved by the society, and ascribed to her a status of ambivalent manhood at best, as a mockery. To quote Dasgupta here:

> The story has more than one moral to preach. If you are a woman and are submissive, you can become a queen and win the appropriate prizes as determined by the men around you. This point is clearly shown by the plight of Ambā, who lost every material reward of life, whereas her sisters became mothers and queens. To drive home the idea of the inestimable value of masculinity, as well as the rashness of attempting to alter one's destined identity, we are told the Yakśa Sthunakarṇa's story. His story thus resonates against the framing legend of Ambā-Śikhanḍin's "unnatural" attempt to overturn her gender-mediated destiny.[184]

Ambā's story expresses her complete defiance of the *dharmaśāstric* ideals, where the maiden has no right to reject the marriage once she is carried by force, as also to try to revenge for anything wrong done to her. Procreation and marriage, both fell out of the purview of her decision-making capacity in the scheme of the *dharmaśāstras.*

The characterization of the two daughters-in-law of Ambikā and Ambālikā is no less interesting. Dhṛtaraṣṭra was married to Gāndhārī, who decided to tie a cloth on her eyes lifelong as her husband could not see.[185] Perhaps by this characterization of Gāndhārī, a new dimension was attempted at to be added to the definition of *pativratā.* A mere glance of Gāndhāri was capable of scorching Yudhiṣṭhira's toe[186] and her curse exterminated the whole race of Yaduvamśīs.[187]

The characterization of Kuntī, the wife of Paṇḍu presents more complexities. She was the daughter of a Yādava chief named Śūra, who gave her to his childless cousin and friend, Kuntībhoja.[188] In the house of her adoptive father, she used to look after the duties of hospitality to *brāhmaṇas* and other guests.[189] Once she was able to please by her hospitality the sage Durvāsā, who imparted to her a formula for invocation and summoning of any of the celestial deities she liked to give her children, who shall certainly approach her and give her children.[190] Out of her curiosity, Kuntī summoned the god Sūrya, who procreated a son upon her even as he restored maidenhood to her.[191] Kuntī, afraid of disclosing her relationship with her son, floated the baby into water.[192] While Kuntī was afraid of disclosing her relationship with Karṇa, who was born out of the same process as her other sons; later her own husband forced her to resort to the same method for procreating sons for him.[193] The later sons gain legitimacy on account of the justification that she was now married and was asked by her husband to beget sons, procreation being important both from the point of view of gaining merit after death, and getting a successor to the kingdom. Again, did Karṇa's illegitimacy rested on the fact that he was begotten on a maiden who was not granted to anyone, and such was not possessed as field by Sūrya? Thus, Sūrya was not the legitimate claimant of Kuntī's procreative powers. However, when she procreates using the same method for her husband's sake, it is considered to be moral in the epic, as then she was the *field* belonging to Pāṇḍu, her husband, who himself used her power of procreation for acquiring religious merit. As pointed out earlier, Kuntī's attitude towards Karṇa stands in complete contrast with that of Satyavatī towards her son begotten before marriage. The arguments advanced by Pāṇḍu to persuade Kuntī to beget sons by using her power to invoke any of the gods[194], speak amply about the existence of a stage of promiscuity before the rules of moral conduct were established. Also, morality is redefined in terms of acceptance from the husband and the demands of patriarchy. The same act committed out of one's own desire, is termed adultery; and when done at the persuasion of the husband, becomes *dharma.* It is ironical, though, that to give legitimacy to his demand from Kuntī, Pāṇḍu is unable to find dharmaśastric sanction, and so he takes recourse to the ancient tradition of promiscuity. None of the *dharmaśāstras* talk of a case of performing *niyoga* when the husband is alive. They are generally silent regarding the birth of progeny in case the husband is impotent. However, Nārada and Pārāśara sanctioned the abandonment of an impotent husband by the wife,[195] thus clarifying that impotence of the husband was not an issue on which complete silence was observed. Again, it has to be admitted that none of the other *dharmaśāstrakāras* has given any rule regarding a case where the husband is impotent and the general ethos of the texts goes against the abandonment of the husband by the wife. Thus, Pāṇḍu's motivating Kuntī to beget sons in this manner was a deviation from the norms laid down. Yet the sons of Kuntī were regarded as legitimate heirs of Pāṇḍu in the epic. The ancient tradition of promiscuity is thus described by Pāṇḍu: "O thou of handsome face and sweet smiles, women formerly were not immured within houses and dependent on husbands and other relatives. They used to go about freely, enjoying themselves as best as they liked. O thou of excellent qualities, they did not then adhere to their husband faithfully, and yet they were not regarded as sinful for that was the sanctioned usage of the time... the practice, sanctioned by precedent is applauded by great *ṛṣis*. The practice is yet regarded with respect among the northern Kurus. Indeed, that usage, so lenient to women hath the sanction of antiquity".[196] Sūrya says the same thing to Kuntī while trying to convince her about the righteousness of a virgin's right to cohabit with a person of her choice. He says, "O thou of sweet smiles, neither thy father, nor thy mother, nor any other superior of thine, is competent to give thee away .... It is because a virgin desires the company of everyone, that she is called *Kanyā* from the root *kan* - to desire .... A virgin is, by nature free in this world."[197] He then tells Kuntī that in co-habiting with him she was not transgressing any *dharma*, "What transgression is there, if people behave according to their desire? All the females are free and so are the males. This is the normal course of the world all others are unnatural barriers".[198] However, it is to be noted that this was against the *dharmaśāstric* injunctions which considered adultery a punishable offence, though in this case a milder offence as it was adultery committed not against the grain, i.e., not in the *pratiloma* but in the *anuloma* way.[199] Again, the *dharmaśāstras* emphasized upon the importance of virginity,[200] and Kuntī's hesitation in relenting to Sūrya's utterances, and later, her fear and shame in accepting Karṇa as her son; amply testify that she was living in a society where virginity was considered important, even if not indispensable. However, Viṣṇu's references to the son of an unmarried girl[201] son received with the bride[202] and pregnant bride[203] prove that adultery was a fact that was happening in the society and there were cases where the girls gave birth to premaritally conceived sons.

In fact, promiscuity must have prevailed in some societies even during the period of composition of *Mahābhārata*, is testified by the references to regions where women were completely independent. It is worth to quote Shah in this regard:

Apart from Uttarakuru, in the *Sabhā Parvan*[204] we get reference to Mahiṣmati and Utsava-sanketa,[205] where women were completely independent. In fact, the term Utsava-sanketa is explained by Nīlakaṇṭha, a commentator on the *Mahābhārata,* as a republic inhabited by the seven tribes of the Utsava-sanketas who had no fixed laws of marriage and indulged in promiscuous intercourse.[206] Were these tribes of Utsava-sanketas matrilineal? It is likely, because in the *Karṇa Parvan*[207] there is a reference to Vālhīka women who are *bandhakīs* (harlots) and where sister's son (*bhagineya)* and not son inherits property. Association of sexually liberated women with a matrilineal set-up is significant – the *Śalya Parvan*[208] tells us that women due to their promiscuous behaviour i.e., *yonidoṣakṛtena* turn into *Rākśasīs*.[209] Equally significant is the fact that Karṇa, representative of an exacting patriarchal moral code, condemns such regions – Madra, Vālhīka and Ārhaṭṭa, for they are populated by such free women.[210] In the epic we get a specific term *svairiṇi*[211] for sexually independent women. Evidently then there were cultures and there was a time when women's sexuality was not controlled.[212]

The second wife of Pāṇḍu was Mādrī. The marriage of Mādrī with Pāṇḍu was one of the many incidences of cross-cousin marriages in *Mahābhārata.* This marked a deviation from the injunctions of the *dharmaśāstras*, which favoured *gotra* and *piṇḍa* exogamy.[213] Mādrī's case also presents an example of *satī* in the *Mahābhārata.* In the *Ādi Parvan* Mādrī tells Kuntī that she must mount the pyre of dead Pāṇḍu because it was in desiring her that he lost life and she was therefore, duty bound to satisfy his desire in the next world.[214] The attitude of the *dharmaśāstrakāras* towards the practice of *satī* was ambiguous, even if not favourable. While some of them did not mention it at all, others left it optional for the women, and yet attached great religious merit to accrue to a woman performing *satī*.[215] Thus Mādrī's having resorted to *satī* does not really mark a deviation to the norm.

The most significant woman character in the *Mahābhārata* is Draupadī, Kuntī's daughter-in-law and wife of all the five Pāṇḍava brothers. The narration of her childhood speaks of the warmth of relationship between her and her father, king Drupada. That no formal education was given to girls is amply borne out by the statement of Draupadī where she says in the *Āraṇyaka Parvan*, "I learned (in childhood) as a sage priest taught it to my brother, while I sat in my father's lap and listened".[216] Whatever knowledge she might have acquired would have been the result of such listening. However, even though she was dear to her father no question of educating her came to the mind of Drupada. This is in consonance with the norms of *dharmaśastras* which carry no provisions for educating the girl children. Manu considers the nuptial ceremony to be the same as initiation for the women, serving the husband equivalent to residing in the house of the teacher, and the household duties as the worship of daily fire.[217] Similar view is voiced in Viṣṇu.[218] *Yama* has prohibited the shaving of heads and recitation of Vedic mantras by women.[219] Atri also says that recitation (of the *Gāyatrī*) and practice of mantras bring about the fall of women and *śūdras*.[220] In the *smṛti* attributed to Dakśa, women are compared with illiterates.[221]

Draupadī's marriage was also in the form of *Swayamvara*, so-called marriage by self-choice, however, putting a condition to it made it rather a pseudo-selection. That the fear of getting someone undesirable existed is testified by Draupadī's refusal to let Karṇa contest in her *Swayamvara*.[222] Drupada's worry regarding the fate of his daughter after the *Swayamvara* regarding the status of the poor *Brāhmaṇas* (Pāṇḍavas in disguise), also attests to this.[223] When his family priest started making inquiries about their family and status, he was promptly snubbed by Yudhiṣṭhira who told him that such enquiries were out of place in the case of a marriage which depended upon a competition in arms.[224] This kind of a marriage did not figure in the forms of marriage recognized by the *dharmaśāstrakāras*.[225] Thus, incidents of such marriages in the epics actually mark out deviations from the norms laid down by the *dharmaśāstrakāras*.

Starker violation to the norms of the *dharmaśāstras* is found in Draupadi's marriage performed with all the five Pāṇḍava brothers. Though polygamy was permitted to males,[226] it was discouraged by the *dharmaśāstrakāras*, specially the later *dharmaśāstrakāras*.[227] Polyandry does not even find mention in the *smṛti* texts. Draupadī's case was not the only one in the epic where polyandry was resorted to. Jaṭilā and Vārkśi are also credited with having had polyandrous marriages.[228] An attempt to explain the reason behind having resorted to polygamy has been made by a few scholars on the basis of the influence of matrilineal tribes on the Pāṇḍavas who had spent part of their childhood in the Himalayan area of Śatasṛnga.[229] But as Kosambi says "It is not necessary to postulate a Tibetan invasion (connection) to explain Pāndava polyandry. The technical term *sādhārani* used for Draupadi as wife in common is also to be found in the *Ṛgveda* for the Goddess Rodasi who was common wife to all the Maruts, indisputably Āryan group God".[230] It is argued that there might have been some connection between polyandry and preservation of property in the hands of women. There can be yet another dimension to it, according to some scholars, that it was practised to ensure that the property rights are in the male line and the overriding principle is the preservation of the joint family property in male hand.[231] It might have been aimed at avoiding the conflicts between wives and sons of different brothers. Shalini Shah writes:

> If we reflect on the material basis of a polyandrous marriage we find that such a marriage could not have been common to a matrilineal set-up. In fact is would have been more of a drain than a benefit to local lineages in societies where women did bulk of subsistence farming and where male wealth was owed to sisters as well as to wives, while it would not have increased future generation of labourers born to a lineage. Poewe suggests that polyandry is usually about communal (non-individuated) access to resources, women and offspring. In the rare cases where it occurs in any significant form, this is in societies where the female contribution to subsistence is insignificant.[232] Seen in this light higher status of women in a polyandrous marriage cannot be presumed.[233]

Whatever be the case, as is proven by the circumstances that follow, Draupadī's polyandrous marriage was in no way a reflection of her having wielded any degree of independence. Whatever independence she exhibited came from within herself instead of emanating out of any of the external structures. In terms of external social structures, she was a booty and therefore, could be equally shared by all brothers.[234] It is told that upon seeing Draupadī, the hearts of all of them became full of desire[235] and fearing a division amongst his brothers, Yudhiṣṭhira said that she should become the common wife to all of the five brothers.[236] Later, when Drupada disagreed to this contention, Yudhiṣṭhira tells him thus: "This thy jewel of daughter hath been won by Arjuna. This, O King, is the rule with us; to ever enjoy equally a jewel that we may obtain. O best of monarchs, that rule of conduct we cannot now abandon. Krishna, therefore, shall become the wedded wife of us all."[237] Draupadī's desire carried no wait in the entire transaction of contentions. Also, the statement of the eldest of the brothers makes it clear that she was being treated as an object to be used at will once having won. The epic does not record the will of Draupadī with respect to her marriage; except for a passing reference to her preferential behaviour towards Arjuna in the

Mahāprasthānika Parvan. When Draupadī fell down dead, Yudhiṣṭhira attributed the reason for her fall to her partiality towards Arjuna.[238] Perhaps had she got any choice, Draupadī might have preferred a monogamous rather than polyandrous marriage.

Ironically, still theoretically virginity was on premium, as it was told that the illustrious princess Draupadī regained her virginity every day after a previous marriage.[239] This tale is later repeated for Mādhavi too.[240] The concern of Satyavatī and Kuntī who do not want their *kanyābhāva* to be tainted,[241] also speaks of the significance attached to virginity of the girls. Such an importance being attached to virginity is in line with the norms in the *dharmaśāstras* theoretically, which consider virginity to be of prime importance.[242] However, that in practice ways were sought to be found out of the bounds of this norm, is evident from false and impossible stories of retention or preservation of virginity.

At the time of Draupadī's marriage, gifts were given to the bride as well as her husbands.[243] Pāndavas received so much wealth from Drupada that Draupadī was described as Śrī[244] (who has been a Lakśmī for them). In fact, we can hardly describe dowry, to borrow Goody's terminology, as an example of diverging devolution (i.e., women's property complex). Dowry in such circumstances cannot be treated as *pre-mortem inheritances,* but has a specific intention of linking the daughter, hence her family with a particularly desirable son-in-law.[245] Thus, where the girl chooses the groom herself, says Manu, she is not allowed to take with her any ornaments given to her by her parents and if she carried them away, it will be regarded a theft.[246] It has to be admitted that in all the other forms of marriage except the *Gāndharva,* the bride was given ornaments and other movable forms of property, which was, in theory, her *strīdhana.*[247] Also, the term used for dowry is *yautakam,* which means separate property. Whether it actually remained an exclusive property for girls has been discussed at length in the previous chapter. As far as the inclination in the epic is concerned, it seems to go towards curtailing women's actual right to property. Śarmisṭhā tells Yayāti that three people can have no wealth – wife, *dāsa* and son. Whatever they earn, belongs to the one who owns them.[248] However, there was one crucial difference between wife and son, while the latter at some stage in his life came into his own inheritance, the wife being a woman remained subservient to different males in her life at all points of time. Karṇa underlines this aspect of woman's life. In the *Sabhā Parvan,* he says that women being always subservient, whatever wealth women have or earn belongs to their master i.e., their husband.[249]

The theoretical entitlement to property granted to women, was nullified as a woman was herself treated as property of the males. This becomes starkly visible in the context of the staking of Draupadī in the game of dice by Yudhiṣṭhira.[250] That the power wielded by the male head of a joint patriarchal household was immense becomes evident with Yudhiṣṭhira's staking his brothers and his wife (also theirs) without consulting anybody.[251] It is to be noted here that in patriarchy, it was not only the subordination of the female to the male patriarch, but also of other males to the head of the household. Thus, as far as this incident is concerned, the epic sought to establish the same definition of *gṛha* as that attempted at by the lawgivers. Further, if Yudhiṣṭhira can thus stake their person, it would not be going too far to assume that he might have had staked all their wealth too, whether it be *strīdhana* or any other form of property. In this context, Shah's observations are worth quoting here:

> In what sense women are property? Where father/husband has appropriative power over girl's/wife's reproductive use value (reproduction of children and domestic maintenance in general) and exchange value (her sexual services)[252] we can refer to women being treated as property. Staking of Draupadi in the game of dice in the *Sabhā Parvan* is often treated as an instance of wife being equated with wealth and thus staked. In the *Mahābhārata* we do get enumeration of women along with wealth[253] - Yudhisthira at one place classifies Draupadi as a *ratna.*[254] The epic also states that both women and wealth are property that could be utilized in difficulties.[255] But the point to be emphasized here is not that Draupadi was staked and to go into ethics of staking, for all the four Pāndava brothers were staked too and then Yudhisthira staked himself. The issue for us is what did the Pāndavas and Kuru clan thought of Draupadi's question of the husband-wife relationship and the rights in that relationship as they belonged to the husband, Bhisma makes an explicit statement that husband may be in any state but his authority over his wife does not cease.[256] Vikarna in his attempt to defend Draupadi says that (a)Yudhisthira had no right to stake her, for, she was not his wife alone and as such he had only part-ownership in her; (b) and then as bonded man he had lost all rights in her.[257] Vikarna's statement is important not for what he says but for what he does not say. His issue of part ownership would imply that had Draupadi been wife of Yudhisthira alone he would have had the right to stake her. The second statement that Yudhisthira was a bondman therefore, had no

right to stake Draupadi would mean that if Yudhisthira had staked her before himself then he would have been correct. In the end Vikarna's defence does not turn out to be defence at all but a mere debate on technicalities. His arguments also do not in any way contradict the general belief that wife is her husband's property. Karna reiterates this belief when he says that when Yudhisthira staked all his possessions as a free man, he already lost Draupadi.[258] He goes on to say that Pāndavas had no right even to the clothes they were wearing. Pāndavas in response start stripping their clothes, thereby agreeing with Karna's position on both counts.[259]

That the husband's right to stake the wife and the right of the winner over the person of the woman who was thus won; was recognized, even though tacitly; or at least not refuted, is proven by the sinister silence that is observed by the entire assemblage of Kuru elders even when the humiliation of Draupadī is taken to the basest level of attempting at disrobing her in front of all.[260] What was the definition of morality, of *dharma* in this society? What made everyone remain silent to such an act. Was it in tune with *dharma* for a husband to have staked his wife, and was it considered in accordance with *dharma* for the winner to act in any way with a woman who was thus enslaved. Even if considered to be a slave woman, could she be disrobed by the masters in front of an assembly? It was only afterwards that Vidura urged upon those present in the assembly to answer Draupadī's question as to if Yudhiṣṭhira, being himself made a slave had the right to stake her, and accordingly whether if she was a slave or not.[261] Bhīṣma's answer to the sorrowful Draupadī is revealing regarding the nature of morality. He says, "I have already said, O blessed one, that the course of morality is subtle. Even the illustrious wise in this world fail to understand it always. What in this world a strong man calls morality is regarded as such by others, however otherwise it may be; but what a weak man calls morality is scarcely regarded as such even if it be the highest morality. From the importance of the issue involved, from its intricacy and subtlety, I am unable to answer with certitude the question thou hath asked."[262] Later, Draupadī was granted two boons by Dhṛtarāṣṭra, whereby she asked him to free all the five of her husbands of bondage.[263] Thus she is imparted an agency in the epic, whereby she emerges in the role of one who is the saviour of her husbands. Karṇa not only acknowledges but applauds Draupadī's role, saying, "Pāṇḍavas were drowning in the sea of misfortune without any support, Draupadī has become a boat for them".[264] Thus, it is Draupadī who protects Pāṇḍavas and not the reverse. It is this that marks out the reversal of the norm to the starkest possible extent.

In the entire sequence of events, Draupadī does not remain a silent sufferer. She repeatedly questions regarding the rights of a husband over her person who had lost his own independence having staked himself.[265] However, even her question tacitly recognizes that had Yudhiṣṭhira not lost himself beforehand, he could have staked and lost Draupadī rightfully, who would then have been the slave. Even the brothers of Yudhiṣṭhira recognise his right over them to have staked them.[266] Another notable thing regarding Draupadī's censure is that she was sorrowful for being brought before the Kaurava assembly in a menstruating state.[267] Previously, she urged Duhśāsana to not to drag her before the elders in 'such a state'.[268] The existence and nature of menstrual taboos as propagated by the *dharmaśāstras* has been discussed in one of the preceding chapters.[269] The *Mahābhārata* does not present a very different picture in this regard. *Rajasvalā* is impure and evil and is forbidden from all religious ceremonies. The *Anuśāsana Parvan* states that such a woman must not be allowed to remain where a *Śrāddha* is being performed.[270] Same as the *Smṛti* texts, the epic tells us that Indra who had incurred the sin of brahmanicide passed on a part of that guilt to woman.[271] Again, in consonance with the *dharmaśāstras*, the *Śānti-Parvan* also declares that after menstruation a woman becomes pure like a utensil cleaned with ash.[272] However, as Shah comments, "All these menstrual taboos in the *Mahābhārata* reach a dramatic height when *rajasvalā* Draupadī is dragged before everyone in the Kuru assembly. Duhśāsana broke the taboo in violating her seclusion."[273] This incident marks the most blatant breaking off the norm, which was theoretically recognized in the epic itself.

Even though the wife in the epic was subjugated by the norms of patriarchy, a different colour was sought to be given to wifehood by the characterization of Draupadī. Thus, though in the *Mahābhārata* also, the common name for wife is *bhāryā* and husband is *bhartā* (the supporter), yet wife was something more than a mere parasitic dependent. Her tremendous capacity is revealed in none other than the character of Draupadī. She stands up to her husbands with conviction and does not really criticize Yudhiṣṭhira initially in the *Sabha Parva*, but later she is vociferous in denouncing his action and calls him a desperate gambler and a fool *(mūḍha)* and attributes her sorrow to the fact that she was his wife.[274] She is not only the one who has the ability to denounce and reject her humiliation on account of being treated as the husband's property; but is also attributed an agency in that she emerges as the saviour of her husbands. Her boon in the *Sabha Parva* from Dhṛtarāṣṭra, freeing her husbands from slavery and recovering their weapons for them[275], is an instance of this role.

Quite in consonance with the ideology enunciated in the *dharmaśāstras*, the epic underlines the existence of wife as central to the household.[276] Wife is described as half the man, the best of friends, the root of the three ends of life and of all that will help him in the other world.[277] It is said that sweet-speaking wives are their husband's friends on occasions of joy, they are as fathers on occasion of religious acts, and they are as mothers in the hour of illness and woe.[278] Draupadi is also described as a "beloved wife, dearer even than life", and the eldest Pāṇḍava states that "like a mother she is to be cherished and like an elder sister she is to be respected".[279] However, in spite of such remarks, he failed to protect the honour of Draupadī, staking her in the game of dice.

That patriarchy was about complete dominance of the male over the woman, specially the wife, is amply borne out by the staking of Draupadī by her husband. However, it was not only gender relations in the sense of male-to-female relationship. Rather, relationships between females were also conditioned on the basis of their position in the patriarchal household. Patrilocality was an important determinant in this regard. It can be actually read as the superiority of the agnates over the woman, which is ensured by patrilocality. Multi-generational dominance along patriarchal lines provided room for sub-dominant roles for women also within the household dominance system. It was this that accounted for the dominance of mother-in-law over the daughter-in-law. It was necessary for the latter to keep the former pleased. Glimpses of this can be found in the epic. Draupadī says in the *Virāṭa Parvan* "Only for Āryā Kuntī did I make sandal paste with my hands".[280] In the *Āraṇyaka Parvan* she says, "Personally do I wait every day with food and drink and clothes upon the revered and truthful Kuntī, that mother of heroes. Never do I show any preference for myself over her in matters of food and attire, and never do I reprove in words that princess equal unto the Earth herself in forgiveness."[281]

Another example of woman being treated as property is that of Mādhavī in the *Mahābhārata.*[282] She is found to be treated as a disposable property by men in her life who alienate her or her reproductive capacity and sexuality at will. Her father Yayāti gives her away to Gālava, so that his sons and grandsons are not destroyed as a result of the curse of a dissatisfied mendicant.[283] It is obvious that the daughter could be sacrificed for the well being of sons and grandsons. Gālava then gave Mādhavī to three other men for producing a son each in exchange for horses for his *guru* Viśwṛmitra.[284] Mādhavī is treated as an object, a *womb on rent* in this entire transaction. She is used as an instrument in social relations created by those with rights in or over her. Continuously in the process of being alienated or disposed, Mādhavī lands up being totally alienated from the male-ordered world where she loses her personhood and becomes only a *womb on rent.*[285] Ironically, she is considered to be a virgin after all that she underwent, having every time become a maiden again,[286] and her father Yayāti arranged for her *Swayamvara,* when she refused to marry and eventually married forest.[287] In other words, she preferred to marry asceticism. The object of men's exchange had finally acquired subjectivity and in the process she repudiated the male world.[288]

That alternative characterizations of women were sought to be presented by the *Mahābhārata,* further becomes pronounced in its characterization of women who found place in other texts also; often having generated more impact in those roles. Thus Śakuntalā of the *Mahābhārata* episode is also courageous like Draupadī and displays a sense of self-esteem, dignity and independence of thought and action. This is in contrast to her characterization in Kālidāsa's play *Abhijñāna Śākuntalam.* In the play when Duṣyanta refused to accept her, Śakuntalā appears to be weak and is thrown into fits of crying, cursing her fate. This is actually the traditional way in which rage and helplessness of women in a patriarchal society finds expression, being rendered voiceless. But in the epic, instead of cursing her fate, she curses Duṣyanta, "May your head break into hundred pieces",[289] and further challenges him that even without his co-operation her son would rule the kingdom.[290] Sakuntalā of the epic does not plead before faithless Duṣyanta. In fact, she expresses clear intention that the companionship of one who lies and abuses trust should be avoided.[291]

Particularly interesting in this regard are the portrayals of Anasūyā, Sītā and Ahalyā. The way these characters are treated in the *Mahābhārata* is actually far more liberal than in the *Rāmāyaṇa.* Ṛṣi Atri's wife Anasūyā finds place in the *Mahābhārata* as a *brahmavādinī* who left her husband with firm intention that she would never again allow herself to be dominated by him.[292] She prayed to Śiva who granted her a boon that even without husband she would have a son who would bear her name and bring fame to her *vamśa.* This is in sharp contrast with portrayal of Anasūyā in the *Rāmāyana,* where she is found lecturing to young Sitā on *pativratā dharma,* telling her that even if the husband is wanton or bad he is still a god for the wife.[293] Anasūyā's portrayal in the *Mahābhārata* is revolutionary in the sense that though procreation of son remains important, the woman is shown capable of doing so without the husband.[294] This is in total contrast to the normative literature where procreation of son was considered important from the point of view of securing heaven for the husband. Also, in the normative literature, there was no place for a woman who abandons her husband. Again, the son of Anasūyā was to bear her name and bring fame to her *vamśa*; in stark contrast with the prescriptions of lawgivers. Though not revolutionary, characterizations of Sītā and Ahalyā also were considerably liberal. In the *Mahābhārata,* Gautama is forgiving about his wife's adultery[295] but in the *Rāmāyaṇa,* Ahalyā is cursed to become a stone statue for an unintended happening,[296] symbolizing a far more rigid patriarchal moral code. Similarly, in the *Rāmopākhyāna* of the *Mahābhārata,* Rāma tells Sītā "O Princess of Mithila whether thou art chaste or unchaste, I dare not enjoy thee, now that thou art like sacrificial butter lapped by a dog".[297] However, it only takes oral testimony of various gods and father Daśaratha from heaven regarding her chastity for Rāma to accept Sītā.[298] While in the *Rāmāyaṇa*, Sītā has to go through fire ordeal to prove her chastity. However, it has to be recognized that among the divergent portrayals of women figures in the two epics, only those showing explicit adherence to norms of patriarchy have been emphasized and disseminated in popular discourse, and hence, have left deeper impressions upon Indian psyche, shaping Indian womanhood on the ideals generated thereby. Thus, it is Sītā and not Draupadī, who is considered as the role model for defining womanhood in India. And even though *Mahābhārata* provided space for a woman like Draupadī who carried a voice, the same woman was shown as involved in an intent description of the religion of the *pativratā* in another context. In the *Āraṇyaka Parvan* Draupadī briefs Satyabhāmā about the *pativratā dharma* thus: "To live under husband's protection is the *sanātana dharma* for women. Husband is God, he is salvation (for women) and he is the only refuge".[299] This theme is repeated constantly in the *Mahābhārata* for instance in the *Umā Maheśvara samvāda.*[300]

Also linked up with the notion of *pativratā* is the issue of chastity. Draupadī tells Satyabhāmā not to wait in solitude even on her grown up sons Pradyumna and Sāmba.[301] This notion of respectable women and emphasis on chastity was taken to a ridiculous extent when *pativratā* was described as one who apart from her husband does not even glance at sun, moon and trees since they have masculine names.[302] However, this was more in theory, and actually, the epic shows various levels of moral response as far as fidelity of women is concerned. Again, chastity was believed to bestow immense powers on the woman. Such was the force of Sāvitrī's *pativratā dharma* that she could actually bring dead husband back to life.[303]

Like the *Rāmāyaṇa,* the *Mahābhārata* also provides glimpses of diverse societies. The cases of Hiḍimbā and Citrāngadā are often cited as presenting examples of matriarchal societies. However, going by the anthropological definition of matriarchy; which implies concentration of dominant power in the hands of women and passing of descent from mother to daughter; both of these cases are not indicative of existence of matriarchy. Hiḍimbā's *Rākśasa* brother Hiḍimba was killed by Bhīma which left Hiḍimbā as the successor of her brother and she requested Kuntī to let her marry Bhīma on the condition that as soon as a son was born from this union she will not pressurize Bhīma.[304] In the case of Citrāngadā, she was a brotherless maiden and, therefore, a *putrikā.* Her father agreed to let her marry Arjuna only on the condition that her first born son would be treated as his heir and successor and not his father's (i.e., Arjuna's) son.[305] However, these two mark deviations from the norms in that marriage with *Rākśasī*[306] as well as with *puritkā* was denounced by the *dharmaśāstrakāras.*[307] It is significant that both Hidimbā's domain and Citrāngadā's Manipura are on the outskirts of the *Āryāvarta* and perhaps its patriarchal norms were therefore, not effective in these peripheral areas.[308]

Though no sure evidence of existence of matriarchy could be found, the *Karṇa Parvan* attests to the existence of matriliny at two places, Ārhatta and Vālhīka.[309] Matriliny means recognition of kinship and inheritance on the maternal line, where the authority over children is exercised not by their father or mother but by the maternal uncle. Thus, matriliny and matriarchy are different in that matriliny implies only following the maternal line with regard to inheritance and kinship. This did not actually confer the rights and powers of the head of the family on the mother. In fact, it was the maternal uncle who remained the supreme head of the family and after him came his uterine nephew. Thus, interestingly, women in matrilineal societies are also subjected to male authority; the only difference being that in this case, the males happen to be their brother and mother's brother. However, the other authorities that they experience are females including their mother and mother's sister. In a patrilineal society by contrast, women are subject to the male authority first of their father and then of their husband. What can be inferred is that women were less likely to be face subjugation and discrimination in a matrilineal set up. Also to be noted is that Vālhīka is also mentioned previously as a place where the sexual ethics do not exist among the women. The existence of matrilineal societies also testifies to the existence of regions beyond the influence of the *dharmaśāstras.* There are also some examples of matrilocal marriage in the epic. Jaratkāru, a sage, married the sister of Vāsuki Nāga and lived in his in-law's house until she conceived from him and their son Āstīka was brought up at his maternal uncle's place.[310] Hindimbā too continued to live in her parental house. In all the above cases brides belonged to same non-*Āryan* tribe viz., *Nāga*, *Rākśasa* etc. whose social institutions apparently differed from the patriarchal model of *Āryan kśatriyas*.[311] It can be inferred that the examples of matrilocal marriages do not come from the heart of the Kuru-Pāñcāla cultural complex but from outside. However, again, these mark out deviations from the norms, and add weight to the hypothesis that the sphere of influence of the prescriptions of the normative texts was very limited and that the social reality was posited somewhere between the ideal and what is practised.

Further deviation from the norms is marked out by the incidences of cross-cousin marriages in the *Mahābhārata*. Based on the kings's list given in the 90th chapter of the *Ādi Parvan*, Shah has given a list of instances which following appear to be cross-cousin marriages, and has inferred that from a record of over fifty marriages, one is definitely a *sapiṇḍa* marriage while three other appear to be so and two are apparently unions of cross-cousins of the second degree.[312] While there does not seem to be any bar against *sapiṇḍa* marriages, these were at the same time perhaps not a preferred type of mating. Indeed, the didactic portions even impose a categorical ban on such unions.[313] However, the *dharmaśāstras* were against *gotra* and *piṇḍa* endogamy.[314] Again, while in theory, the epic owes allegiance to the norms, in practice these are often disregarded.

As discussed earlier, wifehood and motherhood were the only two recommend status of womanhood in a patriarchy perceived by the *dharmaśāstrakāras. Mahābhārata* seems to agree with them on this count. In the *Mahābhārata* we do get references to unmarried women. There is one reference to a daughter of Kunigarga who chose to remain unmarried and performed severe austerities.[315] But she had to marry Śṛngavāna and give one half of the merit to him in lieu of his consent and only then could she attain her salvation.[316] The story is revealing in that a woman remains unable to attain heaven if she is unmarried as she remains devoid of *samskāras* without marriage. Also, consent of the husband is imperative in order to get relieved from the material world. The Śalya Parvan refers to a celibate daughter of Śāndilya who attained heaven but it is emphasized here that she performed austerities that were impossible for women.[317] It is clear that pursuit of salvation was not favoured in the case of women. However, the narration of such cases points towards women actually following the path and thus deviating from the norm. The *dharmaśāstras* actually prohibited performance of penances by women.[318] Further, the barren wife is considered to be worthless.[319] It is said that the gods and ancestors will not accept at the sacrifice that what is offered by a barren woman for it is stained.[320] Again, the gifts that are made by a woman without husband and children rob the receiver of his life powers.[321] Such statements are in conformity to the normative texts.[322]

Like the *dharmaśāstra* texts,[323] the ethos of the *Mahābhārata* is not exactly in favour of widow remarriage. It is stated in the *Anuśāsana Parvan* that one who gives his daughter twice in marriage is born as a worm in next life.[324] It is also said that a remarried widow's son (*paunarbhava*) pollutes the *śrāddha* food; yet he is called a *dvija.*[325] Various terms like *punarbhū, parapūrvā, anyapūrvā* for the remarried widows occur in the *Mahābhārata.*[326] Even didactic portions show familiarity with the practice of a widow marrying her brother-in-law.[327] Again, it needs to be recognized that Nārada and Pārāśara permitted widow remarriage.[328] However, according to Pārāśara, death of the husband after betrothal is the condition when the girl may remarry. It is to be noted that the *dharmaśāstras* were themselves not unanimous on the issue but the ethos of the normative texts certainly goes against widow remarriage. Pārāśara, though permitting remarriage in such a case, in the following verses says that a widow who observes celibacy all through her life after the death of her husband, attains to heaven after death just like the *brahmacārīs*.[329]

The condition of the widow was not much different from that prescribed by the lawgivers.[330] The widow had no right to dress aesthetically. Arjuna saw Yādava widows open haired without garlands and ornaments.[331] The colourless and tasteless living of a widow is indicated by the fact that anything divested of beauty and splendour is compared to a widow – thus appears Dwārikā to Arjuna without Śri Krsna.[332]

To summarize, the *Mahābhārata* presents myriad shades of women characters. The society as depicted in the epic is patriarchal, but existence of divergences and variations from the norms is also pointed at. Women are given no less space in that their voices find expression in spite of the accepted allegiance to the patriarchal norms. The cases of Satyavatī and Draupadī point towards the fact that even if external conditions are not congenial enough, empowerment can come from within oneself. While Kuntī is afraid of acknowledging Karṇa as her son till the end, Satyavatī rears up her *kāṇīna* son and when the need arises, recognizes him to be her son. While Mādhavī relents to become an instrument of male ambition, Ambā throws herself into singular efforts for not only one but also the subsequent birth. Thus the epic provides depictions of characters with multiple hues and shades of personality, as also events and cases with multiple dimensions regarding the unquestioning adherence to or deviation from the norms. It becomes clear that though theoretically accepting the norms, in practice there were several divergences. Thus reality emerges as a complex state of affairs.

Women in the *Śangam* Society

While the epics provide glimpses of the other societies existing parallel to the *Āryan* society, there was a society in the far south, which yet away from the *Āryan* influence, was gradually getting influenced by it. The ethos of this society is reflected in the earliest stratum of Tamil literature now available – the literature of *Śangam* – which forms the first well-lighted epoch in the history of the Tamil land.[333] According to Hart, this large body of poetry antedates for all intents and purposes the incursion of Sanskrit culture into Tamilnad, that the culture which produced it was a continuation of the megalithic culture which dominated the Deccan for the millennium before Christ and its special importance for cultural history is that it describes this civilization, which according to the Allchins was characterized by a very conservative and unchanging culture,[334] before it was appreciably influenced by Sanskritic culture from the north.[335] However, Sastri believes that the picture of the social and economic conditions of the age, the cultural ideas and ideals accepted and cherished by the people, of the institutions and activities which embodied and sustained them; of which the literature of *śangam* gives an unusually complete and true picture; is the unmistakable result of the blend of two originally distinct cultures, best described as Tamilian and *Āryan*.[336] Further, as Vijaya Ramaswamy writes, "For South India the earliest historical evidence that comes down to us is from the śangam age. This period roughly going back to the 3rd century BC and forward into the 2nd–3rd century AD is wholly dominated by Tamil literary sources which range from grammar and Tamil poetics to religious and erotic literature. For this period the other regions of the South throw up no corresponding literary evidence. Kannada and Telugu, which are languages particular to the present day linguistic states of Karnataka and Andhra, emerged only in the 7th–8th century and Malayalam, the language of the Kerala region, in the 10th century. Therefore it would not be inappropriate to extend one's analysis of the *Śangam* artefacts to the whole of South India and talk in terms of a pan-Dravidian culture rather than just the 'Tamil' culture of religion."[337] In the light of the over-view quoted, it can be said with a degree of certainty that a study of the *Śangam* society is sure to provide insights into the regional variations in co-existing cultures in the subcontinent.

The *Śangam* literature essentially consists of two major collections of songs – the *Ettutokai* and the *Pattuppaṭṭu*. The *Ettutokai* comprises the following eight anthologies: *Narrinai, Kuruntokai, Aiñkurunūru, Patirrupaṭṭu, Paripātal Kolittokai, Akanānūru, Puranānūru.* The other major collection, the *Pattuppaṭṭu*, comprises of the following ten: *Tirumurukāruppatai, Porunarārupatai, Ciruppānāruppatai, Perumppānāruppatai, Mullaippāttu, Maturaikkāñci, Netunalvātai, Kuriñcippaṭṭu, Pattinappālai, Malaipatukatām.* In fact, the eight long poems and ten anthologies of the *Śangam* age are considered to be the oldest and most distinguished body of secular poetry extant in India.[338] The two collections together consist of more than 2,300 songs. Out of these, a total of 154 poems carry women's signatures, and it is possible that some of the 102 poems that have not yet been attributed to specific composers were also written by women.[339] Out of the extant poetry two-thirds of the women poets seem to have contributed only one poem each to the anthologies. It is only thirteen women who seem to have made major contributions ranging from five to the fifty nine poems contributed by Auvaiyar to both *aham* and *puram* categories.[340]

The *Śangam* literature got its name from a college or *Śangam* of Tamil poets who flourished under the patronage of the Pāṇḍya kings of Madurai. The literature is divided into three phases – the beginning (Mutal Śangam), the middle (Itai Śangam) and the end (Katai Śangam).[341] The *Śilappadikāram* and *Maṇimekalai*, the two great Tamil epics, are post-*Śangam* works. Aesthetically the poems belong to two genres – *Ākam* and *Puram. Ākam* poems are usually love poems and deal with an inner space, whereas *Puram* poems take everything else into their scope: the yard, the court, the battlefield, and the public life.[342]

Women are central to the entire poetics.[343] The entire *aham* or love poetry of *Śangam* is in five major moods or situation (*tinais*) called *anbi tinai* – expressions of a woman's love and lovers' meetings – *Kurinji*; patient waiting – *Mullai*; pining for the warrior lover – *Palai*; the women's sorrows and secret meetings – *Neydal*; and her sulkiness and anger against marital unfaithfulness – *Marudam*. All the five situations are based on the feminine response. The last *tinai* also sometimes expresses the response of the prostitute to the angry wife.[344] Both male and female poets handle such themes in a common manner except for marginal differences. Accordingly, the *dramatis personae* of the *Ākam* poems include the heroine, the hero, the heroine's mother, her foster mother, her woman friend, the courtesan, the courtesan's woman friend, the hero's friend, passers who witness the event. However, the principle characters remained the heroine and the hero; the heroine being portrayed as young and made for love. Thus, while the love poems set up a fictive situation with the characters portrayed as ideal types; the *Puram* poems deal with historical figures and real events. In the *Puram* poems, women are portrayed as older in age, as mothers of grown up sons, as widows of warrior husbands and as courtesans. It is to be noted at the first place that while love-making before marriage did not have scriptural sanction in the *dharmaśāstric* ideology, there was a complete body of literature dedicated to this theme in the South. As observed by Ramaswamy:

> It is also noteworthy that women seem to have enjoyed considerable autonomy in their marriage partners and there are a plethora of reference to lengthy courtships and elopements in the *aham* themes of all the Sangam anthologies. Elopement was not merely condoned but looked upon as quite natural and hence socially acceptable although not the ideal form of marriage (*Tolkappiyam*: sutra 40: Dikshitar: 1930: 279). According to a *Tolkappiyam* verse the foster mother of the girl is in fact dissuaded from following the eloping couple by the people she encounters on the way (*Tolkappiyam*: sutra 40: vide Dikshitar: 1930: 279). In the *Tolkappiyam* a marriage conducted with parental blessings is categorised as Agattinai and the woman's *Karpu* is held forth as an ideal. By *Karpu* is meant not only chastity but the upholding of the honour of the marital home in acceptance of her role model as the *Illal* the 'maker of the home'. Alternately, a union born out passion and heaving its culmination in elopement is climaxed by parental acceptance and is categorised as *kalaviyal*, *kalavu* meaning stealth or as *kamappuarchchi*, a passionate union.[345]

Thus, unlike the forms of marriage discussed and recognized in the *dharmaśāstras*, marriage by elopement and marriage by parental sanction are the two forms found to be mentioned in the *Śangam* texts. Again, though *Gāndharva* form is close to marriage by elopement in the case of southern society, the difference lies in the fact that while in the *dharmaśāstras*, this form of marriage found only a tacit acceptance,[346] in the *Śangam* texts, such a marriage was considered to be very natural and was encouraged. Again, no equivalents of *Paiśāca* and *Rākśasa* forms could be found in the *Śangam* texts. It may be safely assumed from this that such heinous acts as marriage by capture or rape did not find any existence, leave aside recognition, in the *Śangam* society. Again, one of the most striking aspects of *Śangam* society is the complete absence of dowry or groom price. There are however several reference to bride price in *Śangam* literature.[347] One of the poems in the *Ainkurunuru* mentions the gift of land by the hero from the *Neydal* i.e., maritime tract, to the bride's relatives before marriage.[348] The willingness of a youth form the *kurinji tinai* attracted by a maiden from the *Neydal* tract, to give away plenty of costly jewels and other presents, is unable to gain for him the favours of the maiden's relatives and their consent for marrying her to him; for which he goes on to lament and then to express the hope of being able to please the girl's father by joining him in the salt field and the sea leaving his *tinai* altogether.[349] In the *Narrinai*, the foster mother tries persuade the girl's brothers to accept her lover because according to her, 'even the ruler of Chembian, with the lovely chariot, who conquered Kazhumalam and annexed Urunthai ... is too small and insignificant a price for the girl.[350] Similarly, in *Puram*, the father says that he will not give his daughter to the man even if he receives wealth equivalent to the Chera, port-town of Musiri.[351] The practice of endowing the girls with bride price persists even now among some of the lower castes in Tamil Nadu (and probably also in other parts of the South) and is reflected in Tamil folk songs.[352] It is of great significance that dowry which has been the symbol of women's oppression within the patriarchy down the centuries, was wholly absent in the *Śangam* age and what prevailed widely was the converse practice of bride price.[353] While marriage with bride price (*Āsura* form of marriage), also finds mention and recognition in the *dharmaśāstra* literature, it was generally condemned and disfavoured by the lawgivers, considering it to be one of the unlawful forms of marriage.[354] In contrast to this, it seems to been accepted norm in the *Śangam* texts.

That virginity and chastity before marriage was not on premium is amply borne out by the themes discussed in the *Ṛham* poetry, where the girls and boys are found to be mixing freely and courting each other. The *Akanānūru* writes that the time young girls kept watch over the ripe corn just before harvest was the occasion for romantic dalliance called *kalavu*. The girls would raise the cry of *puli*, *puli* (tiger, tiger) which would immediately bring the youth.[355] This *kalavu* or courtship was an accepted aspect of social life.[356] It appears that it was only with growing Brahmanical influence that South Indian society tended to become conservative and closed.[357]

Perhaps it was due to such social structures that in the *Śangam* society, a female child was as welcome as a male child.[358] One finds a converse situation in the classic patriarchal structure as prescribed by the lawgivers.[359] Further, as Ramaswamy notes, "The welcome extended to the female child is logical in the *Śangam* polity where women and men were co-sharers in the economy."[360]

In *Śangam* literature, which, it must be clarified, is by and large a description of the countryside and rural economy, women seem to have been co-sharers with men both in the domestic and the public spheres.[361] The evidence in *Śangam* texts is widely scattered and meagre; still it makes a significant contribution towards our understanding of the role of women in the early South Indian economy. More than 60 per cent of the agricultural operations were controlled by women. Sowing seeds, cleaning and husking paddy, guarding the crops and pounding and storing grain were entirely women's work, while both men and women were equally important in irrigational operations.[362] Women helped men in cultivating the fields among the low caste Vēlālas called *kataiyār*[363] (meaning 'the last in the society'). The *Purananuru* also refers to these women known as *kataicciyār*.[364] In the *Tolkāppiam* the farmer is referred to as *ulavarand* his wife as *ulatti*.[365] However, the term *ulatti* was applied not only to the farmer's wife, but even to a woman working as agricultural labourer.[366]

Husking and winnowing of the paddy were also done entirely by women. The image of two women standing face to face pounding paddy with a big pestle (*ulakkai*) is a recurrent theme in *Śangam* literature.[367] Besides the above, young unmarried girls were employed to keep a watch over the paddy and millet fields and drive off the parrots and other birds and also stray animals. A pretty girl driving away the parrots the fields is a cliche in *Śangam* poetry.[368]

Further, cattle breeding and dairy farming was a sector of the economy in which women played a leading part. The *Perumppānāruppatai,* which can roughly be ascribed to the fourth century AD, gives a detailed description of the work of a shepherdess in the southern country.[369] The process of setting curds from the milk done by the shepherdess is used as a simile in the *Purananuru.*[371] The *Purananuru* also says that in the Pāṇḍya country the prosperous housewife exchange paddy for the goat meat brought by the shepherdess.[371] At home the *kovalar* woman prepared red *tinarrice* which was consumed with milk and also offered to guests.[372]

In the handloom industry too, women participated actively. The spinning of thread was also done by housewives. In fact, it was by and large the sole occupation of widows and unmarried or destitute women.[373] Such female spinners are referred to in the *Śangam* literature as *parutti pentukal*. The *Puranānūru* uses the expression *parutti pentir pannuvāl* for the thread carded by spinning women.[374] Another profession associated with the handloom industry – the bleaching and washing of cloth, was again a sphere of work in which women engaged independently or actively assisted their husbands. The washer-woman was known as *pulatti*. The *Śangam* texts are replete with references to her. The

Purananuru says that the *pulatti* washed the clothes in the particular area called *kalar* whose mud was a good purifying and whitening agent.[375] The *Narrinai* says that she prepared starch from rice[376] and the cloth was dipped in the starchy solution.[377] Finally, with her long tapering fingers she removed the lumpy or excess starch from the cloth.[378] The *Akananuru* also refers to washing and starching of cloth by the *pulatti*.[379] A solitary reference in the *Purananuru* to the *Vennikuyattiyar*, that is, the potter woman of Venni, who was a poetess and who composed a poem on the victory of Karikala at the battle of Venni[380], may be taken as an indicator of women's involvement in the task of pottery. However, there are more frequent references to basket weaving by women. In a *Śangam* reference pertaining to the sixth century AD, it is said that besides washing, it was the job of the *pulatti* to make baskets out of reeds called *korai*.[381]

The wives of salt makers played an important role in the making and marketing of salt in the *neytal* or coastal region. The *Perumppanarruppatai* describes how the husband and wife extracted the salt and heaped it on the sea shore. It was loaded into a cart and hawked from door to door. The wife drove a pair of additional bullocks to be harnessed in case the ones driving the cart got tired. Women also carried head loads of slat and sold them from door to door. The *Akananuru*[382] says that the beautiful *neydal* women used to exchange salt for paddy from the peasant women. Further, in the *Neydal* region, the *parataiyar* or fisherwomen caught and sold fish. Young girls of this caste kept watch over the fish dried in the sun.[383] The *Ainkurunuru* says that the *valaya* women sold the *varal* fish (regarded as a delicacy) and got year-old white rice in return.[384]

Garland-making and flower-selling were, by and large, the occupation of women.[385] Further, women hired themselves out as cooks, either in private homes or temples. They also made pancakes or hoppers and *appam*, a kind of sweet, and hawked them in the streets according to the *Maduraikkanci*[386] and the *Śilappadikaram*.[387] *Śangam* literature also refers to the employment of women as wet nurses and foster mothers known as *cevilittai*. Though probably only indigent women took to the profession, the nurse seems to have enjoyed the respect as well as affection of the family she served. In the *Kurincippattu* the daughter of the house first confides her love affair to her nurse or foster mother who then convinces the mother and the marriage takes place.[388] Also, women bards and dancers called *viraliyar* occupied a very important place in *Śangam* society. In fact, there is a separate poem called *Viraliyarruppatai* contained in the *Akananuru* which refers to the great beauty and accomplishments of the *virali*. The *virali* were very graceful dancers,[389] while the women who sang were known as *pattini*.

Women could be found in the armoury as cleaners of weapons or as lamp-lighters to which reference is made in the *Mullaippattu* which also says they carried shining spears.[390] However, as Ramaswamy comments, "One does not know whether they actually fought with them."[391]

That women were not relegated to the 'private' sphere of domesticity in the *Śangam* society, rather they were active participants in the public and professional life, is amply borne out by the above discussion. This is in striking contrast to the Brahmanical injunctions, which laid down the sphere of women's activity to be confined to the household and domestic activities.[392] Thus, the society in the South presents a strong variation to the one envisaged by the 'Brahmanical patriarchy', and thus, clearly was away from the sphere of influence of the *dharmaśāstric* injunctions.

Further, it was not only the economic sphere which presented deviations from the normative codes of conduct. There are striking variations and divergences in the way women were perceived in the socio-religious realm.

Śangam literary evidence suggests that the notion of 'pollution' was also foreign to Dravidian culture and the bipolarity of purity and pollution entered the *Śangam* texts as a part of the Brahmanical discourse.[393] It is the Brahmanical text *Achcharakkovai* (circa sixth century AD) which for the first time introduces the notions of purity and pollution followed by references to these categories in the *Kizhkanakku*, a Jain text called *Pazhamozhi Nanuru*. The idea of a female as polluting agent (because of her menstruation, birth 'pollution' etc.) also began to occur around the same period. *Purananuru* describes how an enemy's horses stand terrified like girls who cannot touch dishes (when they are) in the temple of Murugan.[394] Here, the poem refers to the time when they are menstruating. However, unlike the *Āryan* concept, where these periods are considered to be inauspicious, in the *Śangam* society, it was fear that was behind considering these periods to be polluting. The following statement of the foster mother to her daughter makes it obvious:

> 'Your breasts are budding, your sharp teeth shine, your head has a coil on it, and you wear a cool dress (*talai*, a dress of leaves worn by girls after puberty). Do not go anywhere with your wandering girl friends-our ancient

> city Mutupati has (places) with attacking deities. You are protected (i.e., now that you have reached puberty, we must protect you), and should not go outside. You are no longer a little girl, wise, lovely child-at the time of puberty, you stayed outside (while you were menstruous).'[395]

The time of ceremonial impurity after giving birth was called *puniru* and seems to have lasted for ten days, after which the woman bathed at night in the tank.[396] Perhaps a separation had to be observed between the husband and the wife following the period of the birth of a child. This is borne out by several poems which describe the husband avoiding the embrace of his wife while she is nursing their child.[397] Again, poems describing how the hero begins to see his harlot (*parattai*) after his first son is born,[398] also may be pointing towards the hesitation of the husband to make love to his wife in childbed probably because she is impure, or dangerous to his manhood. Crawley observes; "Separation between husband and wife at birth is often prolonged until the child is weaned, the idea being that milk, a female secretion, is specially dangerous vehicle for transmission of her effeminate properties. Hence the infant, from contact with the mother, is also 'unclean', that is, 'dangerous' in the taboo sense, no less than it is in danger.[399] Apparently these seem to hold similarity with the concepts of pollution in the *dharmaśāstras*. However, there is a gross difference between the way pollution is perceived in the two societies, and this difference renders the *Śangam* counterpart of the concept to be a strong variation to, even if not deviation from, the norms of the law codes. While pollution in the *dharmaśāstric* tradition resulted in marginalization of the concerned individuals or groups, in the context of *Śangam* society, it became instrumental in their empowerment. As Ramaswamy observes:

> There was a close connection between polluting forces and power. Spiritual power was vested in the polluting castes like the *Pana*, *Velan*, *Pulayan* or *Pulatti*. It was they who, under the influence of possessions usually by Murugan, foretold good and evil. It was again they who officiated at the bloody sacrifices before Korravai or Murugan. Spiritual power resided in the men and women who lighted cremation fires, danced, lamented or played the funeral drum in the house of death … Thus pollution in their case was a means of spiritual empowerment … The *Śangam* situation was however totally reverse by the Brahmanical patriarchal order. Spirituality came to be identified with purity-*nirmalam/niranjanam,* that is, that which is untainted. This immediately excluded women and the polluting castes

> from the ambit of Brahmanical or Agamic religion and rituals. Thus the Brahmanical emphasis on purity spiritually dis-empowered the two most 'polluting' sections of society – (women of all castes and classes) and the low-caste/untouchable men.[400]

In fact, such an empowerment of the female arose out of the awe in which the power of procreation was held by the society. Surprisingly, in the *Śangam* society, it is not only the virgin but also the barren woman who was considered to be ritually powerful. It is thus interesting that in the Dravidian cultures, the spiritual powers of women were linked to both the fear of pollution and the male fear of female sexuality.[401] George Hart opines that the ancient Tamils defined this latent sacred power accruing out of female's sexual power as *Ananku*, which at certain times became dangerous so that they had to be tabooed.[402] When contained within the paradigm of a chaste wife, the woman's *Ananku* could be auspicious, but outside the marital status it became a deadly and destructive power. However, as Ramaswamy comments, "Hart seems to assign excessive importance to *Ananku* within the context of female spiritual power, an interpretation that may not be entirely borne out by the available evidence."[403] However, she too does not entirely reject it as the *Śilappadikaram* does associate *Ananku* with female spiritual power and personifies it into *Ananku*, the youngest of the seven virgin sisters "who made Śiva dance".[404] The chief source of such power was a woman's chastity (*karpu*).[405] Ramaswamy writes: "Women in the Sangam age also derived their spiritual power directly from their marital status. *Karpu*, which for lack of any other suitable word in the English language can be translated as 'chastity', gave the chaste wife immense spirituality and transformed her into a Goddess – *Pattini-Daivam*, literally Wife-Goddess. Here again the operative force behind the worship of the *Pattini Daivam* is the fear of her spirituality born out of chastity."[406] The power arising out of *karpu* is best epitomized in the *Śilappadikaram* of Ilango Adigal written anywhere between the 2nd to the 4th century AD, which tells the story of a woman, Kannagi, and transforms her into a *Pattini Daivam,* describing her blazing spiritual powers. The core of the story of Kovalan and his chaste wife Kannagi goes thus: The husband falls in love with a courtesan, Mādhavī, and attempts to sell his wife Kannagi's anklet to a craftsman in Madurai who happens to be the king's goldsmith. This goldsmith had stolen the queen's anklet, and he falsely implicates Kovalan as the thief who is then summarily executed. It is at this point that the *Śilappadikaram* equates Kannagi with Korravai and with *Ananku* 'who made Śiva dance'. The fire of her *Karpu* burns the city of Madurai and Kannagi herself retires to Murugavel Kottam in Malainadu (modern Cranganore) where by her penance she bodily ascends to heaven. Reference to the chaste wife Kannagi is also found in the *Narrinai*.[407] It refers to the incident of Kannagi casting off one of her breasts in her fury and calls her *Tirumamani* (as in the *Śilappadikaram*), perhaps the title given to Kannagi after she was installed as the Goddess of chastity.[408]

Further, the spirituality inherent in the chaste woman is deified in *Śangam* literature.[409] There are references which consider the *Karpu* of the wife to be equal to godliness or divinity.[410] Hart makes the interesting observation that the *Karpu* of the wife 'consisted of a sort of *asceticism,* the restraining of all impulses that were in any way immodest… . Clearly the more sexually attractive a woman is, the more power her chastity endows her with.'[411]

The above discussion makes it clear that 'in the *Śangam* age even woman's pollution arising out of gender or the concept of chastity, went towards empowering them rather than controlling them within the framework of male sexual politics as one tends to find under Brahmanical patriarchy.'[412] It is in this that it is a gross variation or even deviation from the injunctions of the *dharmaśāstric* literature. It is also evident that the *Śangam* texts depict a picture where women are co-sharers with men in the economic as well as socio-religious sphere. Thus, this society is the one which was away from the sphere of influence of the *dharmaśāstras.*

Women in the Epigraphic Records

Recently, the importance of epigraphs as sources for studying Indian women's history is recognized, so much so that it is said that the epigraphic records have tremendous potential to make *real women* visible on historical stage.[413] The main argument that is pushed forward in support of such an enterprise is that "the women figuring in contemporary literature mostly emerge from an androcentric perspective and, therefore, are rarely real women."[414] While the importance of textual sources can not be undermined solely on the basis of the above argument, it has to be admitted that a study of epigraphic sources is sure to offer significant insights into the history of women in ancient India. One of the ways in which the epigraphic records can be used is to find and mark out deviations from the norms prescribed by the normative textual literature, thus getting clues to be able to sift reality from myth. This is what is attempted at here.

One of the thoughtful works on epigraphic records as far as women's history is concerned, is the one by Kirit K. Shah,[415] and he has claimed to have prepared a corpus of inscriptions pertaining to women of early India.[416] It is this corpus which is used for the purpose of this study. Thus, for the purpose of the present study, the 'innovation' made by Shah in naming the inscriptions;[417] i.e., to name an inscription on the basis of woman figuring prominently instead of the king in whose reign it is dated; is retained. The inscriptions covered belong to the period between the third century BC and third century AD.

Deviations from the Norm of Ideal Wifehood

As had been discussed at length in one of the preceding chapters, the *dharmaśāstrakāras* laid down a life of perpetual dependence on and subjection to the husband for the wife.[418] The idea reaches its summit with the prescription of worship of the husband, even though he be devoid of any virtues or strength of character.[419] Even a wicked husband is ascribed a divine status. If role-models from the epic literature are added to these references, we could legitimately assume that the women of the period were thoroughly indoctrinated into this patriarchal ideology and faithfully followed the norms set by the lawgivers.[420] However, a study of the epigraphic records reveals that perhaps, there was a section of women that had escaped the indoctrination. As observed by Shah:

> Leave aside the divine status, even the human status of a husband is negated by women like Nāgamulanikā, Śivaskandanāgaśri, Rudradharabhaṭṭārikā, and Sāmaḍinikā, to offer only a few examples. For Bapisiri and Chaṭhisiri, the sole source of identity is her mother rather than her father, who fails to find even a passing mention. In case of north-western India, we have women whose exclusive attribute of identity is their wifely status, and yet, they fail to mention the names of their respective husbands. In fact, if the north-western epigraphy is viewed as a whole, the solitary case of the anonymous *vihārasvāminī* figuring in the Sui Vihar copper plate inscription with her wifely and motherly status would seem to represent a deviation much more than the norm, as all other women disregarded patriarchal norms in constituting their identity.[421]

Details of a few of these is given to support the passage cited:

Bedsa Cave Inscription of Mahādevī Sāmaḍinikā[422]

The inscription refers to the gift made by Sāmaḍinikā. The whole text of the inscription is devoted to establishing the identity of the donatrix. She is referred to as the *Mahādevī*, the *Mahāraṭhinī*, daughter of *Mahābhoya* and the wife of Āpadevaṇaka. The reference to her wifely status comes in the last among the constituents of her identity. It seems that it was added as an afterthought when the whole text of the record had already been finalized and perhaps incised as well. It is surprising that the husband figures without the dignity of a single epithet or even the common honorific *śrī*, while the identity of the wife is highlighted by no less than three royal titles. At least two of these three royal titles are feminine forms of royal titles indicative of her wifely status, but they are preceded by a seemingly proud proclamation of her daughterly status as *Mahābhoyabālikā*. Also, the husband figures in the end as a non-entity. This might have been due to the fact that the husband might have owed his position to the favours granted by the father-in-law. There might have been other reasons, but in any case, this marks a deviation from the norms set by the *dharmaśāstrakāras*.

Kanheri Cave Inscription of Mahāraṭhinī Nāgamūlanikā[423]

The inscription belongs to the post-Sātavāhana period. It is clear from the titles attributed to Nāgamūlanikā that she belonged to a family of *Mahābhojas* on her father's side, though was given in marriage to a *Mahāraṭhī*, a person of lesser rank in political hierarchy. Perhaps this is the reason that he finds no mention in the record. Our knowledge of his official rank is based merely on the assumption that she derived the title *Mahāraṭhinī* from her wifely status in relation to a *Mahāraṭhī* husband. The utter exclusion of the husband and his family from the phraseology of the record again marks a deviation from the norm of ideal wifehood.

Vanavasi Nāga-image Inscription of Śivaskandanāgaśrī[424]

This record also belongs to the post-Sātavāhana period. The first among the four attributes of identity mentioned for the donatrix is *Mahābhuvī* (a variant of *Mahābhojī*). This she has derived from her husband perhaps, who seems to have been a *Mahābhoja*. The next to follow is her status as the daughter of a *Mahārāja*. The third constituent of her identity is expressed by the term *jīvaputā* which is used by a woman whose son or sons are alive. In the fourth attribute she is mentioned as the mother of the crown-prince. It is obvious that she was an appointed daughter and her son owed the status of being the crown-prince in relation to her father. An attitude of utter indifference to the husband is evident in this inscription too.

Nagarjunikonda Āyaka Pillar Inscription of Mahādevī Rudradhara-bhaṭṭārikā[425]

The record stands marked out as a case of self-perception. The identity of the queen is constituted in terms of three attributes, none of which concerns her husband and his family. That she was the consort of the ruling king is obvious from the title *Mahādevī*, but she makes no attempt to derive pride out of being a part of the Ikśvāku royal family. Instead, it seems, that she attached more importance to being an *Ujenikā* (a woman from the city of Ujjain), and *Mahārāja-bālikā* (daughter of the *Mahārāja* of Ujjain). She absolutely ignores her husband and his family while establishing her identity. This again goes against the norm laid down by the lawgivers.

It is clear from the above that power relationship was central to the determination of the importance one is given in the epigraphic phraseology of identity-construction; so much so that the husband was ignored by the wife if his position is insignificant regarding the power relationships. As commented by Shah:

> Almost all of our queens have figured in the familial framework. However, the selection of attributes from the familial framework has been usually guided by considerations of power-relationships. The cases of Nāgamulanikā and Śivaskandanāgaśrī, in which husbands have been absolutely ignored for constructing identity, clearly reflect it. Sāmaḍinikā does mention him but at the fag end and almost as a favour to him in a most perfunctory way. Likewise, Bapisiri and Chaṭhisiri trace their identity on the parental side with an exclusive reference to their mother and indicate the object of benefaction with due regard to her alone. As a matter of fact, the cases of male identity covered by our inscriptions also reveal the role of power relationships in identity-formation. *Mahābhojī* Vijayā is the sole source of identity for her *Mahābhoja* son Khandapālita. Likewise, Usavadāta place his *jāmātā*-status in relation to his lord Nahapāna first in the chronology of his attributes. Understandably, therefore, Dakśamitrā, his wife, prides in her daughterly status much more than the wifely one. Since the consideration of power-relationship was central to the construction of

identity, adhering to the normative ideals was hardly possible not only in cases of self-perception, but, at times, in those of social construction as well ... Viewed in this perspective, Nāgamulanikā, Śivaskandanāgaśrī, Rudradharabhaṭṭārikā, and Sāmaḍinikā represent deviations from the norm much more than an approximation to it.[426]

Deviation from the Norm Regarding the Name of Women

The *dharmaśāstrakāras* were very particular regarding the naming of persons, and issued injunctions with regard not only to the procedure of naming or *nāmkaraṇa samskāra* but to that of selecting appropriate names as well. The excessive importance attached to the names of girls goes to the extent of regarding the suitability or auspiciousness of the name of the maiden to be one of the major qualifications to be chosen as a bride and vice versa.[427] However, as Shah comments, the dichotomy between the textual provisions and their disregard in practice could be convincingly established in respect of proper name itself.[428] According to Manu, the names of women should be easy to pronounce, not imply anything dreadful, possess a plain meaning, be pleasing and auspicious, end in long vowels and contain a word of benediction.[429] Names of women figuring in many of the inscriptions seem to go against this norm. The names Ayakoṭusiri and Vijhaṭhavisiri are not easy to pronounce, and the names like Nāgavasusiri, Nāgasiri, Śivanāgasiri (all mentioned in Nagarjunikonda Memorial Pillar Inscription of the Ikśvāku Queens)[430], Nāgamūlanikā (Kanheri Cave Inscription)[431], Śivaskandanāgaśrī (Vanvasi Nāga-image Inscription)[432], Nāganikā (Naneghat Cave Inscription)[433], seem to have been derived from a snake and inspire terror. Nor do any of these names contain a word of benediction. Further, "the command of the long vowel ending has been disobeyed in most of the cases like Khandasiri, Misasiri, Samusiri, Mūlasiri, Golasiri, to cite only a few. In fact, Paṇḍita, Mūla, Gola, Samuda, and Mahisara can hardly be considered female names, but devoid of the honorific *śrī* they actually are so. No doubt in the Sanskritized version of these names given by Sircar, Rāmasiri becomes Kāmaśrī, Vijhaṭhavisiri becomes Vindhyabodhiśrī, and Ratūsiri or Rantusri becomes Kṛṣṇaśrī,[434] but the names Kāma and Kṛṣṇa are hardly female names whereas Vindhyabodhi has been derived from the name of a well-known mountain, which, again, is in violation of Manu's provision. As regards Manu's injunction against naming a girl after the name of a river, we have already referred to Revā."[435] Further, Shah's observations regarding norms laid down by some of the other lawgivers are worth to be quoted in this regard:

> Yet another scriptural injunction against naming a girl with *dattā* or *rakśitā*-ending, where such suffixes are preceded by the names of a deity[436], has been observed more in breach than in compliance. It might be argued in this regard that most such names figure in the Buddhist inscriptions and the Buddhists were hardly bound by the Brāhmaṇical injunctions. In answer to this we could cite the classic case of *Śakanikā* Viṣṇudattā of the Nasik cave inscription which is Buddhist in religious affiliation, and yet, the forepart of her name leaves not even a shadow of doubt that she was considered to be a gift of god Viṣṇu by her parents, when they selected a name for her. The name of queen Gautamī Balaśri violates other textual prescription requiring names of girls to be of uneven number or of three syllables.[437] If the term Gautamī is taken to be her *gotra*-patronym and suffix *śrī* as the royal honorific, that leaves only Bala or Bālā as her proper name. The fact of her being a devout Buddhist would in no way weaken the force of our argument since her eulogy has much more Brāhmaṇical content than Buddhist content.[438]

It is evident further that the injunctions regarding the naming of girls were not followed in practice; rather there were both variations and deviations, which sometimes depended on religious or regional differences. This speaks well of the limited sphere of influence of the *dharmaśāstras*.

Deviations from the Norms Regarding Exogamy

Besides the variations and deviations noted with regard to naming girls, which seem to be more general, there are specific and obvious deviations with regard to the provisions making exogamy normative. The following records raise a point in this direction:

Nagarjunikonda Āyaka-Pillar Inscription of Mahātalavarī Cāmtisiri[439]

The inscription is a eulogy of queen Cāmtisiri, who figures as the donatrix. The prominent mention of her sisterly status (being his uterine sister) in relation to king Cāmtamūla, the founder of the royal house of the Ikśvākus; is certainly indicative of her being a Vasiṣṭhīputrī. Interestingly, her husband also figures with his metronymic – Vasiṣṭhīputra. This makes it clear that Cāmtisiri as well as her husband had mothers from the same Vedic *gotra*, Vasiṣṭha. This is quite surprising in view of the prohibition of the *dharmśāstras* regarding *gotra* endogamy.[440] As observed by Shah, "Perhaps, the rule was related to a father's *gotra* rather than to a mother's. It needs to be noted in this regard that the practice of *gotrāntara*, that is the change of a girl's *gotra* after her marriage, had not yet begun and we have very many epigraphic references showing that the wives continued to maintain their paternal *gotra* even after marriage. The inscription does not enlighten us about the paternal *gotras* of Cāmtisiri and her husband which may well have been different, and so, their marriage might seem to be in tune with the sāstric injunctions. However, if the fact of their having and identical *gotra* on the maternal side is viewed in the context of the Āpastambian injunction prohibiting marriage between relations within six degrees on the mother's side as well as on that of the father's,[441] their marriage could be termed as a deviation from the norm rather than as a variation. Relations on mother's side in this injunction should be taken as her *sagotras*,[442] more so when she continued to retain her paternal *gotra*."[443] The argument forwarded by Shah proves it beyond doubt that this was a case of deviation from the norm of *gotra* exogamy.

Nagarjunikonda Āyaka-Pillar Inscriptions of Mahadevīs Bapisiri and Chaṭhisiri[444]

The queens figuring in the two records are sisters married to the reigning king Vīrapurisadata. The record tells that the two queens were daughters of the king's, i.e., their husband's father's uterine sister. It is obviously a case of cross-cousin marriage. The fact that the Ikśvākus followed the custom of cross-cousin marriage has already been noted in the aforementioned inscription. The cases of queens Bapisiri and Chaṭhisiri now establish it beyond doubt. Again, this marks a deviation from the norm which advocates *gotra* as well as *piṇḍa* exogamy.[445]

The cases cited above are all the more surprising since the royal records of Nagarjunikonda proudly proclaim the adherence of the Ikśvāku kings to the ideals of orthodox Brāhmanism. Shah comments, "The admission of such a deviation in a public record indicates what we regard as a serious deviation from śāstric norm might, after all, be a norm itself not recorded in any of the available legal texts. Our notion of the Indian tradition, based largely on the literary source, needs, therefore, to be corrected in the light of data contained in the early Indian inscriptions."[446]

Deviations from the Norm: Use of Metronymics

There are several examples where the sons are found using metronymics to establish their identity. In spite of the certainty of father's paternity, descent is found to be reckoned through the mother. How does one explain this anomaly? One explanation offered by Rajvade, whereby he writes: "Perhaps this is due to the fact that prior to *Prajāpati* institution, descent was reckoned through mother and this norm took a long time to erode."[447] Shalini Shah also agrees with this explanation.[448] However, as Trautmann points out, the use of metronymics does not imply matrilineal set-up.[449] Even though the use of metronymics does not imply existence of matriliny, it is significant that such cases existed in spite of the stronghold of patriarchy. The following are a few of the examples where metronymics are being used by the kings or officials, which deserve to be noted:

Nasik Cave Inscription of King Gautamīputra Śātakarṇī and Mahadevī Gautamī Balaśrī[450] *and Nasik Cave Eulogy of Queen Gautamī Balaśrī*[451]

The inscription records the joint donation made by the Queen-mother Mahādevī Gautamī Balaśrī and her son, the reigning monarch, Gautamīputra Śātakarṇī. It is interesting to note that the king uses metronymic for establishing his identity. His name actually always figures with his metronymic Gautamīputra in his own inscriptions as well as those of his successors.[452] Further, it is also interesting to note that the Queen-mother used her paternal *gotra* Gautamī in establishing her identity. As pointed out by Shah, available references indicate that Gautamīputra Śātakarṇī has only one queen and she was a Vasiṣṭhī,[453] thereby indicating the use of paternal *gotra* by her too. Similar observations follow the analysis of the contents of another inscription, the Nasik Cave Eulogy of Queen Gautamī Balaśrī[454], which is ostensibly intended to record the grant of a cave by the queen and a village, to meet the expenses of sculptural decoration thereof by her grandson. However, it actually turns out to be the lengthy eulogy of her son, Gautamīputra Śātakarṇī.

Nagarjunikonda Āyaka-Pillar Inscription of Mahātalavarī Cāmtisiri[455]

The inscription is a eulogy of queen Cāmtisiri establishing her identity in terms of eight attributes, selected from the familial as well as non-familial framework. Interestingly, one of the attributes of her identity is derived from her being the paternal aunt of the reigning king Vīrapuruṣadatta, belonging to the royal house of Ikśvākus, who figures in the inscription solely with his metronymic Mahariputra. Again, the queen's husband Khaṇḍaśrī also figures with his metronymic Vasiṣṭhīputra. Also, her brother, Cāmtamūla, the founder of the house of the Ikśvākus, also figures with his metronymic Vasiṣṭhīputra.

Deviation from the Prohibition upon Performance of Religious Penances, or Sacrifices by Women

Naneghat Cave Inscription of Devi Nāganikā

The inscription has been of overwhelming interest among the epigraphists, as is evident from the volume of literature penned in the process of solving the puzzle regarding the restoration of the mutilated text of the inscription. The name of the queen also has not survived in the available text. However, she is invariably identified as Nāganikā, figuring among the label inscriptions in the same cave. That the inscription can be categorized as Brahmanical with a measure of certainty can be stated on the basis of the first part consisting of an invocation to the Brahmanical deities followed by full biographical details of a queen whose name is lost in the mutilated portion. It has been told in the inscription that the queen was 'well acquainted' with initiatory ceremonies (*dikhā*), vows (*vrata*) and sacrifices (*yana*). It is also said assertively that sacrifices were offered by her (*yanahuta*). Regarding this, Bühler concluded that either 'she performed or caused to be performed, those very acts, with the enumeration of which the second part of the inscription is filled'.[456] However, it was found impossible to believe the performance of more than 20 Vedic sacrifices, including the *Rājasūya* and the *Aśvamedha*, by a woman, and so, he suggested the mention of some male's name in the missing portion, in whose company the queen must have done the sacrifices. Obviously, that man could be none other than her husband.[457] But Bühler could not arrive at a decisive position regarding the one to whom the performance of the Vedic sacrifices could be attributed, for he later conjectures that the prohibition of the *śāstras* regarding the performance of *śrauta* sacrifices, and the blame upon the *brāhmaṇas* who perform such sacrifices for them (*strīyājakas*) does not apply to queens who may be conducting the government of a state, either independently or for minor sons. In that case, the disabilities attaching to sex are removed by the position which the female occupies.[458] Thus, though he postulated the mention of a male's name in the mutilated part before the phrase *yañehi yiṭham* in the text, he thought that there was nothing improbable for a queen, governing independently or conducting the state affairs as a regent, to undertake the performance of Vedic sacrifices on her own, which was otherwise prohibited for her in the scriptures.[459] Behind such contentions of Bühler remained his assumption of the queen as the ruling regent of her minor son, support for which he sought in the non-familial attributes of the queen such as *gahatapasa* and *caritabrahmacariya* indicative of her status of a widow. Technically, the assumption amounts to an automatic exemption from the restrictions on women as she had stepped into a male role.[460]

Mirashi broadly agreed with Bühler regarding the question of her performing Vedic sacrifices, however, he suggested that she had performed all the sacrifices as consort of her husband except the last three, which she performed through her family priest (*purohita*) when the king was no more.[461] Though he quoted the Āpastambian injunction in this context, but reconciled it by repeating Bühler's assumption that the provision was not applicable to independent or regent queens.[462]

Going by the inferences drawn by Bühler and Mirashi, the case of Nāganikā represents a stark deviation from the norms which prohibit the performance of any sacrifice, vow or fast by women apart from their husbands,[463] and where it is specifically laid down that there are no *mantras* for women[464] and that the nuptial ceremony is equivalent to the Vedic sacrament of initiation for women, serving the husband is equivalent to residing in the house of the teacher, and household duties are equivalent to the worship of sacred fire.[465] Nāganikā publicly proclaims not only her mastery of the sacred lore but also the performance of Vedic sacrifices, some of which she undertook singly.[466] As Shah remarks, "If it is also remembered that hers is a case of social construction of female identity, the deviation acquires the character of the norm itself."[467]

Within the Sphere of Influence: The Cases of Identity Construction in Accordance with the Norms

While deviations from the norms far outnumber those in which an adherence to the norms becomes obvious; such cases should also deserve consideration as part of the foregoing discussion.

Nagarjunikonda Image Inscription of Mahādevī Khanduvula[468]

The inscription is a brief dedicatory record of a donation made by an Ikśvāku queen. Among the four attributes constituting the identity of the queen in the inscription, two attributes are conceived in accordance with the ideal prescribed by orthodox Brahmanism for women. The specific mention of *avidhavā* and *jīvasutā* epithets as constituents of the queen's identity reflects that she was fully in tune with the ideology of orthodox Brahmanism or, perhaps, we have a case here of a social construction of identity from the pen or her scribe or teacher. Narasimhaswami, who edited the inscription, has cited several passages from the epic and classical literature in which the twin-attributes have figured indicating that the record represents an epigraphic transcription of ideals set forth in the Brahmanical normative literature.[469]

Among the other records that may be discussed in the foregoing category are the Nasik Cave Inscriptions of Queen Gautamī Balaśrī.

Nasik Cave Inscription of King Gautamīputra Śātakarṇī and Mahādevī Gautamī Balaśrī[470]

In the record, the second constituent of the queen's identity is the epithet *jīvasutā* meaning 'a woman whose son is living'. According to Sircar, the attribute suggests that the king was ill and the people had to be assured about his health, which is why queen mother used this epithet.[471] Even if this be the case, the record suggests the use of a term which indicates adherence to the Brahmanical construction of a woman's identity.

Nasik Cave Eulogy of Queen Gautamī Balaśrī[472]

The record marks the construction of the queen's identity in three sets of attributes, in which the first one was intended to represent her as an idealized version of a Brahmanical widow and the other two consist of a string of titles and an honorific.[473] Verily, the royal scribe seems to be less concerned with constituting her identity than with representing a model of womanhood in Brahmanical terms in order to inspire and exhort contemporary women.[474] However, the inscription itself presents a contradiction as the titles given to her 'have been conceived in terms of her familial status in the royal household, creating an impression of a majestic matriarch enjoying unquestioned authority with a plurality of official positions and, perhaps, power as well, though the nature, content, and extent of this power is not easy to ascertain.'[475] Thus, unlike the

Brahmanical notion of a widow, whose life was considered to be worthless, and, as noted in one of the preceding chapters, who was pushed to the margins of the household life; here the widow seems to have wielded power and authority.

The above instances of deviation are, though sporadic, but reveal that the injunctions were neither strictly enforced, nor completely followed in the society. The injunctions of the text were more normative in nature and not a few number of times were far removed from the social reality. The inscriptions speak not only in terms of marked deviations from the norms, but give the glimpses of social reality by the general attitude exhibited by the women who made donations. That women figured as donatrix, itself speaks of their having possessed some form of property, whether it be movable or immovable. Though most of the times, these were women belonging to royal circles, this was not so in all the cases. The women who joined the Buddhist Sangha, and figure in the records as donatrix, belong to the category of almswoman as well as lay followers. From the paucity of joint grants made by men and women discovered in her study on the inscriptions from Sanchi, Roy concluded that this indicated a relative autonomy of the two in relation to each other, so far as access to disposal of economic resources was concerned.[476] However, that the hold of patriarchy existed on the collective consciousness of women is reflected in the fact that most women of all regions and religions have figured with an attribute from familial framework.[477] Nevertheless, as Shah has concluded from his study of the records, a section of women did break out of the parameters and have figured either by their personal names alone or in a purely non-familial framework.[478] Roy also found out from her study of the inscriptions from Sānchi that the single most common means of identification adopted by both men and women in the Sanchi records is a reference to the place of residence. Of the 218 lay-women figuring as individuals, as many as 102 establish their identity through their association with a place and for the 59 among these, the native place is the sole means of identification.[479] This indicates the importance of the place of residence to be more for these women rather than their identity within the familial framework. Shah has also given a corpus of inscriptions where women do not figure as constructing their identity within the familial framework.[480] Again, as Shah has further pointed out in his study, there were women figuring with professional attributes of identity. Though he admits that statistically speaking, the number of women figuring with the professional attributes of identity is much less than those identifying themselves by royal, religious or familial attributes. However, as he comments, "The very fact that some women perceived their social self in professional terms is in itself a fact of profound significance because the women of this category not only stepped out of the private domain but claimed equality with men in the public space by using the feminine forms of professional attributes to constitute their identity."[481] Shah's inferences are worth to be quoted in this context:

> The paucity of records is more than compensated by the freshness and variety of data that they contain. The freshness of data is evident from the fact that the literary source is practically silent about the technical terms of professional status that we have been able to locate. I.B. Horner devoted a full chapter to the woman-worker on the basis of the data contained in the Buddhist canonical literature, and yet, she could locate only the domestic slaves, the nautch-girl, and the woman-musician as categories of professional women apart from, of course, the familiar figure of a courtesan.[482] We have been able to locate more than ten kinds of women with professional identity, though except for the merchantwoman, we have only one inscription each for all other categories. What we wish to stress is that some women did step into the public domain and were conscious of their professional identity to an extent that they hardly used any attribute from the familial framework to constitute their identity. This is not to deny that in some cases the attributes might well be merely feminine forms of the professional status of the husbands concerned. It is also true that very few professions or services were open to women. The cases of Loṭā and Bhagvatā would show that women were employed for women only. Even the solitary case of *sevikā* strengthens this impression. But Revā was attached to a king and was resourceful enough to finance the making of a pavilion. Again, the cases of Dharmasomā and Sidhi would indicate that the possibility of some women being engaged in trade and commerce cannot be altogether ruled out. An identical view could be taken of the carpenter-women figuring in the Ramnagar Jina-image inscription. In the final analysis, therefore, the corpus of our inscriptions, though small, reflects that a section of women was engaged in work other than that of housekeeping, and the professions they entered into were much more diversified than those assigned to them in literature.[483]

It can be thus established that the social reality was complex, and though the inscriptional evidence points towards the influence of patriarchal norms, it also makes it evident that there were deviations from as well as variations of the norms, and there were women who could dare to move away from the norms of patriarchy.

The following inferences can be drawn on the basis of the discussions in the present chapter:

1. The picture which emerges out of a study of epics reveals that the norms prescribed by the *dharmaśāstrakāras* were not completely followed in the society. There were instances when they were ignored, interpreted differently or even reversed. However, the norms are found to be ignored only resulting in a stricter subjugation of women most of the times. Also, the epics present evidences of existence of diverse cultures and different societies, even with matriarchal or matrilineal traditions. Also, there were women who dared to voice against their subjugation at the hands of patriarchal injunctions.
2. A study of the *Śangam* texts reveals that there were regional differences, and in the South was a society that was away from the influence of Brahmanical norms, and it was only in the post *Śangam* texts, that a gradual influence of Brahmanical norms could be perceived.
3. The study of epigraphic evidences presents striking deviations and variations from the norms and speak of women foregoing the scriptural injunctions as well as testify to existence of remnants of matriarchal influence.
4. The aforesaid amply testifies that the *dharmaśāstras* were not the sole determining texts, and though an attempt was made to strengthen the stronghold of patriarchy, it was not completely successful. Several parallel trends co-existed. Though the women were subjected to an unequal position, the society must not have been as unegalitarian as depicted in the *dharmaśāstras*.
5. Women have not been a homogenous category at any given point of time in history. This stands true for the 'ancient' period of Indian history. Given the existence of diverse cultures and traditions, no universal or general assumptions may be made regarding the position of women at any point of time in history. Rather, women's identity has to be relocated within the existing web of structures and formations.

6. In the *dharmaśāstric* ideology, human relations were defined in terms of possession. One was related to the other either as the possessor or the possessed, thus, either as a superior or an inferior. There was no concept of equality in human relations. Given the stronghold of 'brahmanical patriarchy', such inequality became most pronounced in case of man to woman relationship. A similar picture of society is reflected in the two epics. However, the study of the *Śangam* society and epigraphic records indicates that the degree of inequality might not have been that high or even quite low in some other regions or cultures, histories of which are as much the components of ancient Indian history as the history of Brahmanical society.

Notes

1. Thapar, Romila, *Ancient Indian Social History: Some Interpretations*, Orient Longman, New Delhi, Third reprint, 1996, p. 23.
2. Macdonell, A.A., "'Ramaism' and 'Ramayana'", *Encyclopaedia of Religion and Ethics*, Vol. 10, James Hastings (ed.), Scribner, New York, 1919, p. 574.
3. Winternitz, Maurice, *A History of Indian Literature,* translated from German by V. Srinivas Sharma, Vol. I, 1st revised ed., Second reprint, Motilal Banarsidass, Delhi, 1990, p. 300.
4. Dasgupta, Madhusraba, "Usable Women: The Tales of Ambā and Mādhavi", in Bose, Mandakranta (ed.), *Faces of the Feminine in Ancient, Medieval and Modern India*, OUP, New Delhi, 2000, p. 48.
5. *The Rāmāyaṇa of Vālmīki: An Epic of Ancient India*, translated by Goldman, Robert P., Vol. I, 1st Indian ed., Motilal Banarsidass, Delhi, 2007, p. 4.
6. Ibid.
7. For a discussion of the *Manu*scripts of the *Rāmāyana,* see Bhatt, G.H. (ed.), *The Bālakāṇḍa: The First Book of the Vālmīki Rāmāyaṇa: The National Epic of India,* Oriental Institute, Baroda, 1960, pp. xiii-xxix.
8. Ibid., p. xix.
9. *The Rāmāyaṇa of Vālmīki: An Epic of Ancient India*, translated by Goldman, Robert P., Vol. I, 1st Indian ed., Motilal Banarsidass, Delhi, 2007, p. 5.
10. Ibid., p. 6.
11. Ibid., p. 14.
12. Ibid., p. 23.
13. Kane, P.V., *History of Dharmaśāstra*, Vol. I, Part I, 2nd ed., B.O.R.I., Poona, 1968, p. 396.
14. Winternitz, Maurice, op. cit., p. 494.

15. Kane, P.V., op. cit., p. 396.
16. Winternitz, Maurice, op. cit., p. 446.
17. Hopkins, E.W., *The Great Epic of India: Its Character and Origin*, reprint, Yale University Press, New Haven, 1920, pp. 386–402.
18. Keith, A.B., *The Sanskrit Drama in its Origin, Development and Practice*, 1st Indian ed., Motilal Banarsidass, Delhi, 1992, p. 454.
19. Kane, P.V., op. cit., p. 372.
20. Sukthankar, V.S., *Critical Studies in the Mahābhārata*, Vol. I, Sukthankar Memorial Edition, Karnataka Publishing House, Bombay, 1944, p. 100.
21. Vaidya, C.V., *The Mahābhārata: A Criticism*, Mehar Chand Lachman Das, Delhi, 1966, pp. 1–8.
22. *The Rāmāyaṇa of Vālmīki: An Epic of Ancient India*, translated by Goldman, Robert P., 1st Indian ed., Motilal Banarsidass, Delhi, 2007, Vol. I, *Bālakāṇḍa*: 1:8,9,16,18–19, pp. 121–122.
23. Kakar, Sudhir, *The Inner World: A Psycho-analytic Study of Childhood and Society in India*, OUP, New Delhi, 1981, p. 63.
24. *The Rāmāyaṇa of Vālmīki: An Epic of Ancient India*, translated by Goldman, Robert P., 1st Indian ed., Motilal Banarsidass, Delhi, 2007, Vol. I, *Bālakāṇḍa*: 65:17, p. 249.
25. *The Rāmāyaṇa of Vālmīki: An Epic of Ancient India*, translated by Goldman, Robert P., 1st Indian ed., Motilal Banarsidass, Delhi, 2007, *Bālakāṇḍa*: 65:16.
26. *The Rāmāyaṇa of Vālmīki: An Epic of Ancient India*, translated by Goldman, Robert P., 1st Indian ed., Motilal Banarsidass, Delhi, 2007, *Bālakāṇḍa*: 65: 14,15.
27. *The Rāmāyaṇa of Vālmīki: An Epic of Ancient India*, translated by Pollock, Sheldon, I., Vol. II, 1 Indian ed., Motilal Banarsidass, Delhi, 2007, *Ayodhyākāṇḍa*: 110:33–35, p. 321.
28. *Yāj*.I.3.64, *Pārāśara*.VII.6–10, *Bṛhas*.XXIV.3, *Vasiṣṭha*.XVII.69, 70, *Nārada*.XII.25–27, *Vyāsa*.II.7.
29. *The Rāmāyaṇa of Vālmīki: An Epic of Ancient India,* translated by Goldman, Robert P., op. cit., *Bālakāṇḍa*: 65:15–19, p. 249.
30. *Manu*.III.27–34, *Viṣṇu*.XXIV.17–24, *Gautama*.IV, *Nārada*.XII.38–39, *Śankha*.IV.2–6.
31. *The Rāmāyaṇa of Vālmīki: An Epic of Ancient India* translated by Goldman, Robert P., op. cit., *Bālakāṇḍa*: 65:15–19, p. 249.
32. *Manu*.III.31, *Viṣṇu*.XXIV.24, *Gautama*.IV, *Nārada*.XII.38–39, *Śankha*.IV.5.
33. *Manu*.III.24.
34. *Manu*.III.25.
35. *Nārada*.XII.44, *Viṣṇu*.XXIV.27–28, *Śankha*.IV.3.
36. *The Rāmāyaṇa of Vālmīki: An Epic of Ancient India*, translated by Goldman, Robert P., 1st Indian ed., Motilal Banarsidass, Delhi, 2007, Vol. I, *Bālakāṇḍa*: 65:18–19, p. 249.

37. *The Rāmāyaṇa of Vālmīki: An Epic of Ancient India*, translated by Goldman, Robert P., 1st Indian ed., Motilal Banarsidass, Delhi, 2007, *Bālakāṇḍa*: 65:27, p. 250.
38. *The Rāmāyaṇa of Vālmīki: An Epic of Ancient India*, translated by Goldman, Robert P., 1st Indian ed., Motilal Banarsidass, Delhi, 2007, *Bālakāṇḍa*: 66:15–16, p. 251.
39. *The Rāmāyaṇa of Vālmīki: An Epic of Ancient India*, translated by Goldman, Robert P., 1st Indian ed., Motilal Banarsidass, Delhi, 2007, *Bālakāṇḍa*: 66:17, p. 251.
40. *The Rāmāyaṇa of Vālmīki: An Epic of Ancient India*, translated by Goldman, Robert P., 1st Indian ed., Motilal Banarsidass, Delhi, 2007, *Bālakāṇḍa*: 66:22–25, p. 251.
41. *The Rāmāyaṇa of Vālmīki: An Epic of Ancient India*, translated by Goldman, Robert P., 1st Indian ed., Motilal Banarsidass, Delhi, 2007, *Bālakāṇḍa*: 72:17–23, p. 262.
42. *The Rāmāyaṇa of Vālmīki: An Epic of Ancient India*, translated by Goldman, Robert P., 1st Indian ed., Motilal Banarsidass, Delhi, 2007, *Bālakāṇḍa*: 73:3–5, p. 263.
43. *Manu*.IX.194, *Yāj*.II.143–144, *Viṣṇu*.XVII.18, *Nārada*.XIII.8, *Kātyāyana* quoted in *Dāyabhāga*.IV.I. 5, 6, 13.
44. *The Rāmāyaṇa of Vālmīki: An Epic of Ancient India*, translated by Goldman, Robert P., 1st Indian ed., Motilal Banarsidass, Delhi, 2007, Vol. I, *Bālakāṇḍa*: 76:14–18, p. 269.
45. *The Rāmāyaṇa of Vālmīki: An Epic of Ancient India*, translated by Pollock, Sheldon, I., Vol. II, 1st Indian ed., Motilal Banarsidass, Delhi, 2007, *Ayodhyākāṇḍa*: 4:2, p. 87.
46. *The Rāmāyaṇa of Vālmīki: An Epic of Ancient India*, translated by Pollock, Sheldon, I., Vol. III, 1st Indian ed., Motilal Banarsidass, Delhi, 2007, *Ayodhyākāṇḍa*: 24–27, pp. 135–142.
47. *The Rāmāyaṇa of Vālmīki: An Epic of Ancient India*, translated by Pollock, Sheldon, I., Vol. III, 1st Indian ed., Motilal Banarsidass, Delhi, 2007, *Araṇyakāṇḍa*: 47:15–22, pp. 188–189.
48. *The Rāmāyaṇa of Vālmīki: An Epic of Ancient India*, translated by Pollock, Sheldon, I., Vol. III, 1st Indian ed., Motilal Banarsidass, Delhi, 2007, *Araṇyakāṇḍa*: 58:6–32, pp. 213–215.
49. *The Ramayana of Valmiki*, translated by Hari Prasad Shastri, Vol. III, *Yuddhakāṇḍa, Sarga* 49, 2nd ed., Shanti Sadan, London, 1970, p. 119.
50. *The Ramayana of Valmiki*, translated by Hari Prasad Shastri, Vol. III, *Yuddhakāṇḍa, Sarga* 102, p. 294.
51. Bhattacharji, Sukumari, "A Revaluation of Valmiki's Rama", in *Social Scientist*, Vol. 30, No. 1/2, Jan-Feb., 2002, p. 36.

52. *The Ramayana of Valmiki*, translated by Hari Prasad Shastri, Vol. III, *Yuddhakāṇḍa, Sarga* 114, p. 328.
53. *The Ramayana of Valmiki*, translated by Hari Prasad Shastri, Vol. III, *Yuddhakāṇḍa, Sarga* 114, p. 329.
54. *The Ramayana of Valmiki*, translated by Hari Prasad Shastri, Vol. III, *Yuddhakāṇḍa, Sarga* 115, p. 329, 332.
55. *The Ramayana of Valmiki*, translated by Hari Prasad Shastri, Vol. III, *Yuddhakāṇḍa, Sarga* 116, p. 333.
56. Ibid.
57. Ibid.
58. *The Ramayana of Valmiki*, translated by Hari Prasad Shastri, Vol. III, *Yuddhakāṇḍa, Sarga* 116, p. 334.
59. Ibid.
60. *The Ramayana of Valmiki*, translated by Hari Prasad Shastri, Vol. III, *Yuddhakāṇḍa, Sarga* 117, pp. 335–336.
61. Ibid., p. 335.
62. *Manu*.XI.62–67.
63. *Yāj*.II.24.288.
64. *Bāhas*.XXIII.13.
65. *Bāhas*.XXIII.14.
66. *Pārāśara*.X.26–27.
67. *Atri*.193–194.
68. *Atri*.197–198.
69. *The Ramayana of Valmiki*, translated by Hari Prasad Shastri, Vol. III, op. cit., *Yuddhakāṇḍa, Sarga* 118, p 336.
70. Ibid.
71. Ibid., p. 337.
72. Ibid.
73. Ibid.
74. Ibid., p. 337–338.
75. *The Ramayana of Valmiki*, translated by Hari Prasad Shastri, Vol. III, *Yuddhakāṇḍa, Sarga* 119, p. 338.
76. *The Ramayana of Valmiki*, translated by Hari Prasad Shastri, Vol. III, *Yuddhakāṇḍa, Sarga* 119, p. 339.
77. *The Ramayana of Valmiki*, translated by Hari Prasad Shastri, Vol. III, *Yuddhakāṇḍa, Sarga* 120, p. 341–342.
78. *The Ramayana of Valmiki*, translated by Hari Prasad Shastri, Vol. III, *Uttarakāṇḍa, Sarga* 42, p. 519–520.
79. *Uttararamacharita of Bhavabhuti,* p. 121, cited in Chakravarti, Uma, *Everyday Lives, Everyday Histories: Beyond the Kings and Brahmanas of 'Ancient' India,* Tulika Books, New Delhi, 2006, p. 241.

80. Chakravarti, Uma, *Everyday Lives, Everyday Histories: Beyond the Kings and Brahmanas of 'Ancient' India,* Tulika Books, New Delhi, 2006, p. 241.
81. *The Ramayana of Valmiki*, translated by Hari Prasad Shastri, Vol. III, 2nd ed., Shanti Sadan, London, 1970, *Uttarakāṇḍa, Sarga* 43, p. 522.
82. *The Ramayana of Valmiki*, translated by Hari Prasad Shastri, Vol. III, 2nd ed., Shanti Sadan, London, 1970, *Uttarakāṇḍa, Sarga* 44, 45, p. 523–525.
83. *The Ramayana of Valmiki*, translated by Hari Prasad Shastri, Vol. III, 2nd ed., Shanti Sadan, London, 1970, *Uttarakāṇḍa, Sarga* 45, p. 524.
84. *The Ramayana of Valmiki*, translated by Hari Prasad Shastri, Vol. III, 2nd ed., Shanti Sadan, London, 1970, *Uttarakāṇḍa, Sarga* 47, pp. 527–528.
85. *The Ramayana of Valmiki*, translated by Hari Prasad Shastri, Vol. III, 2nd ed., Shanti Sadan, London, 1970, *Uttarakāṇḍa, Sarga* 47, p. 528.
86. *The Ramayana of Valmiki*, translated by Hari Prasad Shastri, Vol. III, 2nd ed., Shanti Sadan, London, 1970, *Uttarakāṇḍa, Sarga* 48, p. 529.
87. *Kātyāyana*.XVIV.8.
88. *The Ramayana of Valmiki*, translated by Hari Prasad Shastri, Vol. III, 2nd ed., Shanti Sadan, London, 1970, *Uttarakāṇḍa, Sarga* 48, p 529–530.
89. *The Ramayana of Valmiki*, translated by Hari Prasad Shastri, Vol. III, 2nd ed., Shanti Sadan, London, 1970, *Uttarakāṇḍa, Sarga* 95, pp. 613–614.
90. Ibid.
91. *The Ramayana of Valmiki*, translated by Hari Prasad Shastri, Vol. III, *Yuddhakāṇḍa, Sarga* 49, 2nd ed., Shanti Sadan, London, 1970.
92. Ibid.
93. *The Ramayana of Valmiki*, translated by Hari Prasad Shastri, Vol. III, *Yuddhakāṇḍa, Sarga* 49, 2nd ed., Shanti Sadan, London, 1970.
94. Chakravarti, Uma, op. cit., p. 240.
95. Chakravarti, Uma, op. cit., pp. 232–233.
96. Ibid., p. 233.
97. Ibid.
98. *The Rāmāyaṇa of Vālmīki*, translated by Pollock, Sheldon, I., Vol. II, 1st Indian ed., Motilal Banarsidass, Delhi, 2007, *Ayodhyākāṇḍa*: 99:3, p. 249.
99. *Manu*.III.24–26, *Nārada*.XII.44, *Viṣṇu*.XXIV.27–28, *Śankha*.IV.3, *Gautama*.IV.
100. Chakravarti, Uma, op. cit., p. 234.
101. *The Rāmāyaṇa of Vālmīki: An Epic of Ancient India*, translated by Pollock, Sheldon, I., 1st Indian ed., Motilal Banarsidass, Delhi, 2007, Vol. II, *Ayodhyākāṇḍa*: 9:26, p. 98.
102. *The Rāmāyaṇa of Vālmīki: An Epic of Ancient India*, translated by Pollock, Sheldon, I., op. cit., Vol. II, *Ayodhyākāṇḍa*: 17:22, pp. 119–120.
103. Chakravarti, Uma, op. cit., p. 267.

104. *Manu*.III.12, *Yāj*.I.3.57, *Nārada*.XII.6, *Vasiṣṭha*.I.24, *Viṣṇu*.XXIV.1–4, *Vyāsa*.II.10–11, *Śankha*.IV.7–8.
105. *Manu*.IX.80, 82, *Yāj*.I.3.73.
106. *Kātyāyana*.XIX.13, *Atri*.339–340, *Dakśa*.IV.8.
107. *The Rāmāyaṇa of Vālmīki: An Epic of Ancient India*, translated by Pollock, Sheldon, I., 1st Indian ed., Motilal Banarsidass, Delhi, 2007, Vol. II, *Ayodhyākāṇḍa*: 109–111, pp. 317–323.
108. *The Rāmāyaṇa of Vālmīki: An Epic of Ancient India*, translated by Pollock, Sheldon, I., op. cit., Vol. II, *Ayodhyākāṇḍa*: 109: 23–28, p. 318.
109. *Manu*.V.154.
110. *Manu*.V.151,152,156, *Yāj*.I.3.77,87, *Nārada*.XVIII.22, *Bṛhas*.XXIV.8, *Viṣṇu*.XV.2,12–15, *Vyāsa*.II.19,26–27,33, *Pārāśara*.V.20, *Dakśa*.IV.4,5,7,12.
111. *The Rāmāyaṇa of Vālmīki: An Epic of Ancient India*, translated by Pollock, Sheldon, I., 1st Indian ed., Motilal Banarsidass, Delhi, 2007, Vol. II, *Ayodhyākāṇḍa*: 110:3, p. 319.
112. *The Rāmāyaṇa of Vālmīki: An Epic of Ancient India*, translated by Pollock, Sheldon, I., op. cit., Vol. II, Ayodhyākāṇḍa: 110:4–5, p. 319.
113. *The Rāmāyaṇa of Vālmīki: An Epic of Ancient India*, translated by Pollock, Sheldon, I., op. cit., Vol. II, Ayodhyākāṇḍa: 110:10, p. 319.
114. *The Rāmāyaṇa of Vālmīki: An Epic of Ancient India*, translated by Pollock, Sheldon, I., op. cit., Vol. II, Ayodhyākāṇḍa: 110:17–19, p. 320.
115. *The Rāmāyaṇa of Vālmīki: An Epic of Ancient India*, translated by Pollock, Sheldon, I., op. cit., Vol. II, Ayodhyākāṇḍa: 109:9–13, p. 317.
116. *Manu*.V.89–80, *Viṣṇu*.XXIV.7,15, *Pārāśara*.IV.20, *Śankha*.V.8.
117. Chakravarti, Uma, op. cit., p. 226.
118. *The Rāmāyaṇa of Vālmīki: An Epic of Ancient India*, translated by Lefeber, Rosalind, Vol. IV, 1st Indian ed., Motilal Banarsidass, Delhi, 2007, *Kiṣkindhākāṇḍa*:5:19, p. 62.
119. *The Rāmāyaṇa of Vālmīki: An Epic of Ancient India*, translated by Lefeber, Rosalind, Vol. IV, 1st Indian ed., Motilal Banarsidass, Delhi, 2007, *Kiṣkindhākāṇḍa*:25:38, p. 109.
120. *The Rāmāyaṇa of Vālmīki: An Epic of Ancient India*, translated by Lefeber, Rosalind, Vol. IV, 1st Indian ed., Motilal Banarsidass, Delhi, 2007, *Kiṣkindhākāṇḍa*:28:1–8, p. 115.
121. *Manu*.IX. 88, *Manu*.III.12.
122. *Manu*.III.63, *Yāj*.I.3.56–57, *Vasiṣṭha*.I.24–27, *Viṣṇu*.XXVI.5–7, *Śankha*.IV.7–9.
123. *Ramayana of Valmiki,* translated by Sen, p. 580 cited in Chakravarti Uma, op. cit., p. 235.
124. *The Rāmāyaṇa of Vālmīki: An Epic of Ancient India*, translated by Pollock, Sheldon, I., Vol. II, 17, 1st Indian ed., Motilal Banarsidass, Delhi, 2007, *Araṇyakāṇḍa*: 16, pp. 123–126.

125. *The Rāmāyaṇa of Vālmīki: An Epic of Ancient India*, translated by Pollock, Sheldon, I., Vol. II, 17, 1st Indian ed., Motilal Banarsidass, Delhi, 2007, *Araṇyakāṇḍa*: 18:1–11, 30:1–4, 31:1–3, pp. 127, 150, 152.
126. Chakravarti, Uma, op. cit., pp. 225–226.
127. Ganguli, Kisari Mohan, *The Mahabharata of Krishna-Dwaipayana Vyasa*, Vol I, Munshiram Manoharlal Publishers Pvt. Ltd., New Delhi, 2004, *Adi Parva*, p. 215.
128. Ibid., p. 126.
129. Ibid., p. 236.
130. Ibid., p. 210.
131. Ibid., p. 126.
132. Ghosh, Jayatri, "Satyavatī: The Matriarch of *Mahābhārata*", in Bose, Mandakranta (ed.), *Faces of the Feminine in Ancient, Medieval and Modern India,* OUP, New Delhi, 2000, p. 35.
133. Ganguli, Kisari Mohan, *The Mahabharata of Krishna-Dwaipayana Vyasa*, Vol I, Munshiram Manoharlal Publishers Pvt. Ltd., New Delhi, 2004, *Adi Parva*, p. 227.
134. She indirectly got it from Śāntanu, when his son, Devavrata, relinquished his right to inherit the kingdom of his father, and took up the vow of celibacy, to assure Satyavatī of the unchallenged accession of her progeny.
135. Ganguli, Kisari Mohan, *The Mahabharata of Krishna-Dwaipayana Vyasa*, Vol I, Munshiram Manoharlal Publishers Pvt. Ltd., New Delhi, 2004, *Adi Parva,* pp. 217–218.
136. Ibid.
137. Ibid.
138. Ganguli, Kisari Mohan, *The Mahabharata of Krishna-Dwaipayana Vyasa*, Vol I, Munshiram Manoharlal Publishers Pvt. Ltd., New Delhi, 2004, *Adi Parva*, p. 227.
139. *Manu*.IX.160, *Bṛhas*.XXV.41, *Viṣṇu*.XV.10, *Vasiṣṭha*.XVII.21.
140. Ibid., p. 236.
141. Ghosh, Jayatri, op. cit., p. 45.
142. Ganguli, Kisari Mohan, *The Mahabharata of Krishna-Dwaipayana Vyasa*, Vol I, Munshiram Manoharlal Publishers Pvt. Ltd., New Delhi, 2004, *Adi Parva*, p. 218, 222.
143. Ghosh, Jayatri, op. cit., p. 41.
144. Ganguli, Kisari Mohan, *The Mahabharata of Krishna-Dwaipayana Vyasa*, Vol I, Munshiram Manoharlal Publishers Pvt. Ltd., New Delhi, 2004, *Adi Parva,* pp. 222–223.
145. Ibid., p. 223.
146. Ibid., p. 227.
147. Ibid., p. 228.
148. *Gautama*.XVIII, *Yāj*.I.III.68–69.

149. *Vasiṣṭha*.XVII.56.
150. Ghosh, Jayatri, op. cit., p. 44.
151. Ganguli, Kisari Mohan, *The Mahabharata of Krishna-Dwaipayana Vyasa*, Vol I, Munshiram Manoharlal Publishers Pvt. Ltd., New Delhi, 2004, *Sabha Parva,* pp. 135–136.
152. Ghosh, Jayatri, op. cit., p. 45.
153. Ganguli, Kisari Mohan, *The Mahabharata of Krishna-Dwaipayana Vyasa*, Vol I, Munshiram Manoharlal Publishers Pvt. Ltd., New Delhi, 2004, *Adi Parva,* pp. 219–221.
154. Ibid., p. 219.
155. Ibid., p. 219.
156. *Manu*.III.27–34, *Viṣṇu*.XXIV.17–24, *Gautama*.IV, *Nārada*.XII.38–39, *Śankha*.IV.2–6.
157. *Manu*.III.23–26, *Śankha*.IV.3.
158. *Nārada*.XII.44.
159. *Viṣṇu*.XXIV.27–28.
160. Ganguli, Kisari Mohan, *The Mahabharata of Krishna-Dwaipayana Vyasa*, Vol I, Munshiram Manoharlal Publishers Pvt. Ltd., New Delhi, 2004, *Adi Parva,* p. 221.
161. Ibid., pp. 221–222.
162. Ibid., p. 222.
163. Ibid., p. 223.
164. Ibid., p. 227.
165. Ibid., pp. 229,230.
166. Ibid., p. 230.
167. Ibid., p. 227.
168. *Gautama*.XVIII, *Nārada*.XII.81–88.
169. Ganguli, Kisari Mohan, *The Mahabharata of Krishna-Dwaipayana Vyasa*, Vol I, Munshiram Manoharlal Publishers Pvt. Ltd., New Delhi, 2004, *Adi Parva*, pp. 220–221.
170. Ganguli, Kisari Mohan, *The Mahabharata of Krishna-Dwaipayana Vyasa*, Vol. II, Munshiram Manoharlal Publishers Pvt. Ltd., New Delhi, 2004, *Udyog Parva*, p 337–338.
171. Ibid., pp. 336–337, 345–346.
172. Ibid., pp. 342–360.
173. Ibid., pp. 361–362.
174. Ibid., p. 362.
175. *Manu*.V.155, *Viṣṇu*.XXIV.7,15, *Pārāśara*.IV.20, *Śankha*.V.8.
176. Ganguli, Kisari Mohan, *The Mahabharata of Krishna-Dwaipayana Vyasa*, Vol. I, Munshiram Manoharlal Publishers Pvt. Ltd., New Delhi, 2004, pp. 362–363.
177. Ibid., p. 363.

178. Ibid.
179. Ibid., p. 364.
180. Ibid., p. 365.
181. Ibid., pp. 368–369.
182. Ganguli, Kisari Mohan, *The Mahabharata of Krishna-Dwaipayana Vyasa*, Vol. I, Munshiram Manoharlal Publishers Pvt. Ltd., New Delhi, 2004, *Bhishma Parva*, p. 302.
183. Ibid., pp. 302–306.
184. Dasgupta, Madhusraba, "Usable Women: The Tales of Ambā and Mādhavī", in Bose, Mandakranta (ed.), op. cit., p. 52.
185. Ganguli, Kisari Mohan, *The Mahabharata of Krishna-Dwaipayana Vyasa*, Vol. I, Munshiram Manoharlal Publishers Pvt. Ltd., New Delhi, 2004, *Adi Parva*, p. 235.
186. Ganguli, Kisari Mohan, *The Mahabharata of Krishna-Dwaipayana Vyasa*, Vol. III, Munshiram Manoharlal Publishers Pvt. Ltd., New Delhi, 2004, *Stree Parva*, p. 22.
187. Ganguli, Kisari Mohan, *The Mahabharata of Krishna-Dwaipayana Vyasa*, Vol. III, Munshiram Manoharlal Publishers Pvt. Ltd., New Delhi, 2004, *Stree Parva*, p. 39.
188. Ganguli, Kisari Mohan, *The Mahabharata of Krishna-Dwaipayana Vyasa*, Vol. I, Munshiram Manoharlal Publishers Pvt. Ltd., New Delhi, 2004, *Adi Parva*, p. 235.
189. Ibid.
190. Ibid.
191. Ibid., p. 236.
192. Ibid.
193. Ibid., p. 251.
194. Ibid., p. 254.
195. *Nārada*.XII.97, *Pārāśara*.IV.30.
196. Ganguli, Kisari Mohan, *The Mahabharata of Krishna-Dwaipayana Vyasa*, Vol. I, Munshiram Manoharlal Publishers Pvt. Ltd., New Delhi, 2004, *Adi Parva*, p. 254.
197. Ganguli, Kisari Mohan, *The Mahabharata of Krishna-Dwaipayana Vyasa*, Vol. I, Munshiram Manoharlal Publishers Pvt. Ltd., New Delhi, 2004, *Vana Parva*, p. 594.
198. Ganguli, Kisari Mohan, *The Mahabharata of Krishna-Dwaipayana Vyasa*, Vol. I, Munshiram Manoharlal Publishers Pvt. Ltd., New Delhi, 2004, *Vana Parva*, p. 594–595.
199. For a detailed discussion on the treatment meted out to adultery by the *dharmaśāstrakāras*, please see *loc. cit.*, pp. 117–132.
200. *Manu*.VIII.205,224,226, *Manu*.X.5, *Yāj*.I.3.52,54, 10.264, *Vasiṣṭha*.VIII.1.
201. *Viṣṇu*.XV.10,11.

202. *Viṣṇu*.XV.15.
203. *Viṣṇu*.XV.16,17.
204. *Mahabharat (Mbh)*: 2.28.23–24.
205. *Mbh*: 2. 24.15.
206. Vora, D.P., *Evolution of Morals in the Epics*, Popular Book Depot, Bombay, 1959, p. 10.
207. *Mbh*: 8. 392.1.
208. *Mbh*: 9.42.18.
209. In the *Rāmāyana* [3. 17. 24] Rāksasi Śūrpanakhā is given to erotic desires at first glance and has no qualm in stating it.
210. *Mbh*: 8.30.40; 8.387.1 and 8.30.16–18.
211. *Mbh*: 1.114.65 (fn).
212. Shah, Shalini, *The Making of Womanhood: Gender Relations in the Mahābhārata*, Manohar, New Delhi, 1995, pp. 51–52.
213. *Manu*.III.5, *Yāj*.III.52,53, Gautma.IV, *Vasiṣṭha*.VIII.1,2, *Vyāsa*.II.3,4, *Viṣṇu*. XXIV.9, *Śankha*.IV
214. Ganguli, Kisari Mohan, *The Mahabharata of Krishna-Dwaipayana Vyasa*, Vol. I, Munshiram Manoharlal Publishers Pvt. Ltd., New Delhi, 2004, *Adi Parva*, p. 263.
215. *Viṣṇu*.XXV.1.14, *Vyāsa*.II.50–51, *Bṛhas*.XXIV.11, *Pārāśara*.IV.33, *Dakśa*.IV.19,20, Uśanā.III.119.
216. Ganguli, Kisari Mohan, *The Mahabharata of Krishna-Dwaipayana Vyasa*, Vol. I, Munshiram Manoharlal Publishers Pvt. Ltd., New Delhi, 2004, *Vana Parva*, p. 70.
217. *Manu*.II.67.
218. *Viṣṇu*.XXII.32.
219. *Yama*.73.
220. *Atri* 135.
221. *Dakśa*. VII. 26.
222. Ganguli, Kisari Mohan, *The Mahabharata of Krishna-Dwaipayana Vyasa*, Vol. I, Munshiram Manoharlal Publishers Pvt. Ltd., New Delhi, 2004, *Adi Parva*, p. 374.
223. Ibid., p. 383.
224. Ibid., pp. 384–385.
225. *Manu*.III.27–34, *Viṣṇu*.XXIV.17–24, *Gautama*.IV, *Nārada*.XII.38–39, *Śankha*.IV.2–6.
226. *Manu*.III.12, *Yāj*.I.3.57, *Nārada*.XII.6, *Vasiṣṭha*.I.24, *Viṣṇu*.XXIV.1–4, *Vyāsa*.II.10–11, *Śankha*.IV.7–8.
227. *Kātyāyana*.XIX.13, *Dakśa*.IV.8, *Atri*.339–340.
228. Ganguli, Kisari Mohan, *The Mahabharata of Krishna-Dwaipayana Vyasa*, Vol. I, Munshiram Manoharlal Publishers Pvt. Ltd., New Delhi, 2004, *Adi Parva*, p. 389.

229. Jayal, Shakambari, *The Status of Women in the Epics*, Motilal Banarasidass, Delhi, 1966, pp. 314–16.
230. Syed, A.J. (ed.), *D.D. Kosambi on History and Society*, University of Bombay Publications, Bombay, 1985, p. 154.
231. Schmidt, Hanns Peter, *Some Women's Rites and Rights in the Veda*, B.O.R.I., Poona, 1987, p. 61.
232. Coontz, S. and Henderson, P. (eds.), *Women's Work, Men's Property: On the Origin of Gender and Class*, Verso, London, 1986, p. 136.
233. Shah, Shalini, op. cit., p. 77.
234. Sharma, R.S., *Material Culture and Social Formations in Ancient India*, Macmillan India Ltd., New Delhi, 1983, p. 143.
235. Ganguli, Kisari Mohan, *The Mahabharata of Krishna-Dwaipayana Vyasa*, Vol. I, Munshiram Manoharlal Publishers Pvt. Ltd., New Delhi, 2004, *Adi Parva*, p. 381.
236. Ibid.
237. Ibid., p. 387.
238. *Mbh*: 17.2.6.
239. Ganguli, Kisari Mohan, *The Mahabharata of Krishna-Dwaipayana Vyasa*, Vol. I, Munshiram Manoharlal Publishers Pvt. Ltd., New Delhi, 2004, p. 394.
240. Ganguli, Kisari Mohan, *The Mahabharata of Krishna-Dwaipayana Vyasa*, Vol. II, Munshiram Manoharlal Publishers Pvt. Ltd., New Delhi, 2004, *Udyog Parva*, pp. 229, 230.
241. Ganguli, Kisari Mohan, *The Mahabharata of Krishna-Dwaipayana Vyasa*, Vol. I, Munshiram Manoharlal Publishers Pvt. Ltd., New Delhi, 2004, *Adi Parva*, p. 127, 236.
242. *Manu*.VIII.205,226, X.5, *Nārada*.XII.36, *Yāj*.I.3.52,54.
243. Ibid.
244. Ibid.
245. Goody, Jack and Tambiah, S.J., *Bride Wealth and Dowry*, CUP, Cambridge, 1973, p 17
246. *Manu*.IX.92.
247. *Manu*.IX.194, *Viṣṇu*.XVII.18, *Yāj*.II.143–144, *Nārada*.XIII.8, *Kātyāyana* quoted in *Dāyabhāga*, IV.I.5,6,13.
248. Ganguli, Kisari Mohan, *The Mahabharata of Krishna-Dwaipayana Vyasa*, Vol. I, Munshiram Manoharlal Publishers Pvt. Ltd., New Delhi, 2004, *Adi Parva*, p. 180.
249. Ganguli, Kisari Mohan, *The Mahabharata of Krishna-Dwaipayana Vyasa*, Vol. I, Munshiram Manoharlal Publishers Pvt. Ltd., New Delhi, 2004, *Sabha Parva*, p. 137.
250. Ibid., p. 124.
251. Ibid., pp. 122–124.

252. Irigaray, Luce, *This Sex Which is Not One*, Cornell University Press, Ithaca, 1985, p. 173.
253. *Mbh*: 3.79, 26.
254. *Mbh*: 1.187, 23.
255. *Mbh*: 5.37.17 and 1.1614', 1.
256. *Mbh*: 2.60, 40.
257. *Mbh*: 2.61, 23.
258. *Mbh*: 2.61.31, 38–39.
259. Shah, Shalini, op. cit., pp. 29–31.
260. Ganguli, Kisari Mohan, *The Mahabharata of Krishna-Dwaipayana Vyasa*, Vol. I, Munshiram Manoharlal Publishers Pvt. Ltd., New Delhi, 2004, *Sabha Parva*, p. 132.
261. Ibid., p. 133.
262. Ibid., p. 136.
263. Ibid., pp. 139–140.
264. Ibid., p. 140.
265. Ibid., pp. 126–127.
266. Ibid., p. 137, 139.
267. Ibid., p. 128.
268. Ibid.
269. For a detailed discussion on menstrual taboos in the *dharmaśāstras*, please see *loc. cit.*, pp. 108–114.
270. Ganguli, Kisari Mohan, op. cit., *Anusasana Parva* (Part II), Vol. IV, p. 155.
271. Ganguli, Kisari Mohan, *The Mahabharata of Krishna-Dwaipayana Vyasa*, Vol. II, Munshiram Manoharlal Publishers Pvt. Ltd., New Delhi, 2004, *Udyog Parva*, p. 23.
272. Ganguli, Kisari Mohan, *The Mahabharata of Krishna-Dwaipayana Vyasa*, Vol. III, Munshiram Manoharlal Publishers Pvt. Ltd., New Delhi, 2004, *Santi Parva* (Part I), p. 74.
273. Shah, Shalini, op. cit., p. 45.
274. Ganguli, Kisari Mohan, *The Mahabharata of Krishna-Dwaipayana Vyasa*, Vol. II, Munshiram Manoharlal Publishers Pvt. Ltd., New Delhi, 2004, *Virata Parva*, pp. 31–32.
275. Ganguli, Kisari Mohan, *The Mahabharata of Krishna-Dwaipayana Vyasa*, Vol. I, Munshiram Manoharlal Publishers Pvt. Ltd., New Delhi, 2004, *Sabha Parva*, pp. 139–140.
276. For a detailed discussion on wifehood as sought to be defined by the *dharmaśāstrakāras*, please see *loc. cit.*, pp. 84–114.
277. Ganguli, Kisari Mohan, *The Mahabharata of Krishna-Dwaipayana Vyasa*, Vol. I, Munshiram Manoharlal Publishers Pvt. Ltd., New Delhi, 2004, *Adi Parva*, p. 159.
278. Ibid.

279. Ganguli, Kisari Mohan, *The Mahabharata of Krishna-Dwaipayana Vyasa*, Vol. II, Munshiram Manoharlal Publishers Pvt. Ltd., New Delhi, 2004, *Virata Parva*, p. 5.
280. Ibid., p. 36.
281. Ganguli, Kisari Mohan, *The Mahabharata of Krishna-Dwaipayana Vyasa*, Vol. I, Munshiram Manoharlal Publishers Pvt. Ltd., New Delhi, 2004, *Vana Parva,* p. 474.
282. Ganguli, Kisari Mohan, *The Mahabharata of Krishna-Dwaipayana Vyasa*, Vol. II, Munshiram Manoharlal Publishers Pvt. Ltd., New Delhi, 2004, *Udyog Parva*, pp. 226–236.
283. Ibid., p. 227.
284. Ibid., pp. 227–231.
285. Shah, Shalini, op. cit., pp. 29–30.
286. Ganguli, Kisari Mohan, *The Mahabharata of Krishna-Dwaipayana Vyasa*, Vol. II, Munshiram Manoharlal Publishers Pvt. Ltd., New Delhi, 2004, *Udyog Parva*, pp. 229, 230.
287. Ibid., pp. 232–233.
288. Shah, Shalini, op. cit., p. 30.
289. Ganguli, Kisari Mohan, *The Mahabharata of Krishna-Dwaipayana Vyasa*, Vol. I, Munshiram Manoharlal Publishers Pvt. Ltd., New Delhi, 2004, *Adi Parva*, p. 158.
290. Ibid., p. 162.
291. Ibid.
292. Ganguli, Kisari Mohan, *The Mahabharata of Krishna-Dwaipayana Vyasa*, Vol. IV, Munshiram Manoharlal Publishers Pvt. Ltd., New Delhi, 2004, *Anusasana Parva* (Part I), p. 43.
293. *The Rāmāyaṇa of Vālmīki,* translated by Pollock, Sheldon, I., Vol. II, 1st Indian ed. Motilal Banarsidass, Delhi, 2007, *Ayodhyākāṇḍa*: 109: 23–28, p. 318.
294. Ganguli, Kisari Mohan, *The Mahabharata of Krishna-Dwaipayana Vyasa*, Vol. IV, Munshiram Manoharlal Publishers Pvt. Ltd., New Delhi, 2004, *Anusasana Parva* (Part I), p. 43.
295. Ganguli, Kisari Mohan, *The Mahabharata of Krishna-Dwaipayana Vyasa*, Vol. III, Munshiram Manoharlal Publishers Pvt. Ltd., New Delhi, 2004, *Santi Parva* (Part II), pp. 250–251.
296. *The Rāmāyaṇa of Vālmīki: An Epic of Ancient India*, translated by Goldman, Robert P., 1st Indian ed., Motilal Banarsidass, Delhi, 2007, Vol. I, *Bālakāṇḍa*:47:29–32, p. 216.
297. Ganguli, Kisari Mohan, Ganguli, Kisari Mohan, *The Mahabharata of Krishna-Dwaipayana Vyasa*, Vol. I, Munshiram Manoharlal Publishers Pvt. Ltd., New Delhi, 2004, *Vana Parva,* p. 566.
298. Ibid., p. 567.

299. Ibid., p. 474.
300. Ganguli, Kisari Mohan, *The Mahabharata of Krishna-Dwaipayana Vyasa*, Vol. IV, Munshiram Manoharlal Publishers Pvt. Ltd., New Delhi, 2004, *Anusasana Parva* (Part II), pp. 316–318.
301. Ganguli, Kisari Mohan, *The Mahabharata of Krishna-Dwaipayana Vyasa*, Vol. I, Munshiram Manoharlal Publishers Pvt. Ltd., New Delhi, 2004, *Vana Parva*, p. 476.
302. Ganguli, Kisari Mohan, *The Mahabharata of Krishna-Dwaipayana Vyasa*, Vol. IV, Munshiram Manoharlal Publishers Pvt. Ltd., New Delhi, 2004, *Anusasana Parva* (Part II), p. 317.
303. Ganguli, Kisari Mohan, *The Mahabharata of Krishna-Dwaipayana Vyasa*, Vol. I, Munshiram Manoharlal Publishers Pvt. Ltd., New Delhi, 2004, *Vana Parva*, pp. 579–580
304. Ganguli, Kisari Mohan, Ganguli, Kisari Mohan, *The Mahabharata of Krishna-Dwaipayana Vyasa*, Vol. I, Munshiram Manoharlal Publishers Pvt. Ltd., New Delhi, 2004, *Adi Parva*, pp, 322–324.
305. Ibid., p. 421.
306. Though nothing was said explicitly by the lawgivers regarding marriage with a woman outside the *Āryan* pale, however, they must not have had their acceptance can be derived from the fact that even inter-*varṇa* marriages were disfavoured by them and got only a tacit acceptance.
307. *Manu*.III.6–7, *Yāj*.I.3.53, *Kātyāyana*.XXVIII.4, *Hārita*.IV.1–2, *Likhita*.51–53.
308. Shah, Shalini, op. cit., p. 16.
309. Ganguli, Kisari Mohan, *The Mahabharata of Krishna-Dwaipayana Vyasa*, Vol. III, Munshiram Manoharlal Publishers Pvt. Ltd., New Delhi, 2004, *Karna Parva,* pp. 107–109.
310. Ganguli, Kisari Mohan, *The Mahabharata of Krishna-Dwaipayana Vyasa*, Vol. I, Munshiram Manoharlal Publishers Pvt. Ltd., New Delhi, 2004, *Adi Parva*, pp. 98–101.
311. Karve, Irawati, "Kinship Terms and the Family Organization as found in the Critical Edition of the Mahābhārata", *Bulletin of the Deccan College Research Institute,* Poona., Issue 5, 1943–44, p. 146.
312. Shah, Shalini, op. cit., p. 37.
313. Ganguli, Kisari Mohan, *The Mahabharata of Krishna-Dwaipayana Vyasa*, Vol. IV, Munshiram Manoharlal Publishers Pvt. Ltd., New Delhi, 2004, *Anusasana Parva* (Part II), p. 18.
314. *Manu*.III.5, *Yāj*.I.3.52, *Vasiṣṭha*.VIII.1,2, *Vyāsa*.II.3,4, *Viṣṇu*. XXIV.9, *Śankha*.IV.
315. Ganguli, Kisari Mohan, *The Mahabharata of Krishna-Dwaipayana Vyasa*, Vol. III, Munshiram Manoharlal Publishers Pvt. Ltd., New Delhi, 2004, *Salya Parva*, pp. 145–146.
316. Ibid., p. 146.

317. Ibid., p. 148.
318. *Manu*.V.155, *Viṣṇu*.XXIV.7,15, *Pārāśara*.IV.20, *Śankha*.V.8.
319. *Mbh*: 12.79.40, cited in Shah, Shalini, op. cit., p. 69.
320. *Mbh*: 13.App. 14.299–303, cited in Shah, Shalini, op. cit., p. 69.
321. *Mbh*: 12.52'.2, cited in Shah, Shalini, op. cit., p. 69.
322. Āpas.Dh.S.IX.24, *Nārada*.XII.94, Angiras.I.70, *Atri*.299, *Dakśa*.I.24.
323. *Manu*. III.166,167,V.157–162, *Vyāsa*.II.50–51.
324. Cited in Jayal, Shakambari, op. cit., p. 186.
325. *Mbh*: 13.409'.8, Cited in Shah Shalini, op. cit., p. 88.
326. Cited in Jayal, Shakambari, op. cit., p. 183.
327. Ganguli, Kisari Mohan, op. cit., *Santi Parva* (Part I), p. 159.
328. *Nārada*.XII.97, *Pārāśara*.IV.30.
329. *Pārāśara*.IV.31–32.
330. *Manu*.V.157, *Bṛhas*.XXV.71, *Pārāśara*.IV.31–32, *Vyāsa*.II.50–51, *Vasiṣṭha*.XVII.55.
331. Ganguli, Kisari Mohan, *The Mahabharata of Krishna-Dwaipayana Vyasa*, Vol. IV, Munshiram Manoharlal Publishers Pvt. Ltd., New Delhi, 2004, *Mausala Parva,* p. 11.
332. Ganguli, Kisari Mohan, *The Mahabharata of Krishna-Dwaipayana Vyasa*, Vol. IV, Munshiram Manoharlal Publishers Pvt. Ltd., New Delhi, 2004, *Mausala Parva*, p. 9.
333. Sastri, K.A. Nilakanta, *A History of South India: From Prehistoric Times to the Fall of Vijayanagar*, 4th ed., OUP, New Delhi, 1999, p. 104.
334. Allchin, B. and Allchin, R., *The Birth of Indian Civilization; India and Pakistan before 500 BC*, Penguin Books, Baltimore, 1968, p. 232.
335. Hart, George L., III, "Women and the Sacred in Ancient Tamilnadu", in Roy, Kumkum (ed.), *Women in Early Indian Societies*, Manohar, New Delhi, 1999, p. 229.
336. Sastri, K.A. Nilakanta, op. cit., p. 117.
337. Ramaswamy, Vijaya, *Walking Naked: Women, Society, Spirituality in South India*, IIAS, Shimla, 1997, pp. 39–40.
338. Tharu, Susie and Lalita, K. (eds.), *Women Writing in India (600 BC to the present)*, Vol. I, OUP, New Delhi, 1991, p. 70.
339. Ibid.
340. Sundramathy, Gloria, L., "The Women Poets of the Sangam Age", *Journal of Tamil Studies*, 1975, p. 62.
341. Ramaswamy, Vijaya, "Aspects of Women and Work in Early South India", in Roy, Kumkum (ed.), *Women in Early Indian Societies*, Manohar, New Delhi, 1999, p. 151.
342. Tharu, Susie and Lalita K. (eds.), op. cit., p. 71.
343. Ramaswamy, Vijaya, *Walking Naked: Women, Society, Spirituality in South India*, IIAS, Shimla, 1997, p. 53.

344. Ibid.
345. Ramaswamy, Vijaya, *Walking Naked: Women, Society, Spirituality in South India*, IIAS, Shimla, 1997, pp. 55–56.
346. *Manu*.IX.92.
347. Ramaswamy, Vijaya, *Walking Naked: Women, Society, Spirituality in South India*, IIAS, Shimla, 1997, p. 56.
348. *Ainkurunuru*: 147 cited in Nataraja, Devabhoopati, "Courtship and Marriage in the Classical Period", *Journal of Tamil Studies*, Vol. I, Part I, 1969, p. 25.
349. *Ahananuru*: 280 cited in Nataraja, Devabhoopati, "Courtship and Marriage in the Classical Period", *Journal of Tamil Studies*, Vol. I, Part I, 1969, pp. 25–26.
350. *Narrinai*: 234 cited in Ramaswamy, Vijaya, *Walking Naked: Women, Society, Spirituality in South India*, IIAS, Shimla, 1997, p. 57.
351. *Purananuru*: 352 cited in Ramaswamy, Vijaya, *Walking Naked: Women, Society, Spirituality in South India*, IIAS, Shimla, 1997, p. 57.
352. Ramaswamy, Vijaya, "Women and the 'Domestic' in Tamil Folk Songs", in *Man in India*, No. 7, 1994.
353. Ramaswamy, Vijaya, *Walking Naked: Women, Society, Spirituality in South India*, IIAS, Shimla, 1997, p. 57.
354. *Manu*.III.25, *Nārada*.XII.44.
355. *Akanānūru*: 48 cited in Ramaswamy, Vijaya, "Aspects of Women and Work in Early South India", in Roy, Kumkum (ed.), op. cit., p. 153.
356. Ramaswamy, Vijaya, "Aspects of Women and Work in Early South India", in Roy, Kumkum (ed.), op. cit., p. 153.
357. Ibid.
358. *Ainkurunuru*: 257: 1–2 cited in Ramaswamy, Vijaya, *Walking Naked: Women, Society, Spirituality in South India*, IIAS, Shimla, 1997, p. 55.
359. *Manu*.IX.81, *Yāj*.I.3.73, *Nārada*.XII.94.
360. Ramaswamy, Vijaya, *Walking Naked: Women, Society, Spirituality in South India*, IIAS, Shimla, 1997, p. 55.
361. Ibid.
362. Ramaswamy, Vijaya, "Aspects of Women and Work in Early South India", in *Indian Economic and Social History Review*, Jan-March 1989, pp. 82–84.
363. *Tolkappiam* of Tolkappiyar, *Porulatikaram* Naccinark-kiniyar commentary, Madras, 1923, verse 20.
364. *Purananuru*, ed. by U.V. Swaminathaiyyar, Madras, 1935, 61: 1.
365. *Tolkappiam Porulatikaram* Naccinark-kiniyar commentary, Madras, 1923, verse 20.
366. Ramaswamy, Vijaya, "Aspects of Women and Work in Early South India", in Kumkum Roy (ed.), op. cit., pp. 151–152.
367. Ibid., p. 152.
368. *Akananuru*: 48 cited in Ramaswamy, Vijaya, "Aspects of Women and Work in Early South India", in Kumkum Roy (ed.), op. cit., p. 153.

369. *Perumppanarruppatai*, 156–60 cited in Ramaswamy, Vijaya, "Aspects of Women and Work in Early South India", in Kumkum Roy (ed.), op. cit.
370. *Purananuru*, 276:4–5 cited in Ramaswamy, Vijaya, "Aspects of Women and Work in Early South India", in Kumkum Roy (ed.), op. cit.
371. *Purananuru*, 33 cited in Ramaswamy, Vijaya, "Aspects of Women and Work in Early South India", in Kumkum Roy (ed.), op. cit., pp. 153–154.
372. *Perumppanarruppatai*, 166–8 cited in Ramaswamy, Vijaya, "Aspects of Women and Work in Early South India", in Kumkum Roy (ed.), op. cit.
373. Ramaswamy, Vijaya, "Aspects of Women and Work in Early South India", in Kumkum Roy (ed.), op. cit., p. 154.
374. *Purananuru*, 125:1, Also 326:5 cited in Ramaswamy, Vijaya, "Aspects of Women and Work in Early South India", in Kumkum Roy (ed.), op. cit.
375. *Purananuru*, 311:1–2, *Akananuru*, 89 cited in Ramaswamy, Vijaya, "Aspects of Women and Work in Early South India", in Kumkum Roy (ed.), op. cit., p. 155.
376. *Narrinai*, 90: 2–4 cited in Ramaswamy, Vijaya, "Aspects of Women and Work in Early South India", in Kumkum Roy (ed.), op. cit.
377. *Kuruntakai*, 330:1 cited in Ramaswamy, Vijaya, "Aspects of Women and Work in Early South India", in Kumkum Roy (ed.), op. cit.
378. *Akananuru*, 34: 11–12 cited in Ramaswamy, Vijaya, "Aspects of Women and Work in Early South India", in Kumkum Roy (ed.), op. cit.
379. Ibid., 34 and 387 cited in Ramaswamy, Vijaya, "Aspects of Women and Work in Early South India", in Kumkum Roy (ed.), op. cit.
380. *Purananuru*, 66 cited in Ramaswamy, Vijaya, "Aspects of Women and Work in Early South India", in Kumkum Roy (ed.), op. cit., p. 156.
381. *Kalittokai*, Naccinarkkiniyar commentary, ed. by E.V. Anantharaman, Madras, 1925, Marutam, 13–14.
382. *Akananuru*, 390:8–10, also verse 140 cited in Ramaswamy, Vijaya, "Aspects of Women and Work in Early South India", in Kumkum Roy (ed.), op. cit., p. 158.
383. *Akananuru*, 9, 20 cited in Ramaswamy, Vijaya, "Aspects of Women and Work in Early South India", in Kumkum Roy (ed.), op. cit.
384. *Ainkurunanuru*, ed. by U.V. Swaminathaiyyar and S. Kalyana Sundarayyar, Madras, 1944, 47:1–3 and Also *Purananuru*, 343:1 cited in Ramaswamy, Vijaya, "Aspects of Women and Work in Early South India", in Kumkum Roy (ed.), op. cit.
385. Ramaswamy, Vijaya, "Aspects of Women and Work in Early South India", in Kumkum Roy (ed.), op. cit., p. 159.
386. *Maduraikkanci*, 405–6 cited in Ramaswamy, Vijaya, "Aspects of Women and Work in Early South India", in Kumkum Roy (ed.), op. cit., p. 160.
387. *Śilappadikaram* 13: 122–3 cited in Ramaswamy, Vijaya, "Aspects of Women and Work in Early South India", in Kumkum Roy (ed.), op. cit.

388. *Kurincippattu* in *Pattuppattu*, 1–26 cited in Ramaswamy, Vijaya, "Aspects of Women and Work in Early South India", in Kumkum Roy (ed.), op. cit., p. 161.
389. *Ciruppanarruppatai* in *Pattuppattu*, 13–31, 62 cited in Ramaswamy, Vijaya, "Aspects of Women and Work in Early South India", in Kumkum Roy (ed.), op. cit.
390. *Mullaippattu*, 45–9 cited in Ramaswamy, Vijaya, "Aspects of Women and Work in Early South India", in Kumkum Roy (ed.), op. cit., p. 164.
391. Ramaswamy, Vijaya, "Aspects of Women and Work in Early South India", in Kumkum Roy (ed.), op. cit., pp. 164–165.
392. *Manu*.II.67, V.150, *Bṛhas*.XXIV.4, *Yāj*.I.3.83, *Viṣṇu*.XXV.4–6, *Vyāsa*.II.20–25, 28–32.
393. Ramaswamy, Vijaya, "Aspects of Women and Work in Early South India", in Kumkum Roy (ed.), op. cit., pp. 42–43.
394. *Purananuru*: 299 cited in Hart, George, L., III, op. cit., p. 229.
395. *Akananuru*. 7 cited in Hart, George, L.,III, op. cit., p. 230.
396. *Manimekalai*, U.V. Swaminathaier (ed.), Madras Kapir Accukkutam, Madras, 1965, 7.75–6
397. Hart, George, L., III, op. cit., p. 231.
398. For Example *Akananuru*., 16, 26, 66, 176 cited in Hart, George, L., III, op. cit., p. 233.
399. Crawley, E., *The Mystic Rose*, Vol. 2, New York, 1927, p. 198.
400. Ramaswamy, Vijaya, *Walking Naked: Women, Society, Spirituality in South India*, IIAS, Shimla, 1997, pp. 51–52.
401. Ibid., p. 48.
402. Hart, George, L., III, op. cit., p. 233.
403. Ramaswamy, Vijaya, *Walking Naked: Women, Society, Spirituality in South India*, IIAS, Shimla, 1997, p. 48.
404. *Śilappadikaram,* 20: 34–44 cited in Ramaswamy, Vijaya, "Aspects of Women and Work in Early South India", in Kumkum Roy (ed.), op. cit.
405. Hart, George, L. III, op. cit., p. 233.
406. Ramaswamy, Vijaya, *Walking Naked: Women, Society, Spirituality in South India*, IIAS, Shimla, 1997, p. 49.
407. Ibid., pp. 49–50.
408. *Narrinai*: 216 cited in Ramaswamy, Vijaya, "Aspects of Women and Work in Early South India", in Kumkum Roy (ed.), op. cit., p. 50.
409. Ramaswamy, Vijaya, *Walking Naked: Women, Society, Spirituality in South India*, IIAS, Shimla, 1997, p. 49.
410. *Purananuru*: 198 cited in Ramaswamy, Vijaya, "Aspects of Women and Work in Early South India", in Kumkum Roy (ed.), op. cit., *Ahananuru*: 184 cited in Hart, G., *The Poems of Ancient Tamils,* University of California Press, Berkeley, 1975, p. 97.

411. Hart, G., *The Poems of Ancient Tamils,* University of California Press, Berkeley, 1975, p. 97.
412. Ramaswamy, Vijaya, *Walking Naked: Women, Society, Spirituality in South India*, IIAS, Shimla, 1997, p. 55.
413. Shah, Kirit K., *The Problem of Identity: Women in Early Indian Inscriptions*, OUP, New Delhi, 2001, p. vii.
414. Ibid.
415. Shah, Kirit K., op. cit.
416. Ibid, p. viii.
417. Shah, Kirit K., op. cit., pp. 28–29.
418. *Manu*.V.152,154,156, *Yāj*.I.3.77,87, *Nārada*.XVIII.22, *Bṛhas*.XXIV.8, *Viṣṇu*.XV.2,12–15, *Dakśa*.IV.4,8,12.
419. *Manu*.V.154.
420. Shah, Kirit K., op. cit., p. 174.
421. Ibid., p. 175.
422. *A.S.W.I.*, vol. IV, No. VI (3).
423. Ibid., vol. V, No. 29 and *H.I.S.W.K.*, Pt II, No. 36.
424. *H.I.S.W.K.*, Pt. II, No. 37.
425. *E.I.*, vol. XX, No. 1 (B5).
426. Shah, Kirit K., op. cit., pp. 84–85.
427. *Manu*.III.9.
428. Shah, Kirit K., op. cit., p. 172.
429. *Manu*. II.33.
430. *E.I.*, vol. XXI, No. 11 (L).
431. *A.S.W.I.*, V, No.29.
432. *H.I.S.W.K.*, Pt. II, No.37.
433. *A.S.W.I.*, vol. V, No. 1, A-B.
434. *E.I.*, vol. XXXV, No. 1 (A).
435. Shah, Kirit K., op. cit., p. 173.
436. Kane, P.V., *History of Dharmaśāstra (Ancient and Medieval Religious and Civil Law in India*), Vol. II, Pt. I, 2nd ed., B.O.R.I., Poona, 1974, p 250; Sharma, T.R., *Personal and Geographical Names in Gupta Inscriptions*, Concept Publishing Company, Delhi, 1976, p. 8.
437. Ibid.
438. Shah, Kirit K., op. cit., p. 173.
439. *E.I.*, Vol.XX, No. 1 (C3).
440. *Viṣṇu*.XXIV.9, *Vasiṣṭha*.VIII.1, *Vyāsa*.II.3–4, *Śankha*.IV.
441. The relevant provision runs, 'He shall not give his daughter to a man belonging to the same family (*gotra*). Nor to one related (within six degrees) on the mother's or (father) side. Apas, Dh.S. II, 5.11. 15–16, S.B.E. vol. II, Pt. I, p. 127.

442. Kane has quoted the provision prescribing penance of *Cāndrāyana* for marrying a girl having the same *gotra* as one's mother's *gotra*, see Kane, P.V., op. cit., p. 459.
443. Shah, Kirit K., op. cit., p. 56.
444. *E.I.*, Vol. XX, No. 1 (C2) and No. 1 (C4).
445. *Manu*.III.5, *Yāj*.III.52,53, Gautma.IV, *Vasiṣṭha*.VIII.1,2, *Vyāsa*.II.3,4, *Viṣṇu*. XXIV.9, *Śankha*.IV
446. Shah, Kirit K., op. cit., p. 176.
447. Rajvade, Vishvanath Kashinath, *Bhāratīya Vivāha Samsthā kā Itihāsa*, People's Publishing House, New Delhi, 1986, p. 99.
448. Shah, Shalini, op. cit., p. 20.
449. Trautmann, T.R., *Dravidian Kinship*, CUP, Cambridge, 1981, p. 366 (fn).
450. *E.I.*,VIII, No. 8(5), A.S.W.I., vol. IV, No. IX (14) and H.I.S.W.K., Pt. II, No. 13.
451. *H.I.S.W.K.*, Part II, No. 18.
452. Shah, Kirit K., op. cit., p. 38.
453. Mirashi has listed four of her sons, all bearing the metronymic Vasiṣṭhīputra, *H.I.S.W.K.*, p. 36.
454. *H.I.S.W.K.*, Part II, No. 18.
455. *E.I.*, Vol.XX, No. 1 (C3).
456. *A.S.W.I.*, vol. V, p. 66.
457. Shah, Kirit K., op. cit., p. 70.
458. *A.S.W.I.*, vol. V, p 66–67.
459. Shah, Kirit K., op. cit., p. 71.
460. Ibid.
461. *H.I.S.W.K.*, Pt. II, No. 3, pp. 8–9.
462. Ibid., p 8, fn. 3.
463. *Manu*.V.155.

     Gautama also enjoins in identical terms, 'A wife is not independent with respect to (the fulfilment of) the sacred law.' Gaut. Dh. S. XVIII.1.
464. *Manu*.IX.18.
465. *Manu*.II.67.
466. Shah, Kirit K., op. cit., p. 85.
467. Ibid.
468. *E.I.*, vol. XXIX, No. 18.
469. Shah, Kirit K., op. cit., pp. 81–82.
470. *E.I.*,VIII, No. 8(5).
471. *S.I.*, vol. I, p. 200, fn.1.
472. *H.I.S.W.K.*, Part II, No.18.
473. Shah, Kirit K., op. cit., p. 43.
474. Ibid.
475. Ibid.

476. Roy, Kumkum, "Women and Men Donors at Sanchi: A Study of Inscriptional Evidence", in Tripathi, L.K. (ed.), *Position and Status of Women in Ancient India*, vol. I, Dept. of A.I.H.C. and Archaeology, BHU, Varanasi, 1988, p. 221.
477. Shah, Kirit K., op. cit., p. 178.
478. Ibid., pp. 178–180.
479. Roy, Kumkum, op. cit., p. 210.
480. Shah, Kirit K., op. cit., p. 91.
481. Ibid., p. 158.
482. Horner, I.B., *Women Under Primitive Buddhism*, first reprint, Oriental Publishers, Delhi, 1975, p. 87.
483. Shah, Kirit, K., op. cit., pp. 170–171.

5

Conclusion

Interest in the present study was evoked as a response to the raging controversy regarding the role of *dharmaśāstra* texts in defining gender relations in India. Feminist scholars have been criticizing these texts for *tightening the noose around women's lives, being the foundational documents of Hindu way of life that codified both social relations and personal belief as religious imperatives.* According to them, these texts have exerted a deep impact on women's lives and conduct through history, and their teachings have not yet entirely lost force. There is yet another group of scholars who are zealous disciples of the authors of these texts. They consider the *dharmaśāstras* as the *representative texts of Indian tradition*, and seek to justify all that is laid down by the authors of these texts. Adherents to both the views have been criticizing each other for not having read the texts *from cover to cover*, and picking up only those verses from the texts which add weight and impart strength to their preconceived notions and biased interpretations. None, either, or both of them may be fair in such a criticism. A thorough reading of the texts *from cover to cover* requires to be *free from any glasses*; that alone can render possible an *unbiased* exposition of the texts, as well as the contradictory opinions of the scholars. A few myths need to be shredded off before making an attempt to uncover reality.

The *dharmaśāstras* may neither be considered to be *the foundational documents of 'Hindu' way of life*, nor *the representative texts of 'Indian' tradition.* Who was, and is, a 'Hindu'? What can or should be included within the scope of the definitions of these terms which are used so often- 'Indian tradition', 'Indian culture', 'Indian values'? Reflection is needed to find answers to these and many other similar questions. Are 'Hindu' and 'Indian' uniform and absolute categories and rigid singular identities? Is one a Hindu who performs *yajña*, and recites *ṛcās* or mantras to propitiate cosmic deities; or the one who worships either or all of Brahmā, Viṣṇu and Maheśa; or the one who is in the pursuit of the nameless and formless *brahma*; or the one who worships Rāma, or Kriṣṇa, or Kāli in her numerous forms; or the one who is an adherent to any of the several ancient philosophical systems, included within the ambit of Hinduism; or the one who is the follower of the spiritual paths delineated by such savants as Vivekananda and Aurobindo in the modern times? Is 'Hindu' a ritualist or a recluse? Should only that line of thought be included within the scope of 'Indian tradition' which was propounded by the Brahmanical document. Is 'Indian Culture' only reflected by the so-called '*Āryan*' culture? Are only those definitions concurrent with the term 'Indian values' which are based on the ethical principles and moral precepts included in the *Dharma* texts?

No singular identity could be attributed to a 'Hindu' at any point of time in the history of the Indian subcontinent, and with the passage of time, the 'Hindu' has kept on assuming myriad forms and identities. In fact, the term 'Hindu', which has currently become a political weapon in the hands of a few with parochial vested interests, is etymologically incorrect to be used both for the 'ancient' past of the Indian subcontinent, and the present of the Republic of India. Apparently, Hinduism has been a floating mass of diverse beliefs and practices, multiple systems of philosophy and different ways of living. Entering into the spirit of what is called 'Hinduism', it reveals itself as an ever evolving philosophy of life. There can be no evolution without *conflict*, and it shall have to be admitted that conflicting trends did existed during all periods of history within the ambit of Hinduism. Similarly, the folk tradition and the aboriginal practices are as much a part of Indian culture and tradition as the set of principles and ethical values reflected in the Brahmanical or other compositions. Indian tradition is and always has been a conglomerate of many co-existing traditions.

Rather than being the foundational documents of Hindu life, the *dharmaśāstras* should be taken to be one of the many genres of literature produced in 'ancient' India. Though aimed at, these texts could not become the foundational documents of the Brahmanical way of life even during the period under study. This is amply borne out by the deviations, divergences and variations as well as reversals demonstrated by a study of the epics, *Śangam* texts and epigraphs. Though the texts presented the 'ideal', the 'real' was not always in consonance with it. Given the existence of diverse societies with different cultures and traditions, the sphere of influence of these texts would have been very limited. Again, instead of being the representative texts of Indian tradition, these texts represent merely one of the lines of thought, which might have become dominant at different points of time in the history of the Indian subcontinent. The discussion in the preceding chapters however is not aimed at washing away or even negating the influence of these texts on Indian society. It was intended to bring home the fact that other parallel and contradictory trends had always existed side by side.

In order to understand the nature and objective of the *dharmaśāstras*, to understand the meaning of the term *dharma* is imperative. The actual meaning of *dharma* kept changing during the ancient times of Indian history. The word has been used in several widely different senses. In its most general sense, it is derived from the root *dhṛ*, which means, to uphold, to support, to sustain or to nourish.[1] Thus, '*dharma* is what is firm and durable, what sustains and maintains, what hinders fainting and falling'.[2] The word appears to be used in the same sense in a few of the passages of the ancient-most documents of Vedic language.[3] In most of the other cases, the word *dharma* carries the meaning 'religious ordinances or rites'[4]. In some other passages, the contextual meaning of the word appears to be, 'fixed principles or rules of conduct'.[5] It is abundantly clear that the meaning of the word *dharma* passed through several transitions. However, ultimately its most prominent significance came to be 'the privileges, duties and obligations of a man, his standard of conduct as a member of the *Āryan* community, as a member of one of the castes, as a person in a particular stage of life'.[6] It is in this sense that the word is employed in the *dharmaśāstra* literature.[7] Just as duties and obligations of a man were defined, the *dharmaśāstras* also laid down specific duties, roles and a code of conduct for women. Thus, the *dharmaśāstras* sought to define the gender relations. The phrase *gender relations* refers to the relations of power between women and men which are revealed in a range of practices, ideas, and representations, including the division of labour, roles, and resources between women and men, and the ascribing to them of different abilities, desires, personality traits, behavioural patterns, and so on.[8] Further, it is suggested that gender relations are characterized by both cooperation and conflict, and that their hierarchical character in any given context is maintained or changed through a process of (implicit or explicit) contestation or bargaining between actors with differential access to economic, political and social power.[9] It is in this light that the relations between man and woman as sought to be established by the *dharmaśāstrakāras* are studied. What was the division of labour, and the roles prescribed to man and woman within the family? What were the respective degrees of access to resources provided to both of them? Many such related issues have formed the focus of discussion. The following paragraphs below shall provide a gist of the observations and inferences.

The core of the domestic ideology has sought to project the family as *a non-conflict zone*, where members are linked to each other through mutual duties and obligations. According to the ideology, while some members of the family may wield authority, it is nevertheless outside the realm of power. Most importantly, what is actually *paternalistic dominance* within the family with members having unequal access to material assets and the right to make decisions is recast as a consensual arrangement amongst its members.[10] What remains unrecognized or as Chakravarti says, 'systematically obscured and not recognized in the ideological construction of the family'[11], is that power is as much in play while determining relationships within the family as it is in any other social institutions. Family, as it is perceived now, is intended to grow as a protective umbrella for individuals not only as far as physical protection and development was concerned, but also to provide a platform for one's mental, emotional and spiritual development; and the fact that these objectives are achieved in the family, even though partially, cannot be outright rejected. However, the other side of the truth is that family also has been the battleground for the interests of individuals who are the members of the family, the continuous struggle between those who are powerful and the others who are powerless. Just as any other social unit, family also carried within it the seeds of exploitation. Again, this fact also cannot be negated that family has been as much a locus of conflict and exploitation. With the establishment of patriarchy; characterized by male dominance, or more specifically, dominance of the male head of the family; the relations between the two sexes became skewed, leading to the general subjugation of women. A similar picture emerges out of a study of the *Dharmaśāstras*.

What was the domestic ideology enunciated by the *Dharmaśāstraṣ* During the period of the composition of the *Dharmaśāstras*, and may be even before that, the importance of household assumed greater proportions, as is evident from the overwhelming importance that was assigned to the order or stage of the householder as compared to the other three orders of life (*āśramas*). The *gṛha,* i.e., the household; controlled by the patriarch, the *gṛhapati;* is recognized as a central institution in the *Dharmasūtras* and the *Dharmaśāstras.* In fact, the *gṛhastha* was viewed as providing support and sustenance to the rest of the three orders of life. Manu ascribes the origin of other three orders to the order of the householder.[12] So much importance was ascribed to the *gṛha* that it seemed to be the sustainer of the entire cosmos. Accordingly, the functions of the *gṛha* included providing shelter to the other three orders by giving alms, propitiation of the gods and ancestors, extending hospitality to the *atithi* and providing nurturance and shelter to the weak and the dependent. The high importance attached to the household, also ascribed an exalted status to the male patriarch of the household; the *gṛhapati*. Within the *gṛha* too, the *gṛhapati* became the supreme. Also, both production and distribution was carried out by the householder only. All the remaining males and females were subordinated to the patriarch. However, the degree of subordination was far more stringent in the case of the females, as has been borne out by the present study.

Quite in consonance with the importance ascribed to the *gṛha,* the points of entry to and exit from the household were attributed a high degree of significance. The attitude towards women at the points of entry and exit, and while being a part of the household are telling with regard to the position ascribed to the women by the *dharmaśāstrakāras*. A significant point is that while the male remains the member of a household throughout the life, the female has to take exit from one set-up and become the part of an unfamiliar set-up within the initial span of her life. The fact of patrilocality has a defining influence in shaping women's destiny, as the discussion amply demonstrates. Birth was a significant occasion in that it marked as the point of entry to the household.[13] However, the birth of a girl child was not welcomed and number of ways are suggested to secure the birth of sons. That the girl child was not given the ritual status becomes clear from the fact that the sacred rites were performed without the recitation of mantras in the case of the birth of a girl child, and no *upanayana* or initiation was prescribed for the girl child. Marriage was the only ceremony in the life of a woman which was to be performed with the recitation of mantras, and it was considered as initiation for women. So the real entry of the woman into the *Āryan* social order was marked with marriage only. Thus defined, the membership of the daughter within the household would have been at best tangential.

The birth of a son was favoured for more reasons than one. The most important, however, was that he was considered to be the one to liberate his ancestors from hell. In the *dharmaśāstric* world view, the purpose of life was something metaphysical. Deep reflections on the cycle of life and death, and the awe that the phenomenon of death might have evoked; made life after death one of the major concerns of the *dharmaśāstrakāras*. While the son was the one to maintain the family line, to offer oblations to the departed manes, and to save the ancestors from hell; the daughter was to be married off before reaching a certain stage. This further strengthened the position of the son within the patriarchal family. Marrying the daughter suitably would also have been a problem, as the subsequent discussion will amply demonstrate.

Marriage was made central to the life of a woman. Among the many qualifications prescribed for a girl to be chosen as the bride, virginity was held on premium. This was to ensure the purity of lineage and the sustenance of patriarchy. However, Dexter puts forward an interesting theory as to why virginity was considered so important. She says that virginity has a significant function within a "male-centerd society". It is treated as a stage which renders a woman a "store-house" of untapped energy, energy which she will in the next stage (as a matron) transmit to man.[14] In any case, emphasis on virginity resulted in lowering the age of marriage for girls among other things. Also, among the qualifications, one was that the girl should be younger in age to the groom. In fact, the emphasis on marriage of girls before the attainment of puberty; while the boy was intended to marry after the completion of is studies, i.e., after the *brahmacārī* mode of life, resulting in a considerable difference of age between the wife and the husband. It must have been intended at further strengthening the hold of the husband and the agnatic relations over the girl's life. Also, pre-puberty marriages were intended at domesticizing the girls. Girls at a tender age could have been mentally conditioned and habituated to domesticity and subjugation before they could grow up to offer resistance to the intentions of the upholders of the patriarchal social order, or could have their minds opened up to other possible aims of life. Other injunctions like the girl's family should not be superior to the groom's family, must have been intended at ensuring the superiority of the male's family in a marriage. Only a few of the *dharmaśāstrakāras* laid down some qualifications for the bridegroom. These fewer criterion included the boy to be from a higher strata, and regular in the study of *Vedas* and scriptures. Also, his potency was one of the concerns for the *dharmaśāstrakāras*. However, it is obvious that all these were directed towards strengthening the hold of patriarchy. The potency of the groom needed to be tried as procreation was the sole aim of marriage in the *dharmaśāstric* ideology.

An analysis of the various forms of marriage is also revealing regarding the way womanhood was perceived by the *dharmaśāstrakāras*.

While marriage being the turning point for a woman's life in patriarchy, the *dharmaśāstrakāras* do not impart any agency to women at this critical juncture of their lives and define their identity as mere possession of the father and the natal family, rights over whom are to be transferred to the groom's family at the father's will. This transfer of authority over the woman may be in the form of a gift, or a transaction or exchange between the father and the groom. Among the other forms of marriage were those where the girl was subjected to fraud or force. Only the *Gāndharva* form imparts some choice to the woman, but this was approved for the *kśatriyas* only. Though it was considered obligatory for both the man and the woman to get married in the *dharmaśāstric* ideology, the difference lies in the fact that while the man had to choose a suitable maiden for himself after *samṛvartana*, the girl was to be given away by her father. Again, she was imparted the freedom to choose a husband only in case the relations fail to marry her off before the attainment of puberty. This was not intended, however, to impart any agency or power of decision-making to the girl. Rather, it was to work as a threat for the natal family of the girl, and to ensure that the reproductive years of the female are optimally 'used'. Though the *Gāndharva* form was recognized, the scope for it would have been reduced given the low age of marriage for the girls. Further, the inclusion of the *Rākśasa* and *Paiśāca* rites within the list of forms of marriage seems to be unfortunate. Though discouraged, these forms were recognized. Though the *Rākśasa* form is discouraged, it is considered lawful for the *kśatriyas*. Again, Altekar attributes the inclusion of this form among the recognized forms of marriage to the fact that in the pre-historic times, victor carried the bride away and married her.[15] Though it may be true that the lawgivers might have included this form as it might have been one of the forms in practice; yet the inclusion of such a fraud in the forms of marriage poses a question on the idea of justice as viewed by the lawgivers. Manu's description of *Rākśasa* form of marriage is itself heart-rending- 'The forcible abduction of a maiden from her home, while she cries out and weeps, after (her kinsmen) have been slain or wounded and (their houses) broken open, is called the *Rākśasa* rite'.[16] What could have made a society to endorse such an act is quite surprising. Again, *Paiśāca* form of marriage was nothing but accepting a rapist as the husband. Though Manu and others condemn it, it seems unfortunate that even this was considered as a form of marriage. Altekar seems to justify the lawgivers for having recognized it as one of the forms of marriage, on the ground that since virginity was becoming a grave concern in those times, there was no other option, but to marry the girl to the one who blemished her, in order to preserve her welfare.[17] He says that, "They (the lawgivers) seem to have subscribed to the modern view that a culprit should not be allowed to be benefited by his wrong."[18] It seems that in the view of Altekar, the welfare of women consists in getting married only, and by remaining unmarried, there welfare is affected badly. In his view, strangely, the welfare of a girl lies in getting married to a rapist rather than remaining unmarried.

That the daughter was considered a possession or the property of the father is implicit in his right to give away the daughter as gift or to sell her for a price. Though there are verses in the texts which speak of the son also as the property of the father, there are no verses where the father is given the right to make choices regarding his marriage or vocation. In fact, *kanyādāna* was highly eulogized in the texts. It was considered the highest form of *dāna*. It is said that both the giver and taker of the bride stand exonerated from all penalties if the father gives the bride in this way.[19] Trautmann says about the *kanyādāna* complex that marriage by gift begins by presuming the superiority of the groom's people vis-à-vis the bride's. Bride is given by her guardian into the groom's keeping, utterly severing the connection between the bride and her family and transforms her into an extension of the groom and his family. Thus, marriage by gift is also a rite of initiation (into another family) for the woman and a sacrament that creates an indissoluble bond between husband and wife and makes any break impossible.[20] In a marriage like this, alienation of woman from her own family is so complete that she is unable to turn to them at any point in her life.[21] Kapoor provides the justification for *kanyādāna* in these words: "Here, an answer is possible. In a culture that puts greatest premium on renouncing, the giving away of the dearest, most precious object is regarded as the highest sacrifice. A daughter is generally very tenderly regarded by her parents; hence, as a kind of renunciation, *Kanya-dana* is given special importance."[22] However, Kapoor remains unable to bring the *daughter* out of the identification of an 'object' by way of providing this explanation, rather his explanation reinforces the fact of considering the daughter as an object, even though she may be regarded as 'the most precious one'.

Inter-*varṇa* marriages were generally disfavoured, while the *pratiloma* marriage or hypogamy was completely denounced. This reveals the fact that in the *dharmaśāstric* ideology, *varṇa* and gender are inextricably linked. In the words of Ganesh and Das, "Women are regarded as gateways – literally points of entrance – to the caste system. The lower-caste male whose sexuality is a threat to upper-caste purity has to be institutionally prevented from having sexual access to women of the higher castes, so women must be carefully guarded."[23] Chakravarti's words also explain this phenomenon very suitably – "Endogamous marriages ensure the perpetuation of bounded groups reproducing a closed structure of land, women and ritual purity in which the central figure is the woman: without total control over her sexuality, neither land nor ritual purity can be passed on with any certainty. The normative family, within what I have conceptualized elsewhere as Brāhmanical patriarchy, was thus designed to reproduce both itself and the caste hierarchy."[24] Similar link between *varṇa* and gender becomes evident while studying the punishments prescribed for adultery and rape. While advocating *varṇa* endogamy, the *dharmaśāstrakāras* advocated *gotra* and *piṇḍa* exogamy. This was to ensure that the girl had no natural ties or bonds of affection or identification with the agnatic family, ensuring her general subjugation, and also marginalization or even alienation under certain special circumstances.

Neither sexual gratification, nor companionship was the aim of marriage. Procreation, and moreover, procreation of sons, was the *dharma* of both men and women in the ideology enunciated by the *dharmaśāstrakāras*. Manu explicitly lays down, women were created to be mothers, and men were created to be fathers.[25] Further, the *dharmaśāstrakāras* gave a particular definition of procreation, where the woman's womb was imaged as the field, and the male sperm as the seed. Two objectives were fulfilled by giving such metaphors for of procreation. Firstly, the agency of procreation was imparted to the male, thereby reducing the female to the state of a passive receptacle. Also, later it was established that the field as well as the produce, i.e., the progeny belonged to the one who wielded the seed. Thus, both the wife and the progeny were conveniently expressed as and established to be the possessions of the man. This image was further used for legitimization of a particular process of procreation. Thus, it is said that if a seed is sown by someone in the field of another, it belongs to the owner and not the begetter. Thus, the begetter is said to be in loss. Manu has reflected at length and made contradictory points in this regard. But finally, the field-seed interpretation became established. It further prevented adultery, thus ensuring the purity of the offspring.

In accordance with the thinking of the *dharmaśāstrakāras*, who considered women merely as vehicles of reproduction, no education was considered to be necessary for the girls. Marriage was the only ceremony in a woman's life, which was performed with due recitation of mantras and was thus, ritually sacramental. The girls were not initiated, and ideologically lacked identity in the *varṇa* order before marriage, marriage ceremony itself considered to be the initiation for women. Deprivation from getting educated was quite in line with the dominant ideology of the *dharmaśāstra* texts, in which womanhood was recognized and given importance only in the role of the wife, whereby she is expected to procreate, serve the husband and be an appendage to him in some of the religious functions; none of which required her to be educated. Rather, a sharpening of the critical faculties of the woman, which is a natural concomitant of education, could have been detrimental to the purpose of the *dharmaśāstrakāras*. Only an illiterate and uneducated woman could be schooled in and made to internalize the patriarchal ideology.

The sole important identification of women in the order perceived by the *dharmaśāstrakāras* was wifehood. An elaborate list of the duties of and code of conduct for the wife is prescribed. While criticizing the critiques of *dharmaśāstras*, Kapoor has referred to the multiple identities imparted to women in India in the form of multiple bio-social roles.[26] Though this may be true in the contemporary society, in the society envisaged by the *dharmaśāstrakāras*, no duties are laid down for women as a mother or sister or daughter, or aunt. As a mother she is to be revered, and while child bearing is given extreme importance, no mention could be found of a woman's duties towards her children. Rearing up of the child or nurturing the child, which is a matter of great importance, no attention or concern of the authors of *dharma* texts was ever directed to this aspect. In fact, such a silence stands in sharp contrast in a society where in order to qualify as a wife, a woman necessarily had to be fertile.

The duties prescribed for the wife included complete devotion to the husband, i.e., *pātivratya*; settlement of domestic chores; and giving birth to progeny. The role envisaged for the woman was mainly the service role. Manu says that the nuptial ceremony is considered to be the same as initiation for the women, serving the husband is considered equivalent to residing in the house of the teacher, and the household duties are considered as the worship of daily fire.[27] This sentence precisely defines the duties of the wife. The most powerful tool in the hands of the *dharmaśāstrakāras* was the ideology of *pativratā*, in which women were thoroughly schooled, annulling all the possibilities of attempts at inversion of the social order sought to be established and strengthened by them. Accordingly, this is one of the most pervasive concepts associated with womanhood in the *dharmaśāstras*. It shall not be an exaggeration to say that this ideology was the pillar which helped to support the entire edifice of the rigid patriarchal organization perceived by the lawgivers. Quite successfully, it attempted at subsuming all the critical faculty of women and muted them outwardly as well as inwardly. Accordingly, the wife had to serve the husband unconditionally, and also his agnatic line by procreating progeny. The ideology of the *pativratā* was devised as a means to ensuring an unquestioning and unconditional service, that brooked no dissatisfaction or doubt. It negated the very identity of a woman, as well as her choice even in the matters completely personal to her. In order to facilitate unquestioned and complete internalization of this ideology, rewards were said to have accrued to the conformist women, and punishments to those who were deviant or non-conformist. Those who propounded the norm of *pativratā* were fully aware that this *dharma* was nothing short of penance for women. Hence, great rewards were promised to the women in the form of gaining supernatural powers. What was expected out of this was that the women would behave according to the set ideal not only for the sake of *dharma*, but also for the fruits that they were made to believe to attain for practising it.

The role of the homemaker envisaged for the women, left no scope for the need for any education for women, rather their deprivation from self-awareness became imperative. Further, it relegated the women to the 'private' sphere of life, reserving the 'public' for the men, thus working towards the seclusion of women and re-ensuring their general subjection. Since such a division of labour as envisaged by the *dharmaśāstrakāras* has been a phenomenon common to all societies in the world, and hence a like light may be thrown on the phenomenon with a view to highlighting the issue in the context.

While arguing for women to be given roles other than home-making and child-rearing, it has to be admitted that the work women have been doing for centuries is of no lesser value. Also, it has to be admitted that several issues at the home front require serious devotion and time, the most important being caring for the elders, diseased and the children. The right of the individuals to be cared for, is no less important than the right of individuals to be given an opportunity to work towards a fuller realization of their potential. Also to be admitted is the fact that the rise of atomistic individualism which asserts only the rights of individuals to the complete neglect of their duties, is sure to give rise to the same kinds of problems as the West is grappling with today. However, it is to be argued that the onus should not lie solely on the women, who are rendered resourceless and unidirectional in the process. Instead of such a neat division of labour, which homogenizes all women, a division may be worked out as giving a justified sharing of rights and duties between man and woman; giving both of them space to work towards optimum realization of their latent potentials. Coming back to the social division of labour in the context of the *Dharmaśāstrasa*, few things deserve consideration. The texts nowhere speak of child rearing or care giving to elders or diseased as the duties of women. Their sole emphasis is on devotion to husband and management of household. Those who speak in favour of the *Dharmaśāstras* on the basis of 'the emphasis on duty rather than rights' argument, may find this anomaly difficult to get over.

Much in contrast to the duties prescribed for women, no set of duties was prescribed for the husband, except for exercising control over the wife's sexuality and procreating progeny on her person during her seasons. In fact, keeping the women under vigilance was a constant preoccupation with the *dharmaśāstrakāras.* A constant fear of transgression of boundaries set by the lawgivers for women is evident throughout the texts. This apprehension is so deep rooted in the psyche of the authors of *dharmaśāstras* that keeping the wife under control is laid down as one of the foremost duties of the husband. While declaring the eternal laws for the husband and wife who keep to the path of duty, Manu says that even the weak husbands must strive to guard their wives, considering it their highest duty.[28] He further says that a woman should be guarded by her father during adolescence/childhood, by her husband in married life and by her son in old age. The women are therefore, never to be independent.[29] Similar views are expressed by all the lawgivers. Why was an urgency felt to control the women's sexuality is made clear by a statement of Manu himself, where he says that it was necessary to preserve the purity of his offspring *(prasūti)*, virtuous conduct, his family *(kula)*, himself *(ātman)* and his means of acquiring merit *(dharma)*.[30] That women needed to be controlled in order to maintain the purity of offspring and thus lineage, also becomes clear from similar verses by other *Dharmaśāstra* writers. Again, preserving the purity of the offspring was central to the successful perpetuation of patriarchy.

Should or should not there be a control over women's sexual freedom and choice? Indian scholars with adherence to feminist ideology have been criticized by some scholars for advocating complete sexual freedom for women following the Western feminists. Kapoor writes, "Feminist critiques of Indian social reality are flawed in that they assume an absolute, universalist Hindu code. They are also asymmetrical with given Indian reality in that they are derived from the reality of, for want of a better word, western social system which in its history of unbridled sexuality and in it progressive weakening for the institutions of family and marriage and a general ethical collapse is foundationally different."[31] He points towards the fact that sexuality has been handled differently in India and the West and writes:

> "As in other areas of knowledge, in women studies also, we have tried to fit the Indian reality to a borrowed western framework … .Western social condition has been and is very different from ours. Three facts stand out. First of all, the societal attitude to sexuality, both male and female, has been different. Both homosexuality and lesbianism have some kind of legitimacy ever since Plato (*Symposium*) and Sappho, the poetess of Lesbos. Add to this the Old Testament narrative of the two cities of Sodom and Gomorrah and you have a picture of unbridled sexuality – a sexuality not governed by any societal institution or ethical framework. There is a sanction, in Genesis, in the roots of western civilization, for self indulgence and for the gratification of one's appetites and desires. No ethics of restraint governs these. Secondly, as we have already noted, there is an ethical vacuum … . In any case, there never was anything analogous to the Indian system of *sanyama* (restraint) and *niyama* (the right way) … . India has handled sexuality differently. Its reality and its power have been more explicitly recognized than in any other culture (no other culture has a whole *sastra* devoted to it) and no other culture has honoured sexual union as our culture has done (witness its place in temple sculpture). But from the raw reality a basic urge to an honoured fact of disciplined life, there is an orderly upward passage in the form of a rigorous ethical framework, both institutional and general."[32]

The point demands some serious thinking. Feminists do seem to advocate sexual freedom for women. Is sexual freedom tantamount to women's emancipation? Seen solely on the physical plane, the right to choice and freedom cannot be denied. But human beings are not merely physical beings. They are also emotional, mental and spiritual beings. Again, they are also social beings having social identities beyond an atomistic individual existence. This fact cannot be overlooked while dealing with any issue related to human life. Sexual freedom may be advocated if sex merely remains a physical act. However, even if the West denies it to be a spiritual act, even they have to acquiesce in the emotional and mental implications of the act. Excessive indulgence leads to emotional and mental deterioration, is a fact recognized by Western psychology itself. Further, Indian philosophy rightly points towards spiritual degradation of an individual as a consequence of sexual excess. As Kapoor rightly comments, "Sex is an appetite; and its gratification, like that of other appetites such as hunger, has to be regulated as is required by the general philosophy of self-imposed restraint and abstemiousness (*sanyama*)."[33] Equally important is the fact that excessive sexual freedom has significant social implications. Kapoor writes, "But we may note, quite unlike other appetites, its gratification has social, beyond-the-individual consequences. Therefore, apart from the merely personal, there is the need for its social regulation."[34] Excessive sexual freedom may actually result in women and men being identified as sex objects more than as mental, emotional or spiritual beings. This stands truer in case of women, whose identity may, as Kapoor comments, be reduced to the existence as a "Baby-doll with the Marilyn Monroe image."[35] Also, the institutions of marriage and family would be weakened, leading to chaos. Marriage and family have to exist until some superior social arrangement is suggested. So far as the *Dharmaśāstras* would have advocated sexual abstinence or regulation for both men and women, it would not have been derogatory to the women's dignity. However, even though adultery was considered a crime both in case of men and women, men were permitted polygamy. It may be argued that gradually the lawgivers went in disfavour of polygamy. But again, even if it is agreed that sexual control was advocated for both men and women, the distinction lies in the fact that while for women, it was control by the husband and other agnatic relations, for the men it implied self control of impulses. There is a difference between sexual control and sexual abstinence. While abstinence implies self-control, sexual control by others implies the use of force and suppression by them. While men were expected to exhibit self-control as a measure to guard against adultery, women were to be guarded by the male members, and even at times, *other female members* of the household. This is evident from a number of verses which emphasize upon the need to keep women guarded. To quote Shalini Shah in this regard – "What was affirmed through this conception of 'mastery' (over one's self) as ensuring freedom was the virile character of this mastery. Just as in the household it was man, who ruled, it was only right that he alone should exercise self-restraint. Self-mastery was a way of being a man with respect to oneself. This does not mean that women were not expected to be moderate. But moderation in this case was imposed on them by their condition of dependence, in relation to their families, their husbands. *For what was symbolized in woman's chastity was not her own self control as in the male celibacy but the control of her kinsmen over her behaviour* [emphasis added]."[36] It is at this point that the inequality in gender relations as sought to be established by the *dharmaśāstrakāras* lies. The sexuality of a woman was not a matter of self-control by her, but the possession of the husband and agnates. This control over her sexuality becomes further pronounced in control over her procreative power by the agnates, undeniably expressed in the practice of *niyoga*. The other duty ascribed to the husband, i.e., procreating progeny on the wife's person, is quite in line with the dominant ideology of the *Dharmaśāstras* where procreation is the most important task. The only other duties of the male were in his capacity as a householder, where he was expected to function as a sustainer of the remaining three orders. This further confined the women to the 'private' sphere of activity, while rendering the 'public' space open wide for the men. Thus the woman in the form of a wife, is accorded a position of subjection and dependence, leading to uneven and unequal relations between the male and the female.

An important role was played by the menstrual taboos in the creation of a society divided across gender lines, and these helped in ascribing to the women a position inferior to that of the men. Menstrual taboos have been common to all ancient societies and find place in some of the societies even to this date. These mark the customs prevalent in society that publicly restrict the behaviour of woman at the time of menstruation and apply throughout most of a woman's life. The *dharmaśāstrakāras* who were almost obsessed with the notions of purity and pollution, attributed a high degree of polluting effect to menstrual discharge. At the same time, they considered menstruation to be an unequalled means of purification of the female body. The only probable way in which such taboos can be explained is the duality of perceptions regarding this unique biological phenomenon. The life giving power of the menstrual blood was recognized, and as such, it was considered sacred. Being sacred and carrying potency, it was dreaded. On the other hand, it was considered polluting. Thomson thus explains these conflicting views- "Its potency makes it something to be dreaded … . From one aspect the woman who may not be approached is inviolable, holy; from another aspect she is polluted, unclean. She is what the Romans called sacra, sacred and accursed. And hence in patriarchal society, after woman has lost her control of religion, it is the negative aspect that prevails."[37] This has been further explained by some other scholars on the basis of their studies of matriarchal and patriarchal societies. While in the matriarchal societies, menstrual blood is considered to be life-giving and hence received with joy and gratitude when it comes to the girl for the first time;

in patriarchal societies, which lay emphasis on fecundity, it becomes unclean. Sanday on the basis of her study[38] of such male dominant societies like, Hausa, Mundurucu, Yanomamo and Papagoes says that in such societies men attempt to neutralize power (sexual and reproductive – which in turn is linked with menstrual blood) which they think is inherent in women by stealing it, nullifying it or banishing it to invisibility. It is this which explains the menstrual taboos in societies. The notion that woman should be secluded during menstruation and that sexual intercourse with such a woman is polluting for men, results in the physical separation of the sexes. Again, such seclusion in everyday affairs plays a crucial role in the rise of male dominance. It may be inferred that menstrual taboos play a significant role in the construction of a gendered society. Since the *dharmaśāstrakāras* were advocates of a patriarchal social order, and worked towards the firm establishment and institutionalization of patriarchy, menstrual taboos might be considered to have come to them quite naturally.

Further, as Agarwal comments, although gender relations are defined as relations between women and men, gender hierarchies also influence and structure relations between individuals of the same sex, e.g., how two women of the same household relate to one another is affected by the gendered character of their relations with the household men. The relation between a woman and her daughter-in-law is one example.[39] Though not much is said directly in this regard, it holds good for the *dharmaśāstric* ideology too. It was enjoined upon the wife to be respectful and obedient to the mother-in-law as well as the agnatic relations. The ladies belonging to the agnatic group were also expected to keep a guard over the wife.

In the society envisaged by the *dharmaśāstrakāras*, adultery, widowhood, rape, or desertion by the husband amounted to a marginalization within or exclusion from the household for the women. At times, such exclusion was temporary, while sometimes it was permanent. Adultery was considered extremely baneful and every attempt was made by the *dharmaśāstrakāras* to prevent adulterous relationships. However, in spite of all the restrictions placed by them, it would not have been possible to completely stop the occurrence of the cases of adultery, which becomes obvious from many verses. Adultery or incest formed a reason for exclusion from the household, some times only temporary and at other times, permanent; both for the male and the female. However, the difference lies in the facts that firstly, adultery was considered to be *intrinsic* to the women's nature; secondly, while men were expected to exhibit self-control in this regard, women needed to be 'controlled' by the males, and thirdly, men might not have felt inclined towards committing adultery except in case they were attracted towards married women, as they were permitted polygamy.

Further, the link between *varṇa* and gender also becomes clear in this context as the degree of punishment is prescribed for adultery between a woman of higher *varṇa* and a man of lower *varṇa*. In fact, it was the respective status of the two on the social ladder, that determined the degree of severity of the crime, and as such, the punishment prescribed for it. According to Yājñavalkya, the highest form of pecuniary punishment is the penalty when adultery is committed with a woman of the same caste, the second form is the punishment when adultery is committed with a woman of lower caste; and death is the penalty when it is committed with a woman of a higher caste.[40] This was repeated by Nārada and Viṣṇu.[41] Manu explicitly says that adultery is condemned and punishment is prescribed to men who commit adultery with others' wives[42], as by adultery is caused the mixture of *varṇa* among men, from which sin follows and cuts up the roots, causing the destruction of everything.[43] This statement of Manu is quite telling as far as the cause for condemnation of adultery is concerned. It was not morality in the contemporary sense of the term that bothered the *dharmaśāstrakāras*, but the sustenance and maintenance of the social order, while condemning and making tireless attempts at preventing adultery. This also brings one to the way morality and ethics were defined in the *dharmaśāstric* ideology. The injunctions were not laid down with the purpose of preservation of moral or ethical values, in the modern sense of these terms; but ethics and morality were defined in a way so as to act as aids in the preservation of a particular social order. The *dharma* of every individual in any capacity, i.e., as a member of any of the *varṇas*, or as a member of a household, or at any stage of his or her life; was to work towards the preservation, sustenance and strengthening of the patriarchal values as well as the *varṇa* order; what is conceptualized by Chakravarti as 'brahmanical patriarchy'. To the modern mind, therefore, imbued with concepts of individual freedom and rights, these precepts would appear nothing but whimsically orthodox. While inequality will be treated as immoral in the present world, in those times, morality itself was defined by and based upon unequal relations between man and man; and man and woman; as well as woman and woman at all levels. In the *dharmaśāstric* ideology, human relations were defined in terms of possession. One was related to the other either as the possessor or the possessed, thus, either as a superior or an inferior. There was no concept of equality in human relations.

It may be argued that no social institution can survive with perfect equality. Example may be cited of the contemporary West, where, the concepts of absolute equality and freedom, as well as the spirit of *exaggerated* individualism have attained such supremacy as is tantamount to several tensions within the spheres of family and society. The notions of equality, freedom, choice, progress etc. need to be re-examined in this light. It is to be admitted that every individual is born with *unequal* levels of physical, mental, emotional and spiritual capabilities. Also, every individual is presented or confronted with a different, rather *unique* set of life circumstances. Further, every individual deals with the life situations and circumstances on the basis of the *inherent* capabilities; and in this process also develops further capabilities, which is in turn based on his/her capacity to adapt, propensity to learn, ability to apply the knowledge and several related factors. Given such inequalities of *inherent* capabilities[44]; as well as *uniqueness* or *dissimilarity* of life situations and circumstances; along with different degrees of adaptability and ability to evolve; the ideal of absolute equality for all becomes a *Utopia*. Unequal results are bound to follow with unequal inputs and in different conditions. In fact, when arguing for equality, it is not absolute equality which need be sought for. It is equality which is conducive to *justice*. It is equality of opportunity for everyone. Again, it is impossible to ensure even equality of opportunity for all, given the dissimilarity of life circumstances for all. However, it is to be argued that what is sought for is that '*inequality of opportunity* should not be institutionalized, or the social institutions should not be structured in a way as to lead to inequality on the basis of sex, colour, race, religion or the like'. Inequality should not be woven within the fabric of any social structure. But inequality was woven within the fabric of the social organization as perceived by the *dharmaśāstrakāras*. Inequality of opportunity was sought to be institutionalized by seeking to make gender and *varṇa* rigid compartmental bases of discrimination.

There is yet another way of perceiving equality. It is this: not to seek for material equality of all, but to believe in spiritual equality of all. This is not to say that everyone is 'spiritually equal' or 'at an equal stage on the spiritual level', or 'has equal spiritual capabilities'. First, spirituality should not be confused with being religious or being solely in some metaphysical pursuit. An aspiration towards perfection defines true spirituality. This definition holds true if one believes that the creation is not merely *Māyā*, the God's plaything; but has a 'purpose'. This purpose is attainment of perfection. This purpose is the perfect manifestation of the spirit through matter. This purpose is the 'Divinisation of Worldly Life' as Sri Aurobindo has expressed. The entire creation is then in the constant pursuit of evolution of consciousness. Every individual, being a part of the creation, is thus, in the same pursuit. This approach to view creation and life, provides a basis for the equality of perception. Since everyone is on the same pursuit whether he/she sweeps the floor or writes books, and since there is no yardstick to measure how far one has reached, everyone is to be treated as equal. This amounts to the recognition of the fact that everyone is different but equal. In such a scheme, no one is superior or inferior to anybody.

It is argued by some scholars that the *varṇāśrama* organization is quite a scientific resolution of the conflicting pursuits and claims of life. Accordingly, different *varṇas* offered opportunity to the individuals to pursue different aims of life depending on their propensities. An individual who is in pursuit of knowledge shall be able to attain greater degree of perfection if there are others to take care of his security, economic stability and mundane affairs. Similar arguments go for the rest of the three *varṇas*. So one may choose to lead any of the lives depending on his or her propensities and capabilities. This argument does not entirely lack weight. However, this must have held true if the individual would have remained free to 'choose' his or her *varṇa*, and also change it during the course of life. Even if initially the basis of *varṇa* was not heredity, later it came to be so. Also, attempting to homogenize the women as a category and imparting to them the work of the home-maker and to remain at the service of the husband; deprived them of any choice regarding the pursuit of life. Ascribing to the women only the mundane; they were actually denied an existence at par with the men. Again, such a social division of labour amongst the different *varṇas* might not have lead to inequality had there been no hierarchy amongst the *varṇas*. But there was a definite hierarchy, so much so that the one associated with the mundane works, the *Śūdra* was not granted a ritual status by depriving him of the *upanayana* itself. Women, being associated with the mundane pursuit too, *upanayana* was considered unnecessary for them also. Such an inequality of perception manifested itself in myriad ways like unequal access to resources.

Similar arguments may be put forth with regard to freedom. Absolute freedom may lead to chaos in the society. Small children cannot be left free to choose. An insane may not be left free. Precisely, wrong choices may not be allowed even at the cost of limiting one's freedom of choice. This holds good even though there are no absolute interpretations for the terms right and wrong. Every individual or society defines right and wrong depending on the objectives there have in view. It was in tune with the *dharmaśāstric* ideology to restrict the freedom of women. However, a society in which degrees of freedom imparted to its components vary on the basis of sex, creed, colour, race, caste etc.; is bound to be based on unequal relations. So, while arguing for freedom for women, a Feminist scholar may not necessarily intend to argue for absolute freedom for them and freedom for them only.

The connection between *varṇa* and gender again manifests itself in the punishments that were prescribed for the rapist. The degree of punishment was stringent when a woman of higher *varṇa* was raped; while the very act done to a woman of lower caste was considered a minor offence. It is surprising that a concern for the sustenance of the perceived social order was a matter of graver concern for the *dharmaśāstrakāras* than the misery and pain experienced by the victim, which will be the same irrespective of the *varṇa* to which a woman may belong. It is obvious that justice was not viewed in the *dharmaśāstric* ideology in the modern sense of the term.

Widowhood is the most miserable state of a woman in patriarchy. A woman's identity was given recognition, approval and significance only as a wife. Her role as the wife was considered to be the one to lend importance to her life. In roles other than this, her identity and existence was reduced to insignificance. Among her wifely duties, serving the husband and procreation were the most important. Death of the husband ended the possibility as well as requirement of the performance of both of these functions. The very objective of a woman's existence was considered to have been lost. A widow is, thus, of 'no use' to such a society, rather her existence and presence was a kind of disturbance. The death of the husband, therefore, was considered to be an occasion for exclusion of the woman from the household life, or even at times, life at all; in the patriarchal set up. Chakravarti presents a thoughtful analysis of the condition of widow in her recent work. In her words, "The problem posed by Brahmanical patriarchy therefore is: since the wife has no social existence outside of her husband's house, then, as a widow, who or what is she? The texts and rituals attempt to work the problem out. The problem itself is simply that although the widow is socially dead, she remains an element in society; the question then is how to incorporate her. One way could be to constitute a separate community of widows, a non-sexual community, such as that of female ascetics. Another could be to retain her in society but place her on its margins and then institutionalize her marginality. This is what Brahmanical patriarchy did with the widow. The widow's institutionalized marginality, a liminal state between being physically alive and being socially dead, was the ultimate cultural outcome of the deprivation of her sexuality as well as of her personhood. The widow's marginal state meant that she was, in a manner of speaking, functionally incorporated into the household while being considered an outsider."[45]

Accordingly, a bare existence was permitted to the widow. She was forced to live like an ascetic, and differed from him in that he/she could at least move about and do other things freely. Further, *niyoga* or levirate was laid down as one of the duties of the widow by most of the *dharmaśāstrakāras*. A code of conduct for the performance of *niyoga* was laid down and it was believed that the son born out of such a union belongs to both the begetter and the diseased husband of the widow. Such a son would liberate the diseased husband of the widow from hell. No appointment shall be made through a desire to obtain the estate, or out of covetousness. A careful analysis of *niyoga* is important in determining the position of the widow. Some of the historians have favoured *niyoga* as one of the ameliorative measures for the plight of the widow in ancient Indian society. One of them is Altekar, who while accepting that the 'leaders of Hindu society took a step in the right direction in stamping out the custom of *niyoga*, as it was a relic of barbarism and was quite incongruous and incompatible with higher ideas and ideals of marriage, that were held before society'[46]; opines that, "*Niyoga* served a useful purpose in its own days. Men are disinclined to marry widows, though they expect virgins to marry widowers. The custom of *niyoga* solved the widow's difficulty to some extent by permitting the brother-in-law to raise issues on his sister-in-law under certain circumstances. *Niyoga* served as a half-way house between a formal remarriage and an absolute celibacy, especially in earlier days when three sons were allowed to be raised under it … . It also helped in improving the economic condition of the widow. When she had no son, she could get no share in the family property. When she got a son by *niyoga*, she could get a share, *if not as an heiress, at least as the guardian of her minor son* [emphasis added]."[47] Again, Altekar seems to believe that marriage is the only resort for the women, and that small concessions can do good for their lot.

However, it has to be borne in mind at the first place that it was not the welfare of the widow but the welfare of the deceased husband of the widow, who died sonless; that is the primary concern of the lawgivers while declaring *niyoga* as the duty of the widow. The procreation of a son was considered so important that even if one died, he needed to get a son by way of his surviving wife. The begetting of son in this way might have lent a support to the otherwise shattered and miserable widow in a patriarchal set up. However, surprising is the fact that deep silence prevails over the birth of daughter by levirate. Further, *niyoga* was not a matter of choice for the widow. She might have been further subjected to misery on account of males taking advantage of the practice. *Niyoga* did not actually lead to the inclusion of women into the household. It was the temporary deputation of a husband's conjugal rights in his brother or kinsmen or to man considered equal or superior to him. The purpose of *niyoga* was to beget sons. The practice only underlines the procreative role of women to the exclusion of any other and in this sense, this practice represents a degradation of women's position. Woman was the property of the family for producing progeny. After the death of the husband, the rights in the reproductive potential of the woman were transferred to the husband's agnatic heirs. Thus *niyoga* is an expression of ownership of the woman by the husband and his family. As women were treated as an instrument for producing heir for men in their lives, their own desire was not of much consequence. *Niyoga* under such circumstances was a task not a pleasure, the woman and the man she had intercourse with had to perform it without least bit of desire or pleasure. It is evident then that women were treated as property.

However, some of the *dharmaśāstrakāras* have disfavoured *niyoga*. This might be because it might have given rise to several controversies and conflicts of self-interest among the agnatic heirs of the deceased husband. This was also against the norms of patriarchy where the younger male members of the family are also subordinated to the male patriarch. This superiority might have been undermined by the younger brother's getting the right to cohabit with the wife of deceased brother. Again, a widow with children might have found their upbringing an uphill task.

Remarriage of a widow was considered to be baneful. Among the people to be carefully avoided are the son and husband of a remarried woman.[48] It is said in verse 167 that a *brāhmaṇa* should shun at sacrifices these lowest of the twice born, whose conduct is reprehensible and who are unworthy to sit in the company at a repast.[49] Thus, by the exclusion of males associated with remarried widow from the ceremonies meant to sanctify the points of entry to or exit from the household; a mechanism was devised to prohibit remarriage of the widow. Another means adopted included the threat of incurring sin by remarrying. However, the husband whose wife died was told to remarry after having burnt her. Some scholars have justified it by saying that the man needed to remarry in order to maintain the sacred fire. All such mechanisms, as to ascribe to the woman the status of an appendage in the performance of religious rites, were further meant to demean the women's identity. Ironically, some scholars glorify the texts by saying that the wife was given such a great importance that religious rites were not believed to be complete without her presence.

It is obvious that the death of a husband lead to an exclusion of the wife from the household life, while the husband was required to remarry at the earliest for maintaining the fire; i.e.; for maintaining the due performance of the functions of the household. The misery that the life of a widow must have been fraught with, might have led some of them to die with their husbands. Even if the practice of *sati* did not find its origins in the *dharmaśāstras*, it cannot be denied that the misery to which the widow was to be subjected, must have worked towards an increase in the instances of *sati*.

Remarriage was permitted to a woman in case of desertion by the husband. However, again, the period of waiting was longer for the woman belonging to higher *varṇa* and vice versa. This indicates that the regulations were more stringent for the women belonging to higher *varṇa*. Remarriage of a woman in any other circumstance is denounced by the *dharmaśāstrakāras* in general, with the only exception of Nārada and Pārāśara, who allowed a woman to remarry in five conditions. It was considered baneful for a woman to abandon her husband in any case. Also, adoption of a life beyond marriage was denounced. Thus, the woman had no choice of opting out of the household life. However, within the patriarchal order, if women remained subjected and 'devoted' to the sustenance of the order perceived by the *dharmaśāstrakāras*, they were given a mild treatment. This accounts for those verses where respect is demanded to be shown to the women. A women bound by the norms of patriarchy, was to be worshipped!

As far as rights to property on the part of a woman are concerned, it has to be studied in the context of the concept of property in ancient India, and women themselves being treated as the property of the male relations. In the hunting and food gathering stage of economy, there must have hardly been any concept of property. Whatever might have existed is a sense of possession of the implements used in hunting, and that too not in the very initial phase. The sense of possession and ownership must have originated and strengthened only with the beginning of pastoralism and agriculture. The concept of individual ownership must have taken still longer to come into existence. Since the early Vedic society was characterized by the tribal bond of kinship, whatever was recognized as tribal wealth was divided among the constituting clans and subclans. Being mostly pastoral warring tribes, the tribal wealth was counted in terms of cattle. The pastoral societies have, however, greater scope to develop the sense of property and individual ownership since cattle could be preserved and multiplied, used as the best medium of exchange, increased by wars and raids, and divided among clans, families, even individuals. Agriculture was introduced only in the later Vedic age, and even then, land was subjected to joint or corporate holding. So no question of individual ownership or inheritance could arise then. During that period, tribes must have exercised control over the areas they had taken possession of. This right of the conqueror must have been the initial form of land right. The tribes allotted land to the individual families for their utilization. The jungle which covered an unlimited expanse of land, although economically useless, led to another form of land right, namely, the right of the first clearer. The strenuous work of clearing, the necessity of mutual help, small-scale defence measures, and the expansion of the families led, in the course of time, to the formation of villages which in turn led to the regulation of land rights. Two different forms developed in time. The village which had individual land rights consisted of a group of families which had rights to the land on the basis of having cleared it. The claims of the families were limited to the cleared land. The uncultivable land in the vicinity of the village was jointly utilized, but no claims were made to it. It belonged to the ruler who, in later epochs, also granted permission to cultivate the land. In the case of villages which held land rights jointly, the village community claimed the right to all land within the village boundaries and allotted it to individual families for utilization. Thus, both individual and joint land rights took shape at an early period itself. However, landed property, as known in Western terms, did not exist at all. The rights were a privilege granting inheritable utilization rights and included social obligations. With the subsequent formation of state, the ruler assumed the supreme position in all matters. Costs of governing were covered, at first, with gifts. Soon, however, it became obligatory to deliver a share of the grain yield, in other words, a tax was introduced. The king was thus only given a right to a share of the yield, but no rights to the land and its utilization.

While the Mauryas had vast state-administered farms, during the post-Mauryan period, the Sātavāhanas started the practice of donating land with fiscal and administrative immunities to *brāhmaṇas* and Buddhist monks. During the Gupta period, however, the land grants paved the way for the growth of feudal society. Women's entitlement to property has to be seen in this light. At the first place, the introduction of the iron ploughshare increased the importance of male labour as far as agriculture was concerned. Accordingly, land came to be the entitlement of the male who cleared the forest and cultivated the land. Again, when land was donated, it was donated to the *brāhmaṇas* and Buddhist monks who were males. Initially, it was the right to utilization, and land was utilized by the males who tilled it. Later, with the emergence of hereditary rights, males must have become the inheritors too. Also, the society being patriarchal, males must have been the recognized heirs.

In accordance with the state of affairs, the *dharmasūtras* advocated a stringent patrilineal form of inheritance, allowing in the absence of sons, the property to go to the near and remote agnates of the property holder than to one's own daughters. However, it was laid down that the ornaments and such wealth as bestowed upon her by her relations, both agnate and cognate, could of course be absolutely owned by her.[50] Thus, women's right to property varied for the immovable and the movable property. Again, the *Dharmaśāstras* or the *Smṛtis* were the first documents which provided a distinct codification of rules relating to ownership, inheritance and partition. In consonance with the norms and requirements of patriarchy, the daughter was not recognized as the natural heir to father's property. However, some rights to property were conceded to her. A small share in the property of the father was granted to the unmarried daughters. However, it seems that instead of being a matter of natural succession, in the case of daughters, it was moral obligation for the brothers to give them a share.

Besides the cases when the daughter was entitled to a limited share in father's property herself, there are references to the appointed daughter, i.e., the *putrikā.* The husband of the daughter had to be informed of the girl's *putrikā* status before marriage, precisely because begetting a son was considered to be one of the main aims behind marrying as the son was considered to be the one to liberate the father from hell. In the case of the appointed daughter, however, the son begotten would rather liberate the girl's father. It would have been certainly difficult for the appointed daughter to get a husband, also in the wake of the fact that the lawgivers themselves discouraged men from marrying such girls. The case of an appointed daughter is actually not a property right granted to the daughter. It is her son who got the entitlement to the maternal grandfather's property in this way. In fact, the status of an appointed daughter reduced her chances of getting a suitable husband to a considerable extent. This would have made her life miserable in a patriarchy where marriage and procreation were considered to be the sole aims of female existence.

The *dharmaśāstrakāras* are found in a state of confusion regarding the widow's right to husband's property. The right of the widow to husband's property could not be rejected entirely by all the lawgivers, and some of them rather granted her the right to get the husband's property. However, the wife's right was recognized only in the absence of any of the recognized sons. Also, the wife had to be faithful to her husband. Manu has observed silence in this regard. It may be inferred that the issue of widow's rights was not a settled issue, and given the miserable life of a widow and her marginalization, she could not have enjoyed the rights even when granted. Also, there was apprehension regarding the widow's right to husband's immovable property. The mother was entitled to a share in the son's property only if he died sonless and/or without a wife.

It was with reference to the immovable property that the Hindu society was for a long time unwilling to invest the wife with full or exclusive ownership. The main reason for it, perhaps, was the ownership of the community on the land. Also, society being patriarchal, the daughter had to become a part of another clan, so in order to keep the ownership with the same tribe, it would not have been feasible to invest the daughter with the same rights on property as the son. But in case of movable property viz., ornaments, jewellery, costly apparels etc., women's rights on their possession were recognized at quite an early stage. Later on, this particular part of movable property was formally labelled as *strīdhana*. Literally, the term *strīdhana* denotes women's property. Varying definitions of *strīdhana* are being given by the lawgivers. Thus, the scope of *strīdhana* kept on changing. However, in general, six kinds of movable property or wealth was included within the scope of *strīdhana.* These included the property given before the nuptial fire; given at the bridal procession; given to a woman through affection; given by a brother; given by mother and given by the father.[51] The most detailed description of *strīdhana* has been given in the *Kātyāyana Smṛti*. Kātyāyana makes the most elaborate treatment of *strīdhana* making improvement of what was suggested by Manu and Yājñavalkya and his version has been accepted by all digests including the *Dāyabhāga*. Also, much debate raged among the lawgivers regarding the dominion over *strīdhana* and whether it can or cannot be used by the woman's kinsmen. There was also confusion whether the immovable property given by the husband to the wife, or any immovable property purchased by the woman using her *strīdhana* should be regarded her *strīdhana* or not. It can be inferred that the term *strīdhana* might not have been inclusive of all the properties that might have belonged to the women. In fact, if the meaning of *strīdhana* would have been 'all the properties which belong to women', there would not have been any need for the enumeration of items in the descriptions of property.

Strīdhana had a character different from that of the ordinary property of the family. Accordingly, special laws were formulated regarding its succession and inheritance. These laws were complex and based on the mode of acquiring *strīdhana*. Also, the type of marriage had a bearing on the order of succession to *strīdhana.* though daughters have been a party to the inheritance of *strīdhana*, not all the lawgivers have recognized them as the first and sole owners. Also, not much is said to clarify the stands of individual lawgivers. Hence, it becomes imperative to refer to the commentaries regarding the rules of succession of *strīdhana*. However, even the commentaries do not give any general rule of succession to woman's property as different schools of Hindu law have propounded different rules in this regard. However, what could be deduced with a measure of certainty is that the succession to *strīdhana* depends, firstly, on the marital status of the deceased women; secondly, on the form on her marriage, whether it was approved or unapproved; thirdly, on the nature of the *strīdhana* i.e., the source from which the *strīdhana* had come; and lastly, on the schools of Hindu law she was governed by.

Though women were vested with rights to some form of property in the limited sense of the term, it is important to find the extent of the power which women really possessed over their *strīdhana*. This has to be seen in the light of two aspects, one, that to what extent it was regarded as exclusive possession of women, and two, what was the extent of the power of alienation that women had over such property. The early *smṛtikāras* were quite reluctant to invest women with absolute and exclusive right over the *strīdhana.* Thus most of the *smṛtikāras* lay down that woman has absolute and independent ownership over her *saudāyika strīdhana* (gifts from affectionate relations), except the gifts received from her husband. However, she had absolute power to dispose them of only after his death, in case it did not consist of immovable property. However, some of the *smṛtikāras* have recognized husband's right to use his wife's *strīdhana* under exceptional circumstances, when the family is in distress, for religious ceremonies, during illness or in times when some great calamity has befallen. Again, while according to some of them, the *strīdhana* utilized by the husband under the pressure of any of such circumstances should be returned; others, including Yājñavalkya, are rather lenient regarding its repayment.

Much is made of women's right to property in the form of *strīdhana.* However, there is little doubt that though women were granted rights to property, they were more in theory, and were circumscribed by various conditions and indictments by the lawgivers. Also, how much the women wielded these rights in practice is another query. Again, this is quite in line with the existing social order which was largely patriarchal, which was characterized by patrilocality for the girls, and as such, a right of girls over immovable property would have meant a transfer of property to another clan to which the girl went after marriage. Hence, movable property alone was considered to be woman's exclusive property. Again, even after marriage, the hold over the *asaudāyika strīdhana* of the woman was maintained by the males, and her complete authority over immovable property was never acknowledged de facto. Also, in the *dharmaśāstric* view, women were themselves treated as the property of the male relatives, namely, the father before marriage and the husband, to whom the possession was transferred after marriage. Women must not have wielded much authority over their movable property in such a state of affairs. Thus, the limited property rights of women came as a natural concomitant of the patriarchal social structure, and would have actually worked towards strengthening and perpetuation of patriarchy. Besides the property rights, some other rights were conceded to the women by the lawgivers. However, these seem to be more in the shape of concessions or privileges rather than as rights in the modern sense of the term. Also some of these were indirectly directed towards upholding the order only.

The foregoing observations offer a brief outline of the order of the society as perceived and sought to be established by the *dharmaśāstrakāras*. It is clear that there was no uniform body of law, which laid down fixed rules, and though the different *dharmaśāstras* sought to establish and perpetuate norms directed towards similar ends, there were differences, both minor and major, in the opinions of their authors. The degree of stringency with which the norms were laid, also varied in accordance with the difference in the treatment of different issues by different lawgivers. Contradictions are not a rarity in any one single text also. It seems that while an attempt was being made to establish a particular social order, there were points where the rules were stringent, however, at other times, there were attempts at reconciliation and assimilation, without which bringing about uniformity of social structure would have been an impossibility.

Further, placing the texts in the context of the then existing socio-economic and religious conditions, there emerges a picture of a society which is in a state of flux in all its dimensions. Whether it be the political scene, or economic, religious or social scenario; each of them is marked with a fast changing situation. At times, the change leads to chaos, as evident in the political condition; while at other times, it leads to an expansion in activity, which is so obvious in the economic scenario, and also to an extent, in the field of religion. The social structures, besides acting upon each other, act and react to give a response to these conditions as well. Interplay of all these factors, and may be some others more, generate historical forces which gave a shape to the existence of women within the social framework.

This has also to be seen in the light of the fact that the fluidity of the political situation and brisk economic activity had lead to a massive influx of foreigners, posing a threat to the existing social order. The theory of *varna-saṃkara* seems to have been an attempt at reconciliation, and thereby prevention of the breaking away of the threads of the social fabric. However, notably, they were absorbed mostly as low castes and were never given a higher caste status. Even when political exigency dictated it that they be given the status of *kśatriya*, they were only accorded the status of degenerate *kśatriyas*. The attempt to prevent higher *varna* women from being married to lower *varna* men might have owed its origin to the idea of keeping away from a free mixing with foreign population. No doubt again, that power relationships must have played significant role in this case too. This is not to argue that foreign invasions were the sole reason behind the injunctions laid down by the lawgivers.

As Roy comments, "The only concession to historical processes or events is the recognition conferred on invasions, the incursions of 'foreigners' which are invoked to justify almost any and every restriction imposed on women … . What emerges in terms of historical explanation is then, very often, a causal link between patriarchal institutions and the threat of the outsider/other. Thus, there is an implicit and even explicit understanding that patriarchal tendencies are basically a response to external threats or challenges. Hence, Hindu society is logically absolved of any inherently oppressive characteristics."[52] This criticism holds good for those who provide justifications like 'women needed to be protected in the wake of the influx of foreign invaders', for what was actually characteristic of already shaped and formed patriarchy, which was not a result of foreign invasions. However, this is to argue that the Brahmanical patriarchy faced a threat in the wake of changing circumstances, and the *dharmaśāstras* represent efforts at the preservation of patriarchy and *varṇa* order. The existing order also faced a threat from the popularity that the heretical sects were gaining and the emergence of newer sects and modes of worship. Again, a spurt in economic activity imparted economic prosperity and hence power to the *varṇas* who were given a low ritual status in the *varṇa* hierarchy.

An analysis of the social conditions of the time presents a picture where the influx of foreigners and a spurt in economic activity, coupled with developments in religion, set a process of transition in the society. The pressure of the circumstances threatened the disintegration of the existent social order. Attempts at reconciliation led to an increase in the social mobility. However, a closer analysis reveals that the threads of the initial social fabric were loosened and the social reality was far removed from the normative models set by the Brahmanical texts.

While the *dharmaśāstras* might have wielded influence in shaping the Brahmanical society, the same does not hold true for all the diverse cultures and societies co-existing in the Indian subcontinent. Precisely with the objective of delineating the sphere of influence of these texts; a study of the epics, the *Śangam* texts, and the epigraphic records was undertaken. While the *Dharmaśātras* depict the 'ideal', the epics present a picture of the Brahmanical society which is 'closer to reality' since they are woven within the fabric of life situations, where the injunctions are being applied as well as tested. Not a few number of times, the norms are ignored, differently interpreted, or even reversed. The epics also provide glimpses of societies outside the Brahmanical influence and provide ground for comparison of gender relations in the Brahmanical and non-Brahmanical societies. Gender relations in the two epics are studied by studying the character portrayals of women in the two epics and their relations with the male characters. The images and models generated by the epics carry a profound influence on the Indian psyche till date. Rāma and Sītā both present the ideal of manhood and womanhood in India. Rāma is considered to be the embodiment of virtues,[53] and Sītā is portrayed in the Vālmīki *Rāmāyaṇa* as the 'quintessence of wifely devotion'.[54] A stark difference is, however, reflected in the definitions that are sought to be established of ideals manhood and womanhood by setting both of them as role models. While Rāma is defined to be *puruśottama* more in terms of being an ideal son, brother and king; Sītā's idealhood consists solely in being the ideal wife. Rāma's evaluation of being an ideal husband, though attempted at, could not be pushed beyond a point. The only point which could be used to push this idea forward was that he remained monogamous. However, to what extent this should be used to exalt the status of Rāma has to be judged keeping in view that the rest of his brothers were also monogamous. While Sītā is portrayed as remaining singularly devoted to her husband through all the vicissitudes, and even after having been subjected to suspicion, insult and abandonment by him; Rāma's main object behind attacking Rāvaṇa was to avenge the injury done to his pride by abducting his wife. Also, he again and again suspects and abandons Sītā. Rāma emerges as the upholder of Brahmanical order by killing Śambuka. In the end, Sītā's return to the earth, thus espousing death, is symbolic in the sense that though spared out of the earth by Janaka, and thus saved to live; a woman's life was fated to end in misery in a society characterised by rigid patriarchal order. Only death could bring an end to her miseries. Also, the ideal of womanhood is established by deifying Sītā for suffering silently, worshipping the husband in spite of all the excesses she was made to face and finally, putting her own life to an end. A similar ideology of the *pativratā* was enforced in the dialogue between Sītā and Anasūyā, another model of *pativratā*. The definitions of good women who were conformist and bad women who were non-conformist or deviant, were reinforced by villainizing Kaikeyī. In a patriarchal set-up, polygamy would have further undermined the position of women; and would have remained a source of tension; is clear from the story of the epic. Resorting to polygamy had the sanction of the lawgivers, even though they disfavoured this practice. In fact, the disfavour of the *dharmaśāstrakāras* could have been a reaction to the problems that were found to arise because of polygamy. If *Rāmayaṇa* is taken to antedate these texts, the authors of these texts might have taken lessons from the story of the epic, where the root of the entire problem lay in polygamy alone. Thus, the basic ethos of the epic were exactly the same as that of the *Dharmaśāstras*. However, still some variations to or deviations from the *dharmaśāstric* injunctions are found in the *Rāmāyaṇa*, which indicates that the general subjugation of women and the peculiarity of the definition of womanhood must have been characteristic to patriarchy, instead of necessarily being originally propagated by the *Dharmaśāstras*. Secondly, the deviations from the norms seem to indicate that the influence of the *dharma* texts was limited even within the Brahmanical society. This becomes more pronounced in the case of *Mahābhārata*, where almost everything is happening against the norms laid down. The norms are either ignored, or interpreted differently or even reversed at times according to the convenience of the characters in power. All of these reversals of the norm have serious implications for the nature of the moral discourse in the *Mahābhārata* that calls for special attention. Throughout the epic, *dharma* remains an ambivalent category. In the *Sabha Parvan*, when Draupadī was dragged into the assembly of the Kauravas by force, following the defeat of Yudhiṣṭhira in the dice game, Bhīṣma tells the sorrowful Draupadī, "I have already said, O blessed one, that the course of morality is subtle. Even the illustrious and wise fail to understand it always. What in this world a strong man calls morality is regarded as such by others, however otherwise it may really be; but what a weak man calls morality is scarcely regarded as such even if it be the highest morality … "[55] Bhīṣma explicitly admits the role of power in determining the definition of morality.

The *Mahābhārata* tries to reinforce the same definition of womanhood as the *Dharmaśāstras*, by making marriage compulsory for women, denouncing asceticism for women, considering procreation one of the most important purposes aims of a woman's existence, treating women as property of the males; and above all, by giving the same definition of *pātivratya*, by way of the *Draupadī- Satyabhāmā samvāda* and the *Umā-Maheśwara samvāda*. In spite of this, *Mahābhārata* presents women who had minds of their own and voices like those of Draupadī, e.g., Śakuntalā, Satyavatī, Ambā etc. This indicates that in spite of being in the stranglehold of rigid patriarchy, there were women who were *empowered from within*. That alternative characterizations of women were sought to be presented by the *Mahābhārata,* further becomes pronounced in its characterization of women who found place in other texts also; often having generated more impact in those roles. Particularly interesting in this regard are the portrayals of Anasūyā, Sītā and Ahalyā. The way these characters are treated in the *Mahābhārata* is actually far more liberal than in the *Rāmāyaṇa.* Ṛṣi Atri's wife Anasūyā finds place in the *Mahābhārata* as a *brahmavādinī* who left her husband with firm intention that she would never again allow herself to be dominated by him.[56] She prayed to Śiva who granted her a boon that even without husband she would have a son who would bear her name and bring fame to her *vamśa.* This is in sharp contrast with portrayal of Anasūyā in the *Rāmāyana,* where she is found lecturing to young Sitā on *pativratā dharma,* telling her that even if husband is wanton or bad he is still a god for the wife.[57] Anasūyā's portrayal in the *Mahābhārata* is revolutionary in the sense that though procreation of son remains important, the woman is shown capable of doing so without the husband.[58] This is in total contrast to the normative literature where procreation of son was considered important from the point of view of securing heaven for the husband. Also, in the normative literature, there was no place for a woman who abandons her husband. Again, the son of Anasūyā was to bear her name and bring fame to her *vamśa*; in stark contrast with the prescriptions of lawgivers. Though not revolutionary, characterizations of Sītā and Ahalyā also were considerably liberal. In the *Mahābhārata,* Gautama is forgiving about his wife's adultery[59], but in the *Rāmāyaṇa,* Ahalyā is cursed to become a stone statue for an unintended happening,[60] symbolizing a far more rigid patriarchal moral code. Similarly, in the *Rāmopākhyāna* of the *Mahābhārata,* Rāma tells Sītā "O princess of Mithila whether thou art chaste or unchaste, I dare not enjoy thee, now that thou art like sacrificial butter lapped by a dog".[61] However, it only takes oral testimony of various gods and father Daśaratha from heaven regarding her chastity for Rāma to accept Sītā.[62] While in the *Rāmāyaṇa* Sītā has to go through fire ordeal to prove her chastity. However, it has to be recognized that among the divergent portrayals of women figures in the two epics, those showing explicit adherence to norms of patriarchy have been emphasized and disseminated in popular discourse, and hence, have left deeper impressions upon Indian psyche, shaping Indian womanhood on the ideals generated thereby. Thus, it is Sītā and not Draupadī, who is considered as the role model for defining womanhood in India.

The fact is that there was no lesser number of women characters in *Mahābhārata* who remained subjected. The story of Mādhavī is upsetting. She is found to be treated as a disposable property by men in her life who alienate her or her reproductive capacity and sexuality at will. Also, Ambikā and Ambālikā carry no voices. Again, even though Draupadī carried voice, it nevertheless could not reduce her suffering at the hands of patriarchy. Draupadī being staked in the dice game was the most blatant example of women being treated as property. That the husband's right to stake his wife and the right of the winner over the person of the woman who was thus won was recognized, even though tacitly; or at least not refuted, is proven by the sinister silence that is observed by the entire assembly of the Kuru elders even when the humiliation of Draupadī is taken to the basest level of attempting at disrobing her in front of all.[63] What was the definition of morality, of *dharma* in this society? What made everyone remain silent to such an act? Was it in tune with *dharma* for a husband to have staked his wife, and was it considered in accordance with *dharma* for the winner to act in any way with a woman who was thus enslaved? Even if considered to be a slave woman, could she be disrobed by the masters in front of an assembly? It was only afterwards that Vidura urged upon those present in the assembly to answer Draupadī's question as to if Yudhiṣṭhira, being himself made a slave had the right to stake her, and accordingly whether if she was a slave or not.[64] Bhīṣma's answer, cited previously, to the sorrowful Draupadī is revealing regarding the nature of morality. Later, Draupadī was granted two boons by Dhṛtarāṣṭra, whereby she asked him to free all the five of her husbands of bondage.[65] Thus she is imparted an agency in the epic, whereby she emerges in the role of one who is the saviour of her husbands. Karṇa not only acknowledges but applauds Draupadī's role, saying, "Pāṇḍavas were drowning in the sea of misfortune without any support, Draupadī has become a boat for them".[66] Thus, it is Draupadī who protects Pāṇḍavas and not the reverse. It is this that marks out the reversal of the norm to the sharpest possible extent.

Both the epics testify to the existence of societies beyond the Brahmanical sphere of influence. Vālmīki's *Rāmāyaṇa* testifies to the existence of societies at different stages of economic and cultural development. While the inhabitants of Ayodhyā are in the phase of settled agriculture, the *Vānaras* and *Rākśasas* are in the pre-agricultural stage of economic development. Power must have been at play in determining the fate of the women even in the societies outside the *Āryan* influence, which is obvious from Rumā's abduction by Vāli, her husband Sugrīva's elder brother.[67] But the contrast between the two cultures lies in the unhesitant acceptance of Rumā by Sugrīva even after such abduction,[68] while Rāma's reservations in accepting Sītā went beyond all humane considerations and sense of justice. Śūrpaṇakhā is the most significant non-*Āryan* female character. She displayed considerable independence in that she roamed about freely in the forest and could make sexual overtures to men.

Also, she could go to her brothers upon facing insult, which is in contrast to Sītā's marginalization and loneliness after abandonment by Rāma. In fact, the position of women in the non-*Āryan* societies as reflected in the epics, as well as in the *Śangam* history; all of which were in the pre-agricultural stage of economy, indicates towards the fact that with the entry into the phase of settled agriculture, and transfer of property through the male lineage, the position of women deteriorated. The *Mahābhārata* not only mentions the existence of other societies, but also indicates that there were societies where women were enjoying a greater degree of freedom. Thus, in the *Sabha Parvan*, there are references to Mahiśmati and Utsava-sanketa, where women were free to move about. Though freedom to indulge in unbridled sexuality cannot be interpreted to mean a better position for women, but these examples point towards the free movement of women, in contrast to the seclusion women were subjected to in the Brahmanical society. Also, the *Mahābhārata* points towards the existence of matrilineal or matriarchal trends in some societies, including those cited above. Though no sure evidence of existence of matriarchy could be found, the *Karna Parvan* attests to the existence of matriliny at two places, Ārhatta and Vālhīka.[69] Women were in a better position in these societies. However, is it to argue in favour of matriliny or matriarchy? Is this the solution that the feminist scholars propose? Matriliny means recognition of kinship and inheritance on the maternal line, where the authority over children is exercised not by their father or mother but by the maternal uncle. Thus, matriliny and matriarchy are different in that matriliny only implies only following the maternal line with regard to inheritance and kinship. This did not actually confer the rights and powers of the head of the family on the mother. In fact, it was the maternal uncle who remained the supreme head of the family and after him his uterine nephew. Thus, interestingly, women in matrilineal societies are also subjected to male authority; the only difference being that in this case, the males happen to be their brother and mother's brother. However, the other authorities that they experience are females including their mother and mother's sister. In a patrilineal society by contrast, women are subject to the male authority first of their father and then of their husband. What can be inferred is that women were less likely to be face subjugation and discrimination in a matrilineal set-up. The question whether if matriarchy or matriliny is answer to set aright the imbalance in gender relations needs much more probing before answered.

Again, there were number of instances of cross-cousin marriages in the *Mahābhārata*. These also mark out deviations from the norms, and add weight to the hypothesis that the sphere of influence of the prescriptions of the normative texts was very limited and that the social reality was posited somewhere between the ideal and the practice.

While the epics also provide glimpses of the other societies existing parallel to the *Āryan* society, there was a society in the far south which was yet away from the *Āryan* influence or at best, gradually getting influenced by it. The ethos of this society is reflected in the earliest stratum of Tamil literature now available, the literature of *Śangam*, which forms the first well-lighted epoch in the history of the Tamil land.[70] The society represented in the *Śangam* literature gives positive indications regarding the position of women in the corresponding society. Unlike the forms of marriage discussed and recognized in the *dharmaśāstras*, marriage by elopement and marriage by parental sanction are the two forms found to be mentioned in the *Śangam* texts. Again, though *Gāndharva* form is close to marriage by elopement in the case of southern society, the difference lies in the fact that while in the *Dharmaśāstras*, this form of marriage found only a tacit acceptance, in the *Śangam* texts, such a form of marriage was considered to be very natural and was encouraged. Again, no equivalents of *Paiśāca* and *Rākśasa* forms could be found in the *Śangam* texts. Again, one of the most striking aspects of *Śangam* society is the complete absence of dowry or groom price. There are however several reference to bride price in *Śangam* literature.[71] That virginity and chastity before marriage was not on premium is amply borne out by the themes discussed in the *Ṛham* poetry, where the girls and boys are found to be mixing freely and courting each other. Perhaps it was due to such social structures that in the *Śangam* society, that a female child was as welcome as a male child. One finds a converse situation in the classic patriarchal structure as prescribed by the lawgivers. Further, as Ramaswamy notes, "The welcome extended to the female child is logical in the *Śangam* polity where women and men were co-sharers in the economy."[72] Women were not relegated to the 'private' sphere of domesticity in the *Śangam* society, rather they were active participants in the public and professional life.

It was not only the economic sphere which presented deviations from the normative codes of conduct. There are striking variations and divergences in the way women were perceived in the socio-religious realm. *Śangam* literary evidence suggests that the notion of 'pollution' was also foreign to Dravidian culture and the bipolarity of purity and pollution entered the *Śangam* texts as a part of the Brahmanical discourse.[73] Yet there was a difference in the way pollution was viewed in the two societies. While pollution in the *dharmaśāstric* tradition resulted in marginalization of the concerned individuals or groups, in the context of *Śangam* society, it became instrumental in their empowerment. As commented by Ramaswamy, "In the *Śangam* age even woman's pollution arising out of gender or the concept of chastity, went towards empowering them rather than controlling them within the framework of male sexual politics as one tends to find under Brahmanical patriarchy."[74]

Further, a study of the epigraphic records, which are said to have *tremendous potential to make real women visible on the historical stage*, reveals that in practice, there were several deviations from the norms prescribed by the *dharmaśāstrakāras*. There are women donors who have deviated from the norm of ideal wifehood by neglecting the identity of their husband in the records completely. As Shah points out, "Leave aside the divine status, even the human status of a husband is negated by women like Nāgamulanikā, Śivaskandanāgaśri, Rudradharabhaṭṭārikā, and Sāmaḍinikā, to offer only a few examples."[75] There were deviations regarding the naming of women. While, in the *Dharmaśāstras,* the excessive importance attached to the names of girls goes to the extent of regarding the suitability or auspiciousness of the name of the maiden to be one of the major qualifications to be chosen as a bride and vice versa. Deviations also marked the norms regarding *gotra* and *piṇḍa* exogamy, and there were instances of cross-cousin marriages. Also, in some inscriptions, metronymics are used by the donors. Even though the use of metronymics does not imply existence of matriliny, it is significant that such cases existed in spite of the stronghold of patriarchy. The Nāneghāt cave inscription of Devī Nāganikā presents a deviation from the prohibition upon the performance of religious penances or sacrifices by women. There also were, admittedly, some cases where identity was constructed in accordance with the ethos of the *Dharmaśāstras*, like using the adjectives *avidhavā* (one whose husband is alive), and *jīvasutā* (one whose son is alive). However, it is obvious that the social reality was complex, and though the inscriptional evidence points towards the influence of patriarchal norms, it also makes it evident that there were deviations from as well as variations within the norms, and there were women who could dare to move away from the norms of patriarchy.

It may be inferred that the sphere of influence of the prescriptions of the normative texts was very limited and that the social reality was posited somewhere between the ideal and the practice. Thus it is a 'myth' that the *Dharmaśāstras* were the foundational documents of Hindu way of life in any age or that they are the representative texts of Indian tradition. Patriarchy grew in the Indian subcontinent just the way it grew everywhere else in the world. These texts represent a line of thought which emerged partly as a response to the existing conditions. They also held reflections of the then society. This is not to exonerate the *Dharmaśāstras* from the fact of having made an attempt to preserve the rigid Brahmanical patriarchy. But only to acknowledge that both, to criticize or to eulogize these texts, is to attach more importance to them than they really deserve. Also, it may be inferred that women are not a homogenous category at any given point of time in history. This remains true for the 'ancient' period of Indian history. Given the existence of diverse cultures and traditions, no universal or general assumptions may be made regarding the position of women at any point of time in history. Rather, women's identity has to be relocated within the existing web of structures and formations. Given the patriarchal structure of the society, gender equation was skewed in the favour of the males.

Notes

1. Kane, P.V., *History of Dharmaśāstra (Ancient and Medieval Religious and Civil Law in India)*, Vol. I, Part I, 2nd ed., B.O.R.I., Poona, 1968, p. 1.
2. Lingat, Robert, *The Classical Law of India,* Thomson Press (India) Ltd., New Delhi, 1973, p. 3.
3. *ṚV*.I.187.1, X.92.2.
4. *ṚV*.I.22.18, V.26.6, VIII.43.24, IX.64.1.
5. *ṚV*.IV.53.3, V.63.7, VI.70.1, VII.89.5.
6. Kane, P.V., op. cit., p. 3.
7. Ibid., p. 4.
8. Agarwal, Bina, *A Field of One's Own: Gender and Land Rights in South Asia*, edition for South Asia published by arrangement between Cambridge University Press and Foundation Books, New Delhi, 1994, pp. 51–52.
9. Ibid.
10. Chakravarti, Uma, *Everyday Lives, Everyday Histories: Beyond the Kings and Brahmanas of 'Ancient' India*, Tulika Books, New Delhi, 2006, p. 253.

11. Ibid.
12. *Manu*.VI.87.
13. This has to be distinguished from the entry to the life of a householder, which is possible only after marriage.
14. Dexter, M.A., *Whence the Goddesses,* Pergamon Press, New York, 1990, p. 161.
15. Ibid., p. 37–38.
16. *Manu*.III.33.
17. Altekar, A.S., *The Position of Women in Hindu Civilization,* Motilal Banarsidass, 2nd ed., Fifth reprint, Delhi, 1987, p. 37.
18. Ibid.
19. *Vyāsa*.II.8.
20. Trautmann, T.R., *Dravidian Kinship*, CUP, Cambridge, 1981, p. 26.
21. Shah, Shalini, *The Making of Womanhood: Gender Relations in the Mahābhārata*, Manohar, New Delhi, 1995, p. 25.
22. Kapoor, Kapil, "Hindu Women, Traditions and Modernity", in Padia, Chandrakala (ed.), *Feminism, Tradition and Modernity*, IIAS, Shimla, 2002, p. 40.
23. Cited in Chakravarti, Uma, *Everyday Lives, Everyday Histories: Beyond the Kings and Brahmanas of 'Ancient' India",* Tulika Books, New Delhi, 2006, pp. 139–140.
24. Chakravarti, Uma, op. cit., p. 254.
25. *Manu*.IX.96.
26. Kapoor, Kapil, op. cit., pp. 32–33.
27. *Manu*.II.67.
28. *Manu*.IX.6.
29. *Manu*.IX.3.
30. *Manu*.IX.7.
31. Kapoor, Kapil, op. cit., p. 27.
32. Ibid., pp. 28–34.
33. Ibid., p. 34.
34. Ibid.
35. Ibid., p. 32.
36. Shah, Shalini, op. cit., p. 57.
37. Bhattacharyya, N.N., *The Indian Mother Goddess,* 2nd revised ed., Manohar, New Delhi, 1977, p. 286.
38. Sanday, P.R., *Female Power and Male Dominance: On the Origins of Sexual Inequality*, CUP, Cambridge, 1981.
39. Agarwal, Bina, op. cit., pp. 51–52.
40. *Yāj*.II.24.286
41. *Nārada*.XII.70, *Viṣṇu*.V.40–43.
42. *Manu*.VIII.352.

43. *Manu*.VIII.353.
44. The term *inherent capabilities* is not intended at defining *inherent differences in the capabilities of individuals* on the basis of sex, race or any other such categorizing. The *inherent capabilities* of every individual vary irrespective of any classifications.
45. Ibid., p. 157.
46. Altekar, A.S., *The Position of Women in Hindu Civilization*, Motilal Banarsidass, 2nd ed., Fifth reprint, Delhi, 1987, p. 149.
47. Ibid.
48. *Manu*.III.166.
49. *Manu*.III.167.
50. *Āpas.Dh.S*.II.6.14.19, *Baudh.Dh.S*.II.2.49 and *Vasiṣṭha*.XVII.48–9.
51. *Manu*.IX.194.
52. Roy, Kumkum, "'Where Women are Worshipped, there the Gods Rejoice': The Mirage of the Ancestress of the Hindu Woman", in Sarkar, Tanika and Butalia, Urvashi (eds.), *Women and the Hindu Right: A Collection of Essays*, Kali for Women, New Delhi, 1995, p. 11.
53. *The Rāmāyaṇa of Vālmīki: An Epic of Ancient India*, translated by Goldman, Robert P., Vol. I, 1st Indian ed., Motilal Banarsidass, Delhi, 2007, *Bālakāṇḍa*: 1:8,9,16,18–19, pp. 121–122.
54. Kakar, Sudhir, *The Inner World: A Psycho-analytic Study of Childhood and Society in India*, OUP, New Delhi, 1981, p. 63.
55. Ganguli, Kisari Mohan, *The Mahabharata of Krishna-Dwaipayana Vyasa*, Vol. I, Munshiram Manoharlal Publishers Pvt. Ltd., New Delhi, 2004, *Sabha Parva*, pp. 135–136.
56. Ganguli, Kisari Mohan, *The Mahabharata of Krishna-Dwaipayana Vyasa*, Vol. IV, Munshiram Manoharlal Publishers Pvt. Ltd., New Delhi, 2004, *Anusasana Parva* (Part I), p. 43.
57. *The Rāmāyaṇa of Vālmīki: An Epic of Ancient India*, translated by Pollock, Sheldon, I., Vol. II, 1st Indian ed., Motilal Banarsidass, Delhi, 2007, *Ayodhyākāṇḍa*: 109: 23–28, p. 318.
58. Ganguli, Kisari Mohan, *The Mahabharata of Krishna-Dwaipayana Vyasa*, Vol. IV, Munshiram Manoharlal Publishers Pvt. Ltd., New Delhi, 2004, *Anusasana Parva* (Part I), p. 43.
59. Ganguli, Kisari Mohan, *The Mahabharata of Krishna-Dwaipayana Vyasa*, Vol. III, Munshiram Manoharlal Publishers Pvt. Ltd., New Delhi, 2004, *Santi Parva* (Part II), pp. 25–251.
60. *The Rāmāyaṇa of Vālmīki: An Epic of Ancient India*, translated by Goldman, Robert P., 1st Indian ed., Motilal Banarsidass, Delhi, 2007, Vol. I, *Bālakāṇḍa*:47:29–32, p. 216.

61. Ganguli, Kisari Mohan, *The Mahabharata of Krishna-Dwaipayana Vyasa*, Vol. I, Munshiram Manoharlal Publishers Pvt. Ltd., New Delhi, 2004, *Vana Parva*, p. 566.
62. Ibid., p. 567.
63. Ganguli, Kisari Mohan, *The Mahabharata of Krishna-Dwaipayana Vyasa*, Vol. I, Munshiram Manoharlal Publishers Pvt. Ltd., New Delhi, 2004, *Sabha Parva*, p. 132.
64. Ibid., p. 133.
65. Ibid., pp. 139–140.
66. Ibid., p. 140.
67. *The Rāmāyaṇa of Vālmīki: An Epic of Ancient India*, translated by Lefeber, Rosalind, Vol. IV, 1st Indian ed., Motilal Banarsidass, Delhi, 2007, *Kiṣkindhākāṇḍa*:5:19, p. 62.
68. *The Rāmāyaṇa of Vālmīki: An Epic of Ancient India*, translated by Lefeber, Rosalind, Vol. IV, 1st Indian ed., Motilal Banarsidass, Delhi, 2007, *Kiṣkindhākāṇḍa*:25:38, p. 109.
69. Ganguli, Kisari Mohan, *The Mahabharata of Krishna-Dwaipayana Vyasa*, Vol. III, Munshiram Manoharlal Publishers Pvt. Ltd., New Delhi, 2004, *Karna Parva*, pp. 107–109.
70. Sastri, K.A. Nilakanta, *A History of South India: From Prehistoric Times to the Fall of Vijayanagar*, 4th ed., OUP, New Delhi, 1999, p. 104.
71. Ramaswamy, Vijaya, *Walking Naked: Women, Society, Spirituality in South India*, IIAS, Shimla, 1997, p. 56.
72. Ibid., p. 55.
73. Ramaswamy, Vijaya, "Aspects of Women and Work in Early South India", in Kumkum Roy (ed.), op. cit., pp. 42–43.
74. Ramaswamy, Vijaya, *Walking Naked: Women, Society, Spirituality in South India*, IIAS, Shimla, 1997, p. 55.
75. Ibid., p. 175.

Bibliography

Primary Sources

I. Epigraphic

Burgess, J. et al., (eds.) *Epigraphia Indica,* Vols. I to XLII, (Reprint).

——, *Archaeological Survey of South India,* Vol. I (The Buddhist Stūpas of Amaravati and Jaggayyapeta in the Krishna District, Madras Presidency), Trubner & Co., London, 1887.

——, *Archaeological Survey of Western India,* Vol. IV (Report on Buddhist Cave Temples and Their Inscriptions) (Reprint), Indological Book House, Varanasi, 1964.

——, *Archaeological Survey of Western India,* Vol. V (Report on the Elura Cave Temples and the Brahmanical and Jaina Caves in Western India, (Reprint), Indological Book House, Varanasi,1970.

Bailey, H.W. (ed. And tr.), 'Two Kharosthi Inscriptions', *Journal of the Royal Asiatic Society,* No. 2, 1982.

Hultzsch, E. (ed.), *Corpus Inscriptionum Indicarum,* Vol. I, *Inscriptions of Asoka,* (Reprint), Archaeological Survey of India, New Delhi, 1991.

Konow, S. (ed.), *Corpus Inscriptionum Indicarum,* Vol. II, Pt. I, *Kharosthi Inscriptions* (with the exception of those of Aśoka) (Reprint), Archaeological Survey of India, New Delhi, 1991.

The Indian Antiquary, Vol. XXI (Reprint), Swati Publications, Delhi, 1985.

Luders, H. (ed.), *Corpus Inscriptionum Indicarum,* Vol. II, Pt. II (Revised by E. Waldschmidt and M.A. Mehedale), Govt. Epigraphist for India, Ootacamund, 1963.

Mirashi, V.V., *Corpus Inscriptionum Indicarum,* Vol. IV, *Inscriptions of the Kalachuri-Chedi Era,* Govt. Epigraphist for India, Ootacamund, 1955.

The History and Inscriptions of the Sātavāhanas and the Western Kshatrapas, Bombay, Maharashtra State Board for Literature and Culture, 1989.

Sircar, D.C., *Select Inscriptions Bearing on Indian History and Civilization,* Vol. I, University of Calcutta, Calcutta, 1965.

II. Textual

Aitareya Brāhmaṇa, with Sāyaṇa's Commentary, ed. by Kashinath Shastri and H.N. Apte, 2 vols., Poona, 1896.

Bṛhadāraṇyaka Upaniṣad, with Śankara's Commentary, Gita Press, Gorakhpur, VS 2012.

Chhāndogya Upaniṣad, with Śankara's Commentary, Gita Press, Gorakhpur, VS 2011.

Dāyatattva of Raghunandana: Text and Translation, G.C. Sarkar Sastri, Calcutta, 1904.

Hārita Samhitā: Original Text with a Literal Prose English Translation, edited and translated by M.N. Dutt, Elysium Press, Calcutta, 1906.

Hymns of the Ṛgveda, R.T.H. Griffith, 2 Vols., Varanasi, 1963.

Manusmṛti: With the 'Manubhāṣya' of Medhātithi, tr. By Ganganath Jha, Vol. 7, 2nd ed., Motilal Banarsidass, Delhi, 1999.

Milindapañho, being dialogues between King Milinda and the Buddhist Sage Nāgasena, ed. by V. Trenckner, The Royal Asiatic Society, London, 1928.

Mitākśarā, Nirnaya Sagar Press, Bombay, 1918.

Pārāśarasmṛtiḥ: edited with 'Subodhinī' Hindi Commentary, ed. by Daivajñavāchaspati Śri Vāsudeva, 3rd ed., Chaukhamba Amarbharati Prakashan, Varanasi, 1997.

Smṛti Candrikā of Devaṇṇabhaṭṭa, Vol. II, translated by J. R. Gharpure, Bombay, 1918.

Smṛti Candrikā of Devaṇṇabhaṭṭa, translated by T. Krishna Swami, Calcutta, 1867.

Taittirīya Samhitā, with Sāyaṇa's Commentary, ed. by Kashinath Shastri, Poona, 1905.

The Dharam Shastra: Hindu Religious Codes, translated by M.N. Dutt, Vols. I–IV, Cosmo Publications, New Delhi, 1979.

The Institutes of Vishnu, S.B.E. Vol. VII, ed. by F. Max Müller, tr. by Julius Jolly, reprinted, Motilal Banarsidass, Delhi, 1965.

The Laws of Manu, translated by Wendy Doniger and Brian K. Smith, Penguin Books, New Delhi, 1991.

The Laws of Manu, translated, with extracts from Seven Commentaries, by Bühler, G., Clarendon Press, Oxford, 1886.

The Mahabharata of Krishna-Dwaipayana Vyasa, Vols. I–IV, translated by Kisari Mohan Ganguli, Munshiram Manoharlal Publishers Pvt. Ltd., New Delhi, 2004.

The Manusmriti, edited and translated by George Buhler, *The Laws of Manu, S.B.E.,* vol. XXV, Oxford, Clarendon Press, 1886.

The Minor Law Books, S.B.E., Vol. XXXIII, Part I, ed. by F. Max Müller, tr. by Julius Jolly, reprinted, Motilal Banarsidass, Delhi, 1965.

The Mitākṣarā and Dāyabhāga (Two Treatises on the Hindu Law of Inheritance), translated by Colebrook, H.T., Calcutta, 1883.

The Rāmāyaṇa of Vālmīki: An Epic of Ancient India, translated by Robert P. Goldman, Vol. I, 1st Indian ed., Motilal Banarsidass, Delhi, 2007.

The Rāmāyaṇa of Vālmīki: An Epic of Ancient India, translated by Sheldon I. Pollock, Vol. II, 1st Indian ed., Motilal Banarsidass, Delhi, 2007.

The Rāmāyaṇa of Vālmīki: An Epic of Ancient India, translated by Sheldon I. Pollock, Vol. III, 1st Indian ed., Motilal Banarsidass, Delhi, 2007.

The Ramayana of Valmiki, translated by Hari Prasad Shastri, Vol. III, 2nd ed., Shanti Sadan, London, 1970.

The Rāmāyaṇa of Vālmīki: An Epic of Ancient India, translated by Rosalind Lefeber, Vol. IV, *Kiṣkindhākāṇḍa*:5:19, 1st Indian ed., Motilal Banarsidass, Delhi, 2007.

The Sacred Laws of the Āryas, S.B.E. Vols. II and XIV, edited by F. Max Müller, translated by George Bühler, reprinted, Motilal Banarsidass, Delhi, 1965.

The Vyavahāra Mayūkha (A Treatise on Positive Law), by Bhaṭṭa Nīlkaṇṭha, Part I (Sanskrit text), translated by J. R. Gharpure, 1st ed., Bombay, 1914.

The Vyavahāra Mayūkha of Bhaṭṭa Nīlkaṇṭha, translated by P. V. Kane, 1st ed., Poona, 1926.

Uśana Samhitā: Original Text with a Literal Prose English Translation, edited and translated by M.N. Dutt, Elysium Press, Calcutta, 1906.

Vyavasthā Darpaṇa: A Digest of Hindu Law by S.C. Sarkar, 2 Parts, IIIrd ed., Vidya Bhushan, Calcutta, 1883.

Yājñavalkya Smṛti, with the commentary of Aparārka, And. ed., Poona, 1903–4.

Yājñavalkyasmṛti of Yogīśvara Maharṣi Yājñavalkya, by B.S. Bist, Chaukhamba Sanskrit Pratishthan, Delhi, 2004.

Secondary Sources

Aboyer, J., *Daily Life in Ancient India,* Asia Publishing House, Delhi, 1965.

Agarwal, Bina, *A Field of One's Own: Gender and Land Rights in South Asia*, Foundation Books, New Delhi, 1994.

Apte, V.S., *Sanskrit English Dictionary,* (Reprint), Motilal Banarsidass, Delhi, 1976.

Allchin, B. and Allchin, R., *The Birth of Indian Civilization: India and Pakistan before 500 B.C.*, Penguin Books, Baltimore, 1968.

Altekar, A.S., *The Position of Women in the Hindu Civilization*, 2nd ed., 5th reprint, Motilal Banarsidass, Delhi, 1987.

Ardener, Shirley (ed.), *Perceiving Women*, Dent Publishers, London, 1975.

Bader, Clarisse, *Women in Ancient India: Moral and Literary Studies*, 2nd ed., Chowkhamba Sanskrit Series, Varanasi, 1964.

Banerjee, Gooroo Das, *Hindu Law of Marriage and Strīdhana*, reprinted, Mittal Publications, Delhi, 1984.

Banerji, Sures Chandra, *Dharmaśṛstras: A Study in their Origin and Development,* Punthi Pustak, Calcutta, 1962.

Banerjee, P., *Early Indian Religions*, Vikas, New Delhi, 1973.

Bhagavān Dās, *The Science of Social Organisation or The Laws of Manu in the Light of Ātma-Vidyā*, Vol. II, The Theosophical Publishing House, Adyar, Madras, 1935.

Bhatt, G.H. (ed.), *The Bālakāṇḍa: The First Book of the Vālmīki Rāmāyaṇa: The National Epic of India,* Oriental Institute, Baroda, 1960.

Bhattacharyya, N.N., *Ancient Indian Rituals and Social Contents,* Manohar, Delhi, 1996.

——, *The Indian Mother Goddess,* 2nd ed., Manohar, New Delhi, 1977.

Bhattacharyya, Parnasabari, *Conceptualizations in the Manusmṛti*, Manohar, New Delhi, 1996.

Bock, Gisela, "Challenging Dichotomies" in Karen Offen et al. (ed.), *Writing Women's History: International Perspective*, Macmillan, London, 1991.

Bose, Mandakranta, *Faces of the feminine in Ancient, Medieval, and Modern India*, Oxford University Press, New Delhi, 2000.

Boserup, Ester, *Women's Role in Economic Development,* St. Martin's Press, New York, 1970.

Carroll, Berenice (ed.), *Liberating Women's History: Theoretical and Critical Essays*, University of Illinois Press, Urbana, 1976.

Chakravarti, Uma, *Everyday Lives, Everyday Histories: Beyond the Kings and Brahmanas of 'Ancient' India*, Tulika Books, New Delhi, 2006.

Chanana, Karuna (ed.), *Socialization, Education and Women*, Orient Longman, New Delhi, 1988.

Chaturvedi, Badrinath, *The Mahābhārata: An Inquiry in the Human Condition*, Orient Longman, New Delhi, 2006.

Chaudhuri, J.B., *The Position of Women in the Vedic Ritual*, 2nd ed., The Author, Calcutta, 1956.

Colebrook, H.T., *A Digest of Hindu Law, on Contracts and Successions*, Vols. I-IV, J. Higginbotham, Madras, 1864–65.

Coontz, Stephanie and Henderson, Peta (eds.), *Women's Work, Men's Property: The Origin of Gender and Class*, Verso, London, 1986.

Crawley, E., *The Mystic Rose*, Vol. 2, New York, 1927.

Das, R.M., *Women in Manu and His Seven Commentators*, Kanchana Publications, Bodh Gaya, 1962.

Dexter, M.R., *Whence the Goddesses,* Pergamon Press, New York, 1990.

Doniger, Wendy, *Splitting the Difference: Gender and Myth in Ancient Greece and India,* Oxford University Press, New Delhi, 1999.

—— and Brian, K. Smith (tr.), *Laws of Manu,* Penguin Books, London, 1991.

Engels, Frederick, *The Origin of the Family, Private Property and the State*, Foreign Languages Publishing House, Moscow, 1948.

Ghadially, Rehana (ed.), *Women in Indian Society: A Reader,* 10th ed., Sage, New Delhi, 2001.

Goody, Jack and Tambiah, S.J., *Bride Wealth and Dowry*, CUP, Cambridge, 1973.

Greven, Philip J., Jr., *Four Generations: Population, Land and Family in Colonial Andover*, Ithaca, Massachusetts, 1970.

Gulati, S., *Women and Society*, Chanakya Publications, Delhi, 1985.

Hopkins, E.W., *The Great Epic of India: Its Character and Origin*, reprint, Yale University Press, New Haven, 1920.

——, *The Ordinances of Manu*, Trübner & Co., London, 1884.

Horner, I.B., *Women Under Primitive Buddhism: Laywomen and Almswomen*, G. Routledge & Sons Ltd., London, 1930.

Indra, *The Status of Women in Ancient India*, The Minerva Book Shop, Lahore, 1940.

Irigaray, Luce, *This Sex Which is Not One,* Cornell University Press, Ithaca, 1985.

Jayal, Shakambari, *The Status of Women in the Epics*, Motilal Banarsidass, Delhi, 1966.

Jayaswal, K.P., *Manu and Yājñavalkya: A Comparison and a Contrast: A Treatise on the Basic Hindu Law*, Butterworth (India), Calcutta, 1930.

Jha, D.N., *Early India: A Concise History*, Manohar, New Delhi, 2004.

Jha, Ganganath, *Hindu Law in its Sources*, Patna University, Patna, 1931.

Jois, M. Rama, *Ancient Indian Law: Eternal Values in Manusmriti*, Universal Law Publishing Company, Delhi, 2002.

Jolly, Julius, *Recht und Sitte*, translated by Batakrishna Ghosh, Bharatiya Publishing House, Varanasi, 1975.

Kakar, Sudhir, *The Inner World: A Psycho-analytic Study of Childhood and Society in India*, OUP, New Delhi, 1981.

Kane, P.V., *History of Dharmaśāstra (Ancient and Medieval Religious and Civil Law in India)*, 5 Vols., B.O.R.I., Poona, 1930–1946.

——, *History of Dharmaśāstra (Ancient and Medieval Religious and Civil Law in India)*, Vol. I, Part I, 2nd ed., B.O.R.I., Poona, 1968.

——, *History of Dharmaśāstra (Ancient and Medieval Religious and Civil Law in India)*, Vol. II, 2nd ed., B.O.R.I., Poona, 1974.

Kapadia, K.M., *Explorations in the Family and Other Essays.* Thacker and Spinck Co., Bombay, 1975.

——, *Marriage and Family in India,* (Ninth Impression), Oxford University Press, Calcutta, 1966.

Keith, A.B., *A History of Sanskrit Literature*, OUP, London, 1953.

——, *The Sanskrit Drama in its Origin, Development and Practice*, 1st Indian ed., Motilal Banarsidass, Delhi, 1992.

Kosambi, D.D., *Myth and Reality*, Popular Prakashan, Bombay, 1962.

Lerner, Gerda, *Teaching Women's History*, American Historical Association, Washington, 1981.

——, *Creation of Patriarchy*, OUP, New York, 1986.

Lingat, Robert, *The Classical Law of India*, Thomson Press (India) Ltd., New Delhi, 1973.

Majumdar, R.C., *Ancient India*, Motilal Banarsidass, Delhi, 1952.

Manjushree, *Position of Women in the "Yājñavalkyasmrti",* Prachi Publishers, New Delhi, 1990.

Max Müller, *History of Ancient Sanskrit Literature*, Williams and Norgate, London, 1859.

Menski, W.F., *Hindu Law: Beyond Tradition and Modernity*, OUP, New Delhi, 2003.

Meyer, J.J., *Sexual Life in Ancient India*, Motilal Banarsidass, Delhi, 1971.

Mies, Maria, *Indian Women and Patriarchy,* Concept, New Delhi, 1980.

Monier-Williams, Monier, *A Sanskrit-English Dictionary*, reprinted, OUP, Oxford, 1964.

Moti Chandra, *The World of Courtesans*, Vikas, New Delhi, 1973.

Mukherji, P., *Hindu Women*, Orient Longman, New Delhi, 1978.

Narang, B.S., *Concept of Strīdhana in Ancient India*, Parimal Publications, Delhi, 1990.

Nita Kumar (ed.), *Women as Subjects: South Asian Histories,* Book Review Literary Trust, New Delhi, 1994.

Ortner, Sherry and Whitehead, Harriet (eds.), *Sexual Meanings: the Cultural Construction of Gender and Sexuality,* CUP, Cambridge, 1981.

Padia, Chandrakala (ed.), *Feminism, Tradition and Modernity*, IIAS, Shimla, 2002.

Rajvade, Vishvanath Kashinath, *Bhārtīya Vivāha Samsthā kā Itihāsa,* People's Publishing House, New Delhi, 1986.

Ramaswamy, Vijaya, *Walking Naked: Women, Society, Spirituality in South India*, IIAS, Shimla, 1997.

Rosaldo, M.Z. and Lamphere, L. (eds.), *Women, Culture and* Society, Stanford University Press, California, 1974.

Roy, Kumkum (ed.), *Women in Early Indian Societies*, Manohar, New Delhi, 1997.

Saberwal, Satish and Varma, Supriya (eds.), *Traditions in Motion: Religion and Society in History*, OUP, New Delhi, 2005.

Sanday, P.R., *Female Power and Male Dominance: On the Origin of Sexual Inequality,* CUP, Cambridge, 1981.

Sangari, K. and Vaid, S. (eds.), *Recasting Women: Essays in Colonial History,* Kali for Women, Delhi, 1990.

Sarkar, Tanika and Butalia, Urvashi, *Women and the Hindu Right: A Collection of Essays,* Kali for Women, New Delhi, 1995.

Sarkar, S.C., *Some Aspects of the Earliest Social History of India,* Humphrey Milford, London, 1928.

Sastri, G.C. Sarkar, *Hindu Law of Adoption*, Thacker, Spinck & Co., Calcutta, 1891.

Sastri, K.A. Nilakanta (ed.), *A Comprehensive History of India*, Vol. Two, 2nd reprint, People's Publishing House, New Delhi, 1987.

——, *A History of South India: From Prehistoric Times to the Fall of Vijayanagar*, 4th ed., OUP, New Delhi, 1999.

Schmidt, Hanns Peter, *Some Women's Rites and Rights in the Veda,* B.O.R.I., Poona, 1987.

Sengupta, N.C., *Evolution of Ancient Indian Law*, Eastern Law House Ltd., Calcutta, 1953.

Shah, Kirit K., *The Problem of Identity: Women in Early Indian Inscriptions*, OUP, New Delhi, 2001.

Shah, Shalini, *The Making of Womanhood: Gender Relations in the Mahābhārata*, Manohar, New Delhi, 1995.

Sharma, Arvind (ed.), *Women in Indian Religions,* Oxford University Press, New Delhi, 2002.

Sharma, Ramashraya, *A Socio-Political Study of the Vālmīki Rāmāyaṇa*, Motilal Banarsidass, Delhi, 1971.

Sharma, R.S., *Material Culture and Social Formations in Ancient India,* Macmillan India Ltd., New Delhi, 1983.

——, (ed.), *Perspectives in Social and Economic History of Early India*, Munshiram Manoharlal, New Delhi, 1983.

Sharma, T.R., *Personal and Geographical Names in Gupta Inscriptions,* Concept Publishing Company, Delhi, 1976.

Shastri, Shakuntala Rao, *Women in the Sacred Law*, Bhartiya Vidya Bhawan, Bombay, 1953.

Sinha, S.N. and Basu, N. K., *Women in Ancient India: Vedic to Vatsyayana*, Khama Publishers, Delhi, 2002.

Sternbach, L., *Juridical Studies in Ancient Indian Law*, Vols. I & II, Motilal Banarsidass, Delhi, 1965–67.

Strange, Thomas A.L., *Hindu Law*, Parbury, Allen, London, 1830.

Sukthankar, V.S., *Critical Studies in the Mahābhārata*, Vol. I, Sukthankar Memorial Edition, Vol. I, Karnataka Publishing House, Bombay, 1944.

Syed, A.J. (ed.), *D.D. Kosambi on History and Society,* University of Bombay Publications, Bombay, 1985.

Talim, M., *Women in Early Buddhism*, University of Bombay, Bombay, 1972.

Thapar, Romila, *Ancient Indian Social History: Some Interpretations*, Orient Longman, New Delhi, 3rd reprint, 1996.

——, *Early India*, Penguin, New Delhi, 2002.

Thapliyal, Uma Prasad, *Foreign Elements in Indian Society-2nd century BC to 7th century AD*, Munshiram Manoharlal, New Delhi, 1979.

Tharu, Susie and Lalita, K. (eds.), *Women Writing in India (600 BC to the Present)*, Vol. I, OUP, New Delhi, 1991.

Trautmann, T.R., *Dravidian Kinship*, CUP, Cambridge, 1981.

Tripathi, L.K. (ed.), *Position and Status of Women in Ancient India*, Vol. I, Dept. of A.I.H.C. and Archaeology, BHU, Varanasi, 1988.

Upadhyaya, B.S., *Women in Rigveda*, 3rd revised ed., S. Chand & Co., New Delhi, 1974.

Vaidya, C.V., *The Mahābhārata: A Criticism*, Mehar Chand Lachman Das, Delhi, 1966.

Vishnoi, Savita, *Economic Status of Women in Ancient India*, Kusumanjali Prakashan, Meerut, 1993.

Vora, D.P., *Evolution of Morals in the Epics,* Popular Book Depot, Bombay, 1959.

Winternitz, Maurice, *A History of Indian Literature,* translated from German by V. Srinivas Sharma, Vol. I, 1st revised ed., 2nd reprint, Motilal Banarsidass, Delhi, 1990.

——, *History of Sanskrit Literature*, translated by Subhadra Jha, Motilal Banarsidass, Delhi, 1998.

Journal Articles

Bhattacharji, Sukumari, "A Revaluation of Valmiki's Rama", in *Social Scientist*, Vol. 30, No. 1/2, Jan-Feb., 2002, pp. 31–49.

——, "Economic Rights of Ancient Indian Women", in *Economic and Political Weekly*, Vol. 26, No. 9–10, March 2–9, 1991, pp. 507–512.

——, "Motherhood in Ancient India", in *Economic and Political Weekly*, Vol. 25, No. 40, October 20–27, 1990, pp. WS-50–57.

Chakravarti, Uma and Roy, Kumkum, "In Search of Our Past: A Review of the Limitations and Possibilities of the Historiography of Women in Early India" in *Economic and Political Weekly*, Vol. 23, No. 18, April 30, 1988, pp. WS-2 to WS-10.

Godelier, Maurice, "The Origins of Male Domination", *New Left Review,* NLR I/127, May-June, 1981, pp. 3–17.

Jaiswal, Suvira, "Women in Early India: Problems and Perspectives", in Proceedings of Indian History Congress, Vol. 42, Magadh University, Bodhgaya, 1981, pp. 54–60.

Karve, Irawati, "Kinship Terms and the Family Organisation as found in the Critical Edition of the Mahābhārata", *Bulletin of the Deccan College Research Institute,* Poona., Issue 5, 1943–44.

Macdonell, A.A., "'Ramaism' and 'Ramayana'", *Encyclopaedia of Religion and Ethics*, Vol. 10, James Hastings (ed.), Scribner, New York, 1919, pp. 574–578.

Nataraja, Devabhoopati, "Courtship and Marriage in the Classical Period", *Journal of Tamil Studies*, Vol. I, Part I, 1969.

Ramaswamy, Vijaya, "Women and the 'Domestic' in Tamil Folk Songs", in *Man in India*, No. 7, 1994.

Roy, Kumkum, "Defining the Household: Some Aspects of Prescription and Practice in Early India", in *Social Scientist*, Vol. 22, No. 248–249, Jan-Feb. 1994, pp. 3–18.

Sundramathy, Gloria, L., "The Women Poets of the Sangam Age", *Journal of Tamil Studies*, 1975, p. 62.

Thapar, Romila, "Tradition versus Misconceptions", in *Manushi,* Nos. 42–43, 1987.

Young, F.W. and Bacdayan, A.A., "Menstrual Taboos and Social Rigidity", in *Ethnology*, Vol. 4, No. 2, April 1965, p. 225–240.

Index

adultery, 102-4
  and gender identity, 106-14
  by female, 106-10
  by male, 110-14
  vs *varna* identity, 104-6
Agarwal, Bina, 293
Allchin, B. and Allchin, R., 234
Altekar, A.S., 3, 4, 45, 46, 73, 101, 118, 119, 284, 285, 298
Ardener, Edwin, 1

Bader, Clarisse, 3
Banerjee, Gooroo Das, Sir, 6, 162, 163, 166
Bhattacharji, Sukumari, 6, 91, 194
Bhattacharyya, N.N., 6, 155, 156
Bhattacharyya, Parnasabari, 16
birth, 44
  of female child, 44-46
Bose, Mandakranta, 5
Boserup, Ester, 100
bourgeoisie, 2
brahmanical patriarchy, 257
bride price, 68-70
Buddhism, 32
Bühler, G., 14, 15, 251, 252

capitalist society, 2
  stratification in, 2
Chakravarti, Uma and Roy, Kumkum, 3, 4, 5, 7
Chakravarti, Uma, 4, 40, 60, 116, 131, 199, 201, 202, 203, 204, 207, 208, 281, 286, 294, 297
Chaudhuri, J.B., 4, 46
class
  emergence of, as a category of history analysis, 2
Colebrook, H.T., 6
Collier and Rosaldo, 70
Crawley, E., 241

Das, R.M., 4, 7
Das, Veena, 1
Dasgupta, Madhusraba, 217
Dauglas, 98
death/*śrāddha* ceremony, 72
desertion, 123-24
Dexter, M.R., 51, 283
dharma, 9
  sources of, 10
dharmaśāstras, 6, 7
  conjugal relations in, 75-92

economic scenario during the period of, 24-30
gender relations in, 41-42
number and dates, 13-19
origin of, 10-12
political scenario during the period of, 19-24
religion during, 30-32

social conditions during, 32-34
women in, 7

dowry
practice of, 67-68

family history, 2
patriarchal biases in, 2
family
and household, difference between, 42
as a social institution, 40, origin of, 40
female patriarchs, 1

gender relations
in early domestic life/family, 41-42
gender, 2
Ghosh, Jayatri, 210, 211, 213
Godelier, Maurice, 98
Goldman, Robert P., 188, 190
Goody, Jack and Tambiah, S.J., 67
Greven, Philip J., Jr., 2
gṛha
ideology of, 42-43
Gulati, S., 4

Hart, George L., 233, 242, 243
history, 1
women in, 1 status of, 1-2, changes in, 2-3
Hopkins, E.W., 15, 190
household,
emergence of, 42
husband/householder
duties of, 82-92

Indra, 3
inherited property
types of, 166-67
inter-*varṇa* marriages, 57-61

Jainism, 32
Jaiswal, Suvira, 5
Jayal, Shakambari, 4, 75
Jayaswal, K.P., 6
Jois, M. Rama, Justice, 6
Jolly, Julius, 14, 15

Kane, P.V., 6, 7, 11, 12, 13, 14, 17, 18, 19, 190
Kapoor, Kapil, 66, 88, 89, 128, 130, 285, 287, 289, 291
Keith, A.B., 14, 190
Kosambi, D.D., 5, 122, 221

law
concept of, 154, in ancient India, 154
legal rights
of women, 174-80
Lerner, Gerda, 1, 79
Lingat, Robert, 15

Macdonell, A.A., 188
Majumdar, R.C., 20
Manjushree, 7
Manusmṛti, 15
marriage, 46
forms of, 54-57; aims of, 61-65
Marx, Karl, 2
Marxist history, 2

Menski, W.F., 6
menstrual taboos, 94-99
Meyer, J.J., 3
Mirashi, V.V., 252
motherhood
  concept of, 99, in ancient India, 99-101
Moti Chandra, 4
Mukherji, P., 4
Müller, Max, 15, 73

Narang, B.S., 6

paternalistic dominance, 40
pativratā
  ideology of, 75-80
polygamy, 92
  wives status in, 93-74
proletariat, 2
property rights
  in ancient India, 154-55, of women, 155-74
property
  and ownership, in ancient India, 152-54
prospective brides
  qualification for, 47-52

Rajvade, Vishvanath Kashinath, 250
Ramaswamy, Vijaya, 234, 235, 237, 240, 241, 242, 313, 314
rape, 114-15
religion
  in ancient India, 30-32
remarriage, 70-72
right(s), 151
  in legal context, 151
Roy, Kumkum, 86, 100, 120, 254, 308

Śaivism, 31
Sanday, P.R., 99
Śangam society
  women in the, 233-43
Sarkar, S.C., 85, 161
Sastri, K.A. Nilakanta, 234
sati
  practice of, 122
Sengupta, N.C., 6
Shah, Kirit K., 5, 244, 246, 247, 248, 249, 252, 254, 255
Shah, Shalini, 5, 69, 73, 75, 86, 90, 219, 222, 224, 226, 231, 250
Sharma, R.S., 5, 119
Shastri, Shakuntala Rao, 7
Sinha, S.N. and Basu, N. K., 5
Sircar, D.C., 253
social class, 2
Sternbach, L., 6
Strange, Thomas A.L., 6
strīdhana (women's property), 159
  kinds of, 159-62
  scope of, 162-67
  succession to, 167-71
  women's dominion over, 171-74

Talim, M., 4
Tambiah, S.J., 69
Thapar, Romila, 5, 20, 24, 187
Thomson, 98, 292
Trautmann, T.R., 66, 285

Upadhyaya, B.S., 3
upbringing of children, 72-75
Vaisnavism, 30
varṇa endogamy, *57*
varṇāśrama system, 33
virginity
  importance of, in marriage, 50-51

widow's marriage
in ancient India, 45, 120-22 age of, 52-54
widowhood, 115
wife
legal rights of, 177-80
role and duties of, 75-81
Winternitz, Maurice, 188, 190
womanhood, 42
women
in ancient India, 3, studies on, 3-4, 5-6, 7; remarriage of, 70-72; rights of, 155-80; in the epics, 187-90; in the *Sangam* society, 233-43; in the epigraphic records, 243-44
women's history, 3
in ancient India, 6, 7
women's rights
to property, 155-74, immovable, 155-59; immovable, 159-74
women's sexuality
control over, 84-90
women's studies
in pre-independence India, 4-5, 6